A Wartime Journey

★ ∞ ★ ∞ ★

Bail-Out Over Belgium
World War II

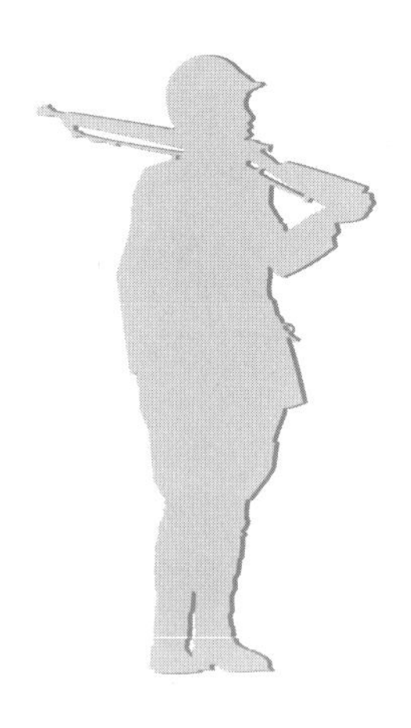

A Wartime Journey

★ ~ ★ ~ ★

Bail-Out Over Belgium
World War II

by
William L. Cupp

SUNFLOWER UNIVERSITY PRESS®
1531 Yuma • P.O. Box 1009 • Manhattan, Kansas 66505-1009 USA

Printed in the United States of America on acid-free paper.

ISBN 0-89745-265-8

Sunflower University Press is a wholly-owned subsidiary
of the non-profit 501(c)3 Journal of the West, Inc.

Contents

Acknowledgments

A DEBT OF GRATITUDE is owed to several people who assisted me materially in bringing this work into fruition. Among them is Professor Jean Tromme, of Liège, Belgium, who made contacts with military authorities at Chièvres and the Supreme Headquarters of Allied Powers, Europe (SHAPE). His phone calls opened communications that made possible the ceremony at which the Belgian helpers of my aircrew were recognized in 1989 by the Air Forces Escape and Evasion Society (AFEES).

Several years have been spent in putting together this book. During that time, the work appeared on two different computer-operating systems and three different word-processing programs. Switching between these programs sometimes caused vexing problems necessitating the assistance of persons skilled in their use. Professor Duane Olson provided help of inestimable value in these matters. Professor Donald Tarr gave significant counsel and help also. Words are inadequate to convey my gratitude for their aid.

It may not be surprising that computer malfunctions presented severe obstacles to the completion of the work. Carl F. Henry came to my rescue when hardware required replacement and in the recovery of lost files. Without his help I might never have completed this book.

Thanks are due as well to my wife, Elizabeth P. Cupp, whose continued interest in the project has encouraged me and who has accompanied me in tracing the routes of my wartime European journeys, enlarging upon my own observations, and providing valuable editorial assistance.

I profited, too, from the generosity of St. Olaf College, Northfield, Minnesota, and the University of Nebraska-Kearney, who granted me leave for research for academic projects. The time spent in Europe also helped me to refresh my memory of the war period, and to locate many of the Belgian and French patriots who made this story possible.

I have received encouragement as well from others too numerous to mention, whose interest in this account has spurred me on. I hope my book will serve as partial repayment for their support.

Foreword

A FRIEND FROM FRANCE, Professor Jean-Claude Vilquin, who at that time was teaching in a Canadian university, prompted me to write an account of my wartime experiences. He had expressed concern that the patriotism of Frenchmen had been portrayed unfairly as self-serving and overly compliant to the will of the Occupation Forces during World War II. During our conversations, he indicated that he had experienced a different characterization, and he encouraged me to tell my story, which might correct the distorted image of the people who had suffered and struggled under the Nazi yoke.

I hesitated at first, for my service in the U.S. Army Air Forces — we still tended to call it the "Air Corps" then — had not shaped a great war novel, nor had yet provided an unknown moral truth.

My experiences with the people of Occupied Belgium and France began when I, as a 20-year-old American aerial gunner, had bailed out of a stricken bomber and literally fell into contact with selfless, patriotic, and brave individuals.

Honoring my friend's behest, I began to write. At the outset, it was my intention to portray the character of the civilians who had helped me and members of my crew, and to describe the wartime situation that, in my view, had made their lives leap out from the commonplace mist in which so many of us live out our days. I soon found that I had taken on a daunting, if not impossible, task. What I had learned from those people in those short months in 1944 was but a faint impression of their true selves and circumstances. I had struggled to comprehend their conversation, as I so very slowly had acquired their language, but there had been much that I had not completely understood — even more of which I had not been told. I had not known the web of relationships that bound them to their extended families and acquaintances.

Nevertheless, I have attempted to deliver a faithful account of a young man, inexperienced in the intricacies of another culture and with a lesser grasp of history. My words, then, reveal my youthful inability to comprehend the fullness of the lives of those about whom I write and the naiveté of my perceptions at that time. If there is a greater moral to be drawn, it must be fashioned from the distance in time, contact, and history that have come with the experience of maturity.

Much of what follows is dredged from the fragments of my memory, refreshed over the years by contacts with many of the patriots whose deeds are recorded in these pages. Only a small part of the story can be corroborated or corrected by persons still living.

The tale begins with my evasion of the enemy, after I had been shot down over Belgium in 1944. My freedom ended upon capture, almost at the edge of Paris. I would travel, as a prisoner of war, through much of central Europe until war's end.

This tale is meant to honor the patriotism, the courage, and the kindness of those stalwart people — all those civilians of enemy-occupied territory, who hid, fed, and clothed me. They richly deserve recognition.

William L. Cupp
November 4, 2001

Chapter 1

The Milk Run

THE SKIES OVER east England bustled with activity during June of 1944. Following the invasion of Normandy on the 6th, bombers accompanied by fighters sped on numerous missions daily to block the movement of Axis supplies and men to the front. Departing in neat formations, the aircraft returned from their sorties as though in a game of tag, hedgehopping fields in exuberance, with the prop wash leaving wakes in the maturing grain below. Detachments of the U.S. Army Air Forces Eighth Air Force played a supportive role, mounting short missions to attack and bomb enemy supply dumps and airfields, whose presence menaced the success of the invasion.

At Debach, in legendary and historic East Anglia — the southeastern part of England — these days were filled almost beyond belief for the 493rd Bombardment Group of the Eighth Air Force. Arriving only in May, fresh from training over the plains of Nebraska, we were assigned to the 861st Bombardment Squadron. We had flown our first operational mission on D-Day, Tuesday, June 6th, to destroy railway

Addy's Crew, 861st Bombardment Squadron, 493rd Bombardment Group (H), Eighth Air Force. Rear, l to r: Lieutenant Robert G. Donahue, navigator; Lieutenant Richard E. Wright, bombardier; Lieutenant Floyd E. Addy, pilot; Lieutenant Douglas W. Hooth, co-pilot; and Staff Sergeant Cecil C. Pendray, engineer. Front, l to r: Sergeant Irving W. Norris, nose gunner; Sergeant Hugh C. Bomar, armorer gunner; Staff Sergeant Frank R. McPherson, radio operator; Robert G. Mathie, tail gunner; and Sergeant William L. Cupp, ball turret gunner.

bridges in Lisieux, France. Our orders were to drop no bombs *unless* the target was visible. The Shrine of Ste. Therèse, in Lisieux, was to be avoided at all costs.

That first day, our target was obscured by clouds, and we flew home with a full bomb load.

On the subsequent days we were at constant alert. Ground crews fine-tuned the bombers to instant readiness, and air crews filled the time between briefings to oil and polish their equipment.

At night, a red-hued glow to the south served as a constant reminder of the fierce intensity of the battle on the narrow Normandy beaches. Now and again, a few crews were called up to mount a low-level attack over an airfield in France. But more frequently than not, those planes were recalled from the runway because fighter aircraft had successfully completed that task.

These were days of irregularity, when men, too dog-tired to eat, dozed in awkward positions on any surface that offered a moment's support. And after a completed mission, they fell into bed for incredible periods of uninterrupted sleep.

A loud voice at our Nissen hut door roused the ten inert forms inside. The non-com shouted it was time to fall out for supper.

A sleepy voice amongst us answered in protest. "Have a heart! We just got to bed for the first time in three days. We ate lunch . . . no one's hungry."

But the non-com insisted. The lunch had been two days before, he told us, and we had been asleep for twenty-nine hours! He shouted for us to get up. "There's a mission for you!"

It was almost 10 o'clock on the evening of June 13th when the speeding jeeps slued into the open space in the squadron area. Quickly, men bearing parachute bags loaded with gear clambered aboard. The jeeps circled, then tore down the road toward the hangar area where the officers hurried into the briefing hut to receive details of the mission ahead. The airmen, during this time, checked their lockers in the supply room, before gathering in small knots to speculate on the mission, smoke a last cigarette, and chat idly to ease the passage of time.

The non-commissioned men of Crew 611 — Staff Sergeants Clyde C.

Pendray and Frank R. McPherson, Sergeants Hugh C. Bomar and Irving W. Norris, and Tail Gunner Robert G. Mathie, and myself — were eager to take our updated Consolidated B-24 Liberator on its first combat mission. The gun mounts had been installed in its Plexiglas side windows, so that they need not be opened in order to fire during flight. The rear compartment was sealed off by a panel wall, with a door providing access to the tail. Together, these improvements made the craft quieter and more comfortable for the crew. The motors and electrical and oxygen systems were in perfect condition, removing the anxiety of malfunctions during the mission. The nose and tail turrets were electrically operated Emersons, replacing the hydraulically operated turrets on earlier versions of the B-24, and responded swiftly to controls.

But we had flown the new aircraft only once, and it had been assigned to us too recently for it to be painted with its eventual name, *My Little Sister*. Lieutenant Floyd E. Addy, our pilot, had suggested the name in honor of his sister who, he said, "could do anything!" And this time, engineer Cecil Pendray remarked, with this plane, everything would be in good condition. No one should black out from a malfunction of the oxygen system, as had happened in the old aircraft assigned to us on our second mission.

"Are you all packed, Mac — in case we have to bail out?" tail gunner Mathie asked Frank McPherson, our radio operator. Mac's parachute bag was stuffed into mountainous proportions. The precautions to be taken in case of calamity was a frequent topic of conversation among airmen. As with the parachutes, we had received instruction, but because we had never actually rehearsed such procedures, these matters always lay gently on our minds.

"You bet I'm packed!" Mac replied with conviction. "If I ever have to bail out, my supplies are going with me."

"It's too bad we can't carry our Colt .45s," Hugh Bomar lamented, referring to the discouraging international agreements that assigned espionage status to airmen armed with handguns or knives. We would at least have some chance against an enemy soldier if we had been allowed to carry a weapon.

Pilot Addy's face was impassive, as usual, as he exited from the briefing. Matter-of-factly, he announced the mission.

"We're to bomb the air base at Athies, near Laon, in the north of France," he stated tersely. "Planes from that field have been harassing the invasion forces. In case we can't see the target, our secondary target is the air base at Beauvais. Command has issued orders that to increase speed and conserve fuel, ball turrets will remain retracted in flight. They're to be lowered only when formations come under attack by enemy aircraft."

I was the ball turret gunner! "It seems you're getting a free ride today, Cupp," co-pilot Lieutenant Douglas W. Hooth amiably commented.

I accepted this news impassively, trying to conceal my disappointment. The ball turret was equipped with an advanced type of gun sight, and I had spent long hours practicing with it.

Lieutenant Addy's face grew grim as his mind turned to the next topic. "But we have bad luck today; somebody in the office has goofed again. We've been assigned a plane consigned to go today to the scrap heap!"

Disappointed not to be flying *My Little Sister*, the ten of us scrambled aboard a waiting jeep, men and gear hanging precariously over the sides, rear, and hood. Amid a cloud of gritty dust blasting from the propwash of freshly fired engines, our driver zigzagged across the airfield. Then piling out of the cramped disorder of the jeep, we somberly assessed the plane assigned to us.

In the dim light of night, she didn't look so bad, if you could discount the slight bend in her fuselage. Lieutenant Addy went around to the left side of the craft and thumped its body with his hand. We heard a *ping*. On the right side, however, the answering sound was a dull *thump*. From the front, her body resembled a whale surfacing from the depths, its body twisted slightly by the effort.

"She'll require extra throttle to keep up with the rest," grunted Hooth.

Just then, Lieutenant Addy noticed the left tail; its lower edge had been smashed when the armament truck had pulled up to hoist bombs aboard.

The bomber's interior equipment had fared little better. The old guns installed for the scrap heap had been warped from overheating during long firing bursts. And later we would find other problems that would surface in flight.

Chinese-style lettering painted on her nose proclaimed the plane to be *Won Long Hop*.

"Her name's appropriate," observed Lieutenant Robert G. Donahue, the navigator.

"This plane has never completed a mission," said Addy. "She had better make it through this one to live up to her name!"

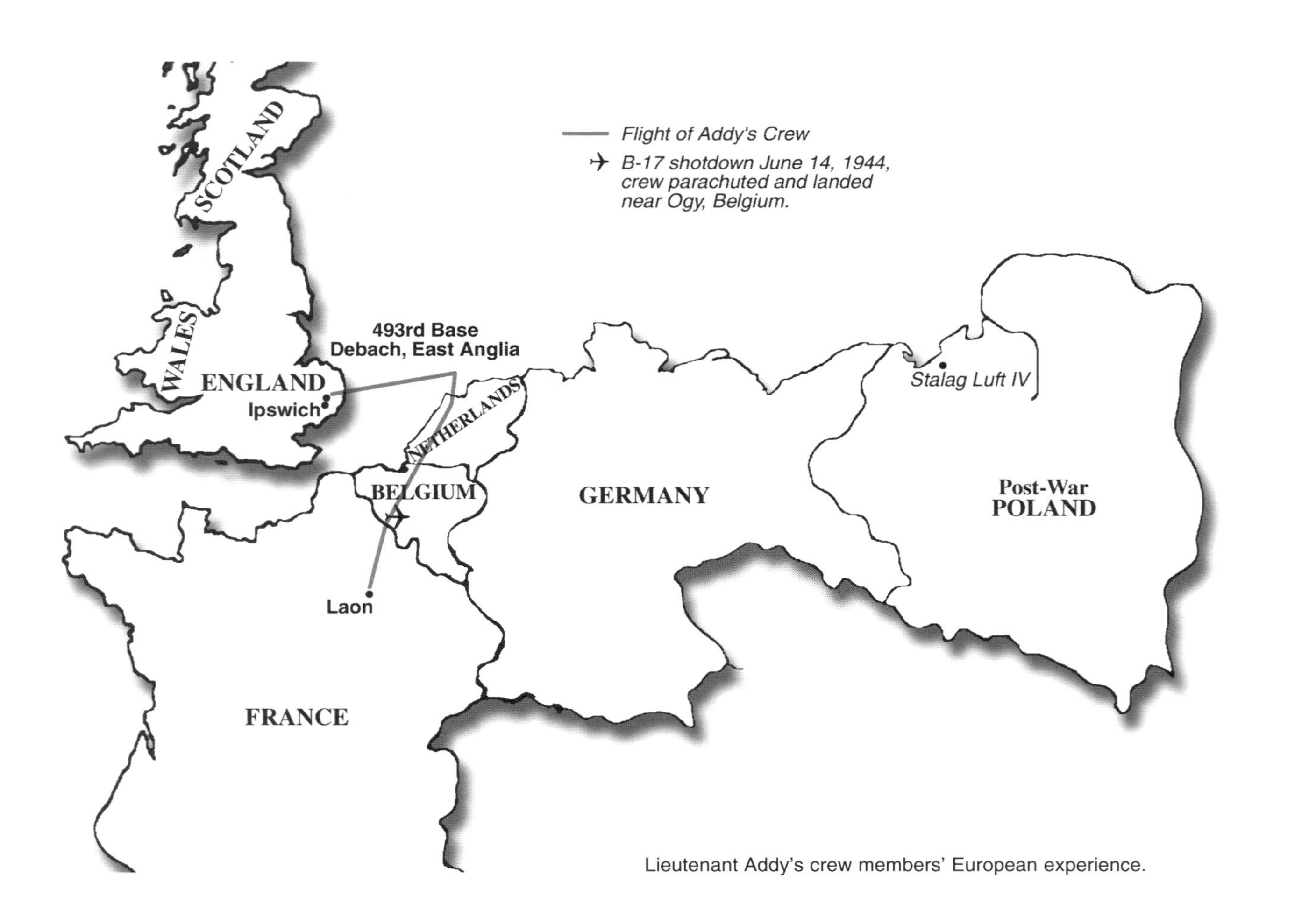

Lieutenant Addy's crew members' European experience.

Somewhat subdued, we entered the aircraft, Addy first. Gear in hand, he stooped low to get through the open bomb-bay doors. The parachute strapped to the back of his lanky frame diminished the clearance between ground and opening. Inside, he stepped up on the catwalk, just ahead of the double tier of bombs, pulled himself up to the level of the flight deck, ducked under the top turret, and took his place in the left seat. He was followed by co-pilot Hooth, whose short stature made the entry seem easy by comparison. Norris, the nose gunner, Wright, the bombardier, and Donahue, the navigator, crawled through a passage beneath the flight deck, by the open hatch for the nose wheel, to their respective stations. Wright tenderly carried his Norden bombsight, and installed it in position, stowing his parachute bag by his side. In his turn, Donahue deposited his portfolio of charts on a small table folded out from the hull.

As they entered the forward part of the massive craft, McPherson thrust his bulging parachute bag into the rear hatch, pulled himself after, stored the bag beside the hatch, and, making his way through the rear compartment and the bomb bay, took his position with the radios on the flight deck. Pendray, the engineer, followed suit before going forward to check on mechanical matters — the fuel and oxygen supplies, the closing of bomb-bay doors, and the retraction of the nose wheel after takeoff. Tail gunner Mathie thrust himself up through the rear hatch, stored his gear behind it, then crawled through the sliding doors into the cramped quarters of his hydraulically operated tail turret.

With my own gear in hand, I ducked into the rear of the bomb bay, stepped up on the catwalk, opened the compartment door, and swung up into the rear compartment to reach the ball turret.

As the plane was being readied for flight, Mathie noticed that his electrically heated gloves were missing from his parachute bag. So were mine. We both knew their importance, for several months earlier, while trying to clear a jammed gun, Mathie had removed his heavy gloves to grasp a small piece, and in the frigid air in the slipstream of the aircraft, his hand was bitterly frostbitten. Deciding that preflight procedures would take several minutes, we jumped from the plane and raced across the field to the supply building. Arriving breathlessly, we disturbed a sleepy supply officer who displayed ill-humor at our request for replacements.

"I have only two pairs in stock," he growled, "and someone might need those tomorrow. Why can't you men hang on to your equipment?"

It seemed pointless to argue that someone had stolen our equipment.

Eventually he grudgingly produced his last two sets of gloves, and we raced back to the aircraft.

We made it just in time, for Lieutenant Addy was ready to taxi to our takeoff station. But once there, we waited. An hour went by. Then another. With the delay, tension mounted. In the dim light, I surveyed my emergency supplies distributed before the mission. On a thick brown envelope was stenciled one word — *France*. Inside were 25,000 French francs, all in large bills. My attention turned to the small clear plastic case, contoured to fit neatly in a coat pocket. This was the "escape kit," routinely distributed on every mission. Carefully removing the sealing tape, I took out the contents piece by piece, laying them on my parachute bag, so that I could easily repack them.

Inside the kit was a sausage-shaped, clear plastic bag with drawstring — a container for liquids. Underneath it was a short section of hacksaw blade, encased in black rubber, which could be hidden in clothing or concealed on or in the body. A compass was included, small enough to be hidden in a body orifice, and matches in a waterproof case. Nestled in the corner of the case was the working end of a razor and its short screw-on handle, Halazone tablets to purify water for drinking, and Benzedrine tablets for quick energy in the event of an exhausting journey. On the bottom of the case, under a tiny sewing kit, lay some thin brown bars — high-energy food I had been told. Making a mental catalog of the contents, I repacked the kit.

Hours passed. To while away the time, the crew broke out the candies supplied to provide energy and allay hunger on a flight. The sweet fruity flavor was agreeable. Then, thirsty, I groped in my parachute bag for the canteen of water I carried to clean the windows of the turret, gulping a cool and refreshing mouthful.

Finally, the order to prepare for takeoff came in the early light of morning. The bomber vibrated in response to new life in its engines, and the silent airfield was charged with the roar of racing engines. A flashlight signaled our turn, and the plane lurched into motion — slowly at first — then with increasing momentum it descended the incline of the runway and laboriously lifted off. The dark mass that was woods at the end of the runway fell away, and we were airborne at last.

On an eastward heading we climbed, jockeyed into a triangular formation, circling left, entering the gray mist of the overhanging clouds. It always seemed a miracle when, emerging above the clouds, we linked immediately on our left with the appointed formation from another base. We were joined, almost simultaneously, by more aircraft swinging in from our right flank. Thirty-six planes merged precisely into battle formation and cruised across the English Channel toward the flak-free entry to the Continent known as the "Hook of Holland."

Over the North Sea area, airmen normally would clear their guns. The procedure involved loading ammunition into the chambers, then firing a few rounds at a patch of open sea to be assured that they were operational. Free ride or not, the ball turret should be prepared for action should necessity so direct. I slithered into the cramped sphere, my face pointing down. The turret could not be placed in a horizontal position until it was lowered, looking for all the world like a globular goldfish bowl glued to the belly of the craft. A short burst into the Channel satisfied me that the guns were in proper working order.

Uncomfortable hanging face-down in the still-retracted turret, I extricated myself and sat on the floor, my support systems plugged into nearby outlets.

The intercom crackled. "We're swinging south toward Mons, on the Belgian border." Lieutenant Addy's voice relayed a command from the mission Commander, Lieutenant Colonel Whitlock. The plane droned on.

"There's not much activity below, though there are antiaircraft emplacements here, according to my charts." The voice belonged to navigator Donahue.

Moments later the intercom crackled again. Hooth, the copilot, directed, "There's some flak off to the right, just off the wings of the right echelon."

The battery presented no immediate danger, but I imagined the scene below. Likely, air raid sirens were sounding, and I pictured sleepy Frenchmen tumbling out of bed, hastily seeking refuge in shelters.

"We're approaching target," reported Donahue.

"The clouds are thick down there," answered the bombardier. "I can't see ground anywhere!"

Lieutenant Addy broke in, "The Commander says to circle right, dropping altitude to ten thousand feet; approach the target on the assigned heading. That should put us under the cloud cover."

"Ten thousand feet?" a voice responded in pointed protest. "That'll make us sitting ducks over the airfield!"

The comment prompted a rejoinder from Lieutenant Addy, who by habit was not accustomed to unnecessary conversation. "Well, now that they know we're in the neighborhood, you had all better keep an eye out for fighter planes . . . be ready at the guns!"

Impatient with my passive role, I thought I saw an opportunity for action. I fingered the microphone button and asked, "Sir, may I have permission to lower the ball turret?"

"Against orders!" came the terse reply. "Just be prepared to lower it if absolutely necessary."

We were in the clouds and still dropping. The right wing dipped again as the formation circled to the north. Sitting idly beside the turret, I switched the radio to the intergroup channel, in the hope of hearing reports that would clarify the status of the mission.

We swung back to the south, breaking below the covering clouds. The plane leveled off. We must have reached the prescribed altitude of 10,000 feet. I glanced out the window and could see the sky was clear, even above us. Had we approached the target 15 minutes later, we might have been able to bomb from a comfortable height.

The radio clicked and an excited voice shouted, "There it is! Beautiful camouflage! *Bombs away*!"

Switching to intercom frequency, I peered below through the window of the ball turret. From the squadron to our left, stacks of bombs were heading downward, their trajectory falling behind the planes. Smoke and dust enveloped a small cluster of buildings below. Was it the target? Our bomb-bay doors hadn't been opened yet. Could that really have been the airfield? Might that squadron have been assigned a target different from ours? . . . Or had someone mistakenly obliterated an unsuspecting farm or village?

The latter seemed all too probable. I felt a little sick, and angry at the awesome finality of the power that could be unleashed from the skies, particularly when that fury could descend impartially and irrationally as result of an error of judgment.

★ ⁂ ★ ⁂ ★

On May 9, 1995, the wartime editor of the Laon *L'Union Journal* recalled that bomb hits had been received at Besny-et-Loisy, about five kilometers southeast of the target area. Because newspapers, managed by the enemy Occupation Forces, had been destroyed when the Germans retreated from Laon in September 1944, the bombing at Besny-et-Loisy could not be verified. However, an elderly woman still living in the village of Besny-et-Loisy remembers no such incident.

Over the aircraft's intercom came orders to open the bomb-bay doors. As they swung wide, my anger turned to the enemy. It was their fault, I reasoned, that we were here where such an error could occur. I thought of their assault on the land over which we passed, and of Greece. I remembered Gus Peropoulos, at whose Sweet Shop in DeWitt, Iowa, I had enjoyed many a soda. The boys had been a bit intimidated by Gus, who never tolerated horseplay from his young customers. But as we enjoyed his ice creams and covetously eyed his expensive chocolates, we were aware of his proud ancestry. Now I imagined his anguished concern over the German occupation of his Greek homeland, too.

I fished in my parachute bag and extricated a piece of chalk. Pulling open the door separating the aft compartment from the bomb bay, I swung down to the catwalk separating the bomb racks. On the side of a 500-pound bomb I scratched "THIS ONE IS FOR GUS." It wasn't much action, but I had done something. Returning to the rear compartment, I slid into the ball turret, and buckled in.

"*Bombs away!*" came Wright's voice over the intercom. Freed from its cargo, the plane lifted suddenly. A blur of objects hurtled past the small round window, then dropped behind the plane. I scampered out of the turret and leaned out of the open window, trying to keep our bombs in sight. Below, they erupted in a succession of puffs on a line down the runway. "Those hits are ours!" came a shout on the intercom.

The plane bucked savagely as flak burst under the port wing. Two bucks, then a lighter bump, as a third burst appeared behind the tail. I scampered back to my station at the ball turret. Over the intercom came navigator Donahue's voice. It was his duty, following possible damage, to conduct an "oxygen check," the euphemism for a report of injury to personnel or damage to the aircraft. Standard procedure began with the tail gunner and progressed forward. All was well until he reached the pilot.

"There appears to be some damage to the port outboard engine. It's losing power, but still running," Lieutenant Addy reported.

Hooth had a word to add. "The Lieutenant also has a shrapnel wound over his eye . . . and he's bleeding."

"It's just a flesh wound," retorted Addy, ending the matter. He fidgeted with the throttles in an attempt to maintain his place in formation.

"Hold on! The leader wants to circle the field again, to see the damage," Lieutenant Addy's voice came tensely over the intercom. "What does he think we have reconnaissance planes for?"

The wing dipped to the right in a narrow circle, and the flight approached the field repeating the same heading. But this time the antiaircraft batteries were ready for us, and the plane shuddered from the shock.

Two other aircraft limped along with us, following the rest of the formation. Someone remarked with rueful pleasure that the leader's plane was one of the laggards. Another oxygen check revealed that all our crew had escaped harm, but that gasoline was streaming from a hole in the right wing. A shell had passed through the gas tank, then exploded above.

The port outboard engine had been hit, and Lieutenant Addy asked Hooth to feather its propeller to reduce the drag. Then the opposite engine cut out for lack of fuel, and as that propeller, too, was feathered, it became obvious that *Won Long Hop* could not even maintain the speed of the other two lagging planes and would have to return alone.

Lieutenant Addy called the navigator on the intercom. "There're plenty of antiaircraft installations along the French coast," he observed. "Can we change course and return the way we came in? Flak there was light this morning."

Donahue answered in the affirmative. "My charts indicate the antiaircraft installations by caliber of weapon. I can chart a course between batteries, staying farther away from the 105mm guns and closer to the 88s."

Addy swung the plane toward the north and, by voice communication with navigator Donahue, threaded his way toward Mons.

The strategy worked well. Occasional bursts of fire appeared just below or off each wingtip, the explosions only gently hammering the plane. Pendray and McPherson, at the waist windows now, broke open the packages of silver tinsel — the chaff — and dropped them from the windows, to deflect the enemy radar.

Suddenly, the flak intensified. An angry red fireball burst just below the tail section, spewing orange flame into a black cloud. Simultaneous with the blast and the sound of tearing metal, the plane lurched violently. Lieutenant Addy ruddered savagely, but two more bursts hammered beside the first. Over the intercom, someone shouted, "They must have moved an antiaircraft battery into the marshaling yards at Mons after we passed here this morning!" Mons lay near the southern border of Belgium. Its marshaling yards were located at St. Ghislain, an important rail distribution center, and they had been bombed on several occasions by Allied forces.

Donahue initiated the oxygen check. "Tail?" he intoned. There was no answer. "*Tail!*" he repeated. Still no response. "*Mathie!*" he called. "Are you all right?"

Faintly, the reply came. "Just let me get this microphone on, so I can answer!" he said. "The glass was knocked out of my turret; the right tail is gone, and the turret doors are jammed open."

I peered out of the ball turret to survey the damage. The floor of the compartment was littered with the bullet-proof glass from the tail turret. How could anyone survive a direct blow like that?

"Are you hurt, Mathie?" Donahue questioned.

"I seem to be all right . . . the glass must have blown around me," came his reply.

My gaze took in Pendray and McPherson. They had exhausted the huge pile of chaff, and had shredded the last small bundle. Incongruous as it may be, they were delicately dropping the last few strands, one at a time.

The pounding continued, viciously. Being of little use at my station, I worked my way along the catwalk and climbed into the forward cabin. As the dialogue between Donahue and Mathie was in progress, Lieutenant Addy was fighting with the controls, forcing the ungainly craft first one way, then another, to evade further damage. The struggling bomber, slowed by its dead motors, its maneuverability hampered by loss of a tail section, virtually defied the attempt to control its movement.

Lieutenant Addy leaned forward, his long frame braced on the rudders, his arms tense at the wheel. His brown leather jacket was wet with perspiration outlined in white from the salt of his body. The oxygen check was completed, the crew faring better than their craft. The superchargers on the remaining engines no longer functioned. But the flak tapered off; the scattered bursts were trailing behind us, and below.

Over the intercom, "Pilot to navigator."

"Navigator to pilot. Go ahead."

"Can you tell me our bearings?"

"Just a minute," answered Donahue. "I lost track during that evasive action."

After a brief interval, the intercom crackled again. "Navigator to pilot, we're almost directly over an airfield called Chièvres. There may be flak."

There was. The first bursts broke well behind us. But successive bursts narrowed the gap and became deadly accurate. Evasive action was to no avail. I huddled behind the protective glass of the turret, acutely aware that the side panels offered little protection. The plane heaved with each burst. Showers of fragments pelted the thin fuselage.

I wondered if we would get out of this. My mouth was dry, cottony. Fishing for the canteen, I extracted a couple of frozen drops. It didn't help much. Images of people dear to me flashed through my mind. My wonderful grandmother, who had passed away in the spring of that very year, seemed vividly present. I had often heard of people who, in moments of peril, had experienced their lives passing before their eyes. I just had not expected that the images could move by so swiftly.

Lieutenant Addy must have had similar thoughts, for his wife, Bobby was expecting their first child in just a few weeks.

We had moved through the flak, and amazingly no crewman had been hurt. The plane, though, was mortally wounded. At an altitude now a mere 6,000 feet, it was losing 500 feet per minute.

"We just might make it to the Channel if we can jettison enough gear," Lieutenant Addy observed, but with faint optimism.

The controls on the flight deck opened the bomb-bay door. Pendray and McPherson struggled to raise the rear hatch. Doubling as flooring, it was heavy, and the men had to lift from the sides, and avoid falling out. Ammunition, machine guns, surplus radio equipment, and oxygen bottles were discarded. Caught up in the spirit of the task, those of us in the rear compartment were at pains to locate other materials to eliminate. Beside the rear hatch, Pendray eyed a bulging parachute bag.

Just then the door from the bomb bay opened as Bomar had vacated his position in the top turret. Urgently, he shouted at me, his voice a scream to penetrate the shrill whistle of air rushing through countless holes in the fuselage. He relayed a message from the pilot. "Tell the others to connect their earphones! Addy has something to say!"

Seconds later, Lieutenant Addy's voice came over the intercom. "We don't have enough altitude to reach the coast," he stated calmly. "We have two options. We can try to land the plane in a field, then high-tail it together for cover. Or any of you who want to can take your chances by parachute."

Nine voices declared the intent to parachute. Copilot Hooth supplied justification. "A crash landing will attract the enemy, and we might all be captured. If we parachute, some of us may get away."

Addy signaled his final communication. "OK, then . . . jump when you're ready . . . and good luck! . . . I'm going to stay with the plane. There are friendly people down there, and I don't want a plane of ours crashing on any of them."

I reached for my parachute bag, unzipped it, and extracted the escape kit and my service shoes. Sitting on the floor, I removed my fleece-lined flying boots and tugged on the laces of the shoes. I was aware of people crouching by the rear hatch. I grasped the bundle that was my chest parachute, taking care to snap it to the harness so that the ripcord would be at my right hand. As I climbed down to the bomb-bay catwalk, I could see that the rear compartment was empty.

The catwalk slanted, indicating the steep descent of the craft, and I steadied myself by grasping the now-empty bomb rack as I surveyed the scene below. A low cover of clouds, broken here and there, revealed patches of open country and occasional habitation. I thought to fall freely would be best, and to delay pulling the ripcord. The chute would be visible only briefly from the ground, and my chances of taking cover would be improved.

I braced myself to receive the expected buffeting of the slipstream. Just then, a blond-headed body clad in a leather jacket hurtled directly from the flight deck into the gulf below. It was Hooth, the copilot. The plane plunged, as the remaining engines cut out. Only a shrill whistle noise remained as the anguished Liberator plummeted toward the ground.

With a slight push of my legs, I followed Hooth.

Chapter 2

Falling into Good Hands

THERE WAS NO blast of wind. Instead, I had stepped into a world of calm and quiet. Gone was the roar of tortured engines; far behind was the scream of air through the perforated fuselage. In order to see how much clearance there would have been between the plane and me had I pulled the ripcord immediately. I counted to three. There would have been ample space. From my position I could no longer see the stricken bomber.

Below extended a bank of clouds. Ever so slowly they tilted and formed a line edged with azure blue, then departed from the field of vision, and all was clear and sunny. Free-fall is a near-dream world, almost without sensation, neither sleeping nor wakefulness — a condition of peace and well-being. Again the clouds leisurely rotated into view. Out of them blossomed a white rose, brilliant with reflected sunlight, then another. With incredible speed they shot into the sky, off to my left. As I craned my neck to keep them in view, they sped aloft and were gone as I was suddenly enveloped in white mist.

The two "roses" had been parachutes of my crew, of course, and the tranquil descent of my free-fall had deceptively concealed both the rotation and the speed of my own descent. The parachutes had not shot upward — I had fallen past them. And the mist was a layer of cloud, which I had judged to lie at an altitude of between 1,000 and 1,500 feet.

Realizing my proximity to the ground below, I worried. What if the chute lines were snarled? Mine was packed in a bundle on my chest, and it would be possible to disentangle the lines, but that would take several seconds. At that altitude, there was little time to spare.

The ripcord was ready by my right hand, and unaware, in the mist, that my head was down and my feet reaching for the sky, I tugged on it. My neck jerked and my body snapped upright as the billowing parachute bit the air, instantly braking the momentum of my descent. In the distance, on the threshold of my consciousness, was the sound of an explosion.

Limply dangling from the harness, I surveyed the unfolding scene below. Only a light haze now dimmed the verdant patchwork of a hundred fields. Along curving roadways the red-tiled roofs of buildings suggested a rural population far more dense than that of my native Iowa. To my left, on the north, was a village. I knew I had to be alert for enemy troops who, upon spotting me, would speed to my projected landing spot. And from the enemy's viewpoint, I reasoned, the most advantageous observation point would be a hill, or a tower.

In my mind at that moment the village church took on an ominous appearance. Situated on a hillside, overlooking the highway between us, it seemed to dominate the countryside. I soon learned that the church was in the commune of Ogy, Belgium, just west of Lessines.

Beneath its slate-black spire the massive belfry housed two cavernous windows on each of the two sides I could see. More importantly for me, should anyone be scanning the countryside from either the south or the east, they would most certainly have a good view of my descent. I knew I must land safely, quickly shed my parachute harness, and get away from the scene as rapidly as possible.

It appeared there were no woods for concealment and I would have to rely on grain fields for the thin screen they offered, traveling quickly, keeping a low profile.

The odds of evading immediate capture seemed good. The church lay a good half-mile to the north, and by either of the two roads winding south,

The author's first sanctuary, the home of Lucien and Denise Guerlus, at Ogy, Belgium.

the distance was farther. The field below me was several hundred yards from each of them.

The three or four acres was framed by a single row of trees, with a wheat field on the edge. Enervated as I was from the opening jolt of the parachute, the risers failed to respond to my feeble tug. The ground seemed to rush toward me at an alarming rate. I wondered if I would miss the tree in the corner of the field. It quickly came directly below me and from among its myriad short branches appeared a massive lopped-off trunk. I knew I would break my legs if I hit that; then suddenly, with a breathtaking thump, I was on the ground. The short branches had sprung back, much like a trampoline, and had diverted my legs from impending disaster. As payment for that service, however, they clasped the limp parachute aloft — a clear marker of my presence.

Several minutes seemed to pass before my breath returned and I could unbuckle the clasps that anchored me to the parachute. Try as I might, I could not dislodge the chute from the tree, and knew someone would see it. Slipping through the fence, I crouched in the shelter of tall wheat and crawled on hands and knees for a short distance before stopping to shed the weighty flying suit. The field of wheat stalks, interspersed with daisies and buttercups, provided a disarming agreeable sanctuary. As I raised my head to survey the scene, at the top of the hill, a man — a civilian — ran in my direction, his arm waving. I wondered if his signal was meant for me or for pursuers, but I could not tarry for the answer. Retreating quickly to the concealing cover of the wheat, I scampered on all fours, cautiously parting the stalks ahead of me to minimize the movement of the foliage. Descending the hill some 100 yards, I lifted my head again to reconnoiter. The man was gone. The parachute, too, had disappeared from the tree. So the man was a friend; his gestures must have been a beckon for me.

Hastily, I gained my feet and ran in the direction in which I had seen him last. Years later, I learned that the civilian was Gilbert Rasson, who lived in Ogy.

The pasture on my right, where my parachute had clung, was quiet. Far on my left, along a file of trees paralleling my route, a woman trotted, a white silken mass trailing from her arms. She was closely followed by two figures dressed in military green. It appeared that the locals were aiding three of us. I wondered about the rest of the crew.

Over the hilltop, a knot of field workers paused, still bent over their short hoes in the tobacco field, all heads inclined toward me. One of them stood erect and vigorously motioned toward a path to my left. I cornered like a cross-country runner, without the merest acknowledgment of thanks. At the foot of the path, screened lightly by trees, stood a farmhouse, its windows framed by green shutters. I ran to the door, which swung wide at my approach.

In relief, I was again, suddenly, very thirsty. "Water?" I asked of the questioning lady inside.

She did not understand me. What language did these people speak? The buildings reminded me of pictures I had seen of the Netherlands. Had we passed out of Belgium during the time we had jettisoned our cargo? "*Wasser*?" I tried again, exhausting my linguistic repertoire. The lady still wore a puzzled expression. Gesturing, I moved my right arm in a pumping fashion.

Comprehension dawned on her face, and she whirled away, disappearing through a stairway door. In a moment she returned, bearing a large bottle capped by a white ceramic stopper. The amber fluid inside had the appearance of beer.

Somehow, a bundle of clothing appeared in my arms and a firm hand ushered me through an adjacent door. To my surprise, inside the bedroom Lieutenant Hooth was pulling on a pair of dark trousers.

"You'd better jump into those clothes — we've no time to lose!" Lieutenant Donahue ordered, buttoning a faded gray shirt.

Rapidly we exchanged our uniforms for clothing like that worn by the workers in the field, pulled on caps, and returned once more to the kitchen. The lady had just come back from the cellar, and with a kind smile, handed me another large bottle, like the one before. I murmured my thanks, wondering again if its foaming contents were what was pumped from wells in this country or purposefully brewed.

In an instant a slender man motioned us out of the house, leading us down the path by which I had come, then through a field to our left. Behind us, a young woman hurried from the house, her arms burdened with our military uniforms.

At some distance along our route, our guide paused; his intent face relaxed as he addressed us for the first time. From his tone, I guessed that it was a question, and to my surprise, Lieutenant Donahue answered him in words the man could understand, even if I could not. The man pulled out a wallet from which he extracted some small paper bills, then fished in his pocket for a few coins, which the three of us shared. With a concluding sentence, our guide again strode on, his erect frame leading rapidly through the field.

When I returned to Belgium, after the war, I learned more about my rescuers. Lucien Guerlus was the farmer who had guided us to the field in which to hide. Madame Denise Guerlus was the person who had brought me beer. The Guerluses did not know the identity of the woman who had gathered up the parachutes of Lieutenants Donahue and Hooth. But I learned that both Gilbert Rasson and Lucien Guerlus had extracted my parachute from the tree.

★ ★ ★

"What was that all about, Bob?" demanded Hooth, who drew us together in a conspiratorial triangle, questioning in hushed tones.

"He had asked us whether we had any money. We have the large French bills in our escape kits, but I was afraid he might ask for a lot of it for his help. And we may need that later on, so I told him that we didn't. He said we might need some to buy our food or drink, and that he was sorry that he did not have more to give us just then, because there wasn't enough to buy tickets in case we wanted to travel by train.

"He gave us Belgian coins, which is what we need here, anyway. He was really sincere. "I'm sorry now that I didn't trust him at first; but we can't be too careful."

Throughout this conversation, our leader had continued along his route, with an occasional glance in the direction of a road paralleling our steps some 200 yards to the left. Abruptly, he swerved to the right, widely skirting a small farmstead, crossing a narrow lane, and leading us to a tree-lined fence bordering a wheat field. After speaking for a moment with Bob Donahue, he was gone.

"What do we do now?" I directed the question to Bob, mindful that I had failed to address him by his rank. Our crew from the first had maintained a casual intimacy, though we enlisted men always, even among ourselves, addressed our officers formally, by rank and surname. Just now, however, the situation seemed to be different. We were out of uniform, and all in the same pickle — a circumstance that didn't seem, at the moment, to require the preservation of protocol.

Lieutenant Donahue was not bothered by the lapse. "The man said to lie low in this field, and we'll probably be out of danger. Someone will look in on us later today. On the bare chance that a search party should look for us here, he said we should try to get away under cover. And he wished us good luck!"

We made ourselves as comfortable as possible, taking care not to disturb the wheat more than necessary. Then we examined our assets. Each of us had identical escape kits, and each was intact. Pulling out the blue card printed with key phrases in French, Hooth and I tried to repeat the unfamiliar words. Hooth's attempt at the first phrase, "I am hungry," sounded like *jay fame*.

With quiet authority, Donahue corrected, "That *jay* is a contraction of the French words 'I' and 'have.' The j has a soft sound, like zhe, so try saying '*zhay*.' The second word should sound more like fam. Try it again."

My interpretation of "Where is the railway station?" came out even worse.

"*Ow este la guerre*?" I intoned, with far less expression than I could imagine.

While Donahue patiently attempted to improve on my diction, I released the stopper from the brown bottle given to me. The yellow-brown liquid had a rather sour, somewhat musty taste, but just a swallow took the edge off my thirst. I passed it to the others, and each took a sip. The second small swallow thoroughly assuaged my craving, and I placed the bottle nearby where all could share. The first round of our language lesson had consumed less than an hour.

In the distance, we could hear a dog barking, from the direction of the farm where we had first found sanctuary.

"I suppose German troops are making the rounds to find out if anyone has seen us," remarked Hooth. "Let's scout around for the best way out of this field, in case we have to run for it."

The field just across from the trees bordering ours looked to be alfalfa, and offered no cover for retreat. Just then, from the hilltop above came the sound of a passing vehicle. There had to be a road up there, running parallel to our field.

I crept closer to the fence line and discovered a large tree with a decayed section almost large enough to conceal a person in a sitting position. A knothole at eye level afforded a view of the road. I pulled myself into the hollow and surveyed the area. No houses were visible in that narrow range of view, but I could scan for passing vehicles and have a head start in case of danger. Two small farmsteads flanked the lane just beyond our field, to the left. Behind us, pasture grasses provided no shelter for retreat, but to our right was another grain field, our best route in case we had to leave quickly.

"If it comes to that, let's scatter and crawl along separate trails through the grain. We'll have better chances separately than together," remarked Hooth convincingly.

Now and then, dogs could be heard barking in the distance. Occasionally there came the sound of a motor. The intervals in between were punctuated by a light, intermittent drizzle. Lying a few feet apart as though nesting in the tiny spaces where our bodies flattened the wheat, we spoke quietly.

"I wonder how many of the others are still hiding out," murmured Donahue.

"I'm worried about Lieutenant Addy," responded Hooth. "I heard a loud explosion when the plane came down. I hope he changed his mind and bailed out."

I thought it unlike the Lieutenant to change his mind about anything, but his chances of surviving an explosion appeared too remote for comfort.

"Maybe he set her down safely, then set her ablaze to destroy the maps and instruments," I hazarded with unfelt optimism.

Between scouting trips to the hollow tree, I searched my pockets again for some useful item. I carried a short nail file — how I wished it were a knife! I had also brought my billfold, in which was a British one-pound note, and my "short snorter" — a small bill of Icelandic currency — signed by a number of airmen who had also flown across the Atlantic. I carried it as my good luck piece, and against the day when I might venture into a canteen and be forced to purchase a round of drinks. However, it was not a good thing to have on my person in the event of capture. Either bill would betray my identity, and the German Intelligence Service would be delighted to connect me to those other signatories on the short snorter.

My companions had been observing my preoccupation, and as I crawled away to bury these mementos, Hooth spoke reprovingly. "You should know better than to carry things like that with you on a mission — that could give aid and comfort to the enemy!"

Somewhat shamefacedly, I slit the earth with the nail file, inserted the billfold and its contents, and carefully pressed the earth back into place. A few gentle pats obliterated all trace of my indiscretion.

A gentle rain gradually saturated our clothing, and the damp chill produced an occasional shiver. We were gratefully surprised, therefore, when two men appeared in the field. The taller one bore an armload of dry clothing. They deposited their burdens, telling Donahue that we were to change clothes, eat, and wait a bit for someone to come for us.

Inside the knapsack, we found cups, sugar cubes, and fried-egg sandwiches. It was 6 o'clock by my watch. After a fast of 24 hours, the egg sandwiches were delicious. There was coffee in a pot, too.

None of us recalled having seen either of these men before, so we took additional comfort in the idea that a number of people must now know our whereabouts, and that they could be relied upon to help us. The whole day had passed, and we still had half of the bottle of beer.

Dusk was falling when the taller of the two men returned to the field, beckoning us to bring our wet clothing and the remnants of our dinner with us. He led us with the calm assurance of habit through the field to the second of the two houses bordering the lane. Inside, a dim lamp revealed two other men. The door closed behind us, and the three occupants hugged us heartily. I didn't understand what they said, and Lieutenant Donahue did not bother to translate. He didn't have to. The mood in the room was clearly one of celebration.

These men rejoiced because we had so far eluded capture. Without a doubt, we owed a large measure of our good fortune to them, and to how many others we could only guess. From the shadows in the room someone supplied a fat bottle, and our bearer of the dry clothing set six small glasses on the table and decanted them with brandy.

The brawny companion lifted his glass in a toast. Inferring that the sense of his words expressed fervent wishes for the continuance of our good luck, I lifted my first brandy ever to my lips and emptied it with the rest. It burned a little all the way down, and I gasped in the attempt to hide a cough. But no one seemed to notice my lack of experience with the ways of the world. Exhaling a hearty breath of pleasure, one of our hosts drew the back of his hand across his mouth and, as though a necessary task had been completed, set his glass firmly on the table.

We later learned that the brawny man was Adolphe Clément, of Ostiches, a member of *Comète*, the Belgian organization engaged in transferring Allied military personnel from behind enemy lines to their proper commands. On another occasion, Adolphe had bravely carried an injured flier several miles on his back.

Adolphe Clément in military uniform, 1940.

★ ★ ★

The brawny man conferred briefly with his companion, then quickly outlined some details to Lieutenant Donahue who translated to us.

"We're going to leave here now, and walk cross-country to a place where we'll be safe for the night. These two men will walk on ahead, but we're to tag closely at their heels. By all means, be quiet. And be on the alert for any signal of danger."

Each of us gave a farewell handshake to our host, and stepped out of the door. One man, already at the gate, signaled that the lane was clear. We were on our way.

The stocky man assumed the lead; his slender companion, now carrying a small-caliber rifle at the ready, lagged a few paces behind and on his left. Behind, we three crewmen trailed single-file. The rain had ceased, and evening's pale light clearly revealed the patchwork of tiny fields — tobacco, barley, wheat, rye, beans, and alfalfa — through which we passed.

From my right side, in a field of tall grain, came a rustle. Alerted, I glanced in the direction of the sound, though saw nothing but a gentle waving of the heads of grain. Plodding onward, my head pointed forward, I swiveled my eyes right and left to catch a glimpse of any stalker. Then, again on my right, I spotted him, a dark-clad man carrying a sub-machine gun. Under the cover of tall grain, he was providing armed escort. I caught up with Donahue, who was ahead, and in a whisper, told him of my discovery. He then scouted to our left while I maintained vigil on our right flank.

A bit later, his arm brushed mine. "There's an armed escort on our left, too," he hissed.

Reassured that we had ample protection, I dropped back to relate this information to Hooth, then fell back into line. We never did learn how many men accompanied us on that trek, whether a lone escort threaded back and forth from one flank to the other, or whether there were indeed two — or more.

Ahead, our leader paused, half-turned, and raised his right hand, palm-forward, as a signal for us to halt. We froze in place while he advanced to the top of a low rise overlooking a highway. He scanned the road carefully, from left to right. All was well to the left. Oddly, for this late hour, a lone woman grazed a herd of cows along the roadside to our right. In answer to a wave from our leader, she shook her apron high, signaling that the area was clear, then turned to urge her cows toward the barn. She must have been stationed there to signal in case of danger.

The leader motioned for us to advance, parting the wires of the fence for our passage. The four of us hurried across the road, the last one pausing at the fence to return the courtesy. Where was our unseen escort? Glancing backward as we strode across the field, we saw no other person cross the highway.

A hundred yards farther, shielded from the road by a hillside, we paused for a moment. Our guides appeared to be more relaxed, and we chatted together, just as we might have done had we shared a common language. A slender man rested his rifle, and from his belt produced a small black automatic pistol. Handing it to me, he said something about "Browning," and "*Belge*" — indeed, a Browning pistol, I guessed about .25 caliber. Fitting nicely into my hand, the gun was a more comfortable package than the bulky Colt .45 still with my gear in England. I showed my approval and was rewarded by a gesture indicating that I could retain it. Handling a weapon again was reassuring, knowing that the offer signified a sense of trust. I later learned that the slender man was Julian Plume, an enthusiastic Résister, who had earlier that evening recovered the injured Frank McPherson from the field where he lay and transported him to a remote farmhouse some distance away.

In the dimming light we changed course, heading in a southerly direction. Giving a wide berth to houses along our way, we crossed a narrow road, traversed a field, then swung left through a pasture. A hiss from our leader brought us to a halt. A strange noise came from someplace ahead. I could not make it out, but it sounded like wires scraping together, and some sort of heavy breathing as well. Our two escorts communicated by whisper, then the leader advanced cautiously. Hunkered down, we listened alertly. The sounds intensified, then all was quiet. Now barely visible in the dark, our leader returned. He had freed a calf that had been caught in barbed wire.

We proceeded with caution on low ground and through the thick grass of marshland. Easing through a fence, we followed a walking path at the rear of several houses, crossed a small road, and were once again in fields. After mounting a hill, we followed an isolated lane to a house, rounded it, and paused at a door mounted in a connecting wall. In response to our leader's staccato rap, the door opened, and we were ushered into a courtyard. A slender man of medium height motioned us to the door of the house. Just before entering, I returned the pistol to its owner.

In contrast to the darkness of the night, the spacious kitchen seemed to be brightly lit. An elderly couple sat at the oilcloth-covered table, while an attractive blonde young woman moved swiftly to place cups upon the table. From the stove she produced a pot of coffee, filling six cups; only she and the older couple did not drink. The man who had met us at the gate appeared to be the host. As he directed questions to our escorts, his warm smile gave way to an expression of earnest intensity. In the lighted kitchen, and in the relief of arriving at a safe haven, it was possible to notice in detail the features of those around us.

Clad in a dark blue coat, his gray shirt open at the collar, our new host was a wiry man of considerable energy. He had a thick mane of black hair, parted on the side, the top combed back from his tanned face. He was young, probably no more than 25 years of age, but his actions revealed an air of self-assurance. With his cap off, our broad-shouldered guide's close-cut, sandy hair was plastered neatly to his head. His rounded face would have appeared cherubic were it not for the firm determination that seemed to burn in his blue eyes. His companion stood behind me, so that I never had a clear view of him. But the young woman moved about the room with easy grace, seemingly aware of unuttered needs, refilling cups, replenishing the coffeepot. She appeared to be too young to be the daughter of the old couple — perhaps 20 or 21 I thought.

Our host was known to me as "Jean," and it wasn't until years later that I learned he was actually Abel Coton, commander of the Résistance group *Battalion 1, Corps 021, Armée Belge des Partisans.* He had married Mademoiselle Berthe Delaunois of Papignies, the young woman who had filled our cups, and a member of the group that maintained this "safe house."

A staccato rap was immediately heard at the gate, the same as that given on our arrival. Our host left the house, carefully closing the door behind. A moment later, the door opened, and in limped our bombardier, Lieutenant Wright. Another man was with him. Wright sagged into a proffered chair, acknowledging our excited welcome.

His chute had come down in a tall tree not far from there, he told us, and he had hurt his ankle in landing. "I had a deuce of a time getting out of the harness and to the ground," he relayed. Then two women ran up and welcomed me. "The little red-headed one kissed me!" he announced, with obvious relish. "Then a man came along and helped me to a farm. . . . Oh, it was this man here!" he interjected, pointing to our host. "A very nice place. They gave me these clothes," he added, rather vainly tugging at his neat gray jacket, displaying his gray flannel shirt with matching button-across tie clasp. In this company, the tie seemed to lend a bourgeois touch to his appearance.

I suppressed a feeling of envy; I wished that I were dressed as well, but of course, my rough farming clothes — the trousers a carefully sewn patchwork from a half-dozen salvaged bits of cloth — was most appropriate for where we had come from.

Wright continued, "A doctor came to the house in the afternoon and bandaged my ankle. I think it's only a sprain, and I can walk on it a little. The people seem to be well-to-do; they have a big house, nice things — and they were very good to me."

In the excitement of seeing Wright, I had not paid much attention to the man who had brought him. Apparently sensing that our greetings were concluded, our young host seized the occasion to bring us up to date on our crew.

"Three men were taken prisoner immediately by the Germans," Lieutenant Donahue translated. "Four parachutes came down together very near a German antiparachute observation post. One man succeeded in making his way into a grain field and eluded capture. Tonight someone will be looking after him. They say Lieutenant Addy is dead. He turned the plane at the last minute to miss the church at Wodecq, then parachuted. But there wasn't time for the parachute to open. No one on the ground was hurt."

It was sobering, saddening news. It did not seem possible that the good luck that had kept Lieutenant Addy from serious injury over the target, and his splendid display of airmanship in eluding the guns of Mons, could have escaped him at the last minute.

Of our crew, three men were prisoners, and the fate of another was in question. Four of us were here. That left one unaccounted for. I wondered who these men were, but it was some time before I learned that the prisoners were Robert Mathie, Irving Norris, and Cecil Pendray. Hugh Bomar had been unaccounted for at this time.

The hour was late, and when Lieutenant Donahue reported that someone was going to show us to our sleeping place, I was ready. It had been a long day.

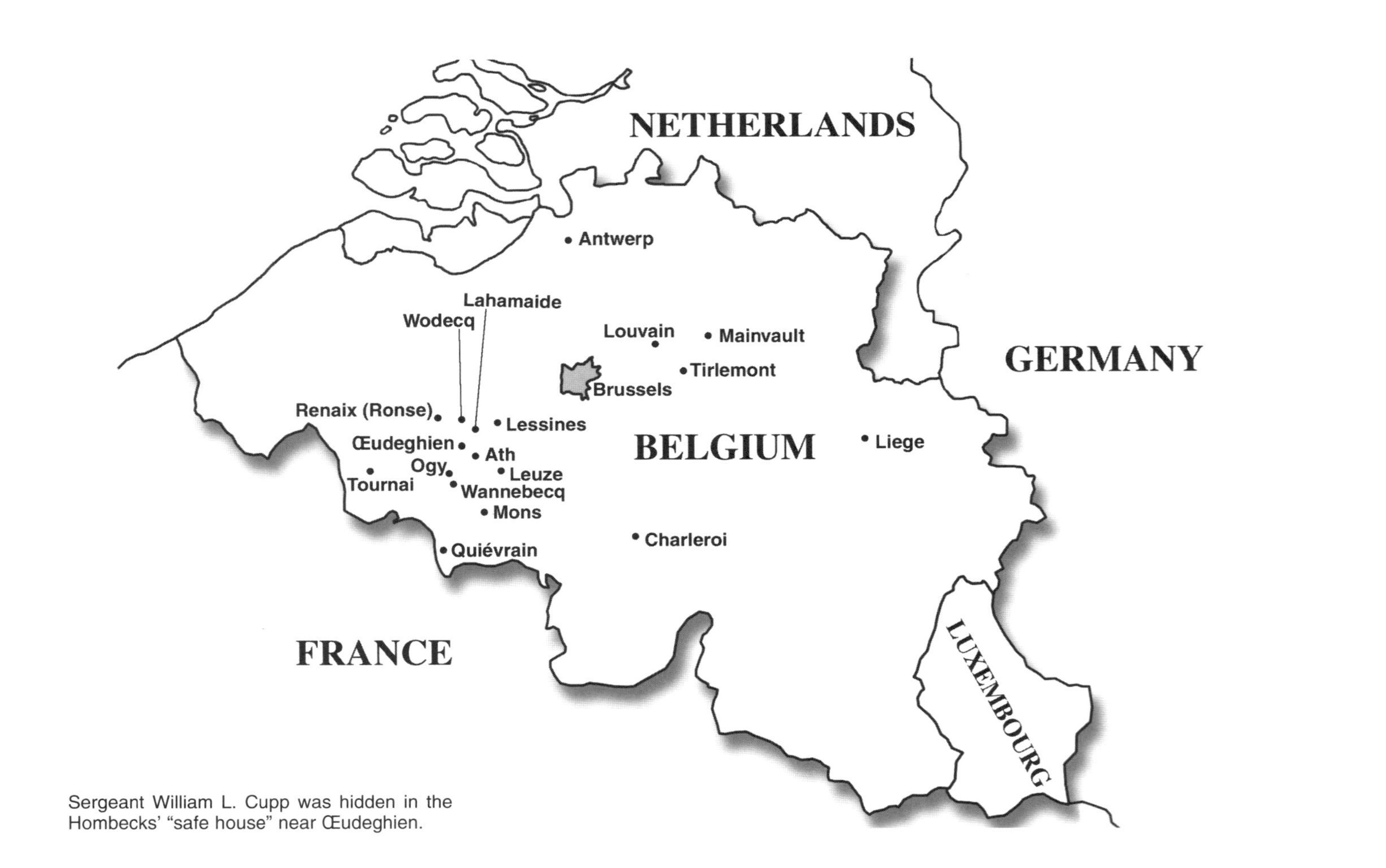

Sergeant William L. Cupp was hidden in the Hombecks' "safe house" near Œudeghien.

Chapter 3

Bucolic Hospitality

OUR BEDROOM THAT night was in a clean and dry section of the brick barn attached to the house. Armloads of yellow straw from a readily available pile served as a soft mattress. Perhaps someone brought us blankets; at any rate, we were comfortable enough. In the dark, the four of us talked for a short while, speculating on the fate of our fellow crewmen.

We thought of Lieutenant Addy, and his wife, Bobby, expecting their baby soon. While the officers probably knew him better than did the non-coms on the crew, we enlisted men were well aware that he was a special sort of man. As aircraft commander, he had always pressed upon us exacting standards for the performance of our duty — not just by urging us on, but by the absence of praise, even when we had excelled, making us aware that, indeed, excellence *was* our *duty*. I remembered a day of aerial gunnery practice for the whole squadron when the tow target had been riddled with holes edged by the colors that had identified the guns of our crew. Did Lieutenant Addy congratulate us? No, he merely quietly stated, "Why, my little sister could do better than that!"

Henceforth, we often heard that his little sister could out-perform us, and it became a sort of rallying cry and slogan of the crew. We had named our first aircraft *My Little Sister*.

Lieutenant Addy always had been businesslike in the course of duty, but shortly before the end of our training in the States, the officers and airmen alike had often met, after hours, in a bowling alley. Sometime during one evening, we had retreated to the bar, where the taciturn Addy, twisting his fingers around a glass as yet untouched by his lips, had begun to speak. And he spoke at length. Only in that setting had he revealed himself as a person of substance, not simply as an assigned Commander.

In the dark of the Belgian barn, as my mind reached back over the day, I seemed to hear Addy's comment of disgust as someone's bombs had obliterated a French hamlet. The thought connected with my memory of his last words, "I'm going to stay with the plane." He had felt it was his duty to prevent the aircraft from hitting a populated area. He had known full well the risk he was taking, and he certainly had a lot to live for. He had succeeded in his objective to steer the craft away from habitation, but had died in the attempt. I hoped his heroic deed would be made known some day.

We must have slept well that night, for it was daylight when we were wakened by the sound of the door opening. Someone called us to breakfast. Cold water washed away the sleep of night, and the morning meal around the kitchen table prepared us for a new day.

Outdoors, the weather had improved. By daylight, we came to appreciate the security of this sanctuary. The courtyard was a protected square, framed on two sides by the house and connecting buildings. A high wall of concrete "boards" screened the remaining sides. Just next to the entry gate, a hay rake nestled against a tall pile of straw. I recalled we had used a later model on our farm in Iowa.

Noticing my interest in the rake, a newcomer to the house that morning came over and pulled it from the straw pile. Then with his foot, he kicked away some straw littering the ground, revealing a metal trap-door. Below, a steep narrow staircase descended into an underground chamber.

Reaching down, the guide fingered a light switch. Far back in the chamber, tiers of shelves were packed with boxes and bottles. Iron-framed bunks were swung up against the walls, providing room for movement.

To understand the explanation, I called to Lieutenant Donahue. "This shelter," he translated, "has space and provisions to hold eight men for a month, if necessary. There is even a ventilator, which extrudes from the top of the straw stack. Guns and ammunition are stored behind the stairway. In case of danger, men can enter. Then someone at the farm covers the trap-door with straw, and pushes the machine against the stack, covering the door."

We didn't learn until later that the farmhouse overlooked a field where the Royal Air Force often made night drops of supplies to the Résistance forces.

Perhaps drawn on by our interest, our tour director reached down into a recess behind the stair and produced a piece of paper. Proudly opening its folds, he displayed a reward poster bearing a poor likeness of last night's host. The poster gave his name as Abel Coton, described his crime as the assassination of some person in the locality, and offered a large cash reward for information leading to his arrest.

"He is an important man," he boasted. "The Germans are willing to pay a great deal to capture him. He bothers them a great deal."

Carefully, the man replaced the paper, closed the trap-door, concealed it with straw, and, rolling the hay rake back in place, motioned us to follow him. While Lieutenant Donahue relayed this information to Wright, Hooth and I followed the man through a cattle gate behind the barn, and to a shed made of prefabricated concrete on the hillside below. Digging with his hands, our friend produced a bundle from the dirt floor of the shed. Upon its unwrapping, we saw a British army revolver and several rounds of ammunition, well protected by layers of oilcloth and cotton. Neither Hooth nor I understood all he had to say, but it was evident that like a Boy Scout, our helper was prepared.

We later learned that our "tour guide" was Gilbert Hoebeke, a member of the Résistance group, who lived with his wife, Lea, at La Cavée, a small, remote settlement fronting a chapel not far from the safe house.

The precious bundle again in its hiding place, we returned to the courtyard just in time for a group picture. In the wrong hands, a photograph could be incriminating evidence, but our hosts acted as though it were a normal experience, so we relaxed and assumed the suggested pose. The elderly couple and the young woman were summoned, as was our young host. We four airmen knelt in front, with our host. The new arrival held the camera, then urged a second sitting to include just the crew members and our young host. As it had been earlier, with the drinks and the coffee, this was a moment of relaxed ritual. Our host introduced himself as "Jean."

Selecting a long straw from the stack, Jean carefully broke it into four segments, requesting that we each draw one. We did, then compared lengths. With Lieutenant Donahue interpreting, he told us that beginning at 11 o'clock, we would depart at five-minute intervals, in the order of the length of our straw. Each was to continue his route until he met someone. We were to greet that person with a password, and he should respond with another. If we were greeted by a different response, we were to smile and walk on. Eventually, we would meet the right person, whom we were to accompany.

Mine was the second longest straw. At five minutes after eleven, I said goodbye to the others and went through the back gate and through the field. A few hundred yards below, among trees bordering a small stream, a man seemed to be inspecting a fence. I recognized him to be our burly escort of the evening before. He gave the correct response to my utterance. We shook hands, then crossed the stream and walked in company. A short time after, we emerged from a field at the edge of a small paved road. Directly ahead, by a walled farmstead, a young man was occupied in changing small triangular-shaped license plates on a bicycle. A second bike leaned against the wall. With scant attention to this man, my guide ushered me into the open courtyard and knocked on the door. A small gray-haired woman, in a gray *tablier* — a smock that served as an apron — covering her black dress, opened the door and waved us in. Closing the door behind us, she embraced me and kissed me on both cheeks. I thought that I had never been made more welcome — even my grandmother had kissed me only once in greeting!

A man, likely her husband, entered the room and repeated her welcome. I thought these people must really be fond of Allied airmen. A few words were exchanged with my guide, then the lady reached into the basement door and withdrew one of those fat dark bottles.

"Cognac," she said, and I gathered enough of her words to think that this treasure had been carefully concealed from the Germans and guarded for just such a great occasion as this. Accepting the toast on good faith, I downed the fiery beverage. Then, offering our thanks, my companion led me to the bicycles. The man who had been switching license plates was nowhere to be seen. We took the bikes and pedaled slowly down the road, with me in tandem.

The cognac eased the bumpiness of the roughly cobbled road, and I settled in for a long excursion. But soon we stopped again, at a small house where the cobbles ended, and where the greetings of the first house were repeated. I left the house with a feeling of euphoria, and we continued on along a dirt track, which wound through surrounding fields.

Once along the route we encountered a party of young people. My guide, apparently feeling that the situation called for a disguise, pulled a pair of spectacles from his pocket and adjusted them on his face. Then he pulled his bike off the *sentier* — the sort of path with which the countryside was laced. Dutifully, I followed his example. Turning his back to the young folk coming up the path, he relieved himself. I did likewise, surprised that the observers discreetly paid no attention to what would have been a serious breach of etiquette at home. It was a mode of concealment, which would serve me well later. Apparently satisfied that all was well, my guide pulled off his cap, revealing a covering of sandy straight hair, and from a pocket produced a beret. When we rode on, my companion had become a spectacled man capped by a beret.

Eventually, the *sentier* led to a village. Passing along the wall of a large building, we crossed a street, pushed our bikes along the building opposite, and entered from the rear. Again, we were met by an older couple — my guide's parents-in-law, Monsieur Ulysse and Madame Maria Rivier, I later learned. Also present was Adolphe's wife, Renée Rivier Clément.

Sometime later, we made exit through another door, opening into a tavern. Hastily, I went out the rear door, unaware that the presence of strangers was not remarkable in that place. By then, the celebrations had produced a salubrious effect, so that I might have ridden on for hours. But I was able to maintain my balance on the two-wheeler, although I had only the slightest recollection of our route. Perhaps it had been planned that way.

We skirted the rest of the village, turning onto another road, then on a much narrower road. Finally, my guide pulled up at a green metal gate beside a small house. In answer to the uproar of barking dogs, the gate was

The morning of June 15, 1944, at the “safe house,” near Rebaix (Hainaut), Belgium. It was not until after the war that I learned the names of our wartime “contacts,” such as Abel Coton. Front, l to r: Lieutenant Robert Donahue, Abel Coton, and Monsieur Ghislain Boucher, with dog. Rear, l to r: Lieutenant Douglas Hooth, Madame Hortense Boucher, Mademoiselle Berthe Delaunois, Lieutenant Richard Wright, and Sergeant William Cupp.

opened just enough for a short, dark-haired woman to slide through. She pulled the gate closed behind her and exchanged a few words with my guide. Then she seized me, kissing me on both cheeks. I was beginning to like this. Turning in tears to my companion, she launched into rapid conversation, plentifully punctuated by gestures. Those I understood, but I could make no sense at all of her language.

As my guide turned away in resignation, she kissed me again in farewell and I pedaled on, following my leader. He seemed to be thinking something over, and he scanned the countryside to the right and left. Finally, he seemed to have resolved the matter on his mind, and he waved in the direction of a small group of buildings on a nearby hill, above which the spire of a small chapel was visible. At the next crossroad, he veered to the left and pedaled along the narrow cobbled road in that direction.

A short, narrow drive curved around the small church, squeezing between it and the wall of the neighboring house. At the gate, which barred entrance to the neat courtyard, two dogs barked furiously at our approach.

"Tomy!" "Rex!" The dogs lapsed into silent vigilance at the command of the short woman, seemingly squarish under her full apron, who answered their bark. From beyond the gate, she peered up at my companion. Apparently, we were unexpected, and it did not seem that these two knew each other. At length, however, satisfied with my guide's explanation, the lady unlatched the padlocked chain securing the gate and led us into the courtyard and around a brick outbuilding, which shielded us from view from the entry drive. There she paused and entered into serious conversation with my guide while I waited anxiously for developments.

As best I could interpret the situation, my guide had expected to lodge me in the small house down the road. When that had proved impossible, he had improvised a plan to request that these people put me up for some period of time. Though he did not know them, he must have had some information that they were trustworthy, and his current task was to persuade them to harbor me. He seemed to be succeeding.

Turning her head toward the adjoining barn, the diminutive lady called, "René!"

From the barn emerged a man, tall by the standards to which I had become accustomed, dressed in wooden shoes and faded blue cotton trousers; under a gray sleeveless sweater the sleeves of his cotton shirt were rolled up to the elbows. Quizzically surveying the scene, he came to

The Hombeck home, 6 *rue du Buisson*, Œudeghien (Hainaut), Belgium, 1949.

the lady's side to acknowledge her introductions. Her arm shading her face from the sun, she spoke rapidly to him, repeating, I supposed, the explanations given to her. René pulled off his cap, wiping a trace of perspiration from the white forehead above his tanned face. As he nodded assent to her remarks, my companion relaxed in relief. Shortly after, he departed, leaving my bicycle in the courtyard.

These kind people were René and Marie Hombeck, whose farm was at the very edge of the commune of Œudeghien, their house adjacent to the chapel of *Notre Dame du Buisson*. Also living at home was their daughter, Eliane Hombeck, just then visiting her grandmother at Brugelette, near the Chièvres *aérodrome*.

★ ☙ ★ ☙ ★

My hosts lost no time in making me welcome and establishing the basis of our relationship. The small, intense woman stood on the lower step leading into the house where her gray eyes could level with mine.

"*Mama*," she said, pointing toward her bosom. "*Papa*," she said with emphasis, pointing to René. He nodded his assent.

So far, I understood. Then, pointing to me she said what sounded like "*feese*." She had me repeat the words, pointing to René and herself. Then she launched into a torrent of words I couldn't fathom. She tried again, emphasizing the last word, which sounded to me like "*Sir*." I looked at René and said, "*Papa*," then added "*Sir*." From their expressions, I gathered that I still had not got it right.

Mama recommenced, this time with gestures. Shaking his head at my lack of comprehension, René stepped out of his wooden shoes — *sabots* — put on a pair of slippers resting by the door, and vanished into the house. When he returned, he carried a faded red book, its frayed cover bearing testimony to frequent use. He leafed the pages of the French-English dictionary to find the key words in his message. "*Fils*" meant son; I gathered that it was pronounced like "*feese*." So I was expected to act as a son should to my erstwhile Papa and Mama. Many words later, the longer message became clear also. A young lady would come to the house — their daughter. Since I was now their son, she would be my sister. Now the message was unmistakable — and I had better treat her as a sister, or else!

The one-story outbuilding connected to the house was equipped with cream separator and a large electric churn. In a corner stood a lavatory, the dipper hanging from a nail by its side suggesting that it be filled from the nearby water pump. I washed my hands and face, drying on the towel draped conveniently by its side. Pulling the stopper, I discovered that the lavatory drained into a bucket underneath. A grate in the floor by the pump could be used to dispose of the contents of the bucket.

As I returned to the door of the house, Mama brought me a pair of slippers to wear always when I entered. The door opened into a kitchen. Taking a chair at the oilcloth-covered table, I watched as Mama pulled dishes and tableware from a large oak cabinet on the wall. Setting them on the table, she went to a door on the far wall. Stepping down, she produced from a shelf a large round loaf of bread, a plate of yellow butter, and a bottle of beer like the one I had been given on the previous day. Then, caressing the bread under her chin much as a violinist in concert, she drew a large knife across it twice, in the motion of a cross. We lunched on bread and butter sandwiches, which she called *tartines*, and light, musty-tasting beer.

The repast concluded, René returned to the barn while Mama showed me part of the house. The kitchen had four doors; on one wall was a door to the *cave*, or cellar. Directly opposite, a door opened on a tiny pantry from which there was no other exit. On the wall adjacent to the court, a door opened into a closet or cupboard, deep enough to conceal a person. Opposite the door to the court, another door led to a room equipped like a dining room. Like the kitchen, it too had four doors. One opened on the walk at the front of the house. To the east was another dining room, somehow more formal than the first. On the far wall, a mantel framed a place for a heating stove.

The only window, on the front, was barred and shuttered. A second door, on the north wall, led to a small bedroom decorated with pictures of film stars. Its only window, barred, looked into the milk house. From what I had seen so far, the only escape route led into the courtyard. That might do in case searchers came to the front door. But what if they came to the rear? My cognizance of my surroundings might save me from capture and even my life. It was time to examine the courtyard and outbuildings.

Framed by a clean brick walk running along the milk house, house, and stable, the neat dirt courtyard was shielded on the north by a large barn, and to the east by a cement wall. Anyone arriving at the gate by the chapel would, because of the milk house, be unable to see movement between the house and stable. There was a small gate in the cement wall behind the chapel, though, at the edge of a one-story addition to the barn. Should anyone approach from the gate, the stable door was clearly visible. I made a mental note to investigate that in greater detail. For now, however, I had better remain in concealment, though there might be a problem of security, for the water closet, or outhouse, was set into the barn, its door just visible from the gate. Walking to the stable door, I noted a barred window marking a room on the side of the house, one which I had not yet seen. Any exit from there would have to be through the dining room, too, past the front door. Only later would I learn that this was to be my bedroom.

The south wall of the stable was an extension of the house itself. The entire stable bore damp evidence of recent scrubbing. The far wall could accommodate a dozen cows. Several calves occupied temporary pens on the near side, adjacent to a hand pump from which water could be procured for the animals and for the task of scrubbing the barn. At the end of a brick walkway separating cows from calves was a connecting door to a stall in which two enormous horses were stabled. Behind them, a small stall could hold several calves. A short hallway led to the courtyard, while an outside door led directly to a manure pit and pasture beyond.

Because this part of the courtyard could be seen from the small gate on the east wall, I delayed examination of the barn and returned to the other end of the stable, noting that midway along the wall a ladder led to an opening in the ceiling. Two doors were situated in the south wall. One led to a large, square room containing a pile of forage beets and a walled compartment housing a motorized chopper. The other door, just inside the entry, disclosed a metal stairway leading to a loft. Remnants of last year's hay could be seen on the concrete floor above the stables. A two-tined fork leaned beside the square opening above the ladder. In the section above the beet room were stored odds and ends of harness, a large wooden trough on legs, several sacks — probably grain — and a variety of other things.

Three wooden steps accessed a door above the house. Clear glass tiles had been placed among the red clay tiles of the roof, providing illumination by day.

The attic, or granary, which I later learned to call *le grenier*, was divided into two rooms. The first was piled deep with grain; in the second, two small windows faced the front, low to the floor. Bunches of dark tobacco hung from the rafters. Except for a few pieces of furniture, apparently in storage, the room was bare. Unless other objects were brought to the attic, it would not offer a good hiding place. Once the hay crop was harvested, though, and heaped in the mow, the prospect could be improved.

René would not permit me to help him milk the cows that evening, but I was allowed to carry pails of warm milk to the milk house. There I discovered that the room had several functions, serving also as a back kitchen and, because of the hand pump beside the cream separator, it was used for laundry and general washing. After starting the electrically powered separator, Mama Marie took the buckets of milk from me and poured the contents through the strainer on top. Even though she performed this task easily, I felt that heavy work of this sort should be left to men, as was the custom in my home. So I waited restively until buckets were full of skimmed milk, and then carried these back to the barn, to be fed to the calves. When this chore was at last finished, we retired to the supper Mama had been preparing between trips to the milk house.

As darkness approached, the windows of the house were shuttered, for Europe like the United States, was in blackout during the war years. René returned from this chore with a strand of the tobacco I had seen curing in the attic above. He went directly to the large *Telefunken* table radio in the kitchen and dialed in a news program, before rummaging for a pipe and taking his seat. As he listened to the news, he untwisted the strands of tobacco, pressing an end into the bowl of his pipe. I watched in curiosity as the several strands that protruded from the bowl ignited, but no calamity followed. A few ashes spilled on the clean tile floor, and others were brushed off his lap. Mama accepted this indiscretion without comment, as René puffed contentedly, apparently oblivious to the acrid stench that began to fill the room. Now and again he commented to Marie as she bustled about, bringing clean dishes to replenish the cabinet.

The newscast apparently finished, René rose to adjust the radio, and the chimes of Big Ben in London announced the news from the BBC. Marie peered apprehensively into the room at that sound, and I thought that René, too, seemed alert for noises from outside the house. As I listened to accounts of the fighting in Normandy, and to other bits of news, which I was unable to discuss, I felt less isolated from my unit and the life I had known up to my hasty exit from the doomed Liberator.

At bedtime, Mama Marie ushered me into the small room behind the formal dining area. The sheets still carried the fresh scent of outdoor drying, and their flannel composition felt good to me in my underwear. The mattress and coverlet had been made of down. This bed was much more comfortable than was the straw in which I had slept the last night. Come to think of it, I had not had so comfortable a bed for many months.

Chapter 4

A Day on a Belgian Farm

DAYLIGHT WAS SHINING through the window when I was wakened by the hum of the cream separator in the adjoining milk house. Tugging on my clothing, I went to the kitchen, not yet knowing whether I dared enter the courtyard unless I was told to do so. Through the now unshuttered window I could see Mama passing by as she carried milk between stable and milk house.

At breakfast, there were *tartines* again — this time with jam — and coffee. Dropping a large square of sugar into my cup, I noticed that Mama and René each dipped their sugar into the coffee, then placed the lumps in their mouths, straining the coffee through it. I made a mental note to copy that. When I got on the road to find my way back to England, I should not wish to be betrayed by non-European dining customs.

Listening to their conversation, I learned that René called Mama Marie. I continued to call them Papa and Mama, as they had requested, which they seemed to appreciate.

Lingering for a few minutes after breakfast, René began a French lesson — just a few obvious words — for wall, floor, and ceiling. Then he was gone, to the field I correctly supposed.

The kitchen was no place for me when Marie began scurrying about her morning household tasks. Once the dishes were cleared, she quickly piled the chairs seat down on the dining table, and with a large thick towel deftly twirled around a handle she began to scrub the kitchen floor. I retreated to my bedroom, but once there, remembered that I would need the dictionary from the kitchen closet in order to construct questions. I would require paper and a pencil too, to write down the words I wanted to find in the dictionary. As I returned to the kitchen, Marie was sweeping water from the tile floor with a squeegee, pulling a small tide through the door that opened on the court. I waited until the floor was dry before entering; it seemed like a good idea. Once her attention was attracted, Marie listened alertly, her head cocked slightly to the side. She grasped my meaning instantly, reached into the closet, and withdrew the dictionary from a shelf. Thumbing through the pages, I located the words for paper and pencil. She nodded, then pronounced the French words several times to be sure that I could say them. Only then did she rummage in the kitchen cabinet to procure the writing equipment for me.

Back in the bedroom, I found and jotted down the word for map — *carte*. I would need one to find out where I was, and perhaps others in order to plan a route. Should I try to travel to Spain and try to get to England from there? It was a lot closer to go to Normandy and to try to contact Allied troops directly, but just how feasible was that? Just before leaving England we had heard that one of the men from our group had hidden in a well after parachuting, and stayed there while the battle passed over him. He should be back at the air base by now.

It seemed risky to try to find the front lines if a safer route were available. How could I travel? By train? How does one buy tickets, and to where? How difficult would it be to cross the border into France?

There were a lot of words to look up. But first, I needed maps. Thumbing through the dictionary, I set about to construct a phrase that would make my request intelligible. Yet finding the right words was the least of the problem. How do you ask a question in French? In what order must the words be placed? The dictionary provided few clues to the matter of word order, but I constructed an alternative way of phrasing the map question. I then began to tackle the matters of the best roads, and how to cross the border into France. The sheet of paper was quickly filled, forcing me to seek out Marie for a new supply.

Cautiously entering the kitchen, I found the table freshly set for lunch. From the small side room came sounds of last-minute preparations, as Marie was removing a kettle of soup from the fire. Just then René appeared at the door, sliding into his slippers in preparation for entry. I thrust the paper with my questions into my pocket. I would ask them later.

As René and I took our seats, Marie brought the savory-scented kettle to the table and began spooning soup into our bowls. I watched as René took an oval slice of bread from the basket. Cutting it in two, he put a half-moon-shaped piece in his bowl, on top of the soup. I followed his lead, and watched as the saturated bread billowed out. At home, we sometimes put soda crackers in soup. The soup, which I was later to identify as leek soup, was delicious, and the soaked soft bread lent substance. Marie joined us, eating quickly before scooping up the dishes and bringing more food to the table — meat, boiled potatoes, and a garden vegetable. When our plates were clean, René pushed his cap back from his forehead in relaxation, and the couple began to converse a bit. I then seized the opportunity to ask about the map.

My question puzzled them; possibly I had not properly constructed the phrase. I tried a different word order, with similar results. Was it word order or poor pronunciation? In frustration, I pushed my paper to René. Gravely, he examined the writing with faintly concealed puzzlement. Showing the paper to Marie, he said something to her. She responded, returning the handwritten sheet to him. Leaning toward me, he pointed to the key word, "*carte*."

"*Oui, carta*," I acknowledged.

"*Cart*," René corrected, omitting the final *e*. So pronunciation must be part of the problem. In the future I would check pronunciation by looking up each word in the French section of the dictionary; it would take time, but I might be able to improve our dialogue.

The subject of my query being identified, Marie quickly went to the kitchen cabinet and from a drawer produced a Michelin road map of Belgium, which she handed to René. Then she cleared the table so that we could spread out the map. With his index finger René began my orientation by pointing to a spot and emphasizing the place name, *Œudeghien.* Words reinforced by gestures demonstrated eloquently that this area was Œudeghien, and was the name of a village, too, which lay off somewhere to the southwest of the house. I repeated his words, indicating my comprehension. Apparently satisfied that I understood this much, he motioned in the direction of the small church next door. "*Chapelle du Buisson*," he intoned.

He continued the orientation by pointing to other place names on the map and waving his arm in their general direction from the kitchen table — Ostiches, Lessines, Ogy, Wodecq. Owing as much to his gestures as to the volume of words he uttered, I gathered that our plane had crashed at Wodecq. That agreed with the information I had received earlier. He said more about it, but I could not understand.

His finger once again on the map, he pointed out Mainvault, then Ath, then a wavy line marked by tiny crosses — the border between Belgium and France — a *frontière*, he explained. It appeared to be about 33 to 35 kilometers to the border. Then, handing me the map, he turned to Marie. Her after-lunch cleanup operations apparently concluded, she urged me gently, but decisively, to my bedroom.

I pored over the map, trying to estimate points where I might cross the border with the least chance of detection. Surely the roads would be patrolled by border guards or troops, and there I would need some sort of identity card or passport. Even if I had the necessary credentials, it would be a risky business. I was not fluent enough in the local pronunciation of the language to answer any questions put to me. So it appeared that a safer route would be through some forested area, where border guards might be evaded. But was there a great likelihood that the enemy had military posts in some of these woods? I would have to find out. I returned to my dictionary, acutely conscious of the fact that I had neglected to ask for an additional supply of writing paper.

★ ★ ★

A short hour after lunch, Marie interrupted my speculation, summoning me again to the kitchen for dessert. At the table, René once more attempted to establish communication. Now and then he switched to speech in which I could recognize a few words. Marie stood by alertly watching for some sign of comprehension from me, and nodding her approval whenever I indicated some understanding. Because I knew only individual words, and only a few of those, it was a slow process. But I did manage to communicate my need for writing paper before René left for work outside.

It was not long before there was a rattling of the chain at the gate. In answer, the dogs rushed through the courtyard to meet the visitor. But they were silent, as though greeting an old friend. While I retreated from the kitchen, Marie went to the gate. She returned, calling to René to meet this guest. I, too, was summoned from the parlor into which I had retreated.

Our visitor was a middle-aged man, dressed in neat and comfortable clothing. We were introduced; he was Gaston Termonia, of Renaix, René's brother-in law. Monsieur Termonia had come by the little interurban train especially to meet me. His mission, he explained in English, was to obtain information about me and my crewmates. He would then relay this news by radio to England. He confirmed the news I had heard earlier from Abel Coton that our pilot, Lieutenant Addy, had been killed when the plane had crashed at Wodecq, and that three of my companions had been captured immediately upon parachuting in the vicinity of an antiparachute lookout station. The rest of us were thought to be still at liberty and under the care of local people.

Monsieur Termonia carefully recorded my name, home town, birth date, and Army serial number, and assured me that news of my evasion would be sent to England within hours.

"Your family will be notified that you are alive and well," he said. "Now," he continued, "you are in good hands here. Marie tells me that you may have been thinking of leaving here to rejoin your military unit. You must not do that. Your General Eisenhower has issued an order for all downed airmen who are in safe hands to remain where you are. It is dangerous for you to leave."

With friendly words to the Hombecks, Monsieur Termonia looked toward the kitchen door. Turning back to me, he said, "I am happy that you are safe. You are in a good home. I shall return in a few days to see you again."

Then he left the house, accompanied this time by René as far as the gate. Marie, intent on reassuring me, told me that Monsieur indeed had a radio, which he kept concealed in his back garden. He was regularly in touch with authorities in London and well aware, she said, of orders emanating from Allied Headquarters. I should heed his advice to remain here on the farm.

I returned to my papers, thinking it a good idea to better understand this French language.

Momentarily, once again the dogs began a clamor at the gate. Gathering the dictionary, map, and writing materials, I withdrew quickly to the bedroom. After silently closing the door, I drew the curtain across the window to the milk house. Marie was already at the gate, commanding the dogs into silence. From the tone of the conversation, there seemed no need for undue alarm. Sitting on the bed, I opened the dictionary and resumed the task of finding the words necessary to ask the questions burdening my mind. This time, after locating a word, I looked it up in the French section and jotted down the symbols of pronunciation.

A few minutes later, Marie rapped on the bedroom door. Whatever the business at the gate, it had not taken long. It seemed unlikely that the visitor had been a close friend, however, for the guest had not been invited into the house. Marie conveyed that she wanted me to move from the bedroom, taking my belongings. That was easy enough. I gathered up my few possessions, escape kit, and the pencil, papers, and dictionary. Spying the escape kit, she asked for it, repeating something about "security." I extracted the tiny razor before surrendering it. I would find a way to ask for its return when I needed it.

Preceding me, Marie took me through the front room to the door on the side opposite, leading to, as I supposed, the master bedroom. At the rear, a door opened upon a small bedroom similar in size to the one I had just left. This one was equipped with a three-quarter size bed and a chair. Hanging space for clothing was provided by several hooks mounted on a board on the wall. A heavy curtain at the window could be drawn for privacy. The room was clean and neat, but otherwise bare. Shielded from prying eyes by the master bedroom, my only exit was through that room. In the event of a search of the house while I was in the room, I would be trapped. Until the time I could leave to rejoin my bombardment group, I knew I would have to find some safer place than the house in which to stay. I determined to explore the large barn during the evening.

Some time after Marie's departure there was a sound at the gate. This time the dogs did not bark. Straining to listen, I identified Marie's voice and the voice of another woman. The conversation seemed to be natural, as though the speakers were on good terms.

Shortly after, in the kitchen, I was introduced to the newcomer. This was my hosts' daughter, Eliane, the young lady whom I was supposed to treat as a sister — *only* as a sister. Now it was easy to see why Marie and René had made such a point of that. Eliane was about my own age, and pretty. When she smiled, crinkles formed at the outer edges of her blue eyes. Her short blonde hair had been neatly marcelled, undulating in symmetrical tiers from the part at the crown of her head. An attractive plaid suit clothed her softly rounded yet slender figure. Introducing us, Marie repeated her point about brother and sister, adding inclusively that with René, we were all one family. That certainly ruled out any other intentions I might have had — but then, I didn't expect to stay there much longer anyway.

A short while later, René returned from the fields, a short-handled hoe — *binette* — in his hand. He bade me join him in the milk house, where he drew water and washed. Toweling himself dry, he motioned for me to do likewise. In the kitchen, Eliane, now clad in a printed cotton frock and apron, was assisting Marie in setting the table for a lunch of *tartines* and beer. René questioned Eliane about her visit — with her grandmother, I gathered — and seemed satisfied with her news. Then, his repast finished, he indicated that it was milking time.

I asked to help, and this time the offer was accepted, with some residual skepticism, I thought. But from the barn René produced a pair of low-cut wooden shoes with a leather band over the instep. He gave them to me, indicating that I was to wear them while in the stable, and to keep my service shoes for outside wear elsewhere. Rather stiffly, I shuffled to the stable.

The rhythmic splash of milk in the bucket provided a welcome change from my forced inactivity. There really wasn't any difficulty with the milking; cows must be the same the world over. But my forearms soon became tired, reminding me that it had been nearly four years since I had attended this task on a regular basis. Soon the cadence of my rhythm began to lag behind René's steady pace. Then the effort became painful as I persisted, determined to perform some useful activity. After milking just three cows, though, I was grateful for René's comment that I had done enough for this time. I busied myself by carrying foaming buckets to the milk house, where Marie insisted on emptying their contents into the cream separator.

Lingering there until the separator discharged buckets of skimmed milk to be fed to the waiting calves, I rehearsed my feeble French vocabulary with Marie, who improved upon it by emphasizing the article attached to each noun. She corrected emphatically, "*Le plancher, le mur, le plafond, la table, le chien*" — the floor, the wall, the ceiling, the table, the dog.

In the stable, René took the buckets from me and poured their contents into small feeding pails for the calves. While he was occupied with this task, I examined the large barn. The door closest to the stable opened onto a small narrow room, which served as the farm bakery. A metal closure concealed a cavernous brick oven on the wall next to the stable. Shelves along the adjacent wall were stacked with tiers of round wicker baskets, possibly for holding dough or freshly baked loaves of bread. Along the far wall, several bound faggots of wood rested on the floor. Only the oven provided a potential hiding place, and that was secure only if a searcher failed to remove the door panel.

The main part of the barn served as equipment storage, and held a two-wheeled cart — a *tombereau;* a mower, a windrower — a device for raking fresh-cut hay into rows for drying, and a wagon for hauling. This section was too open and neat to provide cover. But a sort of loft was formed by the ceiling of the bakery room, separating the oven from the rest of the barn. A few odds and ends were stored at the far end of the loft, and there was a pile of straw at the front. Someone might hide here in case of urgency, particularly if they could silently ease the ladder to the floor after gaining the top; but there was not enough straw yet to provide sure cover.

Opposite the entry from the court, a large double door provided space for wagons to drive directly through the barn. Inset in one of the doors was a smaller door, so that a person had to step high to pass through. Cautiously, I opened it a crack and peered out to be certain that my actions were unseen. Buildings projected from either side. The roadway in the distance was clear, and the door was shielded from direct view from the road close by. I stepped out to investigate.

The building on the left was a sort of open shed, piled high with faggots like those in the bakery. The building nearer the road was a small stable, providing space for chickens to range between the fields and a henhouse in the portion of the barn that I had not yet explored. However, it was not a good hiding place, because entry would startle the hens into frightened cackling. Around the corner of this stable, closer to the road, stood an isolated building, with double doors facing away from the road. If it did offer a possible hiding place, it would still be difficult to get there undetected were the enemy to surround the farm buildings.

On my way back to the cow barn, I was reminded that the doors would be exposed to anyone standing by the gate to the courtyard. Neither did the stable area, its haymow, nor the attic of the house provide a secure sanctuary in the event of a search. On the other hand, the arrangement of the farm buildings themselves offered considerable freedom of movement and a good deal of privacy under ordinary circumstances. If the haymow above the stable had been full, it could offer a good hiding place. But the hay would not be coming in for a week or two, at best. I expected to be gone before that happened.

When I returned to the stable, René was already scrubbing the floor in readiness for the morning's milking. Sloshing a final bucket of water on the corridor, he brushed the water into the shallow gutter running along the rear of the raised platform for the cows, and shoved it to the drain hole at the far wall. That chore finished, he tugged at the bill of his cap, raising it above his forehead, and rubbed his brow before repositioning the cap, a characteristic gesture. It was time to return to the house for the evening meal.

Chapter 5

Fitting in to Farm Life

WE SAT ON THE front steps of the house that evening watching cottony clouds drifting over the jagged tree line to the west. As they assumed rosy hues from the setting sun, René, Marie, and Eliane chatted about local people and normal events. Half-listening, I gathered as much from the unhurried pace of the conversation as I could occasionally understand. They were enacting a scene familiar everywhere — people who, having completed the work of the day, find gentle relaxation in the still, soft light of evening.

A fragrant aroma drifted in from the fields and the call of quail in a distant meadow blended in with the casual tone of the conversation. The utter peacefulness of the setting seemed to mute the pervasive urgency of the war and the stern reality of the threat to these people should an Allied airman be discovered on their premises. At this moment, the Hombecks were synchronized with their environment, exacting from the moment every pleasure the evening had to offer.

Sitting beside them, as I reflected on Monsieur Termonia's message bidding me to remain here until Belgium was set free, I began to sense the optimism that they seemed to feel. For them, there was no question but that the war would soon be over and that the indignities and privations that they had been forced to endure over four long, hard years would be a thing of the past. They expected, without question, that it would end in the defeat of the oppressor, and they were prepared to assume any reasonable task in order to bring that about. Far from rushing pell-mell into rash ventures, they waited with seemingly endless patience, selecting from the opportunities that arose each day those actions most consistent with their overall aim.

Like it or not, I was thrust into their milieu; I wondered whether I should — or ever could — adopt the practical optimism I was witnessing. For the present time, at least, I would have to abandon an attempt to rejoin my Bomb group. It would seem best for me to learn to live like these folk, working on their farm to earn my keep.

A high-pitched thrum of aircraft motors awakened me from my ruminations, and from the northeast, a twin-engine Dornier bomber furtively hugged the ground as it passed toward France. I recognized the German plane from training manuals and flash cards. But this was the first time I had ever seen one in the air. Not so long ago, bombers of that type had flown audaciously over the Continent, and in terrifying numbers. The cautiousness of the pilot on this evening flight seemed to signal the impending eclipse of the vaunted *Luftwaffe*, and to justify the Hombecks' optimism.

Even so, the intrusion of the German plane into an otherwise idyllic evening had served as a reminder of the undeniable presence of the war. As René arose from his seat to perform the wartime ritual of closing the shutters, I was reminded of the conscious activism of people like Adolphe Clément and Jean and those people at the safe house. They followed their daily routines, too, but also persisted in striking actively at the enemy. Might there be some means whereby I could do the same?

★ ∽ ★ ∽ ★

Faint light came through a crack where the shutters met, when I was wakened by a quiet rustling from the master bedroom. Fearful lest I should intrude on their privacy, I waited in bed, listening to be sure that René and

Marie were both up and out of the room. The door to that bedroom opened, almost silently, then closed again. I lay still for a moment to be certain that no one was still in the process of dressing, then pulled on my clothes and cracked the door ajar. The bed was empty, so I made my way to the kitchen. René was already eyeing a plate of *tartines*, while Marie encouraged the stove to bring coffee water to a boil. I joined René at the table for the simple pre-chore breakfast, appreciative of the contrast this made with my boyhood years on the farm. There, upon rising, we virtually rushed to the barns to break ears of corn to stimulate the cows' entry to their customary places. The morning milking had been accompanied by our pangs of hunger, which could not be stilled until the cows had been returned to pasture, the fresh milk run through the separator, and the skimmed milk fed to calves and pigs. Having slept through this part of the morning each day since my arrival here, I had not realized before the simple comfort of milking cows without having a raging appetite.

This Sunday morning the cows were more accustomed to my presence, and my muscles had become readjusted to the task of milking. As the chores progressed toward completion, René expressed approval of having a useful co-worker in the barn. I felt better after that, and noted that the *sabots* now seemed less clumsy on my feet. I managed almost normal movement as I started the electric cream separator and exchanged whole milk for skimmed. In the calf pen, the larger animals greedily butted the smaller ones in their haste to gulp down warm, frothy milk, while René barked harshly at them in what proved to be a futile attempt to restore order.

In the kitchen, as Marie sliced a large, yellow loaf of bread, Eliane deftly spread the pieces from the oval mound of butter that had been marked with a neatly incised design. Then, cutting the slices in half, she folded one piece over the other to make *tartines*. It was apparent from their manner that this "Sunday bread" was a special treat, and its taste affirmed their judgment. Rich in eggs and butter, yet unsweetened, the bread crumbled like a rich cake. It was good when buttered, wonderful when dipped in the barley coffee, and better still when spread with jam.

René lingered at the breakfast table, unhurriedly engaging me in conversation and patiently attempting to improve my vocabulary. From the northeast, church bells from the village of Lahamaide began to toll. They were followed, shortly after, by the bells from the church of Œudeghien in the valley, René explained. Yet no one hurried to prepare to attend the morning service. Perhaps the family was reluctant to leave the house while I was there. Maybe they wished to avoid speaking to casual acquaintances lest someone undependable might guess that something unusual was going on in their household. Well, I reasoned, it was equally possible that they were not in the habit of regular attendance. I would not ask because it couldn't make any difference, and I would probably learn the answer in good time anyway.

The noon meal that day was special, too. Then during the customary Sunday afternoon of rest, someone came to the gate and was admitted to the kitchen. I remained in my room, but Marie found occasion to bring me dessert. Shortly after that guest left, another arrived. The afternoon grew tedious, broken only by the sound of indistinguishable voices from the kitchen and the occasional pounding of antiaircraft fire from the *aérodrome* at Chièvres. It was a relief when the last guest departed and I was invited to help with the chores.

The following afternoon, Monsieur Termonia arrived, carrying a parcel for me which contained two books in English. One was the collected short stories of Edgar Allen Poe, the other a novel by John Galsworthy. Now here was a way to drive away boredom!

Acknowledging my gratitude, Monsieur Termonia offered, "When you have read these, René will let me know, and I shall bring you more." Then, turning to another matter, he said, "I have been in radio contact with London, and have reported that you and your four comrades are alive and in good hands. I am told that another man — very likely from your crew — is lodged in the commune of Isières, but I have been unable to learn his identity. I am told that he speaks French. Do you know who that might be?"

I was confident that our tail gunner Bob Mathie did not speak French, and that if Clyde Pendray, our engineer, did he would certainly have told me. Norris? I didn't imagine that he did, but I couldn't be certain of that. Bomar, I knew, spoke Mexican Spanish, but he had never mentioned any knowledge of French. No, that gave me no clue to the identity of the other parachutist, but I fervently hoped that it was one of them. So far, I had heard of the certain capture of only three of my crew members.

"Perhaps we shall see," replied Monsieur, "though we have poor lines of communication with that commune. But you and the others can rest easily with the knowledge that your families will soon receive the news that you are alive and well."

Then at last accepting the glass of beer that Marie had pressed upon him, he chatted of other matters with the family before remounting his bicycle to return home.

The books went into hiding, concealed at the rear of a low shelf, under a bolt of cloth in the capacious wardrobe in the master bedroom. For days, they were sufficient to relieve the gnawing boredom of my benign captivity.

Late in the morning after Monsieur Termonia's visit, Bob Donahue came to call, this time in the company of his host's son, Raoul Ponchaut. Raoul was an affable young man, tall and athletic in appearance, his face ruddy under sandy hair. He gave the impression of being just under 30 years of age. Quaffing a beer at the kitchen table, he chatted amiably with Marie, occasionally directing a comment to Eliane who, as she readied the noon meal, moved about between the milk house, rear kitchen, and main kitchen. Then, his elbows on the table as he leaned forward to address me, Raoul spoke of his stay at his family farm. Gravely, he turned to Marie, waving his arm in emphasis as he spoke of a German soldier who had been reported in the vicinity. The message seemed to be that his family welcomed Bob and was honored to have him as a guest, but that the situation involved real danger all the same. Then, with a round of farewells, he left, with the news that Bob would stay with us overnight.

That evening, after supper, René produced two small folders of light brown paper. Passing one to each of us, he explained that these were the Belgian *Cartes d'Identités* — identity cards — for which we were waiting. Opening mine, I found my small photo, stamped with an official-looking raised imprint. On the line bearing the legend *Nom* — surname — and *Prenoms* — first name — was penned "Ghislain Néry." The *Etat-Civil* — marital status — was given as *Célibataire* — bachelor, and the age as just a year or two younger than my own. René emphasized that we should keep these with us at all times. The small cards fit neatly in an inner pocket of a coat, so there they went.

Néry Ghislain was the young man whose home was just down the hill to the west of the farm. I did not know at the time that the name was not fictitious, and though I saw him from a distance a time or two, I did not know his identity.

Bob Donahue's visit was a welcome diversion from the narrow routine of recent days, and offered the occasion for fuller communication with the Hombecks. For one thing, we learned that a few months earlier the family had sheltered another downed American, a bombardier, whose name was Charles Lambert. Lambert had been moved by the Underground sometime before the Normandy invasion, and the Hombecks were hopeful that he had arrived safely in England. Naturally, they had no way of knowing whether his transfer had been successful.

Following Bob's departure, Marie expressed satisfaction with his visit, and with evident pleasure remarked that I was making good progress with my French. Inactivity began to weigh heavily however, and I returned to the volume by Poe. I first re-read "The Gold Bug," an adventure tale of pirate treasure. I had read it long before, at an age when I was too young to fully appreciate its depth. Among the other selections were "William Wilson," "The Cask of Amontillado," and "The Pit and the Pendulum." The stories were short enough to be read during brief periods of banishment to the rear bedroom, the plots sufficiently gripping to drive other concerns from my mind. Poe's fascination with themes of human conflict and his flair for providing a macabre twist to the story's ending served to make those frequent hasty exits from the living quarters almost welcome.

Sometimes, when activity in the kitchen was at low ebb, and when a guest had departed before I had finished a tale, I brought the book to the kitchen table in preference to reading alone on my bed. Once, while reading, I looked up as Eliane passed the table on some errand across the room. Impishly, I tugged at her apron string, untying the knot. She responded by shaking a finger accusingly at me and shouting, "Naughty boy!" But the crinkling of her eyes betrayed her good humor about the teasing. I would tease her again, but it would be better if her parents didn't see me.

★ ✤ ★ ✤ ★

Even though I was acutely aware of the periods calling for retreat from the activities around the farm buildings, a pattern of activity was becoming apparent. One day was devoted to baking bread. While René stoked the large brick oven with faggots, heating the interior to just the right shade of white, Marie, buckets of water in hand, climbed the stairs to the space beside the granary. There she mixed a huge batch of dough in a large wooden trough, bent low over the kneading, and fashioned large circular globs, which she placed in the wicker baskets. Being at hand while watching these proceedings, I helped carry them to the baking room, probably saving René a few steps. They rested there while the yeast completed the rising process. By this time, René had raked the ashes from the oven.

Extracting the loaves one by one from the baskets, Marie placed each one on a long wooden spatula, and René expertly distributed them until the oven was full, then replaced the metal cover that served as a door. They baked as Marie cleaned her implements. Some time later, René opened the oven door and inspected the baking. When satisfied, he again used the long spatula to extract the sweet-smelling loaves, which Marie replaced in the wicker containers and set on the shelves to cool. Later they were stacked in the cellar until needed in the kitchen.

There was a wash day, too, which seemed to be women's work. An exception was made for me. I pumped water in the milk house to fill the kettles heating on the gas plate, where potatoes, "fried in the French manner," as Thomas Jefferson described them in the late 1700s, were cooked for dinner. While the water was heating, Marie sorted the clothing, emptying pockets of grain chaff. This work Marie preferred not to trust to men, so standing idly by, my eyes took in a large copper tub used for rinsing. I asked its name. "*C'est le chaudron*," Marie replied. That made sense to me because it was similar to cauldron, an English word, which could designate the same object. "*Répétez le mot*," Marie commanded. She tensed at my response, repeating the word with emphasis. "*Répétez*," she repeated, vibrantly rolling the "r."

With infinite yet evidently hard-tested patience, she conducted this chorus for a full half-hour. By the time she resigned with a helpless shrug from her task, my voice had become hoarse. By then I was willing to continue trilling the "r" on the end of my tongue. Evidently my practice had begun too late in life to reach down my throat for the sound.

Washed and rinsed, the clothing was hung to dry in the court, on lines stretched between the barns. When rain came — mere drizzle did not count — they were pinned to lines permanently installed in the kitchen. In either case, drying was slow in this humid climate.

The following day the clothing was inspected for necessary mending, after which each article was ironed, including stockings. "Then they will be dry when I put them away," Marie explained, as she bent over the kitchen table to press a shirt that opened only halfway down from the collar.

Butter-making was another project scheduled into the weekly routine. Cream, stored in closed cans and kept cool in a tank at the far end of the milk house, was poured into a large wooden churn installed next to the separator. A heavy-duty electric motor tumbled the wooden tub until the task was completed. Pungent-scented buttermilk was drawn off into clean buckets, and the solids were left to drain. Only then were the rich yellow contents extracted, separated into smaller globules, and patted to remove the last clinging drops of buttermilk. Placing a clean, white sheet of wrapping paper on the scales, Marie sized the globules into half- and one-kilogram portions and molded them into loaves. Then with the back of a knife, she incised them with her characteristic markings, wrapped them up, and carried them to the cellar for safe keeping. Those not needed for home consumption were marketed among her special clientele or, I came to believe, in Brussels.

On Saturday mornings, there was no haven in the house for an idle male. I moved here and there to stay out of the path of determined cleaners, who made it clear that this was earnest business. Already impressed by the gleaming effect from daily cleaning, I was astonished by the thoroughness of the weekly campaign against dirt. Mop bucket in hand, Marie entered room after room, stacking chairs on beds or tables, the better to expose the tiled floors. Then with a long-handled squeegee, or *raclette*, she briskly pushed a *torchon* — a large, thick cloth — to scrub every inch of floor. With fresh, clear water she retraced her path, then pulled the water away with the squeegee through the doorway of the next room. Eliane followed her, room by room, dusting everything visible — wardrobes, furniture, pictures, figurines — and perhaps things invisible. As Marie splashed the last of the scrub water through the kitchen door onto the steps leading from the court, Eliane was already standing on a chair and dusting the small ornaments that rested on the shelf above the door to the rear kitchen.

Marie's determined glance led her next to the milk house. While she mounted a furious attack on any germs foolish enough to seek shelter there, Eliane swept the walkway again, around three sides of the court. She extended her toil to the drive between the chapel and house, then swept the sidewalk in front of the house before assaulting the brick path which, together with the drive, circled the chapel. Finally, wearing boots and equipped with soapy water and brush, she fell on her knees and scrubbed the entire set of walks.

As Marie made her exit from the sparkling milk house, her daughter was about to enter. Eliane, with damp wisps of hair protruding from under her kerchief, her face rosy from exertion, hands reddened by scrubbing, and knees splotched with damp soil, now had a new objective — her own cleanliness.

By the time that Marie had brushed the dirt courtyard to remove all evidence that animals or hay had ever dared to impose upon it, Eliane emerged from her ablutions. And a few minutes later, groomed as though she had never witnessed so ignoble an activity as a household chore, she mounted her bicycle and pedaled away to visit her grandmother.

Other than the field work and milking, the time not devoted to these weekly tasks was available for neighbors and other passers-by, and for relaxation — that is, the time left over from the regular activities of the day. Aside from her household duties, Marie fed and watered the chickens and pigeons and gathered eggs as well. In the early evenings, while René and I milked, she worked in the garden. She seemed truly to enjoy that task. Interspersed between the rows of potatoes, peas, beans, leeks, carrots, onions, and other vegetables were planted rows of peonies, bachelor's buttons, roses, lilies, irises, tulips, poppies, and other flowers also. This much I had gathered from peeping furtively from the window of the room where chickens roosted.

The house was strictly woman's domain, but René, too, assumed additional chores around the farm buildings. He pruned the orchard behind the barn, tended the few pigs and rabbits kept as a supplement to the family larder, repaired the hardware, and, I was told, plowed the garden in preparation for planting. I expected to learn more about the life of a farmer if ever I were permitted to go to the fields — permission for which came soon after.

At dinner one evening, René leaned over the table to speak to me. "Tomorrow morning you may leave the house to work with me," he confided. "It has been arranged. I have told the neighbors that a cousin who has never been here before is coming for a visit. If someone speaks to you, just smile; don't say anything to them. I have said that my cousin cannot speak well."

Pleased, I responded with a simple, "I understand."

But did I? Somehow I got the impression that René had let it be known that his cousin had something wrong with him. Could he have told the neighbors that I was an idiot? I would learn later, in fact, that he had told them his nephew was from Flanders and spoke no French.

The following morning René and I walked together through the pasture behind the barn, slipped through the barbed-wire gate where he drove his cows to alternate pasture, and walked a short way down the narrow road to a patch of tobacco. Working side by side with the short-handled *binettes*, we loosened the soil around each plant, clipping tiny weeds as we went. A short time later we were joined by Marie, who fell into position on the row adjacent to René's. He moved from his position to her row, hoeing to meet her. That accomplished, they resumed activity where René had left off, and we worked side by side. Eliane followed Marie to the field, taking the row next to her mother, and a family conversation soon accompanied the work.

My back ached from the unaccustomed stooping, and I wished for a long-handled hoe such as we used at home. When at last we paused to straighten our backs, I had formulated a way to tell them of this happy innovation. They accepted the news with little interest.

Pushing back his cap to wipe the perspiration from his forehead, René observed, "With the *binette* a person is close enough to his work to see all of the weeds." Then, so as not to seem disparaging of an alien custom, foolish as it may be, he added, "Each country has its own ways." That settled the matter; if I wanted to work in these fields, I would have to get used to stooping.

A passer-by on the road dismounted his bicycle, and René interrupted his work to meet his advance. A moment later, Marie and Eliane joined them. From the side, I could see them glancing in my direction — probably explaining my presence, I thought. I stood up, nodding a greeting, and continued my task. Shortly after, the man retrieved his cycle and pedaled off, and the Hombecks rejoined me. That incident had come off all right.

We were seated on the ground sharing *tartines* and beer when a family came to work in the patch next to ours. Eliane arose and went to greet them — a couple, a teenager, and a child. The snack finished, René and Marie joined them briefly, while I resumed hoeing. The talk, when the Hombecks returned, seemed centered on that family and the exchange of neighborhood news. About all I could glean from the conversation was that the name of the teenager was Paula. At about 11 o'clock, Marie left the field to tend the poultry and prepare lunch. We worked on until noon. The afternoon and the next few days involved a routine similar to this, though Marie and Eliane spent less time in the fields on days devoted to household tasks. Paula's family was often in the tobacco patch adjacent, talking together as they worked, and their task, like ours, was frequently interrupted for unhurried conversation with passers-by.

What a contrast that made with life on a farm in the American Midwest! We more frequently worked in solitude in much larger fields and cultivated not by hand but with machinery drawn by horses or tractors. We had less opportunity to encounter neighbors, for we characteristically met only momentarily when our machines coincidentally arrived at the same moment at the end of a row of grain or when they stirred up clouds of dust as they drove by on a quick errand to town. By comparison, our pace was more constant, even swifter.

At home, visits seemed more purposeful, and more hurried, except on Sundays or holidays. Here, in Belgium, each occasion to exchange a word with a neighbor seemed to fit naturally into the expected unfolding of time, as things ordained, as were the tasks for each day. It seemed that these casual meetings wove a living web between friends and neighbors, promoting a deep sense of identity with the community. And for families laboring together in the fields, the sharing of information and sentiment extended as fully to children as to adults. How practical it was to expose children to work as an enterprise in common, to which each contributed and from which each — and all — received tangible benefits and could expect more in the future! While they shared these daily tasks, children were included in matter-of-fact judgments concerning daily and community affairs, instead of leaving those tasks to memorized lessons at school and church.

When Sunday arrived once more and, after the morning chores were finished, René seemed to have something in mind for me to do. Marie had brought a shirt, freshly laundered and pressed, for me to wear, and René, handing me a tie, took great pains to tutor me in the tying of a Windsor knot, apparently the style of choice. Eventually I produced a knot of which he approved, and wearing one of his sweaters, I was ready to accompany him on some mysterious errand.

Together we walked down the narrow road on which I had first arrived at the Hombeck house. At the crossroads we turned to the right, still retracing the path by which Adolphe had led me after departing the safe house. The little house to which Adolphe had first brought me was just ahead, and there René turned and rapped at the green gate. When the rap was answered, I still had no idea what this visit was about. But inside, in a bedroom, sat Frank McPherson, our radio operator, his leg propped up on a pillow. We were surprised and happy to see one another, and we had a lot to talk about. Frank had hurt his legs when he landed, and had rolled in his parachute, right into a neighboring grain field. He had heard his companions, Pendray, Mathie, and Norris, being taken prisoner. But apparently his presence went unnoticed. He had lain all day in that field, but a patriot had come that night and carried him away. A mile or so later, the man found a bicycle and pushed Frank a long distance to a house where he was welcomed.

He was comfortable, he said, but he missed the supplies he had packed expressly for such an occasion in his parachute bag — two cartons of cigarettes and a box of candy bars.

"Just as I was reaching for that bag, Pendray, who was trying to lighten the plane, picked it up and tossed it out the rear escape hatch. If I ever see him again, I'd like to kill him!"

McPherson did like to smoke.

A young man entered the room as we spoke, eagerly displaying several leather patches. I recognized them as the ones we had made in El Paso, to identify our personal flight clothing. They had been sewn onto our leather flying boots and on the sheepskin trousers and jackets, as well. On mine was printed, "W. L. Cupp Gunner." He held up another, "C. C. Pendray Gunner."

"Here is another one," he said. "That man's name is Gunner, too. Are you all brothers?"

McPherson painfully got to his feet to retrieve something from a dresser. He had to support himself by leaning on the furniture. It must have been very uncomfortable to be confined in a single room, without reading material and no change of scenery, I thought. I was grateful for the variety in my own situation. Then, René, who had been conversing with the adults in the house, came to the door, indicating that we must leave. Because we were staying only a half-mile or so from one another, I expected to see Frank again soon.

Just across from the entrance gate, a narrow road intersected the one on which we had approached the house. René led me on this new route, passing a small house at the intersection and, when we were well past this house, we entered a field and walked diagonally across, toward a cluster of farm buildings in the lowland beyond. Reaching the buildings, we circled around to the front, and came into a barnyard. I learned that this was the *Ferme du Chamberlan*, where Bob Donahue's host family, the Ponchauts, lived.

During the feudal age, the *ferme* — farm — had been a dependency of the chateau of Lahamaide, owned by the Count of Egmont. It apparently had been awarded to the Count's Chamberlain — manager — hence the name.

We were expected, and greeted at the door by Néry Ponchaut and his two small granddaughters, Oda and Odette. Madame Ponchaut joined us from the kitchen where she apparently had been preparing a meal, and led me to the dining room. Bob Donahue was just then spooning the last from a large bowl of soup. Rosa Ponchaut, the daughter-in-law of the elder Ponchauts, bustled in, carrying a tureen of steaming soup. Bob accepted a second helping, and I, too, was served. We sat at a long table with dishes in place for a large assembly. As Bob and I finished, the persons who were to occupy those several chairs at the table filtered in.

A middle-aged couple, Rosa's parents, Monsieur and Madame Leleux, arrived at the door, accompanied by another couple. They were introduced as Monsieur and Madame Pilate, the parents of Raoul Pilate, a handicapped young man who apparently was staying with the Ponchauts. And finally, Raoul Ponchaut, the young married son of the family, came in from the barn, saying that he had been caring for the family's horses. It was a bit confusing, trying to keep the names and relationships straight; fortunately, I wasn't tested on that.

Rosa brought soup for the diners. I declined, and Bob indicated that he had eaten quite enough. When the soup plates were taken away, platters of beef, potatoes, and vegetables were brought in, with gravy, bread, and butter, and several bottles of table beer.

At that array, Bob let out a groan, "Had I known that there would be all these things to eat, I wouldn't have had that second bowl of soup," he declared.

There was a salad course, too. The food was very good, and I ate until I was stuffed. Then, while Rosa and the elder Madame Ponchaut cleared away the dishes, the rest of us left the room.

In the parlor, the pretty little twins, Odette and Oda, begged to "ride the horsie." Bob had introduced them to this game, which consists of an adult seated on a chair with one leg crossed over the knee of the other, and a child perched on a protruding foot. The "horsie" was the dangling, wriggled foot. The little girls took immense pleasure in this game, perhaps especially because there were two of us to act as steeds.

Raoul then led Bob and me into a field behind the barns and pointed to a faint depression in the ground. This, he declared, was where another airman had landed when his parachute failed to deploy. It was not a pleasant thing to contemplate.

When we returned to the house, the women had cleared the dishes and we were all shooed into the back yard to have photos taken. Several years later I received small prints of a couple of them. Declaring that our main meal must have settled by now, we were urged again to the table for coffee and a healthy helping of dessert.

It was becoming late, and the farmers now had to return to their chores. I accompanied René back to the farm.

The following day, the tobacco patch having been cultivated for the time being, I found René in the barn, oiling his McCormick-Deering mower. The hayfield was ready, and soon there would be a better sanctuary in the haymow, should it ever be needed. When the task was completed, René harnessed the two massive horses, hitched them to the rake, and headed for the field, a small one — perhaps only four or five acres. He was back before noon, oiling the hay rake.

After lunch, a short nap, and dessert, I accompanied him to the field, just a short distance down a rutted lane bordering the cement-posted fence line directly across the road from the chapel. I hurried ahead of the team to open the gate, and leaned my two-tined pitchfork against the fence for later use — just what use I was soon to learn.

René urged the horses back and forth across the field, gathering hay in the curved, rake-like catcher, and by a foot lever, dropped it into long piles which, after a few passes, became extended windrows. When he had completed three or four of those, he invited me to turn these over, the better for them to dry. This was a new idea for me, for at home the sun quickly baked the hay, making this an unnecessary step. The two-tined fork was a novelty too, and required more mastery than I, being accustomed to a three-tined hay fork, would have guessed. But the work was a pleasant change from confinement in the farm buildings, and the collie, Rex, active in chasing rabbits from the fence row, stopped by between forays for a pat on the head.

Turning the hay over, I was surprised to notice the quantity of chaff from Allied aircraft that had dropped in the field. I would soon discover that this field was not unique in this respect; chaff was evident in just about every field I visited.

In mid-afternoon, René, having completed the windrowing, tied the horses to the fence and, *musette* sack in hand, invited me to sit near a cement utility pole at one end of the field. The leather *musette* was filled with *tartines* and a bottle of light beer. I was becoming used to the sweetly sour, musty taste of the light beer, and knew it to be a good thirst-quencher. As we chatted over this light repast, I couldn't help thinking how this custom improved on its counterpart at home where, when thirsty, we made a hasty trip to the jug of well water and just as quickly returned to work. But having detected signs of visible life in the water drawn from the milk house well, I concluded that the beer just might be healthier to drink than the water.

The snack dispatched, René got to his feet and led me across a deep, narrow ditch and through the fence to a small pasture where several heifers were grazing. Attracted by our presence, they meandered in our direction. I could see why. The small cement tank in the field was nearly empty. From the *sentier* at the corner of the field, René fetched a bucket which had a long rope attached. Depositing it on the ground, he removed the heavy cover from a well beside the tank, tied one end of the rope around his leg, and dropped the bucket, upside down, into the well where it landed with a hollow thump in the water. Bending low, he tugged hand over hand, raising the bucket until he could seize the bail, then sloshed its contents into the tank. A few buckets later, I relieved him of the task, eventually — though wet — overcoming my initial clumsiness. I had just acquired a regular chore, but it would be later that I would come to understand why the rope was to be fastened securely to one's leg. If you ever have to fish a lost bucket out of a well, you are likely to be careful about that in the future. We returned to the hayfield, working on adjacent windrows to turn the hay.

The next morning, while waiting for the sun to drive the evening's moisture from the hay, I assisted René in loading seven-foot-long poles onto a three-wheeled dump cart. Pulled by a single horse, the cart bumped down the lane, and at René's command, halted briefly for us to unload the poles, in groups of three, at various points in the field.

Anticipating my question, René explained, "When the hay is dry enough, we will put it on these poles to finish drying. The air can circulate around it better, and it won't take up moisture from the ground."

As we raised the poles and fashioned them into tripods, I could see that the hay would be partly protected against rain as well, for the outer layer would shed some of the moisture. We finished the morning by turning the windrows again by hand, returning in the afternoon to fork the hay into haycocks, suspended from the tripods. The green-tinged grass would cure there for several days before it was carted to the barn for storage.

Bob came again for a visit, and as the noon meal was being prepared, a guest came to call. Bob and I were hustled off to the formal dining room for the duration of his visit. As often happened, Marie managed to sneak two heaping plates of food to us, right past the nose of the visitor. I eyed the dishes suspiciously, for the contents bore close resemblance to fowl I had observed suspended in net sacks from the stable ceiling a few days before. At the time, Marie had asked if I liked squab, adding that these delicacies were reserved for Bob and me at his next visit. I had tasted pigeon before, but I did entertain misgivings about these, as they had begun to take on a purplish tinge as they cured. Cured? It appeared, rather, that they were becoming rather ill. Well, there was no escaping this dish. Closed up in the formal room, there was no place to dispose of it, except by eating. Surprisingly, the squab was rather good, and we were well on our way to cleaning our plates when there came a sharp, insistent knocking at the front door.

On her way to answer the door, Marie made an urgent gesture for us to leave the house through the kitchen. Bolting through the door, we sidestepped Eliane who, with both arms, energetically propelled the visitor backward through the door into the rear kitchen. The man's eyes bugged with surprise at this treatment, and at the sudden appearance of two strangers impetuously dashing by.

Silently closing the stable door behind me, I followed Bob up the iron stairway to the barn loft, wishing that the haymow were already prepared for this emergency. In its stead, we entered the granary, which we had rearranged, slid into two cramped spaces behind and under boxes, and pulled old comforters casually over the spaces for added concealment. The hiding place was not ideal, but it might pass superficial inspection.

Remembering that my bedroom was bare, I relaxed somewhat at the thought that there was no evidence of live-in strangers left in the house. But how could Marie explain the unfinished plates in the dining room, and would the visitor locked in the rear kitchen divulge our presence?

It seemed that a long time had passed, and still we heard no footsteps mounting the iron stairway. Then Marie's voice called from below, "William! Robert!"

Extricating ourselves stiffly from our narrow quarters, we rearranged the boxes and descended to the kitchen. I never did satisfy my curiosity about that urgent situation, but as if to atone for our inconvenience, Marie plied us with dessert.

Bob and I stayed in the granary much of that afternoon, avoiding visitors to the farm. Although the passage of days had eased our minds somewhat concerning the security of our living arrangements, the incident at noon had served as an acute reminder of the danger our presence imposed upon our hosts. As we whiled away the time by playing simple games of cards we pondered aloud the steps we might take in case a hasty departure became necessary. And since our first conversation on the matter, we now had identity cards.

After Bob returned to the Ponchauts' home, I returned to my reading. But when I went out to the pasture beside the barn after finishing Poe's depressing "Fall of the House of Usher," the sky, which my eyes told me was blue, seemed bleak and gray. I felt wary lest the ground would crack open at my feet. That was enough of Poe for now, I decided.

I was absorbed in watching a stricken, lone Boeing B-17 Flying Fortress elude immediate destruction from the flak battery at Chièvres. Already losing altitude, the B-17's motors were running rough; it would certainly face more flak ahead. Wondering if the bomber would make it back to England, I fervently wished that I was aboard to take those chances.

For the next few days we pitched hay from the haycocks onto a wagon whose curved wooden ends were held high by connecting chain. When loaded high, René urged the horses up the rutted lane, past the front of the house, and halted along the far side of the barn. One of us stood on top of the load, forking hay into a small door midway along the floor of the hayloft; the other ascended into the loft and pitched it back to the end. In the confines of the loft, that was a hot, dusty job, and we exchanged tasks from time to time. When the north side of the haymow was filled to the tiled roof, we reversed our field, stacking it at the beams, which marked off the territory reserved for bread making and general storage.

The last two wagon loads were the toughest for the man in the mow, for the space by the window was narrow and each fork load that arrived blocked any ventilation. Each pitching motion had to be high in order to fill in the center of the loft. But once the task was finished, in a day or two it would be possible to make a good hiding place in the barn!

As the morning chores were being completed, Marie requested that after breakfast I shine my shoes. That task finished, I returned to my room to discover that she had laid out a clean shirt on my bed. Taking the hint, I clothed myself as neatly as possible, then returned to the kitchen, learning there that I was to accompany someone on an errand. I would ride René's bike.

Shortly thereafter, the dogs' furious barking announced a visitor at the gate. It was Jean of the safe house, whom I had not seen since leaving there. He was seated at the kitchen table while Eliane scurried down the steps to the cave, returning quickly with a bottle of beer to quench the thirst he had undoubtedly acquired on the long ride here. Marie then came from her bedroom, wrapping something in wrinkled brown paper. When Jean had finished his drink, that package was thrust into his hand, and together we went into the court, retrieved both bicycles, and rode off together.

Our path took us straight down the road, past the crossroads where I had turned to visit Frank McPherson, past two other farms, then past the Ponchauts' place. Up a low hill farther on, and to another crossroad we traveled. The small road to our left appeared quite secluded, and I took this opportunity to stop Jean and bring up a topic I had been wanting to ask about. I had taken pains to write this request, using the little book, "*J'Apprends l'anglais?*"

Jean seemed puzzled by my request. I had asked if I might be permitted to join in the activities of his Résistance group. I understand now that the word order of my sentences left a good bit to be desired, but he may have had other reasons for failing quickly to accept me as a volunteer. A person who had no firmer grasp of the language and local geography would be a dangerous addition to a little band out to do sabotage. Jean shrugged as though the message were incomprehensible, and we continued on our way. We now took a brick road, winding through a small village, Scaubec, marked by a distinctive little chapel.

Much later, we came upon a small city, Lessines. We entered and rode to what seemed to be the downtown area. In front of a brick building, Jean dismounted, and parked his bicycle in a bike rack. I did the same, then followed him into the building, a café. We took a table and a waiter brought us each a beer, stronger and tastier than what I had grown accustomed to.

Before my glass was half drained, a short, wiry, middle-aged man emerged from a side room and approached our table. No words were spoken, but Jean picked up the package and beckoned me to accompany them into the other room. The mysteries of the package and our errand now seemed clear. The diminutive man pulled out a length of dark wool fabric, pin-striped in blue. Jean and he seemed to agree that it was a suitable cloth, then "the little tailor" as others called him, set to work measuring me for a suit. I still had no idea why I was to have a suit. Of course, the trousers I wore were meant for work in the field, not for visiting, but surely some used clothing would suffice, should René and Marie think I needed something better than I was wearing. However, I was not accustomed to questioning the actions of my hosts.

Jean and I returned to our tables, quickly quaffed our beer, and pedaled back to Œudeghien.

Chapter 6

A Festive Event

RENÉ WAS NOW frequently absent from the farm, working in other localities. My brief, though distant, exposure to neighbors as I worked alongside the Hombecks had served to make my presence commonplace. I was free to range farther from the farm buildings. There was work to be done, and the variety of those tasks dispelled the boredom I had experienced during the first days of confinement to the house and barns.

With the scythe, I ventured along the roadside, cutting grass to feed the rabbits. The fence around the pasture next to the barn needed mending, and I learned to attach the fence wire to the cement posts by passing a short length of wire through a hole in the post and bending it tautly around the woven wire. The dog, Rex, accompanied me when I went to refill the water tank in the pasture, his playful antics threatening to tumble me into the well. At other times I lent a hand to Marie by gathering eggs, washing the cream separator, and carrying bread dough from the mixing place to the bakery room.

If variety dispelled feelings of boredom, the sounds of pastoral life imparted a sense of peaceful well-being. A rooster greeted the dawn; a hen proudly announced the triumphant delivery of an egg. Guinea fowl from a neighboring farm chorused in the grating sound of a rusty hinge; from afar sounded the yapping of a dog. In the pasture a cow bawled admonishment to her straying calf. A quail, from the tree line by the ditch inquired after "Bob White," and was answered from a nearby meadow. And as she washed dishes in the rear kitchen, Eliane's alto voice lilted a popular melody.

Sometimes, though, the drone of hundreds of aircraft engines directed my attention aloft, where condensation trails converged, etching a broad white path across the sky. Later in the day the engines thundered as smaller formations returned at a lower altitude, just out of reach of pursuing bursts of flak.

There was variety of food on the table, as well, where Marie's ladle poured out savory soups concocted of leek, chervil, onion, potato, and — after churning — a sweet-sour delicacy of buttermilk, thickened with rice flour and laced with sugar. The most surprising thing to me, though, was the array of meats that found their way to our plates. In those days, before farm families in the American Midwest had become accustomed to the luxuries of community cold storage facilities and home freezers, fresh meat came as a treat only when we killed a chicken, returned from a successful hunt, or when we had freshly butchered an animal. In the absence of low-temperature preservation, the pork not immediately consumed was converted into sausage, or cured as bacon or ham. The remaining meat, whether pork or beef, was cooked in bite-sized chunks steeped in savory gravy and cold-packed in quart-sized glass jars for preservation. Cold-packed meat resembled chunky roast beef or pork in its own juice. Appreciation of its delicious flavor paled, though, through the monotonous regularity with which it appeared at mealtime.

Marie's menus alternated between fresh beef, pork, and lamb, and fowl, cold cuts, and ham. Had they butchered an animal, I surely would have known. But they had not; nor was I aware of special trips to the market or of the arrival of a grocery truck. How the Hombecks acquired so rich a variety of fresh meat remained a mystery to me, but a puzzle with which I was quite content.

★ ∾ ★ ∾ ★

My suit had been cut and basted, and when it was time to go to Lessines for a final fitting, Jean led me to the café, cycling along the same route we had taken earlier. In the back room, the little tailor eased me into a single-breasted jacket with narrow lapels and flapped pockets adorned with inverted pleats. The back was scalloped, cowboy-style, across the shoulder with a pleat on either side, extending from the scallop just below the shoulder to its belted back. I could now see that the charcoal-black worsted cloth had a blue stripe, edged in white, at half-inch intervals. Marie would be pleased; I had seen no one here wearing a suit so handsome.

Satisfied with the fit of the jacket, the little tailor contemplated the drape of the trousers. Jean had his own ideas about the proper width at the knees and cuffs, and the two discussed the matter as if it were they who would wear the suit. Soon the apparent compromise was marked with pins, and we made ready to depart. The finished suit would be delivered; I need not return.

Emboldened by the uneventful passages through these streets, I pedaled confidently beside Jean as we returned by the now familiar route. I might have been less at ease had I been aware that the cement water tower we passed near the edge of Lessines had been considered as my hiding place that first night — or had I identified the raised platform to our left a bit farther on as the observation tower from which my companions' chutes had been spotted just before their capture.

★ ★ ★

A letter delivered in the morning mail attracted René's studied interest. It seemed that René did indeed have a nephew or cousin who lived at some considerable distance, and the letter announced that he would be coming to spend an extended visit. He shared this news with Marie, and nodded in agreement with the soundness of this decision.

"He is a young man, and should be permitted to finish his schooling," he asserted. "If he stays at home during the summer vacation it is probable that he will be impressed into labor in Germany. If he comes here, it isn't likely that he will be found; and even if he is, the fact that he is doing useful work may delay his conscription. Then he can return to school in the fall."

Emile arrived a few days later, and took up residence in the milk house, where a cot had been installed for his use. He was a tall, blond fellow with the slenderness of youth. He had little familiarity with farm work, but he possessed the assets of willingness and the ability to speak French, so he would and could learn. Those qualities, plus a genial nature, made him a welcome addition to the farm.

Emile had barely settled in when disturbing news came from another quarter. Dabbing her reddened eyes with a damp handkerchief, Marie met René returning from a field. René's brother, Michel, and Raoul Hombeck, his son, had been arrested. There had been grounds for the suspicions that brought the agents to their home in Ogy, and the ensuing search had turned up a parachute, hidden in a doghouse.

At the time, I had suspected that it had been my parachute. Years later, however, Michel showed me the tree in which he had found it. I now believe that the chute must have been Hugh Bomar's.

Apparently the parachute was taken as tangible evidence of proscribed behavior, and the two had been arrested on the spot. As he listened to the message, René's shoulders sagged in despair. He had a good idea of the treatment in store for them.

The next morning, there was little chatter at breakfast. Apparently no one had slept well the night before, and all went about their work as though their minds were somewhere else. René did not even scold the calves as they slopped milk from the bucket in their gluttonous effort to rob the smaller ones of their feed. Eliane ceased to sing at her tasks, and Marie's quick pace had slowed to a shuffle. In the past they had expressed sympathetic concern for victims of the Occupation Forces, but this time the news had come very close to home, producing profound sadness.

I spoke to Marie, saying that they had experienced enough grief, and that it would be better for them if I left. She would have none of it, and brought the matter up to René, who insisted that there was nothing for me to do but to stay. I waited for another opportunity to talk with Marie alone and, changing my tactics, asked if I might have my escape kit, which would be helpful to me in the event that I were forced to leave suddenly.

"It is safely hidden under the altar of the chapel," she told me. "It is locked behind the grill, and I have the key. If you ever need it, I will get it for you in time."

★ ★ ★

A few days later my new suit, in wrinkled brown paper wrapping, arrived at the farm. I was as eager to try it on as Marie and Eliane were to see the finished product. I donned a clean shirt, and at the dining room mirror carefully adjusted a tie in the Windsor knot, which René had so carefully taught me. I even dared to pull on my heavy Army shoes while still in the house, and stepped into the kitchen to model the new apparel. Marie stood back, critically examining the cut of the coat. When I turned so that she could see the back, she called Eliane's attention, approvingly, to the belt, scallops, and pleats. I looked down at the trouser cuffs, wincing as I noted that their generous cut almost concealed my shoes. Eliane's eyes twinkled. Did she share my judgment that the legs were too wide, or was she merely amused at my reaction? Marie had taken no notice of this pantomime, and cooed her pleasure over the general effect. Later, she expressed her satisfaction to René. The suit had come in time, she said, for some outing which I was to take a few days later.

When I returned to visit the Hombecks in 1949, Marie produced that suit from the family wardrobe, saying, "This is yours to take home with you now."

I was waiting when the sturdy Adolphe Clément, arrived to accompany me on an excursion. At Marie's urging, I had bathed, shined my Army shoes to a lustrous brown, borrowed René's best tie, and dressed in the new suit. Marie satisfied my curiosity as to the plans for the day.

"You are going to a reunion with your crewmen," she told me excitedly. "The parachutists who are hidden all over this area will be brought together to have dinner with men of the Résistance."

I was surprised to see Adolphe again, for Jean had become an almost regular visitor to the house. But I was glad he was there, and we greeted each other warmly.

Slipping on the trouser clips to protect my new suit against grease from the bicycle chain, I found that the wide pant legs wrapped neatly around my ankle. I need not have worried about them getting caught in the sprocket. Adolphe pedaled easily, surveying the fields with the calm ease of a Sunday voyager. We were to meet Bob Donahue at the *Ferme du Chamberlan*. Then the three of us biked along the roads by which Jean had led me to Lessines.

Perhaps a mile beyond the *Ferme* though, Adolphe took a different route, which rejoined the main road some distance farther. I recognized it as the one we had traveled on by the far edge of the little hamlet of Scaubec, with its quaint old chapel. By now I was convinced that Adolphe had deliberately chosen a twisting route in order to confuse us. In case we were ever interrogated by the enemy, we should be unable to identify the places we had visited. If that were true, he had certainly succeeded. When we left the main road a few minutes later, we traveled east, on a road quite new to me.

Many years later, I learned that Adolphe did not deliberately lead us astray. In the interest of security, we had taken minor twisting roads to our destination, easily confusing to a stranger.

Eventually Adolphe paused. A solid metal gate concealed the buildings of a farm fronting on an open area, known as Perquièsse. I recognized it as the same place where I had acquired a bicycle on the day after our plane had been shot down.

Our guide dismounted, invited us to do likewise, and swung open the gate. Inside, the courtyard appeared deserted, but in a shed to our right, nestled in a mound of loose hay, a speedy automobile was visible. When we entered a barn in order to conceal our bikes, it became evident that a number of cyclists had already arrived. As he closed the barn door, Adolphe's manner became wary. Approaching the house, he motioned us to stand aside. Withdrawing a pistol from his belt, he rapped it sharply on the door. The door swung wide to reveal a Sten gun pointed at Adolphe's menacing pistol. In recognition, both men lowered their weapons, reached across the threshold in a friendly handclasp, then bade us enter.

Inside, a knot of men stood by the door conversing. Jean disengaged himself from this group to greet us and introduced us to his companions in general, failing to call them by name. Shaking hands with each in turn, I recognized one of them as a man I had seen somewhere on the day we had parachuted. Behind the men at the door, others arose from their seats at a long table, which reached across the wide room. As we shook hands, Doug Hooth hurried to meet us. Though his face was pale, Doug's broad smile gave testimony to his well-being. "It's good to see you fellows," he exclaimed. "I haven't spoken English with anybody since we separated at

Evaders and helpers at the Vifquins' farm, Wannebecq, Belgium, 1944. From l to r: John Wilson (evadee), Madame Victoire Vifquin-Deltenre, Lieutenant Richard E. Wright, Monsieur Hilaire Vifquin, Lieutenant Douglas Hooth, and Madame Marie-Louise Deltenre-Auverlaux.

that Résistance farm! Here, I want you to meet the chap I was talking to when you came in."

Neither of us had ever seen the man with his leg in a cast, who lounged in an overstuffed chair at the end of the room. We learned that he had broken his leg while parachuting some weeks before our plane had crashed, and had been taken at night to a doctor who had set the broken limb. Until today he had not encountered another flier with whom to share experiences, and until Bob and I arrived, he had been making up for lost time with Hooth.

But now Doug profited from our meeting to hurriedly tell his own story as though he feared that it might be interrupted before its end. "I'm staying at a house only a few minutes by bike from here. The couple who are hiding me are very nice, but it's a small house. There's no back exit, and the only door opens onto a road, so I can't go outside, even to the bathroom. The man goes to work every day at a quarry in Lessines, and the lady stays at home all of the time because of me. I can go out at night, to the garden sometimes, but only with either Emile or Marie-Louise. If I go with Emile, one of us has to dress like a lady, even at night, so if a neighbor sees us they will think that it is the couple going out together.

Emile Deltenre and his wife, Marie-Louise Deltenre-Auverlaux, Doug's hosts, resided on a small acreage in the commune of Wannebecq. We had walked through this village on our journey to the safe house.

Hooth was interrupted by the sudden awareness of tension in the room. Two men picked up weapons and stood at ready, flanking the door, while a third, machine gun poised for instantaneous action, prepared to open it. For the first time I was conscious of the fact that the rest of the partisans were seated at the ends of the long table, away from direct exposure to the door. A couple of men rose quietly and came to the windows near where we were seated. Leaning against the windows were several rifles and a Sten gun or two — the kind that was supplied to Résistants through British air drops. The window sills were piled high with ammunition and hand grenades.

The room resettled into casual order when it appeared that the visitors were expected. Dick Wright, our bombardier, entered with his guide, and a general round of handshaking followed before we could speak to him.

Briefly, because women appeared to set the table for dinner, the injured airman was introduced to Wright; then each of us told what had occurred since we last met.

"I'm staying on a farm in Lahamaide. That must be near to both of you," Dick contributed. "The place is fairly isolated, in a hilly area with lots of woods around. I've been able to get outside and help my host and his two sons with some of the farm work." That was as far as his story went, for Jean called everyone to the table.

When we all were seated, a young man commanded attention. "We are very pleased to host you today as you gather to meet your friends," he said in English. "You may call me Jacques. I shall be your translator today, to interpret the words of welcome by our officers and to relay to the others anything which you want to say to them. We are sorry that Sergeant McPherson will not be present today. His leg is not yet well enough to ride a bicycle, but he sends you his greetings."

Jacques stood back then, as Jean and others voiced their welcome and lifted glasses in toast to this occasion. There was a word of caution, however. This was an important gathering, and the Germans would be pleased to find so many Allied fliers here, and so many patriots as well. In case of trouble, the situation was in good hands; a sentinel would sound an alarm. The guest airmen were to lie low until the Résistants had taken care of the intruders. With a British accent, Jacques interpreted very well, I thought, as I emptied my glass a second time.

I later learned that Jacques Empain, a resident of Ath, was assigned the task of placing explosives during acts of sabotage.

"Since your pilot has died in a heroic attempt to save the lives of Belgian civilians, the copilot is now the commander of this group," Jacques interpreted. "It is fitting that he say some words in return."

Doug Hooth came to his feet, expressing our gratitude for the generosity and fearlessness of our host families and the patriots now present, and for others like them. In conclusion, he raised his glass high to toast not only this grand occasion, but the quick and successful completion of the war. It was an impressive performance. In the States, when the crew had met together at a bar, Doug had politely but quietly sipped a Coke; he couldn't have had much experience in the art of toasting.

The preliminaries finished, the company dug voraciously into the food. A couple of the partisans, renouncing normal etiquette, speared savagely at large chunks of beefsteak, and with the points of hunting knives, thrust huge morsels into their mouths. Had they been too long away from the graces observed at a family table, or was this merely an attempt to impress us with their toughness?

Setting down his glass, Doug Hooth remembered an addition to the story he was telling when interrupted by Dick Wright's arrival. "I'm usually alone in the house," he continued, "but often we're visited by a lady called 'Madame Victoire.' That's the name of a woman who was famous in the history of Ath, so this lady has taken that name for the duration of the war. My hostess says that Madame Victoire does all sorts of things for downed airmen — she gets clothing for them and sees to it that there is plenty of food in the houses where they stay. The other day she brought me a basket of fruit and a bottle of wine."

None of the rest of us had met the lady; we thought perhaps we had something to look forward to. In actuality, the lady's name truly was Victoire Vifquin. A sister of Doug Hooth's host, she resided on a farm near the Deltenre home.

At that moment in our conversation, from upstairs, the sharp crack of a gunshot brought instant reaction. I saw men grab for weapons and empty the window sills of ammunition. While men crouched at the windows and beside the front door, others left by way of the kitchen. All became silent in the room, straining to hear sounds from outside. But it was silent there, also. Then someone came in from the kitchen, and the men smiled in relief as he announced a false alarm. In the attic, the sentinel's gun had accidentally discharged. A moment later, Jean reentered the room, his face resolute as he spoke to Jacques.

The partisans had already resumed their meal when Jacques explained to us, "An observer in the attic has been careless and fired his rifle. There is no danger, and if you will please excuse this interruption, you may continue your dinner. The offender is being punished for his carelessness."

From across the table, the flier with the broken leg whispered loudly, "He'll receive stern punishment; there'll be no dinner for him today."

It was a good party, with the chance to visit with my compatriots, eat abundantly of good food, meet a company of lively yet earnest men, and to experience a bit of excitement. But like all good parties, it had to come to an end. Stopping to drop Bob off at his home, we tarried a few moments with the Ponchauts before Adolphe led me back to the Hombecks. Marie didn't seem surprised that I had little appetite for supper.

★ ೋ ★ ೋ ★

Chapter 7

A Rap at the Door

FOR SOME REASON René, Emile, and I were standing in front of the chapel when we saw a large touring car passing along the road from Œudeghien. The experience was exceptional because it was the first car I had seen on any road since landing in Belgium — more singular still because of the black-clad figures riding stiffly at attention ahead of its folded top. As the car passed from view behind the neighboring house, Emile hurried to the courtyard to summon Marie and Eliane to witness the scene. They arrived in time to see the vehicle round the curve beyond a more distant farm.

"That's a carload of Belgian *Gestapo*," René explained. "They must be after someone close by." Turning to me, he added, "The Belgian *Gestapo* are bad business. They are worse than the Germans."

The car had dropped from sight momentarily into a shallow valley. Reappearing on the hill beyond, it met a truck speeding from the opposite direction. The car turned right at the next road and suddenly halted, disgorging black figures that separated and encircled a large building that dominated the hilltop.

"Its stopping at La Laiterie," breathed René, giving the local name for the site of a former brewery, now out of business. The site was a bit less than a mile away as the crow flies, and though we could see little more than the building with the car parked near its front, we could already hear the crisp crackle of gunfire. From behind the nearby farm buildings, the truck rumbled pell-mell in the direction of Œudeghien.

"It's the truck from the Œudeghien brewery," René pointed out. "They must have sensed trouble, and are heading for home."

A few minutes later the gunfire ceased. Black figures converged on the car, and it glided away. The countryside was peaceful again, but somehow it didn't seem that way. La Laiterie, no longer a brewery, continues to bear the same name long after the building had ceased to serve as a creamery, from which its name had been derived.

How does it happen that a day may seem to be virtually electric with suspense? There is a commonplace expression that "the air is charged with tension." Can it be that Nature is sensitive to disruptions in the affairs of humans so that birdcalls become muted, and the very wind seems to wait in breathless anticipation of some yet unknown but dreaded occurrence? Or is it more likely that humans themselves, in unspoken knowledge that one event surely precipitates another, attend with sharpened senses any sound or movement that can signal the awaited unfolding of the dramatic sequence of events?

I had no doubt but what my own sense of apprehension was nourished by the apparent preoccupation of the others in the household that afternoon and evening. Marie moved about silently, her head cocked slightly to one side, as though listening, still, to those sounds of distant gunfire. She spoke only rarely, and then in short, staccato phrases. Eliane, her singing voice muted since her kinsmen's arrest, emulated her mother. Emile's thoughts, too, seemed to be on other things, and René went stiffly about his chores, gesturing rather than speaking to his animals, as if awaiting some far-off signal. Perhaps my own uneasiness produced in me an acute awareness of the mood of others in the household, and that, in turn, sharpened the tension I felt.

The next morning, when the milking was done, I went with Emile to drive the cows to pasture in the hayfield; no breeze was stirring. In front of the chapel the yellowing barley stood tall and still. Yet, by the roadside there was a sudden rustling, and a man, Sten gun strapped to his back, hurried, crouching, across the road and disappeared again. A moment later the field was motionless; the wake he left behind in the tall grain had disappeared, as though he had never passed. Where was he going? What purpose prompted this civilian to carry a weapon in broad daylight I could only guess. I knew only that he was headed in the direction of yesterday's battle.

Several times that day the scene was repeated; always a man alone, armed, moved swiftly and cautiously, and invariably through the fields. But these men moved, seemingly, at random, coming from north, and east, and west, scurrying toward different destinations.

René had news adding perspective to these events. The old brewery had been used by an Underground organization as a sort of headquarters. The Germans had somehow learned this, and the *Gestapo* was dispatched to the scene. Luckily, only three members of the Résistance were in the building at the time; but they had all been killed in the attack.

The German assault was the result of increased vigilance in the Mainvault area after Gaston Durand, the *Bourgmestre* — the town or commune administrator — of Mainvault, had been assassinated by the Résistance. He was suspected of being a member of an ultra-conservative political party that advocated amalgamation with Germany and sent Belgians to join the *Gestapo* and troops to fight alongside the Germans. His assassination had been carried out in the Chicago style, as portrayed in American gangster films. A fast car had driven up in front of the *Bourgmestre*'s house, and the door was kicked open. Shots rang out. Then the automobile sped away, leaving the victim dead and the door ajar. In a final insolent gesture of defiance, the light beaming brightly through the shattered door violated a strict prohibition imposed by the authorities of the Occupation.

One harsh event had led to another. But was the matter ended? René didn't think so, and he was concerned. So were the rest of us. Perhaps Nature was, too, for the air seemed to spark with dread anticipation.

By my watch, just after 4:30 a.m., I was awakened by hard battering at the front door. I jumped out of bed, running barefooted toward the exit. Marie, already dressed, met me at the door of the master bedroom. "*Germans!*" she uttered in a loud whisper. The pounding resumed, louder, if that could have been possible. There was no time to retrieve my clothes from the chair. Racing through the living room, I pulled the kitchen door closed behind me, rushed pell-mell to the stable, taking just enough care to open and close doors quietly, dashed up the stairs, vaulted into the haymow, and slid down the narrow chute to my hideaway. I did remember to pull a little loose hay into the opening behind me, the better to conceal my route.

Inside the tight tunnel, I breathed heavily, taking in huge gulps of sweet-scented air. The knocking had ceased. I suppressed breathing in order to hear. A man's voice, loud and brusque, seemed to be questioning. Faintly, I could hear Marie respond. The words were not audible, but her voice sounded calm and steady. So far, so good. But what would happen if they came across my room, with its empty bed and clothing still draped over the chair? Then, remembering the Army shoes beside my bed, I felt a little ill. What would happen next? I thought I knew all too well.

The hay felt scratchy through my thin summer underwear. From a distance, I could hear the drone of engines. Trucks, I concluded, quite a few of them. I looked at the luminous dial of my watch. It was not yet 5 o'clock. If those trucks were carrying troops on a general house-to-house search, they were likely to find some other strange guests still in beds. It would be a sad day in many households.

Marie's voice could be heard again. The sharp clack of hobnailed boots sounded in the courtyard, and the opening milk-house door squeaked in protest. The man's voice spoke again, harshly. There was no answer from Emile. Where was René? It struck me that I had not heard his voice. And he had not been in the bedroom, either, as I sped through. Why had Marie been already up and dressed at this early hour? From the east, a truck engine groaned as it labored up a hill. Below, a man's voice raised in sharp inquiry; he asked about the empty beds. Marie's answer was loud, rapid, and voluble. I could hear something about working in fields, and Ostiches. That was all.

The man barked a command, and the sound of boots clattered rapidly into the court, coming from the direction of the chapel. The footsteps continued on to the stable, then paused. From below, the door to the beet storage room grated open. Muffled sounds. Then footsteps again, this time on the brick aisle leading to the horse stall. A pause. Back they came, toward the stable door. The bolt slid open on the stairway door, and hobnails grated on the iron steps. The attic door ground open. Was he looking in the pile of boxes for the makeshift shelter Bob and I had constructed? It sounded like it. Now he was back in the corner where Marie kneaded bread. There was a rustling of the hay. I tried hard not to breathe.

Chht! . . . Chht! . . . Chht! It sounded like a pitchfork being thrust into the hay. Heavier rustling, as though someone was climbing to the top of the loft. Deep in my hollow within the hay, I had no fear that a pitchfork would reach me. But might he discover my entry route? *Chht! . . . Chht!* The sound was almost above me now.

The voice from the courtyard came loud, in German — a question? From above, the shouted reply sounded like, "Nothing yet." The answer from below sounded like a command. There was a sliding sound, a thump, then the thwack of hobnailed boots, followed by the grating thump of rapid descent. The door slammed, and the footsteps retreated. From the front of the house, car doors slammed, a starter whined a motor into life, and the vehicle swung around the chapel and disappeared down the road past the garden.

I could hear nothing from below. Had Marie been taken away in the car? What about Emile and René? Eliane, I now remembered, had left the farm yesterday to visit her grandmother. Perhaps the departure of the car was a ruse; some soldiers may have been left behind to capture anyone who came out of hiding when they thought the danger was past. I would wait a good long time before going down to investigate. My watch told me that it was almost 6:00 a.m. Trucks still rumbled in the distance.

The hay seemed more prickly now, but in case someone was posted in the barn below, I repressed the urge to scratch — it wouldn't do to make noise — even a little bit.

Muted footsteps sounded in the courtyard, coming toward the stable. The door opened; then the stairway door, quietly, because the soldier had not thrown the bolt upon leaving. Soft footsteps padded on the stair. "*William!*" I relaxed at the sound of Marie's voice.

"Yes," I answered, as quietly as possible.

"They are all gone now. It is all right. You may come down." Her voice was calm.

Scrambling up the steep slope of loose hay was harder than sliding down. Taking care to conceal the entrance, just in case, I hurried back to the kitchen. Marie was already there, making *tartines*. "Hurry now, and dress." She silenced my barrage of questions. "You will need to eat, and I have something to tell you."

In the bedroom, my clothes were just as I had left them. Apparently no one had picked up the shoes for closer examination. Hastily, I dressed and hurried back to the kitchen to find Marie dishing fried eggs onto my plate.

"Eat this while I talk to you," she directed. "The German officer looked all over the house. He wanted to know why the beds were empty, and I told him that the men had gone early this morning to work in the fields at Ostiches. That was true, because René woke Emile and left just after 4 o'clock. I said that all three men had departed. The soldier who searched the barn saw that the horses were gone from the stable, and found no one in the barn, so they believed me.

"Is it a good breakfast? Have you had enough to eat?"

It was good, and I had eaten plenty.

"Fine, then. I have something for you. You may need this." Marie handed my escape kit to me, ready when I needed it, just as she had promised.

"And here is your little razor, too; they belong together. Now, take this with you," she added, handing me a package of *tartines*. "It is time now, and you must go. Go to the fence in the pasture behind the barn. You will find someone waiting for you." She might have added — but didn't — "Good luck!"

I had arrived at the Hombecks' hospitable safe house on June 15, 1944. It was now the 5th of July.

There was no one waiting at the pasture fence. Well, I could do the waiting; I had nothing else to do. Trucks were still moving on roads to the east and north. I could hear them, but none were visible from where I stood. To the east, three men were running in this direction. They appeared to be civilians. Was that lanky one Frank McPherson? Indeed, it was, and also a young man whom I believed had been staying at his house. The third man looked familiar, but before I could be certain, I was climbing the fence to join them as they crossed the field ahead. Mac was wearing heavy rubber boots, and seemed intent on setting a record for a half-mile run. I sped across the field to intercept them.

Mac panted, "This fellow knows the way, so come on!"

Across the next fence row the short stubble gave way to an oat field. The lead man in this mad dash, whom I now recognized as the chap who had been visiting Mac on my last visit, stopped at the field, pointed his hands ahead as though in the act of diving, and crawled into the field.

"Follow me, but do not leave a trail," he urged. We followed his curving lead until he stopped, about 20 yards from the edge. "Now, catch your breath. We wait here for a long time," he gasped.

We lay close together; the oat straw, mashed beneath our stretched-out bodies, formed a thin mattress under us.

"Your leg seems to have healed in a hurry," I joshed at Mac. "Only three days ago you were hobbling around, leaning on furniture for support, and now you're doing the mile run — wearing boots, yet!"

Mac's pock-marked face twisted in a wry grin. "You would do pretty well, too, if your house were surrounded by Germans. I couldn't find my shoes, and these boots were handy by the door. We got out of there in a hurry, and no one fired a single shot!"

Oscar, an English-speaking Belgian, crawled carefully back through the curving trail by which we had followed him into the field. A moment later, assured that no one was about, his head and shoulders could again be seen above the grain. He retreated, inspected the field, then inched his way back to where we lay.

"It is good," he reported, speaking mostly in French. Perhaps I had overrated his command of English. He continued, in the same vein, "Unless they knew we were here, no one would see where we entered. We can widen this spot to give us more room."

It was a good idea; the morning dew still hung heavily on the grain and the dampness had penetrated our clothing. Soon the sun would dry the mashed-down grain and we could lie on that.

Oscar crawled back from a scouting trip to the edge of the field. "Two men are coming," he warned. "We will lie quietly. It is possible that one of them is your comrade, Robert — he is expected."

A short moment later, a whistled birdcall sounded, not far away. Oscar repeated the call, explaining, "That is the signal. I will go now to speak with the messenger. You stay here, please."

When he returned, Bob Donahue crawled along behind. He, too, had heard the trucks, but no Germans had visited his farm, at least not before he had left.

As the morning passed, we whiled the time away by becoming acquainted. McPherson had been staying at Oscar Carlier's home. Though I didn't know it at the time, I believe that his parents had been McPherson's hosts. Oscar carefully sidestepped questions about his past, but related something about the present.

"I am Lieutenant in the *Armée Blanche*, the White Army," he offered. "The *Armée Blanche*, you may know, was organized by men of the Belgian army who got out of uniform when the army was demobilized at the Armistice. Some men who were prisoners of war in Germany also joined after they were repatriated, and others who had been too young to be in the army joined later. I am one of those."

In response to our curious questioning, he continued. "What does the White Army do, you ask? We carry on the résistance to the enemy in every way possible, and shall continue to do so until our country is free again. Sometimes I have orders to destroy a railway bridge, or to damage a lock so that military supplies cannot be moved on the canal. At other times my orders are to attack a convoy. Orders of this kind are not issued every day, you understand. Much of the time I must lie low and stay in contact with my organization. At such times I am free to do as I please, within reason.

"We must not upset the Germans unnecessarily, for then they take measures against ordinary civilians. So when I am not on special assignment, I often go to a railway station or to a café and listen to what German soldiers say there. Sometimes we learn something of importance. When it is possible, my companions and I distract the attention of a German soldier, while one of us steals his rifle. That is a good way to get weapons." He chuckled, adding with obvious relish, "And very embarrassing to the Germans, too."

At the sound of nearby voices we became silent. The voices passed beyond our entrance to the field. Delaying until they were far in the distance, Oscar crawled to the edge of the field to investigate. On his return he carried a khaki *musette*. "A couple is hoeing in the beet field above us. They left this here for our lunch," he reported.

"Are you sure they left it for us?" queried Bob. "If that's their lunch, they will be downright suspicious."

Oscar reassured him that dependable people knew we were here and would arrange to care for us, for as long as was necessary. "If they intended to eat this themselves, they would have taken it to the field where they are working," he reasoned. "Here, let's see what they brought.

"Ah!" he exclaimed as he peered into the bag, "Besides the two bottles of beer, there are cheese sandwiches. And here is a deck of playing cards. Do you play whist? You do not? Then later, I shall teach you."

After we had eaten, Oscar returned the *musette,* with one empty bottle, to the spot where it had been left. The afternoon passed slowly, even though we had the cards. A coat spread upon the matted barley provided a surface upon which to play, but soon we became tired of lying on the ground.

I showed my escape kit to the Belgian, and Oscar, quick to see the practicality of the small packet, marveled over each item and the compact way in which they fit together in the small case. But that novelty was eventually exhausted, and conversation became desultory. Only occasionally now could truck engines be heard, and the sounds came from a great distance. We speculated on their location, but not about what might be happening there.

Late in the day, the empty *musette* was gone. In its place, stacked neatly on a pile of blankets, was another. The blankets were a welcome padding for the ground, which felt hard now through the thin mat of dying oats. And there was enough food in the bag to satisfy all of us for supper.

Oscar left us at twilight, saying that he had an appointment with a messenger. From our entrance in the field, two figures could be dimly seen in the near-darkness, apparently conversing beside a cattle shed a couple of hundred yards away.

When he returned to our nest, Oscar was full of news. One old man had protested the intrusion, and had been shot — not mortally, but in a sensitive spot. It would be some time before he would be comfortable in a sitting position. Contraband had been discovered in another house, and members of that family were suspected of aiding Allied fliers. The family members were assembled together, and the women, one by one, had their fingers inserted into a door jamb; when the door was closed, the fingers broke, also one by one. Still, everyone remained silent, so in the end, they all had been shot — the whole family. To Bob and me, the description sounded like the family who had first given us refuge, and clothing. Years later I would learn that they had not been the victims.

It was a sorrowful tale in any case, for if by giving us aid, a family had exposed themselves to this kind of tragic consequence, I felt that we bore responsibility for their fate. I would not want to cause suffering to anyone, least of all to the Hombecks, who were like second parents to me. But it would not do to discuss this in the present company. I would speak to Bob later.

★ ★ ★

Sorrow and regret were not the only emotions evoked by the news of the German atrocities. We reacted in indignation, bitter resentment, and fierce anger to this reported savagery. I could readily understand why so many people were heedless of the risk in acting against the enemy, but what discipline could have restrained them from mounting a suicidal attack on the Occupation Forces? Chewing on an oat stem, I turned this question over in my mind. Here were five young men, angry enough to seek vengeance, yet here we lay, compliantly obeying the counsel to hide out in this field.

Four of us, certainly, had been trained in some arts of warfare. I was a good shot with a rifle, could fire a pistol (not well), and operate a machine gun. But I didn't have any of these weapons, and what real training I had was as a gunner shooting at enemy aircraft, not in terrestrial maneuvers. I had boxed at school, however, enough that I could use my fists; and I had seen enough training films to have an idea how to strangle a man, and perhaps almost overcome my sense of fair play, possibly well enough that I could fight dirty. Well, why was I lying in hiding instead of seeking out a German soldier and attacking him?

Even more to the point, why wasn't Oscar doing that? After all, he was an officer in an organization devoted to resistance against the enemy. He was accustomed to risk, too, and willing to sacrifice for the cause. Hadn't he moved away from his parents and wife, electing to sleep in strange beds just so that he could continue the fight? Maybe Oscar acted on the principle that he could be more effective in cooperating with others in the destruction of military targets than in striking out blindly, and alone.

What about René Hombeck, then? Surely he was courting avoidable risk by harboring me. Why hadn't he joined in active resistance, if indeed he hadn't? Well, he did have obligations to his family, and those he took seriously. He also had a sense of responsibility to his livestock and his fields. It just might be that he felt that he was contributing something to the cause by producing food for the civilian population. That might help account for the remarkable restraint exercised by many of these people. It was even possible that some others might not feel the resentment expressed by the ones I had met.

I didn't know at that time of the many months René had spent in France when Belgium had been overrun by the enemy, or of the hardships he had faced in his travels south. Nor did I know about the many farmers who had been taken from their homes and sent to Germany to work on farms or in factories. I had little inkling of the conditions those men and their families had experienced, and how difficult it had been simply to exist. Had I known more, I might have been better able to understand how responsibilities for those closest to them produced severe restrictions on the courses of action they might be able to contemplate.

Even so, many of these people were resisting the Occupiers in daring ways, as opportunities arose.

When the stars began to appear, Bob Donahue pointed out prominent ones by name, showing us how, with the naked eye, it was possible to find directions and steer a course at night. Under the blankets sleep came easily, and when the early light of dawn finally stirred us into wakefulness we found that the covers had protected us from the heavy dew. But the grain around us was damp enough to discourage movement, so we dozed in our nests while the sun dried our little environment. The blankets, though, had picked up moisture from the ground. By enlarging our sanctuary just a little, and by lying on the blanket tops in the new location, the sun could reach into our bed. When that was dry, we returned, spreading the bedding to dry in the new area.

The day passed, a near-duplicate of the one before. Food appeared at regular intervals, and we ate, talked, and played whist. Someone remarked that our Fourth of July had passed us by. We could not celebrate the day of American Independence. No flags were flying, no bands had led a parade down our avenue. The only fireworks we heard came from the flak battery at Chièvres.

I thought how American Independence was an established fact, but what mattered at present was the restoration of our European Allies' independence. That play was unfolding, we had no doubt, but our seats gave us a poor view, at best, of the theater. Even the nightly news bulletin relayed to Oscar at the cattle shelter had a sameness about it.

The house-to-house search seemed to have abated somewhat, though there had been more arrests and more violence. We would remain in our hideaway for the time being.

When daylight stole over the field, our arrangements of yesterday provided the pattern for a routine. Lounging until our blankets dried, we moved into temporary quarters in the drying place, then breakfasted in the nesting quarters while the blankets steamed in the sun. But the routine was somewhat limited for comfort; my companions, their faces now stubbled with a two-day growth of beard, had a rather seedy look. My own face felt bristly against my hand, and how I itched to take a bath!

But how much better to itch here than in a prison, and how preferable it was to lie here warmed by the sun, with the sweet scent of earth permeating the air, than to have done something rash and to have provoked retaliation against some unknown civilians. It wasn't as though the Nazis were getting away with it all — their internment camps; their Stukas dive-bombing cities; their herding of civilians into the path of opposing armies; their cruel suppression of countless populations; their taking of hostages; the Medieval torture they imposed in interrogation; their unfeeling requisition of foodstuffs from subjugated peoples; and more. No, someone was doing something about it. We could tell that from the thunder of bombers passing overhead.

At dusk, the now-familiar signal beckoned Oscar to the cattle shed. In a moment he was back, with word that we would sleep in beds tonight. The blankets folded, we walked upright through the yielding grass, heavy with its burden of oats. I carried a *musette*, never thinking that it wasn't really mine to keep, only that the bag might come in handy in the future.

Adolphe was waiting for us by the small shed — "Adolphe Café," Oscar had called him, explaining that it was a *nom de guerre* or alias, like his frequent change of disguise, a subterfuge to conceal his real identity. I wondered if the name could be associated in some way with the café where he had taken me on the way to the Hombecks. If an alias identified a person with his home or usual hangout, wouldn't that offer a dangerous clue to the enemy?

Adolphe said that he would accompany Bob and me to the *Ferme du Chamberlan*, for this was not yet a good time for me to return to the Hombecks. He shook hands in farewell with the others, leaving them in the custody of Oscar for their own return. We parted company with the casual assurance of men whose friendship was well cemented.

"Now that you can travel, Mac, drop in for a visit now and then," I invited, fully believing that I soon would be seeing these three again.

A warm welcome awaited us upon our arrival at the Ponchauts. Apparently they had been as concerned for our safety as we had been for theirs. The twins, especially, were enthusiastic in their greeting, and waited only for the adults to award their embraces before begging us to "play horsie" once again with them. Adolphe tarried just long enough to tip a toast to the occasion, then cycled off into the darkness.

"Yes, the Hombecks are fine," Monsieur Ponchaut assured me, "and are eager for you to return to them. Perhaps that will be possible tomorrow. René will let me know."

He turned to lavish goodnight kisses on Oda and Odette as Rosa scooped them up on their way to bed.

Neither stars nor clouds hung over the bed Bob shared with me that night, but under us was a comfortable thick mattress. I felt better now, having both shaved and bathed before sliding between the clean sheets. I felt still better in the morning, neither stiff from lying on hard ground nor was I damp with dew. There was hot coffee with the breakfast, and conversation unrestrained by concern that it might be heard.

Bob and I were to stay in the house, a day in which to while away the hours until the countryside settled down once more to its normal state of guarded tension. In the living room I gave close inspection to the vast display of trophies and medals, which had been awarded to Monsieur Ponchaut's horses and cattle.

The young Raoul Pilate profited by our leisure by displaying his own creations, small crosses cleverly carved from tough scraps of Plexiglas that had been salvaged from our plane. The miniature crosses bore ornamental designs painted in several colors, and were pierced to dangle from a necklace chain. Verbally handicapped though he was, he communicated

July 6, 1944, at *Ferme du Chamberlan*, Ostiches (Hainaut), Belgium. Front, l to r: Augusta Leleux, Rosa Ponchaut-Leleux, with Odette and Oda Ponchaut. Middle, l to r: William L. Cupp, Robert Donahue, and Raoul Pilate. Rear, l to r: Monsieur and Madame Pilate, August Leleux, René Hombeck, and Monsieur and Madame Néry Ponchaut.

a great deal by gestures, with only an occasional addition from Madame or Rosa when they happened to pass by.

Yet even with the distractions provided by good food, the playful overtures of the twins, and the family's loving attention, the hours seemed to drag by. Late in the afternoon, Monsieur came to say that I was to be their guest for yet another night, but that tomorrow I was to return to the Hombecks, and Bob was to go with me.

This time Oscar accompanied us to the Hombecks. When asked why Adolphe had not come as he had promised, Oscar told us that Adolphe had been captured the night before. German soldiers had broken down the front door of the café and taken him to a prison. Oscar took care to lead us through the fields. Except for that, it was like any other walk we had taken between our houses. Until, that is, we approached the little road between where Mac stayed and the crossroad.

"*Germans!*" Oscar almost spat the word out, flinging his arm toward the east as he plunged headlong into a drainage ditch. I dove behind him, reaching for green cover, and heard Bob's thump as I landed. Through the low foliage I caught a fleeting glimpse of a truck driven by a gray uniform. On the back sat a soldier manning a mounted machine gun. The truck rolled on, toward the *Ferme d' Orlincamps*; in its field we had found sanctuary for the past several days. Oscar picked himself up, rubbing his hands. "*Orties*," he explained. I was luckier than he; I didn't yet know that nettles could sting more than thistles.

Oscar, his prudence vindicated, kept to the fields, following close by the small ditch that bordered René's hayfield. He circled the chapel at a distance, and when satisfied that there were no vehicles parked near the house nor visitors at the chapel, he led us back to the gated entrance to the court. We were welcome, indeed, and the Hombecks seemed little the worse for wear from the recent events. But they knew more about the fate of René's brother and his son, and their concern showed in their demeanor.

After the two had been taken prisoner, René's brother, Michel, had been incarcerated in the dreaded Brandonck prison, in Ghent. His son had been sent to the concentration camp at Buchenwald, where he subsequently died.

As twilight came, René led us to the small outbuilding behind the barn. "For tonight," he said gravely, "it is better that you sleep here than in the house. It is not very comfortable, but there is a roof overhead, and you can bed down in clean straw from the barn." He helped us carry armloads of straw, and to strew them in a protected corner of the building.

"It would be a good idea," he added, "to scatter just a little straw between the barn and this building. Then if you are found here, it will seem that you just came here for the night, and that we know nothing about it."

When we were alone, Bob and I discussed again, as we had done both earlier and these past two days, the chances of our getting back to England. My narrow escape from the early morning search, our flight to the field, and the reports of reprisals against families in the area seemed to outweigh Monsieur Termonia's counsel for us to stay put until the Liberation. Our meeting with the army truck on the nearby road and René's wariness in showing us to the outbuilding for the night seemed to clinch the matter.

"If people like the Hombecks are worried now about keeping us," Bob observed, "our presence here is a real threat to them. I wouldn't want anything to happen to them."

I agreed. "They've already had enough worries with the arrest of their relatives."

It really was a matter of consensus; neither of us urged the other. We acknowledged that it was time to leave.

"No matter how much we would like to, we can't let them know we're going. Every time I've mentioned leaving, they have insisted that I stay," I told Bob.

It would be hard to leave, but it was for the best. We would wait until the family had gone to bed, then go out through the fields and head for France. The prospect of trying to steal an airplane at the Chièvres *aérodrome* now seemed to depend too much on luck to be practical.

When we entered the court through the barn door we came upon Eliane, uncharacteristically free of work. Picking up a small ball from someplace nearby, we coaxed her into a game of catch.

A bit later, having come upon a way to say goodbye, I disengaged myself from the game and went to the house. Upon a scrap of paper taken from the bedroom armoire I penciled a crude anonymous note, non-incriminating in case it fell into the wrong hands. However it came out in French, I intended to say, "Thanks for your hospitality. We leave now, and expect to return." How soon? . . . I thought that if we did get to England, and were reassigned to the Pacific Theater, it might be a long time before we were free. It would cost a lot of money to get back here from the States, too, enough that it might take a long time to save. And so I ended with, ". . . in five years." The folded note fit into Marie's facial powder box, just under the powder puff. There it was unlikely to attract attention by anyone except Marie. It was a distant farewell, but it would have to serve the purpose — for now.

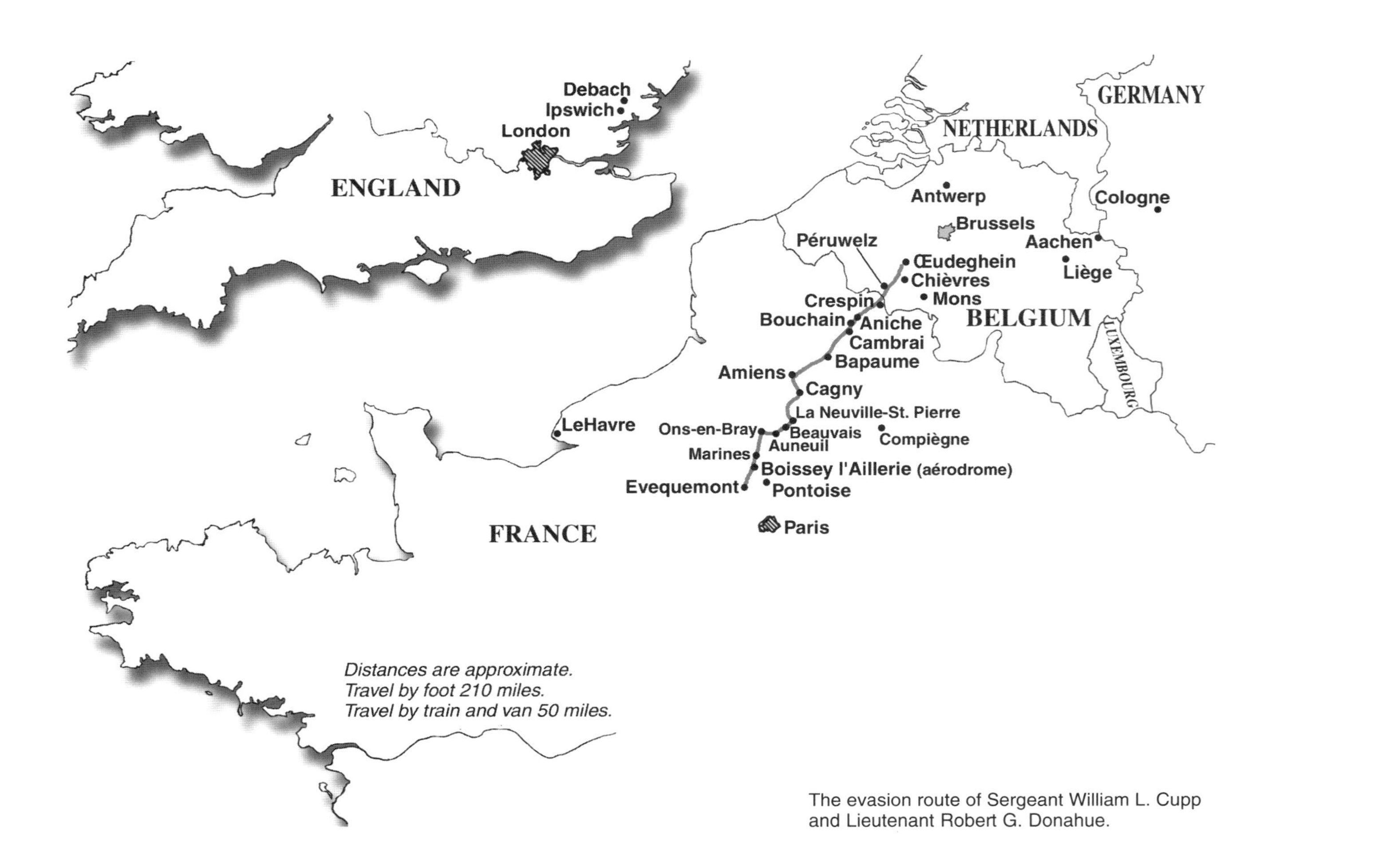

The evasion route of Sergeant William L. Cupp and Lieutenant Robert G. Donahue.

Chapter 8

Across Unknown Fields

A CLEAR SKY DELAYED the onset of nightfall. Inside the little brick stable time passed slowly as we lay, sleepless, waiting for darkness to send the last farmer to his home — darkness sufficient to conceal the movement of two men on foot through unaccustomed fields. The outbuilding was close to the road, too close to permit conversation. Stretched out on the soft straw, I tried to foresee the main elements and hazards of our trek, but each general detail seemed to depend on eventualities of that place and moment. It would be necessary to act quickly and appropriately to each situation, and I could only guess what those would be. I found it more satisfying to dwell on concrete things, like the Hombecks and others whom I had met, had appreciated, and was now about to leave without proper thanks or goodbye. Their kindness, extended with unflinching courage, deserved more than that. But given the perils they faced should their helpfulness to us become known to the enemy, the best repayment I could offer was to steal away in the night.

Up through the light layer of fresh straw wafted a dry, acrid odor of urine deposited there by untold generations of Hombeck bulls. Sleep would not have been easy in that shed. But watchfulness, not sleep, was uppermost in my mind. We would have to start as early tonight as feasible and travel as far as possible before daybreak. But only after we could be reasonably sure that we would not be seen by a farmer out late at his chores. Light still showed through a crack under the door.

I glanced at my wristwatch. Its luminous dial registered 8:45, too early yet to chance our departure. My ears strained for any sound of footfalls on the cobbled road, for the clang of a metal bucket, the opening or closing of a door — but I heard only the sounds of the summer night. Prudence required us to wait only a short while longer.

The minutes dragged ever so slowly by, but straining ears detected no new sounds. My watch indicated that it was just after 9 o'clock. At my nudge, Bob turned on his stomach and crawled silently to the door, inching it slowly open. Outside, a soft twilight lingered. I gathered my *musette* and we crept out through the door. Bob motioned me to proceed around the south side of the building, while he inched along the north wall. Bright moonlight illuminated the evening, but revealed nothing suspicious ahead, or as far as I could see to my right. I peered around the corner of the stable, just as Bob's head appeared there. He signaled that all was clear, and I responded in like manner. We moved cautiously toward the fence bordering the road.

The strands of barbed wire stretched chest-high, and began too close to the ground to wriggle under. Selecting a point midway between two fence posts, I planted a foot on a middle strand. With my hands I lifted the strand above. The fence parted just enough for Bob to bend and pass through. From the other side he repeated the courtesy for me. Fearful of detection from the farmstead across the way and wary of the sound of our footsteps on the cobbled road, we strode quietly a short distance on the tall grass at roadside. By the garden area behind the chapel we tiptoed across to the opposite fence, repeated our fence-breaching procedure, and hastened across the small meadow.

A few yards to the south, and across another fence lay the farm road leading to René's hayfield. The moon was bright enough for us to locate and cross the fence. Hurrying down the little road, we angled toward a farmstead silhouetted on the horizon ahead. Beyond the hayfield stood a low hill. Rows of forage beets lay across our path, necessitating frequent sidestepping of leafy tops and into neighboring furrows. Then a field of grain, followed by a small pasture, before we reached the curving road. Our apprehensions about barking watchdogs were unfounded; no sound came from the farmstead.

Quickly we crossed the road, then giving the buildings a wide berth, we turned south. A short distance later we came upon an embankment angling across our path. At the top, we discovered a narrow-gauge rail line. This must be the little tram whose whistle had sounded so often from the south and west. Crossing the embankment, we scrambled onward, angling in a more westward direction.

Above, stars were dimmed by the brightness of the moon. We were in open fields now, our way illuminated by moonlight. A bit farther, a large dark mass loomed to our left. That would be Mount Mainvault, over which several times I had witnessed straggling bombers heading toward England, mercilessly tracked by antiaircraft fire from the batteries around the Chièvres *aérodrome*. We veered a bit south to give ample clearance to a cluster of buildings. Soon, on our right a spire rose out of a dark mass. That would be the church of Œudeghien. We had never seen that, either, for it lay over the brow of the hill from the Hombecks' home.

There were more fences to cross. Then ahead stood a lone house just beyond the grayish line that marked a road. Selecting a spot at some distance to the south of the house, I stepped on a wire of the fence, lifting the barbed strand above with my hand. Bob passed through and once again I followed. Warily, lest a sound might waken a sleeping dog, we tiptoed across the cobbled road, breached the fence, and strode into the adjoining field.

Though the terrain sloped upward, we were in fields of grain and the climb was easy. A dark blot on the horizon marked a grove of trees. In the sky above, a cloud reflected a searchlight beacon on a southwest-to-northeasterly direction. In this time of strict blackouts, the beam was markedly visible, perhaps emanating from a Nazi airfield, we conjectured, probably serving as a night navigational aid, to preserve radio silence. The searchlight's trajectory roughly coincided with the direction we had chosen, and it would guide us as long as we could see the sky. But that would be possible only when we were walking in open terrain, we learned, as we entered a wood. The leafy canopy overhead obscured not only the sky, but our pathway as well.

We walked single-file, Bob in the lead. When he ran head-on into a tree or when our feet encountered occasional underbrush, we stepped to the side to find freer footing. Those little deviations from our route threatened to disorient our sense of direction, and periodically we stopped while I checked the tiny luminous compass, which I had extracted from my escape kit. It would prove to be a dependable guide.

Bob paused, and I came beside him. Faint light had revealed a narrow sunken road lying across our path. All was silent. We heard no voices, footsteps, nor any other indication that we were not entirely alone. Still, the grayish road, bordered by high, steep embankments and flanked by dark woods on either side, made us nervous. Once we set foot upon the road we would not easily elude capture if it were guarded.

But our destination lay on the other side, so we scrambled down the precipitous slope, catching ourselves by grasping shrubbery along the way. Our own footsteps clapped harshly on the cobbled road.

To the east, foliage concealed the upper reaches of the road. To the west and below us, a faint luminosity marked the edges of the wood, probably at the bottom of the hill on which we stood. We trod as silently as we could in the direction of that open space. The roadway flattened beneath our feet. The trees on either side formed an archway under which we stood in shadow, almost as a window through which we could peer, hopefully unseen.

Bright moonlight bathed the landscape, revealing a lone house a short hundred yards ahead, on our left. All seemed serene as we approached, then passed, that house. Luckily again, we had aroused no dogs. Behind the house, silvery in the moonlight, was a field. We traversed the field and started up the slope, parallel to the woods flanking the road we had just crossed.

A safe distance away from that house, the fear of encounter dissipated; our pace increased, and we walked with greater confidence. Trees appeared ahead, and to avoid woodlands that would slow us, our steps were diverted to the southeast. Sometime later, in order to avoid walking across furrowed fields, we followed a road that led us to a village — a single row of houses flanking a narrow street. Warily we walked on, fearful that a barking dog might bring curious townsfolk — or worse — to investigate. After what seemed a very long time, though it was truly a small community, we passed again into open country without having been accosted. When the terrain again permitted, we left the road and returned to fields, following the trajectory marked by the aerial beacon.

Descending a long, rolling hillside, we spied an embankment cutting across our line of travel. From a distance it appeared to be a train track, and that it was. The full-gauge railway was unattended, and the embankment permitted us a view of the way ahead. Perhaps 150 yards distant and paralleling the track lay a wide highway. Along it, to our right, lay several farm buildings, a sort of local community. Beyond lay fairly level land, spotted by what appeared to be small mounds surmounted by trees. The walking should be easy, we concluded, and the small copses should offer us shelter if rest were required.

We approached the highway, keeping our distance from the farm buildings. At the fence we surveyed the road in both directions. Satisfied that no one was about, we passed through the fence then hurried across the highway, which seemed broad enough to accommodate three lanes of traffic. A dark blot on the horizon to our right suggested the location of a town. Could it be Leuze? We knew from our study of road maps that Leuze lay almost midway between Ath and Tournai, both connected by a main highway. Surely, this must be that highway.

We headed due south now, avoiding the town and the connecting highway to the south, assuming that we had correctly identified our position. That other highway should lead to the town of Peruwelz, along the border between Belgium and France. We hoped to cross that border a bit to the east of Peruwelz, in a wooded area.

By the time we reached another east-west road, we were both tired and hungry, but we were intent on moving ahead. It would be easier, however, to walk along the road for awhile, so we did.

Some time after midnight we came across a country church, isolated from other dwellings, except for a large square house that we took to be the home of clergy. Bob considered this to be a fortuitous occasion to ask for help. If it were a priest's home, he reasoned, we might well encounter compassion. If not, and if our pleas were rebuffed, we could still quickly melt into the landscape.

We entered the grounds and came to the door. No lights were visible, even around the edges of the windows. Bob rapped soundly at the door, then again. From inside, we could hear someone stirring, then an inside door slammed, and footsteps approached. The drawing of a bolt could be heard, and the door was opened by a large man, robe hastily drawn over his sleeping costume. His face somewhat agitated, he warily asked us our business at this late hour. Bob replied, saying we were farm hands on our way to France, and that we were very hungry. Could he spare a *tartine* and cup of coffee?

Dutifully, the man complied, boiling water mixed with the dark concoction that passed for coffee during those days of austere rationing. He sliced a round loaf of bread, smeared two slices with butter, halved each, and folded them into sandwich form.

We sat at the table, glad for the rest, and hungrily devoured this small meal. Our host remained standing, not solicitously seeing to our appetites, but rather as though he must endure unwelcome intrusion into his slumbers. The priest, if that is what he was, must have concluded it would be wise to know very little about us. Even though Bob's vocabulary and grammar made his meaning clear, he had not yet acquired the singsong intonation of local speech. Very likely our host concluded that we were not exactly as we had represented ourselves, and he chose not to pursue the matter further. In the absence of a warmer welcome, we, too, chose to let the matter lie. Somewhat refreshed, we expressed our thanks and resumed our way.

It soon became apparent that the woodland that bordered our road to the south was forcing us farther to the east than we had hoped. An opening in the trees beckoned us, but we could see by the light of the setting moon a large house or estate. We retreated, turned back in the direction from which we came, and when the house seemed sufficiently distant, we deserted the road and plunged into the woods.

The darkness concealed both tree trunks and bushes, so we were forced to use our hands and arms to feel ourselves through the dense obstacles. Often we had to pause and check our bearings by the tiny compass. Then suddenly, Bob, who was in the lead again, uttered a startled gasp as he plunged into a stream. Alerted by his fall, I merely slid into waist-deep water.

We waded to the other bank and, with the aid of bushes at the side of the stream, pulled ourselves up. Shaking off what water we could, we moved on, stockings sloshing in our shoes. The water now seemed even colder as it evaporated.

During my turn as lead, I unfortunately repeated Bob's experience. The ground suddenly was no longer beneath me, and I fell forward into a stream. On land again, I rechecked our compass to determine whether we had circled back and fallen again into the same stream. Our heading checked out by the compass, and thus we proceeded.

Eventually, faint light indicated that we were nearing the edge of the woods. We could see a wheat field, and we waded in and lay down. In that woods we had stumbled into water a total of seven times. Could there have been that many streams? Had the woods really taken us more than four hours to traverse? I looked again at my compass. The indicator had slipped from its rest; it was jammed. Perhaps we hadn't crossed seven streams, but the same stream several times.

I took off my shoes and wrung the water from the stockings which had wadded up at the toes. My feet were cold and wrinkled. I put the stockings and shoes back on — that was somewhat warmer — then I lay down in the dew-drenched field. We wondered if we should rest there during daylight hours and travel only at night. We both lay wet and shivering, hoping that sleep would erase the discomfort and that the rising sun would dry our clothes. Tired as I was, I was too cold to sleep.

★ ∽ ★ ∽ ★

A sudden roar from the south of our resting place interrupted the songs of morning birds. Staccato bursts from machine guns, punctuated by blasts from small bombs, were accompanied by the throaty roar of revving motors. With a swoosh, several U.S. P-38 Lightnings swooped over the fence line near us and passed low over our heads. The twin-engined, twin-nacelled fighter planes had executed a bombing-strafing mission on an adjacent airfield.

Surprise gave way to longing — the desire to be with them, only 50 feet above. And they would be back in England in only a matter of minutes, with a feeling of pride in what they had accomplished. Too bad, it turned out, the *aérodrome* was merely a decoy! But we didn't know that yet, and the likely presence of an enemy camp adjacent to our resting place was disquieting, at best. If there were enemy troops, they would, just now, not be in a tolerant mood toward suspicious-looking strangers.

We decided to risk travel in daylight, and hurried westward, distancing ourselves from the airfield. Coming to a north-south road, we walked briskly to the south. An intersecting road led us again to the west, and eventually to a larger road, this time on the north-south axis. To this point we had not passed near any houses, which was a source of some comfort. But now, in the daylight, people were likely to be out, at work in fields, or passing by on streets or roads, and strangers such as ourselves could be detected at some distance.

A *borne* — a marker — at the side of the road carried the name, Peruwelz. We could not consult the Belgian road map in my pocket, for it would most certainly draw attention to us. We soon came upon contiguously joined houses, and now and then a storefront, with living quarters above, occupied the ground level.

I thought it would be nice to have something to eat, but dared not risk entering a grocery to ask, in my poor French, for something to sustain us. We passed a sort of square on our left, flanked on the other side by shops. I felt uneasy walking in the open street, dressed more fittingly for heavy farm work than for an urban promenade. From the stiffness of his walk I sensed that Bob was uncomfortable, too. But few people were on the narrow sidewalk, and none of them near us. Ahead, the street narrowed abruptly into a lane ascending the hill ahead.

By that time, Bob and I had developed a means of communication for when we might be under scrutiny. With lips only slightly parted, one would mumble a statement or question. The other would respond with a short "uh-huh" or "no." To alter direction, one simply shifted posture and/or pace and the other quickly followed.

We approached a crossroad, and the way to the right appeared small and less-traveled, though we could see a broad avenue rising in the distance to a sort of basilica. A sign on the house at the corner proclaimed this to be the road to Bon-Secours. We chose the broader route. Along the avenue were large, pretentious houses including a spacious brick mansion set in a manicured lawn surrounded by an iron fence. We continued up the hill, noting that a number of people were looking at windows in shops that lined the street. In our country clothes, we felt daringly out of place.

At the crest of the hill, as I moved closer to the curb, I could see men in uniform just beyond the last visible building on the right, and directly across from the basilica. Bob saw that, too, and we quickly arrested our ascent and, feigning casual interest, peered into a shop window — surely we wouldn't be interested in purchasing jewelry! We turned and looked in another window, glancing back to see whether we had aroused curious stares. Apparently we had not, so we strolled back down the avenue.

How could we exit? The first opportunity appeared to be at the the large mansion we had passed. We pushed on the gate. We entered and closed it behind us. Assuming a pose of familiarity, we strode along a pathway to a circular flower bed adjacent to the house. We bent over a rose bush, feigning nurturing care of the garden. No one accosted us. A trail led into the woods, and we strolled along it, disappearing from view of anyone in the house.

The woods were calm and comfortably cool. Huge beech trees dominated the forest, their smooth gray trunks frosted on the north side by light green moss. Overhead, leafy branches provided a canopy that all but concealed the sky. Underbrush had been carefully cleared, leaving only a low growth of ferns, though some more than waist high. Birdcalls relieved the stillness and the tension that had gripped us since we had first entered Peruwelz.

Our path seemed likely to lead to a roadway just south of the basilica, uncomfortably close to the soldiers or police we had seen, and thus we left the path, wading deeper into the forest.

Eventually we came upon a service road, which paralleled the broad avenue leading to Bon-Secours. Still bent on crossing the border into France in a woodland we judged to be some distance to the east, we followed the road in that direction and came across an intersection with a highway. After careful scouting, we crossed and hurried along. We stumbled onto the remains of an old campfire, but saw no evidence of anyone else within the woods. Then, finally, wanting to rest, we left the path and sat among the ferns, beside a large tree.

I took the opportunity to take off my shoes and stockings again. Still damp, they had wadded up once more in the toes of my shoes, and the right big toe was red and sore. I knew the socks would not dry out in the few minutes we took to rest, but exposure to the air might help.

We were hungry, and explored the contents of our escape kits, which contained concentrated foodstuff. One variety resembled pasty-colored peanut brittle. Although it didn't taste very good, a nibble would have to do for now. We washed the food bar down with water from the ceramic-capped beer bottles each of us carried in our *musette*. Purified by Halazone tablets, also from our escape kits, we gulped it in confidence. Then, on my road map, we located our position as the forest of Bon-Secours. The woods ended just to our east, and a short distance beyond, a canal curved from south to east, parallel to the French border.

Ready to resume our travel, we proceeded to a fence, climbed through and walked a path that followed the course of the canal. We passed along lowlands toward a nearby village. The canal was spanned by a bridge, which we crossed to enter the town. Bob suggested we contact the local priest to request aid.

We were forced to ask directions to the home of the priest, but Bob handled this task well enough. An elderly woman answered our knock and informed us that the priest was in a meeting. She would tell him that we wished an audience with him.

We were disappointed to be ushered into what appeared to be the dining room, where the priest was seated with several other men in priestly garments. We had to make our request to this gathering. Bob felt obliged to conceal the fact that we were Allied airmen, so the urgency of our need to cross the border was made less forcefully than we wished.

The priest told the woman to prepare coffee for us, and we were taken into the foyer. My gratitude for the hot drink was countered by regret that we had been unable to secure assistance in crossing into France. And our hunger was becoming more insistent.

Leaving the house, we continued along the canal. Though this course brought us face to face with a few villagers, our clothing was more appropriate to the village than it had been to the larger towns we had just passed through, and we walked on with greater confidence.

The terrain on the opposite side of the curving canal gave way to marshland, girded by a brush-covered embankment. Fields were on our left, and we saw no one on the path. My shoes, though drying, remained damp, and the stocking on my right foot persisted in working forward and balling up at the toe. We stopped in the grass at the edge of the path, and my big toe, once exposed to view, was blistered and inflamed. Since there were no bandages in the escape kit, there was nothing to do but again pull the stocking on carefully and hope that it would stay in place. We rose to our feet and continued on our way.

We wandered on, searching for a place to breach the boundary to France. We crossed one bridge, then another, becoming apprehensive as our path became a street in a town. Aware of curious stares, we walked steadfastly ahead, our eyes cautiously glancing to the side for signs of danger and possible routes of escape. A street intersecting with the one we traveled led to a bridge and a uniformed patrol. It might be a border crossing, but we dared not proceed in that direction, so we continued on.

At another intersection, our road ended, pushing us to the right. Dead ahead, a Nazi flag hung from a large building. We forked to the left, behind it.

Soon pasture land and fields flanked the road on the left, and in time we came upon houses on our right. From the barn behind the second house came the sound of hammering. One man, alone, was visible through the doorway. Bob and I agreed that we must ask for help. If this man became hostile, we felt that the two of us would have to disable him and seek some way to cross the border unassisted.

Entering the barn, we found the robust man was perhaps in his mid- to late forties. At our greeting, he laid down his tool and turned toward Bob. I edged to his side, awaiting any negative reaction. Quickly, Bob described our situation and asked for aid in crossing into France. The man seemed accepting of our story, and his response gave us reason for growing confidence in his trustworthiness. He asked if we were hungry.

Going to the yard behind the house, he summoned a teenage girl and asked her to pick cherries for us to eat. He then explained that we would be safest taking a train from the neighboring town, to get at least a few kilometers away from the border. He would get train tickets for us and take us to the station after his return. He departed, leaving us with the girl.

We assured ourselves that there was a rear exit to the barn. Then we positioned ourselves inside, out of the sight of passers-by, at a point where we could see anyone approaching. Our tired bodies welcomed the rest, and we relaxed as we ate the fruit the girl had brought us.

Chapter 9

Breaching a Border

WE HAD RESTED but a short time when the man, who had so quickly grasped our need and willingly responded, returned to the barn. Summoning the girl from her cherry picking, he spoke to all three of us.

"You are to board the train in Crespin. These railway tickets are valid to Somain, where you are to get off the train. You must go directly to the street. If you hurry along, no one will notice you. Then turn left to the next street. Turn left again, and go to the fourth house, where you will knock on the door."

He handed us the tickets and gave us a password, which would gain us entrance at the house.

"Good patriots will answer your knock," he added, "and they will take care of you."

Bearing a large sack of cherries, the girl came to the barn and thrust the sack upon us.

"The four of us must now take the path to the border. When the way is clear, we shall walk to the station. We will stroll along, the pair of you together. I shall lead, and the girl will follow."

We filed out of the small door at the rear of the barn. A faint trail descended down a gradual slope toward a stream, and we crossed on a crude footbridge. As we ascended the steeper slope on the other side, our guide turned, his finger to his lips to signal silence.

"We must wait until the way is clear," he whispered. After peering through sheltering shrubbery, he drew back. "A soldier is guarding the border here."

To the girl he said, "Go and distract the guard; stand on the other side of him so that he cannot see us cross the street."

Quickly, she slipped through the shrubbery and strode saucily down the street toward the soldier. From the back, she seemed less the young girl we had first encountered than a carefree teenager. With a toss of her head, she spoke to the soldier, initiating a conversation. She moved subtly, as though to go along on her route, but tempted to prolong the contact. So convincing was her ruse that the soldier's attention never wavered from her presence, and she lingered there. Following the signal of our guide, we walked quickly ahead and crossed the street. We turned on the next street, paralleling the one fronting the border.

Bob and I strode ahead, our companion watching out for trouble. At the next intersection we saw our feminine companion walking in our direction. Soon she fell in step with the man behind us. We continued on, wary, but without event, perhaps making a jog back to the border street. Eventually we arrived at the railroad station, a brick building on our left. We turned, and saw our companions nod that we were doing the right thing.

A train was waiting on the track. Near us were dingy wooden cars. A bit farther away was a shiny blue-and-yellow one, each door emblazoned with the number "I." We headed for that one.

A hiss came from behind us. Our companions urged us toward the wooden cars. As we quietly changed direction, we saw two Nazi officers stride briskly toward the blue-and-yellow car; ours was for second- or third-class passengers.

On board we settled onto straight wooden seats, Bob on one bench and I on the other, next to the window. Other passengers peered into our compartment, then went elsewhere. Soon the car must have filled up, for a man and woman and two children joined us in the compartment, carrying a wicker basket, its contents concealed under a cloth. Keeping space between themselves and us, they made room for another person or two. We ignored their curious glances, and soon they interested themselves in their own affairs.

The train inched out of the station, passed a gaggle of buildings, and gained momentum. A breeze blew in through the open window. Bob passed me the sack of cherries and we sat back, comfortable and comforted; we munched the ripe fruit and spit the seeds out of the window. Our fellow passengers chose to ignore us.

I wondered who these kind people were who had just helped us. Was the man the proprietor of the barn where we had met him? Was the girl a neighbor? His daughter? I was not sure even of the town in which they lived, and I realized that in parting, I had not even thanked them for their generosity. I hoped that our gratitude had showed in our demeanor.

Whistles announced the arrival of the train at the station in Somain, France. Military uniforms were abundantly visible as we strode toward the exit. After handing our tickets to the attendant, we disembarked quickly on the sidewalk and walked up a low hill and in a direction different from most of the people at the station. As we neared the top of the hill we could see an open space, groomed like a park. A soldier was standing guard. Our directions had been to turn left at that point and knock on the door of the fourth house. But that would be clearly visible to the sentinel. In the event that no one answered the door, would it seem odd that people clad as we were would knock there, then depart? What would we say if we were challenged? What if the person who answered the door would turn us away? Would that arouse the soldier's suspicions? And if we were turned away, just where would we go next?

These questions passed through my mind, and I expected that Bob was having similar thoughts. An alternative would to be walk confidently past the park then turn at the street beyond. Continuing in our direction, we strolled by the posted guard. We had decided not to risk going to that door. The option was still open to return there later.

We walked to the far side of the street, away from the sentinel, crossed the road that led away from the town, passed a block of buildings on our right, then turned down the street. That had not been the best choice, however, for the street dead-ended after a hundred meters. This was not a good place to loiter while waiting opportunity to go to the house to which we had been directed. Yet, we could not know what lay ahead if we returned to the street away from the railway station.

The soldier posted at guard had his back to us. We decided it was a lesser risk to return to and take the road leading out of town. With some apprehension we retraced our tracks, rounding the corner by the block of buildings, and headed south. Relieved that the guard did not call after us, we proceeded on the way. But we had been unable to make contact with the potential helpers.

The street sloped downward — agreeably, for our tired legs and sore feet. We met very little traffic along this road in either direction. A truck or two passed us, each carrying a large tank at the rear of the driver's compartment, in which coke was converted to a material agreeable for combustion in the former gasoline engine.

An open space came into view on the right, then Somain gave way to another town. Passing the last house that blocked our view to the left, we saw a small pasture, then more houses beyond that.

Near the whitewashed buildings bordering the pasture were several deep craters, possibly ten-feet long by five- or six-feet wide. Had this area been bombed? As we neared them, it seemed instead that the craters had been plowed up by a salvo of unarmed 500-pound bombs that likely had been released in order to lighten a crippled bomber. Luckily for those on the ground, they had just missed the dwelling.

The sign along the road announced this town to be Aniche. We knew nothing about it, and had not had an opportunity to consult our maps since crossing into France. But a church spire was visible ahead and to our left. By that time it was almost a must to seek help at a church, for we were thirsty, tired, and hungry.

We passed between rows of houses on either side. To minimize suspicion we kept our eyes averted as we met the few people along our walk. Between houses on our side of the street was a small gateway, and through the opening we could see the rear of the church. Ahead, on our right waved the Nazi flag — probably, we thought, the Nazi command center. There seemed to be little to do other than pass by with all the circumspection possible, but my apprehension mounted as we came abreast of the building on the corner. No one was posted in front. We turned the corner opposite, relieved to discover a broad open space leading to and opposite the church.

The little square was empty, and Bob was able to whisper to me, "Just follow me and do as I do."

I trailed after him as he turned onto the short walk, up the steps, and opened the door to the church. Inside, a service was in progress. Bob walked directly to a vessel mounted on the wall, dipped his fingers in the Holy Water, and, with a shallow bow toward the altar, touched his damp hand to his brow and made the sign of the cross. I copied his actions to the best of my ability, and followed him to the last row of chairs, where he made a deep bow toward the altar, chose an empty chair, and knelt as the others were doing. I followed and knelt at the adjoining chair, relieved at last to be off my feet.

I was unable to understand anything that was occurring, but watched those about me and imitated their actions. I felt hungry and weak. Bob must have felt the same, for he whispered that he was leaving, but would meet me after the Mass concluded. I continued to follow the actions of the congregation through a service that seemed to last for a long time. Eventually, though, it ended, and I followed some of the people out of the church, again trying to echo their actions. Most of the congregation turned toward the west side of the church, where they broke into small knots of conversation.

Bob was nowhere in sight, so while waiting for him to appear I lingered at the fringe of a cluster of people speaking with the priest. As the group became smaller, I became even more conspicuous among the rest, marked by my shabby clothing and perhaps by my youth. While waiting to speak privately with him, he addressed me. But just then he was joined by two relatively well-dressed men, so I replied in a tone as low as I could that I was in need of assistance. Though there was no reply from either of the priest's companions, their facial expressions were of surprise and consternation. I assumed that my accent had given away my identity. The priest's head moved almost imperceptibly, suggesting that I should leave without delay.

I was saved from the necessity of extricating myself from this situation by shouts from the rear of the church.

"*Robbers! Robbers!*" called a young boy. My attention turned in that direction, where I saw Bob emerging from a cellar doorway where he must have been resting. His unseemly appearance certainly was cause for alarm, and the crowd surged toward him. I met him on the run. Looking for a way of escape, we spied a small path leading toward the road on which we had entered the town. We sped down it, passing gardens on the right and the left. As we neared the gateway to the street we slowed to a walk, not eager to give the impression that we were fleeing the clamor behind us. Bob reached the gate first, and opened it. As I stepped through, I bumped into a German soldier.

"Where are the robbers?" he asked in French.

"Back there!" we replied quickly, and in unison, hopefully disguising our language skills.

As he ran up the path, Bob closed the gate, and we walked briskly toward the corner we had passed earlier. A soldier and civilians stood at the door of the building displaying the Nazi flag, their attention directed toward the church beyond us. We crossed the street quickly, continued past a road that went over the railroad tracks, and on to a spot on the right, out of sight of those at the corner. We stopped for a moment to assess the situation, then concluded that the road we had just passed offered our best opportunity to leave Aniche. Hoping that we had eluded special attention, we turned and walked again toward the sinister corner. There, by the railroad track, we turned and walked down the road and out of town.

A mile later, there was no evidence of pursuit. We wondered why not?, for some in the after-church crowd had seen our path of departure. And if the soldier who had gone to investigate had been informed, surely he would have concluded that we, whom he had bumped into, were the quarry. In addition, the onlookers at the steps of the Nazi headquarters might have noted our passing, for there were few alternatives to the route we were taking.

Was it possible that someone who commanded respect at the church had calmed the crowd? And if so, could it have been the priest who had signaled me to leave the area? Concluding that we would probably never learn the answer to that question, we continued on our way.

The July sun beat down on the cobbled road before us. My socks were again balled up, cramping the toes of my right foot. There had been no opportunity since leaving the train to adjust them. Still thirsty, we chose to risk begging something to drink from a family outside the front door of their house. Kindly, they offered us what passed for coffee and seemed to accept our explanation that we were Belgians en route to work as field hands. I knelt and removed my shoes, adjusting my socks. We thanked the family and returned to the road.

Sometime later I heard the rattling of a bicycle on the road behind us. We refrained from turning to look, and the cyclist passed on our right. I recognized the slim black-clad rider as the priest from the church at Aniche. Strangely, he seemed to ignore us. The road led only in this one direction, so by continuing on we followed him until he disappeared from view.

Eventually the road ended in a choice of the right or the left. The way to the right seemed to bear evidence of greater use, so we chose that direction. Some time later we came upon a town. Mysteriously, people stood in the doorways of each house, silently watching our passing. Uncomfortable in their scrutiny, I wondered whether the priest had alerted them to our coming — and if he had, why didn't someone say or do something?

There were no side streets by which we could avoid this main street, so we continued on, walking with heads pointed directly ahead. Abruptly, a street intersected with this one, and the way ahead was blocked by a building. We were near the village church, but no person was visible. We turned to the left, then found the road to turn to the left again, describing a horseshoe-shaped path through the village. The town may have been Marq-en-Ostrevant, for when I returned to that area many years later, the route and place seemed familiar. But I could not locate the small road leading south of the village.

We were close to the edge of the village, and the road seemed once more to dwindle in size. We turned south on the cross street and saw immediately a young man on the edge of the road, by the corner house. He held a book in his hand, though evening was nigh and there was little light to read by. Wary, we edged to the opposite side of the road and passed him, giving no sign of notice.

He called, "I would not go that way if I were you."

Turning back, Bob asked, "Why not?"

"There are many Germans in that direction," he replied, closing his book and getting to his feet. "Would you like something to drink? Are you hungry?"

Under the roofed shelter at the rear of the house, this young man — he might have been 19 — brought out a long loaf of brown bread, *pain gris* we later learned, and a large jar of strawberry preserves. As we slathered the preserves on the slices, he asked us details of the route we were traveling. We told of having walked through fields, woods, and on roads for we were not certain of our route. The young man listened gravely, then proposed that we would find the roads preferable.

"I shall give you *binettes* — hoes," he told us. "Carry them in your *musettes*. There they will announce your intent to do farm work. If you think that someone on the road may wish to interrogate you and you wish to avoid them, just enter the nearest field and begin hoeing."

Fortified by the sandwiches and coffee, we were inclined to believe him and heed this advice. We gobbled more bread and preserves and drank more coffee. Our young helper was possibly five feet, eight inches in height. He was slender, yet muscular, and his demeanor suggested self-confidence and maturity. Wisps of dark brown hair — the color of his eyes — showed from beneath his cap. Other than his work clothes, no distinguishing features set him apart from other young men we had seen. Friendly though he had proven himself, we did not divulge our identity to him, nor did we ask for his name. Bob and I had agreed to be cautious about learning the identities of those who helped us, lest, if we were to be captured, we might be tortured into revealing them.

When we had devoured all that good breeding would allow us to take from a well-wisher, we once again offered our thanks. Then, returning the remnants of the bread, preserves, and coffee to the house, our erstwhile host spoke once more to us. "It is not safe for you to stay here tonight, but there is a haystack in a field not far from here where you may make a comfortable bed. Then you may be on your way in the morning. I will show you the way."

Picking up two *binettes*, he handed one to each of us.

He took us back to the road in the direction that he had first said would lead to us toward a concentration of the enemy. Perhaps a bit more than a quarter-mile later, he led us into a field on our right. Less than a hundred yards into the field, stood a large haystack. In the waning daylight he led us to the far side of the stack, reached up, and pulled out a large tuft of hay.

"Make a hollow here, and use the surplus hay as a cover. That will keep you warm and hide you, too," he said. "In the morning, return by this road to the corner where we first met. Go east, and follow that road toward the next town. Pass through it, and follow the main road on your way to Cambrai. Good night . . . and good luck!" With that, he turned and left us.

Reaching upward, we were able to part strands of hay until at last we had a hole large enough to hold us both. Squeezing under, we concealed the entrance with hay. Because we were clothed, the hay didn't seem scratchy; it provided a soft, warm, and fragrant bed.

Lumpy ground under my bed prodded me to wakefulness. It was still dark outside as I shifted my position to find greater comfort, and drifted off to sleep once more. Later, when repeating this procedure, the gray light of early morning filtered in through the hay. Bob was stirring when I awoke again. He sat up as best he could in the cramped quarters and stretched. I rolled toward the opening and peered out. By morning light I could read the dial of my wristwatch. It was nearly 7 o'clock. I reported that to Bob, and we moved out of the haystack, ready to continue on our way.

Chapter 10

Hunger, Thirst, and Fatigue

As WE CLAMBERED down from our lofty nest, we took stock of our position. The town on the road ahead of us was Bouchain — a minor town, according to our map. The road south from there intersected with the road to Cambrai. From there we would head south toward Amiens. We each took a drink of water from our bottles, made sure that our newly acquired hoes were secure in our *musettes*, then shouldered them and set off.

We paused by an embankment while I adjusted my socks; they still persisted in inching forward and balling up by my toes. By keeping to the larger of the alternative roads, we eventually entered the town. The streets seemed quiet, but soon we saw well-dressed people hastening on. Our unshaven faces and work clothing would seem even shabbier when compared with them.

Tolling of nearby church bells identified the reason for the fine dress of local passers-by. It was Sunday, and they were bound for church services. Not only our soiled and shabby clothing set us apart from the locals — our *binettes* were inappropriate for Sunday. Reluctantly, we discarded them in a small alleyway along the street.

The road through Bouchain was longer than I would have guessed from its portrayal on the map. Still, we soon had passed through it. We had earlier decided to continue a routine of walking for an hour, then taking a rest, but that became impossible when we reached the highway between Valenciennes and Cambrai. The route was flanked by buildings, mostly houses, interspersed by an occasional shop or café. Here and there, small knots of people loitered in the sunshine, and we often met pedestrians on the walkways. Our progress was made more difficult by the tension induced from the fear of being accosted as a stranger. But we saw no German soldiers along this route, to our relief.

At last the solid row of dwellings came to an end. At some distance from these houses, we halted and rested on the grass along the walkway. By that time, the bunched stocking had so irritated my right toe that these stops were as welcome for the readjustment as they were for rest.

When we finally reached the edge of Cambrai, we saw a large monument, surrounded by a circular base of flowers in a park. I lingered only a minute or two — not long enough to read the entire inscription. I was curious about this old city of which I had read. I don't know exactly what I expected, but certainly there should be some evidence of a medieval town, with strong crenelated walls and perhaps a few turrets. The street just beyond the park had many businesses.

We hurried on, impelled to quickly pass through the city in order to avoid too much notice. However, those we met passed their eyes over us with indifference. Cambrai seemed to be a fairly large city — at least, it offered few opportunities for us to pause and rest our weary legs. But we kept to the road, following traffic signs that directed us toward Amiens.

To my eyes, unpracticed in the art of detecting the remains of formerly fortified cities, I still had not seen obvious remnants of Cambrai's historic past. Nor did I note the devastation of a *blitzkrieg,* which I had expected to be discernible. However, the buildings along our route displayed evidence of neglected maintenance during these five years since war had swept over them, resembling some of our American towns during the depths of the Great Depression of the 1930s.

By the time we approached the southern edge of the city, hunger and thirst joined our fatigue. Just ahead, on the right side of the street, we spotted a café. The word conjured up images of cafés in the American Midwest — places where one could order a meal, or at least a sandwich, and beverage. Bob and I decided to go in.

No sooner had our eyes become accustomed to the dimmer light of the interior than we discovered about a dozen German soldiers at ease at the tables. Beer seemed to be the featured part of the menu, so in hopes of deriving some nutritious benefit from that, we each ordered one. We paid with some of the coins given us by the Belgian man, who had helped us across the border. There were few civilians in the café, and Germans occupied the tables adjacent to our own. By silent consent we avoided display of our accents, sipping our beer in silence. Then, arising from my seat to leave, I discovered the perils of drinking strong beer on an empty stomach. Quite giddy, I steered myself uncertainly around the several tables between ours and the door, trying not to jostle the soldiers on my route, and thrust myself back onto the sidewalk. I think that Bob must have had a similar experience.

Giddy or not, hunger pangs remained with us, and we spoke of searching out a meal, even though it might require dipping into the large notes making up our escape money. At the very edge of town we spied a lone building bearing a sign proclaiming it to be a restaurant. Discovering the closed door to be locked, we turned away, when a man clad in work clothing rounded the building, wanting to know our business.

"We would like to buy a meal," Bob told him. His response suggested that another hour — or day — might be more suitable. Bob persisted, telling him that we were hungry, and asking whether we could buy a *tartine*.

"Do you have ration cards?" the man demanded.

Of course we didn't. The Army Air Corps had been so generous in providing us with passport photographs, maps, and money to assist us in evading capture. How could they have overlooked so basic a need as ration cards? For two such seedy-looking characters as ourselves to produce thousand-franc notes in order to procure a simple meal risked intensifying the man's suspicions. We chose not to take that risk, and walked on.

As the buildings of Cambrai thinned out, the route stretched straight before us. The two-lane thoroughfare was flanked by shade trees, seemingly placed to provide comfort to pedestrians and draft animals, which might have pulled burdens along its course. Though rays of the afternoon sun did not beat down with the intensity of a summer day back home, the shade furnished comfort, not only in itself but also as a token of the thoughtfulness of those who had planted them.

When the city seemed a safe distance behind, we sat down to rest by the roadside. In the adjacent field young beets were growing. Our hunger made them the more tempting. Since we were quite alone, we crept into the field, each of us picking a single beet. If they were satisfying, we could uproot more. We dusted dirt off the tubers, cleaning them as best we could. Later we would know by their shape that they were sugar beets. Had we correctly identified them and expected them to be sweet, our taste buds might have been even more disappointed. Hungry as we were, we discarded them in distaste and sought no others.

This time, however, when I rose to my feet, my legs were stiff, and I strode heavily up the first few steps of the shallow hill. But the stiffness soon abated, and I was able to resume a rapid stride.

Ahead, the stone framework of a church steeple pierced the skyline. I had never seen such a building, and it was only as we drew near that I discovered it not to be the wreckage of recent war, but quite likely the product of the architect's plan. A sign along the road identified this place as *Fontaine Nôtre Dame*. At an intersection, set in an open place by the roadside, was a statue of an angel. The setting was peaceful enough, yet placid villages like this had been, and still might be, places of danger. We did not tarry. We passed signs marking the presence of a British cemetery, unseen, to our right.

The gentle hills through which we had been moving gradually gave way to more pronounced swells. Signs directed visitors to other cemeteries of an earlier war that obviously had failed to bring such battles to an end. We pushed on, in hope of arriving at the canal marked on our road map. There, we reasoned, we could wash the visible grime from our bodies and shave the stubble that now covered our faces.

The sun was low in the sky as we approached the canal. Several teenagers appeared to be using its bridge as a trysting place. We approached slowly, seeking to assess the slope of the banks where we would scoop water for our ablutions. Shockingly, the canal bed was dry, accommodating only a thin crop of weeds. Most of the bridge had been destroyed and had fallen into the dry channel below, but repair had made it passable to traffic. Should we move beyond the bridge? The teenagers displayed faint curiosity at our presence, but that interest might intensify into suspicion if we turned back. This situation required discussion. We stood there briefly, surveying the canal bed; then we returned in the way we had come. Once out of earshot of the teens, we examined the options.

Beyond the bridge, perhaps a half mile up the hill, stood a large brick building, certainly a shelter for us. But it was also large enough to house several platoons of soldiers. We did not want to chance an encounter with the enemy. A little bit of potable water remained in the bottles in our *musette*s, which should suffice until morning, but it could not be spared for washing ourselves. If we pressed on, where would we spend the night?

At last we chose a slit trench, dug to provide shelter against aerial strafing. Upon inspection, it offered but scant comfort, for the bottom was lined with calcareous stones. Wheat shocks in a field across the road supplied bedding, and we carried several bundles to the slit trench and piled them on the floor. We opened our escape kits and ate a bite or two of the hard, brown substance intended to serve as concentrated nutrition. Then we settled down, still hungry, to sleep.

I had not slept long before I was wakened by raindrops falling on my face. They wakened Bob, too, and we soon decided that improved shelter was required — the dark and now deserted bridge! We climbed off the roadside and scouted the bridge underside. The old span tilted down from its mooring, creating a low shelter. But the ground beneath was lumpy and hard, and thus we returned to the wheat field for additional sheaves, which now served as both mattress and blanket.

We adjusted our positions so that our heads were on the upper slope and tried to sleep. I awoke several times to readjust my position. On one of those occasions the rain had stopped, and at last the outline of the bridge was detectable in the faint light. Still too early to depart, I rolled over to await full daylight.

★ ∽ ★ ∽ ★

The ground was wet when we clambered out from under the ruined span that had sheltered us for the night. We did not return the sheaves to the field, but left them under the bridge. Stiffly, we shouldered our *musettes* and plodded up the hill.

At the top, perhaps a half-mile from the empty canal, stood the brick building we had noticed the day before. As we walked on the left side of the road, a clear view of it was obscured for a time by a low bank of the roadside ditch. But no smoke curled from the tall smokestack at the far end of the structure. Did that mean that the building was unused? Could it now be used to quarter troops or military equipment, either of which would not require a great fire to heat the place? We would later learn that this was a brickery, and five years after, upon meeting my wife and me, the manager of the brickery, Mr. Totis asserted that he would have known in an instant that Bob and I were not Belgians as we had represented ourselves. He said that he would have offered us a place to stay in the cavernous chimney of the brickery, had he been there that day, for though not in use at that time, other refugees had been sheltered there.

Moving closer, we could see no windows on this side of the building — unlikely that it would be used to quarter troops, and the approaching road seemed not to have been heavily traveled recently. That evidence suggested the place might not be dangerous. Then, getting closer, we could see a small house on the front of the property made of cement tongue-and-groove "boards" set between vertical posts, the same sort of construction that we had seen in farm sheds in Belgium, and the fence bordering the Hombecks' barn lot. Remarkably, a bright array of flowers surrounded the house. Garrisoned troops were unlikely, we thought, to take such care in a building serving only as their temporary quarters.

Our concerns much allayed, we left the road and approached the house. A short, smiling woman answered Bob's rap at the door. After greeting, Bob explained that we were Belgians, traveling south to avert German soldiers. The woman appeared to think that this was a perfectly natural thing to do, so Bob proceeded. As she could see, we needed to clean up a bit, shave and, if she could, would she please give us each a cup of coffee?

"Come in," she replied, extending her arm through the doorway, and waving us into the small kitchen. At the table sat a young girl, lingering over the remnants of her morning meal. The child eyed us impassively. She pushed her plate away and watched her mother deal with these strangers.

Our hostess filled a teakettle and placed it on the stove.

"Be seated," she said. "Shaving water will be hot in just a minute, and you may take a basin back there," she continued, nodding her head toward the door to an adjoining room. As the water heated, she made an effort to put us at ease.

"I am from Italy," she said, "and I do not yet speak French like the people from here." That seemed to explain her olive-hued skin and raven hair, a strong contrast to the general run of people we had met in Belgium.

Satisfied that the water was hot enough, she poured a quantity into the basin and handed it to Bob. With grateful acceptance, he took it and the hand towel she offered and disappeared into the wash room, closing the door behind him. Adjusting the fire to prevent the remaining water from boiling, our hostess pulled her chair around to address me, now seated by the doorway.

"Your companion will be hungrier after he has attended to his toilet," she observed, quite naturally filling in any awkward silence that threatened the ease of the situation. "I shall brew coffee for you both and make you each a *tartine*. When did you last eat?"

I replied that we had eaten a bit of bread yesterday morning and had a glass of beer in the afternoon.

Madame clucked sympathetically and observed, "You will have no need of an aperitif, then. For a long time my daughter Norina had no appetite. She became very thin — much thinner than you see her now. A lady from the next town advised me to give her a small dose of St. Raphael's Quinquina just before mealtime. Then she had some appetite, and began to put on weight. Now she no longer needs an *aperitif*, and you probably won't either. But, whenever you do," she added, "St. Raphael's Quinquina is very good for you." That was advice I have never forgotten, though I have yet to taste that elixir.

Bob emerged from the wash room, his face clean and shaven. He returned the basin to our hostess, who replenished the water and gave it and a hand towel to me. The simple wash room boasted a sink with a drain, a shelf, and mirror. Eager to erase the grime that had accumulated in more than two days, I removed my jacket and shirt, extracted my plastic escape kit from the interior pocket of the jacket, and placed it, open, on the shelf. Then I splashed water on my hands and face. A small piece of gray soap lay in a dish on the shelf. This was not the first time I had seen wartime soap; it produced few suds, but contributed nevertheless to the desired end product. In due course I worked up sufficient lather to shave with the short-handled razor.

Finished, I toweled myself off, then sloshed the dirty water around in the basin before pouring it down the drain. Fully dressed again, I peered in the mirror as I combed my hair. Under the circumstances, I felt presentable again. As I returned to the kitchen, our hostess interrupted her conversation with Bob. In my absence she had buttered two large slices of bread, which she now offered to us. Then she poured the wartime variant of coffee for us. Our famished stomachs welcomed the hot liquid and tasty bread. My stomach cried for more, but the bareness of this kitchen counseled me to be silent about the craving. Very likely, she had given us the very bread intended for her luncheon meal.

As Bob and I ate, Madame gave us pointers for our journey. "Be cautious in passing through Bapaume," she said. "There are German soldiers there. You must go through the town — there is no other practical way. Act so as not to arouse suspicion."

Now that our exteriors were clean, I expressed concern that our tattered clothing might draw the attention of people along the route.

"You would need ration coupons, of course, in order to buy clothing," she replied. "But if you are in dire need of a clean and new shirt, some shops sell shirts made of paper. They hold up well for a time, and I believe they can be bought without coupons."

Signaling that our stay had come to an end, Bob placed his empty coffee cup on the table. Following him to his feet, I set mine down beside it, and, in my halting French, thanked Madame for her hospitality. I knew no words adequate to express the depth of my gratitude for what to her may have seemed only normal hospitality. The child Norina remained in her chair, silently nodding a discreet *adieu*. Our hostess followed us to the door, bidding us goodbye and wishing us a good route.

★ ★ ★

Back we trod toward the road, past the rows of flowers that embraced the little house. At the highway we stole a last glance back at the scene of the tranquil interlude we were leaving. Then we turned to the left and strode swiftly down the road, refreshed and confident in the knowledge that our faces were clean and free from stubble, less likely to attract unwanted attention.

The terrain had given way to a more gentle undulation after a long climb up the hill from the canal. My early morning stiffness was now gone, and we both swung easily into a rapid gait. Alone on the road, we were able to speak freely to one another.

"There is a village ahead, along the road," Bob observed.

I replied that it seemed to be a small one, not very forbidding. "Madame made no point about this village. She mentioned only Bapaume, which must be another ten miles ahead," I continued, as much to reassure myself as to comfort any anxiety Bob might have about passing through another inhabited area.

The mileage marker at the village edge announced our presence at Boursies, indeed a small and not very prosperous village. Another sign indicated a British cemetery to the south; I concluded that it must have been a cemetery from World War I. I felt a sense of relief when we had passed through the village without incident.

A short distance later, a road sign indicated that the town of Beaumetz and another British cemetery lay off to our left. We paused to rest at the side of the road. A glance at our road map revealed that our route shifted slightly southward at Bapaume, passing through Albert before it led to Amiens. To stay on course, we should be alert to road signs pointing to either of those destinations.

Our route passed through two more villages before we saw the larger town of Bapaume ahead. As we began the descent through the town I remarked to Bob, "The larger part of Bapaume seems to lie to the right of our road; maybe we will bypass much of it. I will feel more comfortable if we don't encounter many people."

It was a vain hope. At the bottom of the hill, at the junction of this and a cross street, stood a monument. The road to Amiens turned abruptly at that point. Following this new direction, we had little time to read the inscription on the monument, but it seemed to refer to events during World War I. Not yet did we know that this site had been in the front battle lines in that fierce conflict.

Ahead on our path lay the main shopping street of this town. We would need to move along quickly, alert to avoid encountering anyone who might single us out as unwelcome strangers. Shielded at the corner by a large building, I saw the red swastika-emblazoned banner that signaled a Nazi headquarters. By the steps leading to its door, a soldier clad in the green-gray uniform of the *Wehrmacht* — the German armed forces — stood at smart attention. Because it was on the opposite side of the street from us, we stood less risk of encounter. I knew Bob's body had tensed, as did mine, and by mental telepathy alone we maintained our purposeful gait, glancing toward the stores on our left as we passed the dreaded building. We both relaxed imperceptibly, but retained our alertness, as we strode up the inclining street.

A small knot of people blocked the sidewalk ahead. Brushing against my shoulder, Bob extended his arm, pointing toward a shop on the opposite side of the street. Though his lips moved conversationally, he uttered no sound which might betray our accent, and we angled across to the window he had singled out. We paused only briefly, as if to inspect the wares on display, then shrugged as though the prices might be beyond our means, and continued on our way.

The buildings here appeared to be better maintained than those in the previous towns. It did not occur to me then that they might be much newer replacements for buildings destroyed by war only 25 years earlier. The street seemed to stretch out endlessly, and my sore foot was begging me to give it a rest. But we simply could not stop until we were free of pedestrians and habitations.

Some time later, after a bend in the road, the presence of a café reminded me that I was thirsty, too; but I didn't care for a repetition of the earlier stop, where most of the customers had been German soldiers. We plodded on, surmounting a slight rise of the street. Ahead at last we saw the shaded roadway to Amiens.

At a short distance from Bapaume, we rested at roadside, shaded by the line of trees bordering the two-lane highway. From the *musettes* at our sides, we extracted the beer bottles that held our water supplies and drank gratefully but sparingly. Almost ritually it now seemed, I took off my shoes and readjusted my stockings, wadded again at the toes. The blister on the toe of my right foot had broken long ago, and the flesh under and around it was an angry red. How convenient it would have been to have a supply of band-aids in that kit! But having neither those nor a longed-for medication, I replaced the stockings with care and laced up my shoes. We had to press on.

Perhaps a hundred paces down the road, the stiffness that always returned during our stops left us, and we resumed our steady gait. We paused by the sign that proclaimed a low-walled cemetery as the final resting place of British soldiers. It seemed fitting that the grounds were neatly maintained, and at that moment I felt drawn closer to our Allies — nearer to the safety of friends and home. I considered that a cemetery like this could be a place to rest, or to spend the night. But it appeared too open for a sanctuary, for if espied, we would be hard-pressed to escape. We resumed our pace.

A sign on our right pointed to a British Memorial, apparently in a wooded copse some distance from the road. As we walked on, other military cemeteries lay beside or not far from the road. The feeling that we were near friendly territory continued to give me comfort, despite the nearly constant tension under which we had been since that morning in Belgium, when an imperious rapping at the door had propelled me for the last time from the comfortable bed at the Hombecks.

The road took us southwestward through several tiny, worn villages. Then we saw the spire of a large church, which marked the site of Albert. The road jogged in the town, affording a good view of the tall, thin steeple surmounted by a golden figure. There, for the first time, we saw wooden buildings, vertically sided with wide boards, that were badly in need of paint. Why would there be wooden buildings here, when we had seen no others like them in Europe? Then we spied the railroad station, remarkable for its roof line, stepped in the Flemish fashion. Our road made a sharp turn to the left before we came to the station, leading us out of town.

At our next rest stop we drained our supply of water, heightening our concern that another source be located shortly. Yet our map showed only one stream ahead, and that was 15 kilometers away. We had not seen an isolated household for many miles. It appeared that farmers lived in the villages, leaving to tend their flocks and till their fields. Only two villages lay by our route; the second of which was located by the stream. We needed to find water soon, though we hesitated to request any from a householder, especially in an inhabited area.

At our next stop, Bob felt the call of nature. A small cement cattle shelter stood perhaps 200 yards off the road. We reasoned that would provide seclusion sufficient for the task. I grasped the top wire of the fence, putting my foot firmly on the second wire to allow Bob room to get through.

Because of the urgency of his errand, Bob didn't bend low enough. A resounding rip opened the seat of his trousers, revealing enough to elicit comment from anyone following. He slowed enough to help me through, then sped for the cattle shelter. There were no cows in the field, but the cement watering tank in front of the building was half full of algae-covered water. It would have to do.

I unstopped the bottles and plunged one, opening-down, through the thick green scum. When twisted to its side, the bottle filled. I pulled it out, flipped a bit of scum from the top, and inserted a Halazone tablet from my escape kit. Only tiny fragments of algae were visible in the bottle. I did the same for the second bottle. The Halazone would require a full hour before the water would be safely potable.

By that time, Bob's discomfort had passed. The cattle shed provided a secluded spot for the repair of his trousers. Fortunately, our escape kit contained a small sewing kit, and the trousers — already oft-patched — soon looked as sturdy as before.

Now we recrossed the field to the road, taking care this time to avoid disaster on the barbed wire.

★ ♒ ★ ♒ ★

Back on the road, we took a glum view of the long stretch of highway. Amiens lay a dozen kilometers ahead, and we would probably need to walk through the entire city before we could sleep that night. If only we had bicycles! Better yet, if only we could get a ride. We had seen very few vehicles on the roads, but to our amazement there, in the distance behind us, came a truck.

"Let's hitch a ride," I suggested hopefully.

As the vehicle loomed closer, it was apparently an old one, moving slowly along the highway. Along the passenger side, by the running board, was a black funnel-like device for burning coke fuel, similar to equipment we had seen on earlier vehicles. To our delight, the truck responded to our hailing, then slowed and stopped beside us. The man in the passenger seat bade us climb up in back. As I hauled myself up, I noted that we were not alone. Seated in the coal dust, for the vehicle must be returning from a delivery, sat a gray-clad German soldier. I sat down in shock, silently nodding to him. I feared we would be unable to escape conversation, and that we would be discovered and arrested.

Right behind me, Bob had thrown his leg over the side of the truck. As the second leg followed, he opened his mouth to signal that we were ready. "Okay," he intended to shout. Then, seeing the soldier, he halted in mid-word. "*Bon!*" he shouted in correction.

The truck lurched ahead. Conversationally, the soldier addressed something to us in French. We couldn't have had better fortune, for just then, it began to rain. Bob drew his coat collar over his head and turned toward the back of the truck. "*Il pleut*" — It's raining — he replied. Grateful for his example, I did the same. The soldier returned to his solitude as the truck rumbled on.

Chapter 11

Close Encounters

LIGHT RAIN PELTED my back, its penetrating power reinforced by the forward motion of the truck. Peering from under my raised collar, I watched fence posts slide back into the distance. Though we may have moved along at only 30 miles an hour, the pace was a great improvement over our pedestrian speed, no matter how hard we had pressed. Even with the coal dust from the truck and the pelting rain, this mode of travel represented comparative luxury.

Through the slit of my half-closed coat I watched as we passed a church in the nearby village. Even with an enemy soldier for a traveling companion, this was the first time I had relaxed while passing through an inhabited area. The village behind us, I settled into the shelter of my jacket and relished each and every 100 yards we would now be spared from traveling on foot.

The truck rumbled on, turning left in descent of a hill, then right again to cross a bridge, and left once more. The truck slowed to a halt before a low grayish building. A man alighted from the cab of the truck and entered a doorway. Our German companion, like us, stared silently at the doorway. What was the trucker's mission here? We were not to learn, for he returned after only a short delay and clambered aboard. The truck lurched into gear and began the ascent up the side of the valley. I retreated again into the shelter of my coat collar and hunched my back to extract maximum protection against the slowing drizzle.

Had I fallen asleep? The brakes were squeaking as the truck pulled to a stop at an orange and white barrier stretched across the road. On either side, a forest extended beyond waist-high embankments. Two German soldiers, rifles at the ready, stood by the barricade. One approached the cab on the passenger side, obviously requesting the occupants' identification and other papers. I tensed, then concluded that flight would be unsuccessful. I waited, prepared to show my Belgian identification card. But knowing that it had not been stamped at the border, I resigned myself to imminent arrest. Bob's body language told me that he had arrived at the same conclusion.

The soldier's attention turned to those of us on the rear of the truck. Acknowledging that our fellow traveler's presence was permissible, the sentry barely glanced at us. Did he assume that the soldier had screened us? Or that coal-smudged laborers such as we posed no threat? He stood back, signaling his companion to raise the barrier. The truck grumbled into gear and proceeded on through the woods. I breathed a sigh of relief.

A short distance into the forest, the underbrush had been cleared out. Stacks of gray barrels suggested the presence of fuel storage; large boxes made of new wood could possibly contain a cache of munitions or spare machine parts. In the hope that I might later be able to pass this on to Allied officials, I made mental notes of the location of the matériel.

The sentries quickly passed us once more at the far edge of the woods. A few kilometers later, we drove into the northeast edge of Amiens. On our right side we approached a fortress-like building, a huge hole gaping in its front wall. How could so great a destructive force fail to have produced more devastation than a breach in so limited an area? Aerial bomb damage would surely have flattened the top of the wall and, likely, much more. There was no visible activity around the building, and our truck rolled on past, allowing my mind to return to matters closer at hand.

It was much later that I read an account of a RAF raid precisely designed to open a particular spot in this prison wall in order to free espionage agents being subjected to harsh interrogation. A plane had swooped low, releasing a bomb aimed at the base of the wall.

The truck slowed, turned into a gateway on the left side of the street, and halted to discharge us passengers. We quickly and silently parted company with the soldier, and continued on foot down the mostly residential street. The sloping thoroughfare eventually flattened, forming a long arch over a waterway and shipping facilities below. We stood for a moment, surveying the barges moored along the canal. What a boon it would be if we could gain passage on a canal boat sailing toward the coast, and from there contact a ship that would aid us in crossing to England! It was a chancy idea, but I was sure that it had been done. But how could we approach a boatman in full view of others? And what could we do if we met with a hostile rebuff? Unprepared for these contingencies, we continued on our way.

The street widened beyond the bridge. A sign posted parallel to the canal indicated that the intersecting road led northwest. The route toward Breteuil lay straight ahead. In our path, a series of log barriers blocked vehicular traffic and shunted pedestrians in a zigzag line past a control point manned by two German soldiers. Too late to turn back without drawing attention to our evasion, we joined the line slowly moving through the maze. Those ahead of us displayed their identity cards for examination. Our Belgian ones, not stamped at the border, were sure to give us away, so we left them in our pockets. With heads bowed and covered with a film of coal dust, we shuffled, unchallenged, past the sentries.

We ascended the street with relief and renewed vigor. Amiens was a city too large to traverse before the curfew hour. We would attempt to locate a source of food and lodging for the night.

We passed a number of business buildings, then a curious tower-like structure seemingly encrusted with small stones. Farther along the area became more residential in character. Should we await the chance encounter with someone in their doorway, or boldly enter a building, stating our need in relative privacy, which might ensure our escape should the householder be affronted by our query?

At this moment in my own deliberations, the clatter of boots on the stairs of the building beside us announced a squad of soldiers. Apparently lodged in the building, they may have been responding to the dinner hour. Quickly they formed a double column and marched in the direction from which we had come. Fearing that others might be housed nearby, I lost my enthusiasm for entering just any doorway.

Bob and I scanned the side streets as we came to intersections, looking for some sign that might suggest a welcome. But again and again I saw nothing favorable. After what seemed a very long time, the route turned west, opening on a wide avenue, which seemed to be deserted at that hour. The buildings within our vision were residential, set away from the street, forbidding approach.

Somewhat dispirited by the growing possibility that curfew would fall upon us while we were still in the city, hungry and without shelter for the approaching night, we looked for a shorter route that would take us out of town. Once in the countryside we might find shelter in a field. A street on our left appeared promising in this respect, so we set out in that direction. The urgency of the hour goaded our tired legs on until we came upon an intersecting street paralleling the crest of a hill bordering the town. A short distance ahead, two German soldiers stood by a barricade of tangled barbed wire. As we watched, one consulted his watch in apparent readiness to close a narrow road leading down the hill and into the farmland. We kept our brisk pace, giving the soldiers a wide berth. Their eyes followed us, and one fingered the handle of a hand grenade fastened to his belt. But they did not accost us. As we passed and headed down the country road, the two swung the barricade into place. We had gotten out of town in the very nick of time.

A few hundred yards farther on, the curvature of the hill concealed the barricade and us from view of the soldiers as well. Resigned to another night of hunger, we entered a field of wheat bundled and shocked for the harvest. We could lie on the bundles and pull others over us as protection from the dew and chill. But first, we needed to slake our thirst. We fished the water bottles from our *musettes*, uncorked the stoppers, and gulped greedily. The Halazone tablets we had added to the greenish water from the trough had done their job. The fluid had a sort of antiseptic taste to it.

As we were then about to select our exact spot to bed down, Bob spied a man on a bicycle riding slowly up the hill toward Amiens. Because he was alone, we felt comfortable in approaching him. At our hail he stopped, no sign of fear nor surprise on his face. Bob told him we were Belgians on foot in France to find work, and asked if there was a farmhouse nearby where we might find shelter for the night.

"Of course," he replied. "At the foot of this hill, on the left, lies a road leading to a village. It is not far from here, and there you will surely find a place to stay."

Gladly we abandoned our preparations to bed down in the field and set out quickly to the bottom of the hill. As he had said, a small road led to the east — our left — and soon we saw a fork in the road, each winding up the incline of a low hill. A small house was set back a bit from a lawn. An elderly woman bent at a pump at the edge of her garden looked up as we came to the wire fence. Bob greeted her and repeated the story he had told to the bicyclist on the other road. It was quickly apparent that she wanted nothing to do with two vagabonds, but told us that there were Belgians in the village and that we should inquire there. They lived just up the hill, on the main street. We were to turn left at the intersection, and they would be found on the far side of the street, at the third gateway.

Bob protested that the curfew hour was near and couldn't she spare us a place in an outbuilding? But she had stated her position, and with a wave of her arm sped us off to find the Belgian family.

Many years later, in trying to retrace the route, I discovered that Amiens had expanded to the south, and that the nearest town I could locate was Cagny — of course, much larger than I remembered. Some of the landmarks had been obliterated as well.

A commotion could be heard even before we rounded the curve at the intersection ahead. At the crossroads, a noisy knot of young to middle-aged men milled about. Beside them, on the right, the red and black swastika waved from a brick building. We did not escape notice, and someone in the crowd called to us, saying I know not what, but clearly we were identified as strangers. Though the street to the left was empty, our entry into a building there would be noted. It seemed too risky to chance a visit. With the crowd dead ahead, we turned to the right, directly in front of the *Wehrmacht* headquarters. As we passed, a soldier mounted on a fine gray-dappled steed approached a window in the headquarters building and listened to an officer within.

We walked quickly on. Soon the clip-clop of the horse's hoofs could be heard on the paving behind us. We turned at the next intersection in hopes of avoiding contact with the rider. But the horseman turned too. We continued on, and were relieved when the horseman turned on the next intersecting street. But he paused and called to us. "Where is the *Maire* — the townhall?" he asked.

"Marie," I had heard him to say, must be a very well-known person, I thought, if even a ragged workman is expected to know where she lives.

"In the third house on your right," I called, hoping that by the time he had found out otherwise, we would be out of sight.

The road curved to the bottom of the hill, revealing that we had come full circle, ending again at the home of the old lady to whom we had first talked. In the failing light, she was still in her garden. She was even more impatient at Bob's request again to let us stay the night.

"I told you to go to the house of your countryman," she scolded, waving her arm toward the intersection by the *Wehrmacht* headquarters. "Now go and do not bother me again!"

There seemed no alternative but to comply, and with deep foreboding we trudged again up that hill. The boisterous crowd was still in the intersection, and as we came into sight one of the men shouted, "And where will you sleep tonight, tramp?"

That triggered general laughter and a series of loud remarks from the others. At the commotion, a window in the *Wehrmacht* headquarters was raised, and we could see the uniformed figure inside as he called to the horseman, who had now returned from his mission. Just then we reached the intersection and hurried toward our destination, the barked order of the officer ringing through the twilight. Immediately the sound of hoofbeats on the cobblestones followed in our path. As the horseman came nearer, Bob lunged for the door in the brick wall and thrust it open. As the horse's shoulder came even with me, the soldier reached out and grasped my coat. Somehow I wrenched free and propelled myself through the doorway, slamming the door behind me.

A space between the house and barn formed a narrow walkway, exiting to the rear. We moved slowly away from the door, waiting to see whether the soldier would open it and continue his pursuit.

"If he enters, we'll have to make a break for it out to the rear. We can separate at the corner of the buildings, so he can chase only one at a time," Bob observed. "The one who gets away should circle back to trees directly behind this place and wait for the other. Let's allow thirty minutes for the other one to come before going on alone."

But, inexplicably, we were not followed; no one tried the door. So we went to the steps leading to the house door. Bob's knock was answered by a slender woman, drying her hands on a white cloth. She did not question our Belgian origins, nor did she welcome us as fellow countrymen. Rather, she said that our needs must await the return of her husband, who was just then out drinking with the Germans.

We didn't receive that as the best of news, but this did not seem a good time to venture back into the street. Was the husband a collaborator, or merely a man trying to maintain a favorable image with those in the vicinity who now wielded supreme power? We assented to wait for him on the doorstep, especially after she had inquired if we had had supper. Of course we hadn't, so she turned to her kitchen stove, edging past two husky teenagers listening attentively in the kitchen. The woman placed bread into two bowls, poured in a quantity of warm milk, pulled two large spoons from a drawer, and offered these to us.

With genuine thanks and ravenous appetites we made short work of these provisions. Only then did we ask to wash our faces and hands. The need for that was obvious to anyone, and we soon stood next to the small outbuilding, splashing ourselves generously with water from the pump and drying on a coarse towel suspended from a nail near the wash table. Our caps now in our *musettes*, we combed our hair, reflected in an old mirror above the table. With our stomachs full, our hands and faces clean, and our hair combed, we felt better. We sat on the doorstep awaiting the return of the householder.

I grew increasingly uneasy as time went on. Surely the curfew must already be in effect. Down the street the banter had stilled, suggesting that the noisy crowd had dissipated. What special relationship must this man have with the Germans to permit him to be out so late? I worried that we had ventured into a situation that might lead to our arrest.

What position did he hold in this town? I worried. Was he socializing with the top officers of the local military government? If his sympathies lay with the conquerors, what would he do about us? Rewards were offered for turning in Allied airmen. If the relationships he maintained with the Germans had the objective of easing potential losses of livestock or other hardship, though, his loyalties might not lie firmly with those who now occupied his country. If so, he might be willing to help us, but only in secret, for he would wish to preserve the favorable reputation he had acquired. Perhaps his relationship was with enlisted men rather than officers. If that were the case, he might have fewer qualms about aiding Allied airmen. I wondered.

After what seemed like an unduly long interval, the wooden door at the street swung open, and in came a man who, in spite of a slightly unsteady gait, strode with the air of proprietorship. At the doorway we gave way to let him pass. With an almost imperceptible pause on the step he looked us squarely in the eye. Then with what seemed unnecessary loudness, he made his presence known in the kitchen. He did not stay there for long. After his wife had explained our presence, he told her to hold dinner until after he had finished with Bob and me. Then, with evident agitation, he returned to the outside corridor, stationed himself by the small outbuilding beside the wash table, assumed an interrogative pose, and addressed us.

Very quickly he concluded that we were not truly Belgians.

"Who are you?" he raged. "The Germans must have sent you here to test my loyalty to them!"

To forestall a decision by our interrogator to turn us over to the enemy in order to preserve his good standing with the Germans, Bob hastened to declare our true identity. "We are American aviators," he said. "Our airplane crashed in Belgium, and we are trying to return to our airfield."

"What proof have you of that?" demanded the anxious farmer.

In response, I reached in my breast pocket for the small packet of Benzedrine tablets I had earlier extracted from my escape kit. I waved the package of stimulants at him to show the instructions, written in English.

He frowned. "Anyone can get a thing like that. The Germans must have cases of them. They could have given them to you so that you could masquerade as Americans to fool me, and then discredit me!"

Bob then produced his escape kit, knowing that the same logic might prevail. But Bob spoke calmly, arguing that the local Germans would be unlikely to have access to such kits, and in all likelihood held the farmer above suspicion of harboring their enemies.

It may have been Bob's earnestness that diminished the man's uneasiness. Or perhaps it was his appetite. At any rate, he consented to let us spend the night. "But only in the barn. And you must be very quiet, and leave this place before six o'clock in the morning."

He started toward the kitchen where his wife, having heard these proceedings, had already prepared two sandwiches for us to eat on the morrow. Grateful, we stuffed them in our *musettes*. Her husband stopped to offer us advice. "Go out the back way and cross the marshy field behind. By the railroad tracks, go south. Just a few kilometers in that direction is a large town. It is dangerous there, so before reaching it you must turn west and circle around it. You will discover a road that will lead you in the direction you wish to go. Now, be very quiet, and good night," he intoned as he turned toward his dinner.

Bob and I took the few steps to the barn door, eager to lie down. We had not slept well the night before on the rocky bottom of the slit trench, nor on the bumpy remnants of the fallen bridge. In the darkness of the barn we could detect a layer of fresh straw. How welcome a bed that would be! As we arranged ourselves, it became apparent that we were not alone. A furry tail beat against my arm; a wet tongue lapped at my face. A small puppy was shut in with us, and he was in serious need of companionship. He whimpered as I pushed him aside, and instantly fawned over Bob. His need for attention was so insistent that a gruff rebuff failed to deter the attentions he lavished upon us. Perhaps if we stroked him he might stretch out beside us and let the three of us sleep. That did not work either. When shoved, he whimpered, then redoubled his amorous attentions. I'm sure that we both must have given consideration to throttling him, but that seemed as ungrateful to our hosts as it would have been inhumane to the puppy.

We had no trouble waking before six o'clock. In truth, neither of us had slept. Bob's utterances of "*allez!*" even if in good French, had gone unheeded by the dog. And Bob's voice — and the puppy's damp tongue — had kept us both awake. So at ten minutes before six, we put on our shoes, shouldered our *musettes*, carefully closed the puppy in the barn, and tiptoed quietly to the rear gate. There was another fence to negotiate, and then we were on the uneven surface of an extensive marsh.

Walking was difficult, so we continued up to the raised roadbed of the railroad track, scrambled to the top, and followed the roadbed. Of course, a train did come along, so until it had passed, we returned to the marsh. Ahead, several smokestacks reared above the shadowy buildings of a town. Mindful of the Belgian's advice, we recrossed the marsh to a road on the other side. Finding a small intersecting road, we traveled westward until brighter light revealed another southbound road. Turning, we were thankful for the trees that screened the view even of the town we were avoiding. The town was probably Boves, situated at some distance southeast of Cagny.

In the quiet of morning, we passed a couple of cottages, complete with gardens. At one of them, ducks floated on a small domestic pond. What a peaceful place! But we had to press on. Eventually, we came to a larger road bearing to the west. That should intersect with the route from Amiens to Beauvais. We turned and followed that until another intersection revealed a large boulder at the edge of the woods. My feet seemed perpetually sore, and it was time for a rest. We trudged to the boulder, clambered on top, and surveyed the tranquil scene about us.

A bicyclist, head down, eyes fixed steadfastly forward, pedaled westward. His stance reminded me of Adolphe on the day he had guided me through the back roads and paths of Belgium. That may have been no coincidence, for trailing behind him came a second cyclist, this one dressed in the forest-green heated suit currently in use by the Air Corps. I sat transfixed, hesitating to signal our kinship for fear of drawing unwelcome attention to him from some quarter nearby. After he had passed, I wished that I had whistled a few bars from some known Air Corps tune, and flashed him the "V for Victory" salute, though it may have been better that I hadn't. Still, I had a good feeling knowing that others in circumstances similar to ours were still being cared for as we had been when we were first downed.

Soon the road left the woods and we walked through farmland. Sometime later in the morning we climbed what seemed like a steep hill and passed through a village, probably St. Fuscien. Just then I craved a drink of water — or better, something to eat. But after our previous experience at the café and having learned that ration stamps were necessary to purchase food, we dared not try to seek out a restaurant or grocery. Not knowing when we next might eat, we were saving our sandwiches. We plodded on, eventually approaching a village which, as we came nearer, seemed to be intersected by a major route. A high brick wall bordering the road enclosed a large enterprise. We approached with what was now customary caution, fearful that enemy troops might be stationed in any large building. Almost hugging the wall, we peered around the corner to survey the area. A curve in the road concealed the full extent of the village, but we saw only a few houses, so we assumed that it was small. Still, the major road — doubtless the highway to Beauvais — was wide, and with a café or hostelry on the next corner on our intended direction, we would be uncomfortably conspicuous.

There seemed no alternative but to take this road, so we crossed the highway and turned southward. No one was seated at the open-air tables at the café just then, so we walked quickly by, crossed the next street, and continued on our way. My relief to have passed through the village without incident was amplified by *bornes* reassuring us that we were indeed on the road toward Beauvais, less than 60 kilometers away. When we were a safe distance past the village, we paused for a much-needed rest.

When my watch indicated that ten minutes had elapsed, once again we got to our feet, continuing on. We regained our habitual cadence, probably about three and one-half miles per hour.

We walked through a small farming village, its buildings badly in need of paint. Not a single person was in evidence. Later, when our bodies signaled that it was time for another rest, we spotted a large house set back from the road. Its access road, flanked by narrow bands of trees, bid us welcome. Wary that so imposing a dwelling might harbor the enemy, we avoided walking up the road. Instead, we passed through the adjacent field, then crept into the brush under the trees. There we relaxed in delicious seclusion for the ten minutes we permitted ourselves to rest.

The highway stretched southward across a landscape of hills rising in long, steep slopes. Narrow strips of woodland stood along the hilltops and spilled down hillsides deemed too steep to cultivate. Though the wooded areas appeared to offer a screen from detection, because of the steep slopes of the banks through which the road was cut, they seemed too difficult to reach just for a short rest period.

As we trudged up a steep slope, a broad valley lay on our right. On the far slope a large but solitary farmstead seemed to beckon. As yet, we could locate no way to get to the farm. Tempting as it was as a possible haven, direct access was blocked by a precipitous incline at the edge of the road. As we neared the top of the hill, we came upon a narrow road leading from this highway to the valley below. Sliced from the hillside, the roadway accounted for the steeply graded drop from our highway. I estimated the distance we would have to traverse just to get to the farm. Considering the steep slope of the return route if we were turned away, we elected to bypass this alluring temptation.

Over the crest of another long hill we could see a church spire almost directly ahead, probably in the town of Breteuil. We would be relieved if the road continued in a straight line, and we might be able to bypass much of the town. Unfortunately for us, the purpose of roads in those days was to direct travelers to the centers of living and commerce. At the top of another hill, the road veered sharply to the left to enter the town.

Now faced with the prospect of walking some distance before an opportunity to relax once more, we sat under a tree at the edge of the road and rested our weary bodies. Then, somewhat refreshed, we followed the road into Breteuil, coming at length to its market center. For local people it could have been a pleasant street on which to meet neighbors, for even with wartime shortages, its shops appeared neat and reasonably well stocked. There were a few people on the street, and we passed through without confrontation. Still, it was with relief that we came to the end of the market area, turned, and passed into and through another residential area.

A few kilometers farther on we were quite ready for another rest. It had been a long and tedious day, and we had already walked about 60 kilometers. Just where we would rest was decided for us by three men conversing by the side of the road, ahead of us. Two of them, at least, had bicycles. We did not want to encounter them, so at that spot we entered an adjacent field and busied ourselves at weeding rows of sugar beets.

It was not a comfortable situation, for we possibly would be recognized as strangers, even at a distance, especially if they were acquainted with those who customarily worked this field. If we were to be accosted, our presence there would be difficult to explain. My next thought was that no easy route of exit led from that field — just more fields, and no nearby woods or buildings. I hoped that the men would quickly terminate their conversation and go away. Soon, they did.

We returned to the highway, wistfully considering the prospects of acquiring bicycles of our own, a way to multiply the distances we could travel in a day, and minimizing even further the risks of encountering persons who might betray our fugitive status. Certainly, we had funds sufficient to purchase bicycles, yet for persons dressed like ourselves to produce such quantities of money — even if a bicycle could be found for sale — would most likely raise questions. Once again, the size of those escape kit bills appeared to act as a barrier to our spending that money in any way except as payment for a guide through the Pyrenees.

Could we steal a bike, and leave an appropriate amount of money in its place? Under favorable conditions, we might ride safely away before the theft was detected; by having paid for it, we would feel less guilty. But because in these past few days we had not seen a single bicycle unguarded, the prospect seemed dim. Still, we could keep our eyes open.

At the square in the next small town, two bicycles leaned, untended, in front of a café. What a surprise! Without a word, Bob and I each walked purposely toward the bikes. Just then, across the square we spied two men in conversation. They were eyeing us intently. Though we might grasp these bicycles and pedal past them, the risk of eventual apprehension seemed too great. Disappointed, without a word we veered off and strode rapidly out of town.

A few kilometers beyond, and just past the lowest point between hills sat a solitary house, possibly vacant. Just below that house we stopped beside a *borne* indicating that Beauvais lay 14 kilometers ahead. Across the road, a lane led up to a tiny village on the next hilltop. From this resting place we could observe no sign of life at either habitation. Not only were we tired, but we were ravenously hungry as well. Now seemed a good time to eat the two *tartines* packed for us by last night's hostess.

I seized this opportunity to take off my shoes. It was light enough to inspect the damage. The big toe on my right foot was shorter than the other toes; it seemed to have been pushed back nearly an inch into the foot. The skin over the joint was worn away and the bone, surrounded by bloody red flesh, had a polished appearance. No wonder it still hurt. I sat there barefooted, exposing it to the warm, dry air.

With *tartines* in hand and bottles of water to wash down the bread, we spoke. Fourteen kilometers still to Beauvais? That was a large city; we would need to plan our route beyond. Just then, Bob remembered what it was that he knew about Beauvais. The *aérodrome* had been our alternate target on the day we were shot down. That was sobering information, for our road map bore no indication of an airfield. A military airfield would signify a concentration of enemy troops, which we would do well to avoid. Without an idea of their location, we could easily blunder into danger. In any case, we would not continue to Beauvais tonight.

As we were finishing our snack and contemplating our continuing hunger, a small car purred up from the south and stopped beside us. From within, a German officer addressed us, saying something which neither of understood. Turning in his seat, he spoke to the other occupant of the coupe. He leaned in our direction and called out something. I could distinguish his language as French, but his accent was different from that to which we were becoming accustomed. Responding to our shrugs of incomprehension, the officer bolted from the car, whipped his Luger from its holster, and began questioning.

Bob had not budged from his seat, so I pulled on my shoe and got to my feet. In answer to his question, I replied.

"We are Belgian," I stated, hoping to provide convincing explanation for our deficiency in language, "and we are on our way to Beauvais. Our uncle and cousin are working at the *aérodrome* there, and we hope to find work there, too."

I edged toward him as I spoke, recalling hours of practice in disarming companions wielding Colt .45s. If it came to that, I would try to overpower him. But his pistol differed from the ones we had used for practice; it was loaded. Was that why the business end of the smaller Luger seemed so very large?

The interrogator seemed to be satisfied with my explanation, but had a further ritual to fulfill. "Do you have papers?" he asked. "Yes, sir," I replied, fumbling in my jacket pocket. In truth, except for the Belgian *carte d' identité*, not stamped at the border, my pocket contained only road maps. With apprehension, I stepped toward him as I fumbled in the pocket.

"Good," he exclaimed with a flourish of his pistol. "Be on your way, then."

As he reentered the car and continued down the highway, I went back to where Bob was seated and sank limply at his side. It had been a narrow escape!

Chapter 12

Compassionate Hands

UP TO THIS time we had seen no activity at the house nearby. Concluding that it was empty, at least for now, we considered alternative means of obtaining help. In the field behind us, a farmer was pitching bundles of wheat onto his hayrack. He must have been nearly finished, for the bundles were already heaped high on his wagon. Except for a small boy as his companion, he was quite alone in the field. With no one nearby to whom he could report us, it seemed prudent to approach him for assistance.

"You go talk to him, Bill." I was surprised to hear Donahue's urging, for up to now he had handled matters of communication ably by himself. "You managed that last situation well enough. I'll just rest here for awhile. You might as well tell him," he added, "that we're Americans."

The worker was just finishing his loading as I walked up, so I easily caught his attention. I told him that I was an American flier, and needed a place to spend the night. "There are two of us," I said. "My companion is by the edge of the highway."

Receiving this information more with anxiety than antagonism, he shrugged his shoulders and made a helpless gesture with his free arm. He replied, shortly, that it was impossible, then turned and led his horse and wagon toward the highway. There was little for me to do but follow. By then, the young boy, had emerged from behind the wagon. He must have heard our conversation, for he tugged at my arm, asking, "Are you American?"

At my affirmative answer he hurried to his father and tugged at his coattail. "*American, Papa. Oui, oui!*"

There may have been more words that I didn't know or didn't remember, but the result was that the worker shrugged his shoulders in acquiescence. When we came to the highway, he motioned for Bob. Together we trailed the wagon up the hill.

After a large, green metal gate set in a high wall was opened, the horse and load of bundled wheat passed through. Bob and I followed the boy into an extensive barnyard. The gate was closed behind us and the rack driven up by a barn. Asking the boy to tend the horse, the worker rapped at the door of the house just to the left of the gate.

The top half of the Dutch door swung inward, revealing a dark-haired woman. To her, our worker-guide, hat in hand, spoke quietly. I did not hear the words, but guessed that he told her what he knew about us. We were ushered inside and our guide dismissed.

My eyes quickly swept our surroundings, ever searching for an escape route. We were in a long, narrow room. Opposite the door was another, leading into a room that I supposed to be a kitchen. On the north wall, two stairs led up to a closed door. The opposite wall had a door also, at the same level as the floor in this room. At the center of the room stood a square table with an oilcloth cover; four chairs were drawn up to the table, by which we stood. Under the window by the entrance door was a sewing machine. Our hostess had apparently been sewing when she had gone to answer the door.

The lady, of above-average stature and only a little plump, smiled benignly as she asked who we were and where we had come from. As she talked, she brushed the palms of her hands against the flowered *tablier* protecting her dark dress, as if to smooth it. She readily accepted our explanations, and divining that we were both tired and hungry, she asked if we would like something to eat. The *tartine* we had eaten by the roadside had barely filled a corner of our appetite, and we agreed heartily.

Seating us at the table, she busied herself in the adjacent room, rather quickly setting before us each a hearty sandwich filled with cold-packed beef. Could we have asked for more? Her wholesale acceptance of and response to our plight put me entirely at my ease. I bit into the sandwich with full appreciation, and abruptly dozed off.

I was awakened by a noise — was it the scraping of a door? Opening my eyes, I found my head resting on the plate, pillowed by that delicious half-eaten sandwich. Our hostess and a young woman were standing over me. I soon discovered that they had been making up a sofa bed in the adjacent dining room. With a rueful glance at the uneaten food, Madame beckoned us to follow her into the neighboring room and indicated the bed, with white sheets turned back for us. This was good fortune, indeed; we had slept in a bed only once during the past nine nights. Almost as quickly as the women had left us we undressed and fell into the bed, to sleep soundly.

I opened my eyes at some movement in the room. My surroundings seemed unfamiliar, dreamlike. By the far wall of the room a slender man dressed in work clothing walked over to a buffet, picked up a cruet and pulled out the stopper, which he laid on the table. This was a strange dream, indeed. I pulled myself up on one elbow and pinched my arm to wake up. The action continued. The man brushed back flowing mustaches, lifted the cruet to his lips and took a big swallow. Then as he replaced the stopper, he turned, seeing me watching him.

"Ah, good morning!" he called. Then, summoning words that I expected to hear only in a dream, he continued, "Will you have '*am* and *ecks*?" He came nearer and leaned over our bed. "I learned some English in 1917," he said. "And this, too," and he broke out with several bars of "It's a Long Way to Tipperary."

Bob, was fully awake by then, and we bolted out of bed. Of course we would have ham and eggs! Pulling our clothes on quickly, we hurried to the room into which we had first entered the house. The sound of sizzling ham was accompanied by the equally agreeable aroma of smoked meat on a hot skillet. With zest born of deep hunger we attacked our plates. Hot food warmed my gullet, and I savored the taste of the ham and the eggs, which I interspersed with bites of crusty brownish bread smeared

A portrait of Monsieur Georges Debailleux, La Neuville-St. Pierre (Oise), France.

with fresh unsalted butter, washing it down with sips of hot wartime coffee.

During breakfast we became acquainted with the family. It was not until many years later, in 1967, that I would learn the names of these new benefactors — Monsieur and Madame Georges Debailleux. Madame, aided by her daughter, Jacqueline, busied herself with tending to matters of food. A dark-haired girl of about 20 years of age, Jacqueline was out of school; she appeared reticent to break into the conversation of the men at the table.

Monsieur Georges Debailleux quizzed us briefly about the mission on which our plane had been lost. What was the target? The date? Where had the plane gone down? In what type of aircraft had we been flying? How many men were in the crew, and what had happened to the other members? With cup poised between table and his mustache, he asked why we were unaccompanied on the road, and why was it that we were arriving here just at this time, when we had been on the ground for nearly a month?

Unlike the transplanted Belgian in the village near Amiens, Monsieur maintained a relaxed manner during his questioning. He conveyed a sense of trust in our identity, a sincere interest in our experiences. Yet he was thorough.

As we learned later, he and his village La Neuville-St. Pierre (Oise) had been under careful German scrutiny, so it was important that he make no mistake by harboring spies in his home.

After breakfast, Monsieur led us on a brief tour of the several buildings in his farm enclosure. The sides of the outer buildings formed a surrounding wall, concealing the activities of those inside from view by outsiders. The barn directly across from the house and adjacent to the gate housed young cattle, most — if not all — of them heifers. It was apparent that the farmer would have, in other days, shown great pride in the size and robustness of his herd. Instead, he spoke about how the Germans came frequently, demanding some of his cattle.

"The cows are my capital; the heifers my future herd. And," he complained, "the *Boche* take my animals without consideration for the future of the enterprise."

Next, we entered a horse barn, though half of it was equipped for the raising of large, white hogs. The pens were remarkably clean. Parallel to the heifer barn was a timber and plaster building in which a quantity of fowl occupied wire cages. Behind that, still, was another barn equipped for the housing and milking of cows. We were not led beyond that barn, possibly because of what appeared to be an occupied house close by and next to a street. Could the occupant have been a farm worker?

Apparently most, if not in fact all, of the residents of this village were employed on the large Debailleux farm, encompassing more than 2,000 acres. Though horse-drawn machinery was in use, the work demanded a great deal of manual labor.

We returned to the house, for it seemed that we were not needed for the farm work, and probably the less visible we were, the better. Meanwhile, Madame and her daughter busied themselves about the affairs of keeping house. Our help was accepted for shelling legumes, but it was all too easy to be in the way, otherwise. To keep out from underfoot, we found a deck of cards, and began an on-going game. Tedium was interrupted by calls to the table, welcome in any case, but especially so because of the hunger pangs we had experienced during the past several days.

After supper that night our host spoke to us of his work with the British armies during the first World War. He had traveled much farther from his home than I had imagined. Still, my limited command of his language — and his of mine — confined the details he might have told, just as it restricted my comprehension of the places he had been and events he had seen.

Soon it was time for bed, but before leaving us to our privacy, Monsieur Debailleux told us that we might expect visitors tomorrow — men who could help us on our journey. With that reassuring news we readied ourselves for sleeping, rather eager to sense once more the comforts of a good mattress and smooth sheets.

The next day brought few surprises, unfolding as it did within the two now-familiar rooms of the house and a few steps into the courtyard. Madame and Jacqueline bustled about their normal household routines, seemingly pleased by the opportunities to serve us at the table. But they kept pretty much to their own business, as did our host. Late in the afternoon, however, our continuing card game was pushed aside by the entrance of the visitors for whom we had been waiting.

The two men were greeted in the courtyard by Monsieur, then courteously at the door by his wife. Ushered into the dining room, our host introduced them to Bob and me. Monsieur signaled them to take seats at the far side of the table, asking us to sit opposite them. Taking his accustomed seat at the head of the table, our host facilitated the questioning that would reveal the authenticity of our story.

Clad in work clothing, both clean and neat, the guests bore no marks that might distinguish them from any other workman. Yet their manner evidenced assurance and their questions conveyed the impression that they were experienced in interviewing men like ourselves. When at last they had gathered the information they wished, they asked for tangible proof of our story. At that point, we surrendered our dog tags so that Résistance authorities could check and return them later. My civilian wristwatch, which resembled a military watch, bore an inscription that further identified me. I called this to the attention of our visitors. One of them seemed to be very interested, and offered to exchange his own for mine. In surrendering my watch, I was under the impression that the exchange was temporary. That turned out not to be the case. Still, this new watch was more in keeping with my disguise as a European worker.

As the visitors stood up to leave, they told our host that he might expect news from them in a day or two, as soon as our information was confirmed. Confident that our stories would be corroborated, we turned once more to our idle pursuits, waiting for the next episode in our evasion.

Tiring of our card games, we seized the opportunity to become better acquainted with our hosts. I hesitated, though, to learn very much about them. The encounter with the German officer on the main road below the village served as a constant reminder that in the event of capture, my captors would want to know who had given me aid. And I had every reason to expect they would be far more severe in their interrogation than that of the Résistants and Monsieur Debailleaux. It would be better, I thought, not to know the identities of the persons to whom I was indebted than to risk exposing them under the pain of torture. I was making a conscious effort to actually forget the names of all our helpers in Belgium as well as France The daughter, Jacqueline, was a bit older than I had expected. She had completed the French equivalent of high school, and might even enroll for more advanced studies. Beyond that information I learned only a little bit about her social skills.

Her mother had already impressed me by generously accepting us two young strangers, a perilous thing to do under the German Occupation. That attested to her courage. The good order of her house, her sewing, and the taste of her cooking spoke well for her homemaking skills. I assessed her as a woman capable of decisiveness, but she nevertheless deferred to her husband on matters in which her family was represented in the community.

Though my judgments were based on a very short acquaintance — and that filtered through my rudimentary command of French — I entertained no doubts about the warm compassion that Madame Debailleux had exhibited in distinguishing our needs and quickly tending to them.

Reflecting on the balance between any benefit that might come from sheltering us and the risk they faced if that became known to the enemy, it seemed that the Debailleux family had little to gain by taking us in. Simple hospitality seemed an insufficient explanation, given the peril of being caught. On the contrary, if exposed, the family risked almost certain execution or, possibly even more painful, brutal incarceration. While in their care we had devoured their precious food and added immeasurably to the work of the household. I believed then that the United States would, if informed of their assistance, compensate the family for our food and lodging. But with the probability of our returning safely to American Forces, that appeared chancy — at best inadequate — pay for their part of the bargain. If their kindness was not motivated by hope of remuneration, then it must have been prompted by feelings of patriotism, there being few other ways to strike back at the massive force of the enemy.

My belief that those who helped downed airmen would be compensated by our government lay more in the realm of rumor than in fact. None of our helpers ever received monetary compensation, nor was any attempt made to calculate the largesse of our benefactors. Most, if not all of them did, however, receive a certificate of appreciation signed by the then General Dwight D. Eisenhower at a later time.

Two days later when someone came to the gate in the afternoon, Bob and I remained in the protection of the house until it became clear that the visitors posed no threat. Our host opened the gate so that the two men representing the Résistance could park their vehicle in the courtyard. They were ushered into the house, where we exchanged greetings. Yes, our stories had been checked and found to be accurate. Lodging had been procured for the two of us, and we could leave immediately for this new destination.

Bob and I thanked our hosts for their hospitality, and I promised to answer mail from them "after the war." Then we gathered our *musettes* containing our meager belongings, and followed the Résistants out the door.

Though we did not learn the identities of these men until long after the war's end, the driver was Georges Vitasse, of Beauvais. The other man was Pierre Schapendonk, a native of the Netherlands. Both men worked as mechanics at the Beauvais *aérodrome*.

Our escape vehicle was a commercial delivery van, on a sedan chassis resembling a car; its rear window areas were of metal, thus opaque. A blanket or tarpaulin lay on the floor of the back compartment. We were asked to lie there with the cover pulled over us. After the men were seated in front, the van pulled out of the courtyard and rolled bumpily down the hill toward the highway.

Eventually the van swerved to the left and the ride became more even on the highway heading toward Beauvais. Looking past the driver, I saw a church and a few housetops as we passed through a village. I settled back again on the floor.

The van slowed. Looking ahead, I saw the orange-and-white-striped barrier of a roadblock. I leaned back hurriedly, pulling the canvas over my head. Even a perfunctory search of the delivery vehicle would expose us, I knew. But the voices I heard were not those of command; they even sounded friendly. *Were we being turned over to the enemy?* I didn't understand the conversation, but there was laughter from both parties.

Then, to my relief, I could see the barrier rise. The van moved slowly past it, but did not pick up road speed. That in itself was disquieting. The driver leaned out his window, shouting a greeting to someone at the roadside. The reply came in an accent distinctly not French. Past the driver's shoulder I could see the blue-gray cap of a German soldier. These people are on disturbingly good terms with the Germans, I thought; perhaps they are taking us directly to some enemy headquarters.

Just then, peering ahead, I saw a flight control tower. I concluded we must be on the *aérodrome* at Beauvais.

Knowing we were at the center of a German installation, it did not seem prudent to try to escape the car through the back doors. My apprehension did not diminish, for I expected momentarily to be delivered to the enemy.

The van rolled to a halt. The voices sounded casual, friendly, as though the sentries were not being alerted for action. Then we were rolling again. The driver's companion turned his head and addressed us. "We are in the city now. You are the twenty-seventh and twenty-eighth airmen we have successfully transported through the *aérodrome!*" It was obvious that he was well pleased. So was I.

Then the driver, now relaxed, turned to speak to us. "We will stop at my home, and my wife will prepare tea for us."

A short time later, the car pulled to the curb. Following the two men, Bob and I clambered out the front door and trailed them through the door of a house. We were admitted by a pleasant lady who bade us be seated, our backs to the doorway, in a comfortably furnished room. Two small children politely restrained their curiosity toward us, inclining their bodies toward their parents.

With alacrity the hostess excused herself and left the room. The clatter of metal in her wake and the sound of water rushing from a tap suggested that tea was being prepared. Our host, the driver, proudly explained this unusual offering. The tea came from supplies dropped by the British for use of the Résistance, he told us. Canisters, dropped by air, contained not only weapons and ammunition, but also tools and explosives for sabotage. Plus, he added, such rare luxuries as tea, coffee, and cigarettes. Many of the latter goods were supplied to evadees who had, like us, found their way into sympathetic hands. And we were now to benefit by drinking a cup of British tea — and cookies, too.

When Madame returned, she was bearing a tray with tea for the four of us men. The children, apparently eager to help, followed her back into the kitchen. Madame returned to the room with a teacup of her own and the children's beverage. The larger child followed their mother, proudly bearing a plate of cookies — scones, I believe — from which we were served. The smaller child graciously supplied all of us with napkins — a curious nicety, compared with the rough clothing that Bob and I were wearing and our circumstances.

In spite of the relaxed atmosphere in the room there was something ceremonious about our tea-drinking this particular afternoon. In contrast to the weary days we had spent on the road, wishing for food and drink, here we sat at our ease partaking of food and drink that were almost unattainable luxuries in war-torn Europe. The absence of tension in this room stood also in stark contrast to the constant and apprehensive vigilance Bob and I had exercised on many occasions since the day our plane had been downed and on our long walk. I savored this aura of gentility perhaps as much as the flavors that touched my lips.

Throughout the visit, conversation orchestrated by our hosts moved at a snail's pace to oblige their visitors. I was able to grasp only parts of it. Still, it was polite conversation and, as a warm March zephyr serves as a harbinger of the coming spring, this setting bore memories of a normalcy to which the world might again, one day, return.

After a pleasant interlude, the cups were put down and gathered up, farewells expressed, and we returned to the delivery van. Bob and I drew the cover over us. The doors slammed shut, and the motor purred to life. I lay back and relaxed as the vehicle pulled slowly from the curb.

From our point of concealment there were few landmarks that revealed our route, should that information ever be demanded. We did drive along for some time on what appeared to be city streets. Then the hum of the motor quickened as the van accelerated on the road out of Beauvais. The route passed over and down some hills, but I sensed very little about the route. There appeared to be no other conveyances on the highway.

After some extended period of time the van slowed, then turned to the left. When the wheels bumped over what felt and sounded like railroad track, I stole a glance out of the window opposite the driver. Ahead loomed a large brick building topped by a chimney and a smokestack, that disappeared from view as the van turned again to the left and began a descent down a shallow hill. Slowing to a halt, the driver's companion climbed out. The sound of metal rasping on metal signified that a gate was being swung open. I raised my head to see an impressive iron gate held open, as the van edged slowly through and angled to the right. With my head raised, I could see the facade of a large brick building. As we pulled up beside it I could hear the rasp of gate hinges. The gate closed with a solid *thunk!* The van pulled forward a few feet, and our driver beckoned us to alight.

Chapter 13

The City House

THE LITTLE DELIVERY van had drawn up between a house and a long, low outbuilding on its southern flank, quite out of view from the street. At the rear of the building a caged dog was furiously contesting our right to invade his territory. We were joined just then by another man, whose sharp command sent the little beast cowering into a far corner of the cage.

The owner of this commanding voice was a short, wiry, slightly bent fellow with wispy, thinning hair, which had probably been black in his younger years. I inferred that he was the householder. With him in the lead, we used a doorway at the rear to enter the house.

Across a wide hallway and in a room appearing to be the kitchen, we were met by a stately blonde woman. Introductions followed; our hosts were Monsieur and Madame Lucien Dupas. The man who had met our delivery van was, as I had surmised, the householder.

As had been true at La Neuville-St. Pierre, where we had first met the men who transported us, the names of our transporters were unmentioned, as if to preserve the anonymity. I was content with that omission, and expected that Bob was as well.

In contrast to our new host's undistinguished costume, Madame Dupas was carefully coifed and dressed in a pale green silk sheath. During these preliminaries, the six of us lingered in the kitchen, accepting some sort of beverage — was it tea? — to commemorate the occasion.

Before our drivers departed we were made to understand that we would soon be visited by a man who would assure that all arrangements would be made for our stay. I was uncertain about just what was meant by that statement but gathered that this forthcoming visitor was highly placed in the Résistance. Then our two companions left, backing their van to the wide area in front of the gate, while Monsieur opened it for their departure.

Madame Dupas seized upon this time to show Bob and me to our room. She led us to the stairway leading to the second floor at the front of the house. Later, I was to learn that this upstairs floor was referred to as the first floor. The ground floor is called the *rez de chaussée*.

The room that Bob and I would occupy was at the front on this level. It was furnished with a double bed, two chairs, wardrobe, and chamber pot. A large roll-top desk nearly dominated the north wall. Just down the hall was a bathroom, fully as large as our bedroom, stocked with a toilet, lavatory, bathtub, and a curious fixture resembling an elongated toilet, but lacking a seat. Later I was to learn that the name for it was *bidet*, but I never received instructions on its use.

At nearly four-feet high, a glass shelf extended almost entirely around the room. On it were arranged a truly astonishing display of toiletries. Below the shelving were affixed a number of towel racks, on which several clean towels were hung.

Bob and I retained the cautions acquired by our experiences with the enemy and any possible informants, so we busied ourselves with checking for possible escape routes. A window on the east wall of the bathroom looked out on a narrow court and, adjacent to that, an extensive garden. The rear and lateral sides of the garden were bordered by a tall brick wall that provided privacy. Still, in the event that a search of the house occurred, there appeared no safe exit except by dropping from the bathroom window — a perilous and potentially noisy signal of our presence to

The wartime home of Monsieur and Madame Lucien Dupas in Auneuil (Oise), France.

any soldiers on guard. Some alternative means of escape or concealment was necessary. This situation would require further exploration, soon.

With lunchtime approaching, Madame suggested we rest for awhile. She called us for *déjeuner* — lunch — in the room where we had first assembled. Monsieur was evidently away, tending to his regular business in the town. Madame, now clad in a well-worn brown kimono, joined us at the table for a light repast. As the meal was finished, she suggested that we retire to our room.

"You must be tired after your journey," she said. Most likely, she had her regular household routine to complete, and could accomplish it much easier without the two of us underfoot.

Dutifully, we lay on the bed in our room, speaking quietly of our impressions of those we had met today and conjecturing on what might still lie ahead for us. So far as we knew, there was no secure exit from this house should it be surrounded by the enemy. With our minds still fixed on this problem, my gaze turned to the huge roll-top desk against the wall of our room. It seemed large enough to conceal a man with the top closed. Examining it carefully, it was large enough for that purpose, should it be needed as a last resort. We were somewhat comforted, though a sure exodus from the house would be far preferable.

Letterhead stationery in the desk indicated that Monsieur Lucien Dupas was a coal and lumber retailer. I didn't suppose that there was a great supply of those commodities during the scarcities of the Occupation, but the furnishings in the house suggested that the family was far from impoverished. Evidently the business flourished, or Monsieur had some additional source of income.

At long last we were summoned to dinner. Monsieur joined us at the table that evening. During the day he had gathered some news. The following evening a man from the Résistance would come to visit. Apparently, he would make some special arrangements for our stay.

The fluid in my glass was hard cider. I had never encountered that before; it had the aroma and taste of vinegar. I didn't enjoy it. Apparently, that displeasure showed on my face, for Monsieur questioned me about my reaction. Didn't I like the cider? Wasn't I in the habit of drinking cider at home? No? What did I drink, then? Milk! Certainly, that was out of the question for a French household; only babies drank milk! In the end, I drank the cider before me, as did the others.

As Madame cleared the dinner dishes from the table, Monsieur led Bob and me into the adjacent room. On the street side of the house, the windows looked out on the front court. Dominating the room, in its center, was a long, rectangular table. Various other furnishings of dark, highly polished wood were positioned around the room. Against the inside or southern wall stood the largest grandfather clock I had ever seen. An enormous pendulum swung in its oaken cabinet, the counterweight of which must have had a diameter of more than nine inches. With each arc it produced a solid tick. The chime struck on the quarter hour, its sonorous notes audible throughout the house.

Placing himself at the table, Monsieur opened a large box, producing from it the biggest checkerboard I had ever seen. Having played both checkers and chess in the States and in England, I was accustomed to a board with eight rows of squares. This one had, or so I seem to remember, ten squares per row and an equal number of rows. Foolishly, I thought I might adapt to that, but the difference in number of pieces on the board was only the first of a series of surprises in store for me. Monsieur's pieces seemed to move in astonishing trajectories, taking my pieces with alarming rapidity. Nor was that all. When one of his pieces attained the opposite end of the board and was crowned, it was now free to move with utter abandon. As a result, my pieces were in play for so short a time that I never got the hang of the game, called *Dames*. Monsieur was delighted with my ineptitude and challenged me to a game whenever his spirits were low. My play never failed to serve as an antidote for his worries.

The evening seemed still young when Madame suggested that Bob and I should retire for the night. Not yet ready for sleep, we talked quietly in our bed, establishing a pattern for the nights to follow. Up to this time the social gulf between officers and enlisted men had constricted our discourse to the surface matters confronting us. Bob had always been referred to as Lieutenant Donahue, until the time we had been thrust together as evaders. Now the barriers ceased to apply, opening up vast areas of experience, aspiration, and conjecture between us with which to pass the evenings.

Madame's call to breakfast woke us and sent us scurrying into our clothing and, with razors in hand, to the bathroom to prepare for the day. Monsieur was nowhere to be seen this morning, and Madame had eaten also. A small table by the inner wall of the family dining room was set with places for two. On a plate sat an enormous cup, which was soon filled by Madame with steaming coffee, or what passed for coffee those days. A plate of whole wheat bread, sliced into long, diagonally cut pieces, was between us, as was a generous bowl of butter and a sauce dish of fruit spread. Buttered and dipped into the coffee, the crispy-crusted bread tasted simply wonderful. It seemed unlikely that any jelly, jam, or fruit preserves could improve on the taste. We ate our fill.

After breakfast we listened to the radio. The BBC carried the Armed Forces Network, featuring frequent newscasts and the music of the Glenn Miller Band. The music fairly lifted our spirits, as did the frequent news of Allied advances in Normandy.

We took occasion to poke about our surroundings, too. The rear door of the house looked out on a small patio on which stood a white metal table and chairs. Behind the patio, a high brick wall enclosed a large household garden. Secure as it appeared, there was offered no way to escape in the event that enemy soldiers should call at the house. For that reason we thought it prudent not to venture often into the garden.

Almost adjacent to the patio and just past the north end of the house stood a fairly large brick building that appeared to have stabled the family horse, and perhaps other animals, too, in earlier years. Another building stood between the stable and the street. Under its shed-like rear section, we could see a barrel of miscellany — brass shell casings, bits of copper wire, and so forth.

On the opposite side of the house, where we had first alighted from the van, was a long, low building that may have served at one time as a chicken house. A notice posted on the door to the building announced that this was a depot for the collection of metals, regulated by the Forces of Occupation. Wondering what those metals might be, I read on, concluding that those substances included brass, copper, and related materials strategic to the war effort, but which were permissible to use in agricultural manufacture. The door to the building was fastened securely, perhaps to be opened only when Monsieur was on the premises.

Just before the time for dinner, Monsieur came up the courtyard from the front gate. Pushing his bicycle, which he leaned against the rear wall of the house, he unfastened five unwrapped loaves — *baguettes*, I had learned to call them — from the carrier on the rear of his bicycle, and brought them into the kitchen. I wondered if the purchase of such a large quantity of bread by a household of two persons had caused any comment at the baker's. Certainly, Bob and I had voracious appetites when it came to French bread!

At the dinner table, Monsieur produced two bottles of Alsatian beer, proudly brewed in France. Quite apparently, he had sensed our dislike for cider, and brought this as a substitute. The beer tasted better than the cider, though I didn't appreciate its flavor, either. I had grown accustomed to the table beer brewed in Bassilly, Belgium, and though few savants would have rated it highly, I now associated that musty taste with the proper flavor for beer. I tried to restrain my negative reaction to this generous attempt to please non-paying house guests, but our absence of enthusiasm for the drink was duly noted, as would become evident to us later.

As the dinner dishes were being restored to their rightful places, the muffled purr of a motorcycle was heard from the street. Any sound of a passing vehicle was a rare occurrence. Monsieur immediately left by the side door. Shortly after, a man emerged into view pushing a motorcycle into the courtyard and around to the rear of the house out of sight from the street.

Monsieur accompanied this visitor into the family dining room, where Madame, Bob, and I were waiting. The most notable thing about the man was that he was dressed entirely in black — black leather jacket and black trousers tucked into black puttees. As he strode into the house, he was stuffing his black gloves into the pocket of his jacket, his black leather helmet dangling from his hand. Clothed as he was, he appeared to be robust, but not unusually tall.

The man seemed to be no stranger to the Dupases, but greetings followed in the formal manner, and the man was introduced to Bob and me, unnamed, simply as a chief of the Résistance.

His name, I would later learn, was Gilbert Thibault, by trade a minor official whose job it was to repossess unpaid-for goods. For that reason, he was quite knowledgeable about the general area and its inhabitants. He was considered to be trustworthy, making him especially well-suited for the role in which he was now engaged.

We moved into the formal dining room and, when we were seated around the table, Madame swept into the room with a tray and set about to serve coffee for the five of us.

As we savored the drink, Madame inquired as to the difficulty our visitor might have eluding the wide net cast for him by the Occupation army. It did present certain problems, he replied. He never slept at his home, nor at the same house on successive nights. Madame murmured some acknowledgment of sympathy at this news of fractured familial life. "But Madame Thibault does sometimes visit the home where I will be staying the night," he added.

Having sipped from his cup, our visitor settled back in his chair and asked Bob and me whether we were adequately cared for in this household. Well, truly we were quite comfortable here, and with the recent memory of hardships along the route from Belgium, I considered myself to be in a fortunate situation. At our affirmative reply, he pushed on, asking about any special needs we might have. From the corner of my eye I noticed Monsieur shift forward in his seat, almost imperceptibly, as though he expected some particular response. Was he concerned lest I would complain about the cider? Certainly, I would not mention that! I told him that I could use a razor blade, if that were possible. We were assured that the necessary toiletries would be forthcoming.

"Do you need cigarettes?" he asked. In unison, Bob and I tried to put him at ease, telling him that we did not smoke. To our dismay, although the Résistance Chief was put at ease by that knowledge, Monsieur fairly slumped in his chair, his face showing a slight trace of anguish. Of course! As much as he was willing to participate in the Allied cause by accepting the hazard of hosting us, he was eagerly awaiting an opportunity to share in the tobacco supply available to the Résistance forces. What bad luck this must seem for him, harboring two American non-smokers, for our visitor had it surely in his power to provide an ample supply for us — and for our host, as well.

After that, the interview quickly terminated, and announcing that our toiletries would arrive in a few days, our contact with the Résistance returned to his motorcycle. Monsieur accompanied him to the gate and presumably checked to ascertain that no one was on the street before allowing him to take his leave. The activities of the day now being concluded, Bob and I retired to our bedroom for the night.

We awoke with the knowledge that this was the 14th of July, a full month since we had parachuted into Belgium. A whole month, and we were still on the Continent, with no clear prospect of a quick return to our airbase. Well, we could consider this an anniversary of a sort — we had still eluded capture by the enemy.

At breakfast, Madame exclaimed, "This is July Fourteen, Bastille Day!"

I knew of Bastille Day and of its significance in the overthrow of Louis XVI and the aristocracy, but until then I had no idea that Frenchmen attached the same sort of significance to it as Americans did to the Fourth of July. Madame went about her routines with uplifted spirits, sometimes humming the "Marseillaise," the French national anthem.

Bob and I spent part of the day listening to the Armed Forces Network on the radio and playing rummy at the table on the patio. Next, we investigated the contents of the metal depository room, having obtained

Monsieur's permission. It was filled with old shell casings, ornamental brass containers, candelabra, copper wire, and so forth. Close to the door, though, was a barrel into which miscellaneous small objects had been dropped. We hesitated to disturb the contents, but our interest was piqued by a large quantity of old coins distributed loosely among the items. Later we would ask Monsieur Dupas whether we might sift through those old coins, just to see what was there.

When he arrived home during the afternoon, Monsieur Dupas brought not only the customary several *baguettes*, but also something wrapped in paper. We would discover what it was at dinner.

With the glow of pleasure on her face, Madame brought a serving dish to the table and put one fairly large leafy ball at each plate. I had never seen such a vegetable before, and Madame seemed to enjoy sharing this treat.

"They are artichokes," she gushed, and proceeded to show us how to extract the leaves, one by one — dip it in a small dish of spiced liquid butter set with each plate, and place it in the mouth, using the teeth to scrape off the delicate fleshy underleaf. I imitated the demonstration, and acknowledged that it was, indeed, good. Deleafing the artichoke seemed a slow process, but at last, between sips of wine and bites of delicious bread, the core of the plant rested, denuded, on the plate. I soon learned that the heart of the artichoke is every bit as delicious as the fatty underleaf.

As the servings on the table became exhausted, Monsieur opened a door to the cellar, reached up to a shelf overhead, and produced a large glass container of golden fruit.

"These are fermented cherries," he told us, "sealed in this container in 1917." This is very likely the last Bastille Day when we shall suffer under the Occupation. Now seems to be the right time to open it."

As Monsieur opened the jar, Madame brought four sauce dishes to the table. Into each she ladled a generous portion of cherries and set them before each place. We spooned them into our mouths, spitting out the seeds. They were tasty and left a warm glow, reminiscent of those brandied cherries to be found in chocolates, but less sugary. This was indeed a special dessert. But that was not all. When our sauce dishes were empty of cherries, the juice was decanted into small cordial glasses, and we drank a toast to Bastille Day and to the liberation of France.

After leaving the table, we men went into the formal dining room. From the bureau, Monsieur brought a flat nickel-plated device to the table, and a sack of tobacco. For some minutes he demonstrated how he could roll his own cigarettes. He did not finish the task until the sack was empty. Carefully, then, he gathered the finished cigarettes and stored them neatly into a small box. Only then did he bring an ashtray to the table. Lighting a cigarette, he inhaled deeply, then relaxed back in his seat. Before the evening was over, he trounced both Bob and me in games of *Dames*.

The weekend brought guests to the house — Monsieur's brother, his wife, and teenage daughter, from Paris. The household soon acquired a level of activity far more intense than I had seen previously. The Dupas *frère* seemed younger than Monsieur Lucien; he showed energy, joy, and enthusiasm in his greetings and storytelling. Both Monsieur and Madame listened eagerly to his report of the Bastille Day observation in Paris. His wife, too, by sharing news of Paris and of mutual acquaintances, brought a semblance of buoyancy into the demeanor of Madame as the two busied themselves preparing food. The daughter, an attractive, reedy blonde girl, maintaining an air of discreet decorum, remained near her elders, responding promptly when they requested help with the activities. Bob and I sought other pastimes to stay out of the way

As we returned to the room for dinner, the brother Dupas was entering through the kitchen door, triumphantly brandishing two bottles of champagne. "We shall drink to this occasion," he said. "There is plenty more of this in my cellar in Paris." Turning to me and Bob, he added, "When the war threatened, I laid in a supply of champagne. I have the largest supply in Paris."

It seemed likely that he exaggerated, but this was the first champagne we had seen in Europe — and for me, anywhere. I was not disposed to dispute his statement.

The dinner began with toasts to the health of the hosts, to the American guests, and to the quick defeat of the Nazis. I had learned by now to mimic the actions of others at the table, so was able to follow suit. Then Madame absented herself momentarily in the kitchen, returning with a platter of thin pancakes. For my benefit, she explained that these were *crêpes*. Hearing a somewhat familiar word, I asked, "Are these *crêpes Suzettes*?"

"No," Madame replied with a smile and a glance in the direction of her niece. "These are *crêpes Georgettes!*" Now it would be hard to forget the name of their niece. The *crêpes*, layered with strawberry preserves, then carefully folded and refolded into an elongated roll on our plates, were very tasty. And the supply was plentiful. There probably were other dishes at that meal, but the delicious *crêpes* had made a lasting impression.

When the dishes were cleared away and washed in the kitchen, the tempo of conversation abated, then grew to a sudden crescendo of leave-taking, and the visitors departed to take the evening train back to Paris.

We had learned that day that Monsieur Lucien had received a military pension as a victim of a gas attack during World War I. The pension, plus the added fact that the house in which they now lived had been in the family for many years, may have preserved the appearance of greater income than they actually had. If it were true, as I suspected, that not much profit was to be gained from the wartime commerce in coal and lumber, these other facts could help explain how the Dupases maintained their present scale of living. They relied, of course, on their substantial garden, but we young Americans they harbored had healthy appetites. And we never left the table hungry.

The following morning when the sun was already high in the heavens, Madame, dressed as usual in her faded brown flannel robe, summoned us to *petit déjeuner*. Breakfast was a welcome meal for me each day. I savored each bite of the delicious bread, slathered with butter and dipped into the rich coffee. It was equally good when coated with fruit preserves, and after eating a piece embellished in one of these ways, I often switched treatments for the next piece.

On this morning my attention was diverted from my eating by a hoarse call from the old parrot roosting on his perch by my chair. Suddenly feeling a bit guilty for my inattention to him, I broke off a small crust of bread and offered it to him. His head darted and his beak pecked my hand. I withdrew my hand in startled pain, as the bread dropped to the floor. Apparently, I had invaded his private space, and he had made me pay dearly for it. I would be careful never to violate his territory again.

Having secured permission from Monsieur to search through the barrel of small items in his metals storage area, our rummaging yielded some 200 coins, only a few of which were duplicates. These we carried to our room, where we sorted them by type. We moved them from our bed to a nearby table, taking care to keep the piles separate.

When Monsieur returned home that afternoon, he hurried almost immediately to the far end of his garden. He returned a bit later, bearing two green leaves of tobacco. Almost feverishly he thrust them into the oven, then waited with tested patience while they cooked to the crisp. At last he deemed the task complete, and extracted grayish imitations of the yellow-cured tobacco leaves, so often portrayed in magazine advertisements. He pinched them, assuring himself that they were stiff and crisp, then tested the scent by sniffing.

"Ah," he exulted in satisfaction.

Hurriedly, he entered the dining room, withdrew the roller from its box, extracted his book of cigarette papers, spread a newspaper over the tablecloth, and set about once more to manufacture cigarettes of his own confection. Crumbling the stiff tobacco leaves in his hands, he piled the results, stems and all, on the table.

The first cigarette had hardly been formed before his trembling fingers thrust it into his mouth, and he ignited it with a match. There was a brief flare-up, but then the end began to glow. Monsieur inhaled deeply, sighed, and let the cigarette dangle between his lips as he proceeded to convert the tobacco into the form he so deeply coveted. When the task was finished, and the last ash dropped from his cigarette, he gathered up his equipment. His countenance seemed to say, "This was not nearly as good as an American cigarette would have been; and not as good as the French ones we might get these days, if we could; but it is far better than having no cigarette at all."

Now that this immediate and compelling task was ended, he could hear of our concerns. We told him of the coins we had discovered, and he gave us permission to appropriate any coins in which we were interested; none of them were valid as currency at that time, but that fact made them all the more interesting to us. We rummaged in the barrel, extracting only the coins, which we then dropped into a small white cotton bag. At last, we returned to our room where we arranged the coins on the bed, sorted by date and, as other characteristics became evident, by country.

The oldest in the array appeared to be a small silver coin of Swiss mintage, stamped in 1654. Many were large copper French *centimes*, minted in the 20th century. Though most of the coins were French, some were of German, Dutch, Belgian, and other origins. We left the coins in those piles while we ate lunch.

When we returned we sorted our treasure still further by condition of wear. Now, our appetites for collecting sharpened, we elected to rely on the toss of a coin to apportion them between us. We tried to be as fair as possible. We took turns pitching and calling the coin on the coverlet of the bed. When the task was finished, we each had a similar collection. Finding a second small sack, we each poured our collections into our bag and put them away with our other possessions.

We whiled away the afternoon on the patio, playing rummy as usual and listening to the sweet tones of the Glenn Miller Band. The swing tunes played on our memories, and we found ourselves whistling them as we played cards.

Monsieur returned from his afternoon activities, wheeling his bicycle to the rear of the house; he removed several *baguettes* from the carrier and entered the kitchen. Shortly after, as on many occasions, he hurried past us and went down the garden path, seemingly on an important errand. Moments later he returned, bearing two small, freshly harvested green tobacco leaves. Bob, whose chair faced the garden and who was in a position to witness what had occurred there, muttered, "Monsieur is hurrying to the oven for a quick curing of those leaves."

I felt a brief pang of regret that our disavowal of the tobacco habit had deprived him of a vital supply. But he had failed to indicate that he might be relying on us to obtain cigarettes through the Résistance, and to share them with him. Had I ever experienced the pangs of nicotine withdrawal, I might have been more sympathetic with his urgency.

After dinner and his after-dinner smoke, Monsieur beckoned me to follow him to the small barn in back of the house. Inside was a hand pump. He grasped the handle and gave several vigorous strokes. As water gushed into the receptacle beneath, he caught some, then thrust it up so that I might see.

"It is clear," he said. And, pumping more, he splashed it about. "See, there is nothing in it. It will be good to drink. You and Robert may have a pitcher at the table."

A few hours later I was doubled over with stomach cramps. It was about then that I discovered Bob to be similarly distressed. We took turns for several hours attempting to alleviate our anguish, almost stumbling over one another in our haste to give Nature her rein. Our discomfort did not go unnoticed in the house, especially when each of us refused meals. When it became apparent that Bob was now too weak to stand, the Dupas sprang into action, and summoned a doctor, who would honor their confidence. However, it seemed prudent for me to remain in the background. I could get around, so I loitered outside our bedroom door while the doctor made his examination. Though the door was closed, I could hear and understand much of what was said.

"Ahh, have you been drinking too much cider?" he asked. Bob replied that he hadn't been drinking cider of late.

"Then, too much beer?" No, to that also.

"Too much coffee?" he asked again.

"Not too much," answered Bob.

"Then, what have you been drinking?" asked the doctor, in a tone of frustration.

"Water," replied Bob.

"Water!" shouted the doctor. "Any idiot knows better than to drink water!"

Upon his departure, the doctor left a prescription with Madame, and a caution against permitting the patient again to drink water. Though my illness lingered on, I was able to be up and about. But it was lonely without Bob's companionship.

I went to the upper floor, determined to improve my billiard play for some future date. But the click of balls on the table seemed both loud and out of character with the noises of the neighborhood. Concerned that the clatter of the game might attract the attention of neighbors, I abandoned the cue and went downstairs.

Seeing my restiveness, Madame assigned me to clean the parakeet cage in the vestibule. Accompanied by the alarmed fluttering of more than a dozen love birds, I changed the paper lining the floor of the cage, then added water and birdseed. I listened to the "Voice of America" on the BBC, and then found a few additional distractions.

Bob remained in bed on the following morning, too. But something of interest caught my attention later in the day. Someone had brought a long, linked band of .50-caliber ammunition, evidently cast off from an aircraft in trouble, to the metal depository. That fact evidently accounted for this later visit from a man arriving in a curtained horse-drawn carriage. He tethered the horse in the side yard, then joined Monsieur in the shed nearby. As I watched, they extracted the projectiles from the casings, emptying the gunpowder into a milk bucket; the empty casings were poured into the barrel of metal from which Bob and I had collected our coins. The task finished, the visitor placed the bucket of powder into the carriage and drove off.

That night we were awakened several times by distant explosions, each coming from a different direction. Whatever the targets were that night, the blasts were aimed at the Third Reich. It was heartening to know that ammunition discarded from aircraft under duress could still serve a useful purpose.

Breakfast time was dull on the next day. Without Bob's company I was at loose ends, mostly watching Madame fondle her pet dog. The pampered creature was a small pug-nosed lap dog with honey-colored fur, which I supposed to be a Pekingese. Her counterpoint was an equally small black and white dog whose fur was just a trifle shaggy; though no one told me so, I believed this one to be a Pomeranian. The interplay between these pets and Madame seemed to reveal that the black and white dog had at one time been the mistress's favorite. With all the attention a childless woman could lavish upon it, its place had been supplanted by a new acquisition, the little Peke. Secure in the knowledge that she was now the apple of her mistress's eye, she acted very much like a terribly spoiled child. Madame selected choice tidbits from the table, placing them delicately in the mouth of the Peke, while the Pomeranian crouched in the background, succeeding quite well in appearing to be victimized. Eventually, when a scrap would be tossed to the Pomeranian, the Peke threatened to snatch it, as if all good things truly belonged to her

When that activity ceased to interest me, I sought other amusements. Again, I climbed the stairs to the third floor room and tried to improve my billiard playing. However, as before, the sound of the balls clicking against one another and rolling across the slate table seemed perilously loud, so I went to the window to see if anyone could be seen. No one was in sight, but pedestrians or bikers would be concealed from my view behind the front wall. And there was a small house just beyond the metal depository; someone there might think it odd that, with Monsieur away at work, anyone would be playing billiards. I put the cue away a second time and left the room.

Later in the day, I spied a newspaper lying on a small table in the eating area. By now, I could read a few words of French, but only with difficulty could I understand the entirety of an article. What did capture my attention were the editorial-type cartoons, which dealt principally with evil persons whose actions — even their very existence, it seemed — posed a threat to the authorities and to good people everywhere. Some of these were saboteurs, pictured as ogres dressed in rough clothing, who wrought senseless destruction inimical to the welfare of all. The others, even more hideously portrayed, were Jews, who were apparently evil simply by being Jews. Despite my understanding of the exaggeration of these propaganda cartoons, the message they carried came as a bit of a shock. By frequent and consistent repetition of the themes and in the absence of evidence to the contrary, I imagined that the message might become believed. Obviously, the press was controlled by the Nazis.

By the time Bob became strong enough to come downstairs again, I had contrived to whittle a likeness of the guard dog caged at the rear of the house. Neither of the Dupases appeared to be overly impressed by my accomplishment. Of course, the work was crude, but I fancy that they did not hold that particular animal in high esteem.

The family from Paris visited again, and for a sort of birthday celebration. No, I learned, it wasn't Georgette's birthday, but recognition of the Saint's Day of Georgette's patron saint, Saint Therèse. After several questions, which fully displayed my ignorance, I learned that Georgette did not celebrate her own birthday, but that of the Saint honored on the day of her birth. Saint Therèse's birthday was on a day different from Georgette's. And who was Saint Therèse? There was much I did not learn that would distinguish her from other revered women, but I did discover that her shrine was located at Lisieux — the important shrine that our 493rd Bombardment Group had orders not to expose to risk during the time of the Allied invasion of Normandy. Our first target, a railway bridge, had been obscured by clouds, and we had returned to our base with bomb bays fully loaded. I could understand the importance our French Allies attached to that shrine. And now that the D-Day landing had come to a successful conclusion, I was glad that we had not destroyed it in the attempt to deter the enemy from bringing tank reinforcements by rail.

Bob, his complexion still a bit ashen from his recent ordeal, had joined me downstairs — a companion welcomed by all who were present. The younger Dupas brother had left the house, to cool the champagne, I correctly guessed, and the Dupas wives were busily moving about between kitchen and dining room. They must have sensed that Bob and I, talking to Georgette, were in the way, for the three of us were ushered into the smaller room that served as a parlor. Suddenly aware that her daughter would be unsupervised in a room with two young men, Georgette's mother placed her on a settee and bid Bob and me to sit on another one, facing her. Then, glancing back at us all as she prepared to leave the room, she must have become aware of two young men facing her daughter, whose shapely knees, revealed by her short skirt, invited attention. Mother Dupas, her face now florid in embarrassment at her manifest concern, charged back into the room and rearranged our seating and posture so as to remove her knees from consideration. She left the room so charged with tension that the ensuing conversation was nothing less than stilted. Perhaps that was, after all, the mother's design.

Conversation at the table was in a festive mood, appropriate to the celebration of Saint Therèse's Day, to the honor accorded to Georgette, and in response to good news from the battlefields. However, it would be almost a year before the Nazis were ejected from France. The Occupation had been long and hard, but the memory of freedom to conduct national and local affairs according to the dictates of Frenchmen remained, and the prospect of a return to that normalcy was sweet indeed. Eventually, the party came to a close and the Paris Dupases bid their *au revoirs*. I did not consider at the time that for Bob and me this parting would be our *adieu* as well.

With Bob rejoining me once more at breakfast, we easily fell into our customary routine. The BBC's Armed Forces Network again aired a fine program of music featuring the Glenn Miller Band, including tunes both catchy and new to us. Those tunes had drummed in my head for hours after I had first heard them, and more than once I became aware that I was whistling; Bob was, too.

That evening, Madame cautioned us once again about that whistling; it seemed that a neighbor, having overheard our less-than-conscious exuberance, had asked whether the Dupases had young boys as house guests. Madame replied that it was probably Monsieur that she had heard; he often did that, she said, when he was happily at work. That evening, during his regular search for near-mature tobacco leaves, Monsieur's wretched attempt at whistling made Madame's explanation untenable.

★ ★ ★

When the closed carriage entered the courtyard the next afternoon, Bob and I, who had been told at lunch we would be leaving, were ready. Our coin collections were stashed in our *musettes,* alongside our escape kits. Our farewell to the Dupases did not fully express our thanks for the hospitality they had extended to us.

Once we were concealed behind the curtained sides, the carriage entered the street, and the gate closed with an emphatic metallic clank.

Chapter 14

Warm-Hearted Country People

THE DRIVER TURNED the carriage to the left, back in the direction by which we had come to the Dupases' house in the delivery van. The horse's hooves clattered in a clip-clop cadence on the hard surface of the street. Soon the carriage turned to the right, and we crossed the railroad tracks, continuing a short distance before turning once more onto a smoother surface. This, I thought, must be the road toward Beauvais, for the vehicle had turned to the right once more.

Not surprisingly, we had not been told of our destination, for security reasons. Unable to see out, we relied for orientation on the motion of the carriage, the sounds of the horse's hoofbeats, and of the road under our wheels. We soon concluded that the carriage had turned off this road onto another, traveling west. Although we were alert also to the sound of voices to tell whether we were passing through a village, we heard none except the soft voice of our driver, urging his horse onward.

Later, we turned right again, staying on that course for a

good length of time. We turned again to the left — westward, we judged — and held that course for several minutes before turning sharply and coming to a halt.

We could hear our driver descend, then voices and the sound of an opening gate. The carriage advanced a short distance and came to a stop. Our driver opened the curtain on one side. We climbed out of the carriage and stood at the yard gate of a large, brown brick house — our destination at last.

A short, wiry man stood beside our driver, his shirt sleeves rolled up to the elbows, his dark hair windblown and the stubble of a beard on his face. Towering over him and peering from behind was a stout woman, whose dark hair was pulled back severely and rolled into a bun. A light-colored *tablier* covered most of her dark dress, unlike the brightly flowered ones worn by Belgian housewives.

Our new hosts were beaming, as though they were honored by our presence. After introducing them as Monsieur and Madame Croizé, our carriage driver climbed aboard and departed. As we were ushered across the threshold, we saw two young men in the background — one sturdy and taller than our host, the other slight, and seemingly younger. A fat, gray-barbed hen screeched, scurrying toward the door as we entered the kitchen. The large room was furnished with an oblong table flanked by several time-worn chairs. On a wood-fired range parallel to the east wall, a large pot emitted a cloud of vapor. Beside it stood a blackened metallic coffee pot.

At the dinner table, I had a better view of the younger Croizés, René and Marcel. René, the older, about 21 years of age, was about 5 feet, 10 inches tall, had powerful sloping shoulders, straight black hair, and an air of earnest friendliness. His younger brother, Marcel, was of a slight build; his brown hair curled in wisps across his face.

Silence governed at the table as the diners avoided prying into matters we might consider invasive. A much older lady, frail with age, sat with us. She was the boys' grandmother, we learned, though I never understood whether she was Monsieur's or Madame's mother.

The family attended to the food on their plates — boiled potatoes yellow to the core, green string beans, and savory meat, cut into small pieces. The slices of whole wheat bread had the familiar French shape, but the loaves were thicker than the *baguettes* to which I had become accustomed at the Dupases. There was no dessert, but I kept my eye on the ignored coffeepot — not so much that I wanted coffee, but because I was curious, for the pot occupied a fairly central place on the stove top.

As Madame Croizé attended to the dishes, the men led us to the stairway in the hallway, off the kitchen, and to our room for the duration of our stay. The merest glance revealed that the interior of the house had not been maintained at the same level suggested by its exterior. The wallpaper was dingy, and some hung from the ceiling in long, asymmetrical strips. The staircase, of solid hardwood — was it oak? — no longer revealed its finished color; the passing of many feet had worn faint hollows in the treads.

At the top of the stairs, René opened the door and bade us enter. The large room was furnished principally by a bed with bolster pillows; evidently it had not been used for many years. The bedding and floor were layered with dust more than a half-inch deep. Bob was quick to remark that the room could not be used in that condition and would require cleaning. René reacted as though that idea had not occurred to him. When we stood our ground, René hurried downstairs and reported this development to his parents. Even from the upper level, I could hear the consternation that resulted from that announcement. A broom? But where would they acquire one? In the end, René was dispatched to the village to borrow one from an acquaintance.

In René's absence, Bob and I set to work. Carefully, we lifted and carried the top bedcover with its load of dust downstairs. There we shook it and draped it to air. The bolsters were the next to follow, then the rest of the bed clothing.

I remembered a passage in Paul Bunyan's *Pilgrim's Progress* where the hero, given the suffocating task of sweeping out a similar room, had ultimately sprinkled water to lay the dust. Seizing upon this idea, we enlisted Marcel to bring us a pail of water and a small vessel from which we could sprinkle small areas. And how to be rid of the dust? In the absence of a dust pan, Marcel provided a grain shovel.

We were quite ready to proceed further when René returned triumphantly with a broom. The sprinkling of water worked quite well to guard against the raising of clouds of dust. The grain shovel served more than adequately to pick up the piles the broom had collected. We emptied the shovel into an old box which, when filled, was carried out and emptied in the barnyard.

When the room was cleaned to our satisfaction, the bedding was carried back upstairs and returned to its proper place. Now we took our leisure to examine the vistas from the windows. At the front, or south side, of the house we looked out over the road by which we had come. Across the road was a pasture, bordered on its eastern margin by a wall that edged an orchard. A farmstead, though not easily seen from the room unless a person craned his neck to peer to the right, could just barely be discerned at some distance to the west. I satisfied myself that there was no vantage point through which a person stationed in front of the house could see into our room. The other window looked out to the east, on another small pasture. In the distance I could make out yet another farmstead. But if I could not see distinctly to that distance, neither could anyone else, I concluded. We were satisfied there was no risk of discovery from the outside.

Still afflicted with the gastric disorder brought on by our appetite for drinking water, Bob and I had unexpected opportunities to tour the back yard, where just behind the brick wall enclosing it was the family privy. Trips to that destination acquainted us with a well-tended garden, accessible through the same gate used to make these still frequent errands. Row upon row of potatoes, peas, and greens were separated by cleanly tilled dark soil. The garden's western edge, the barn wall, sheltered several espaliered fruit trees. We dined mostly on the garden's produce during our stay with the Croizés. The geese, chickens, and Guinea fowl, which watered at the old washtub in the house yard, would be a welcome supplement to our meals.

The fowl seemed eager to appear as part of our repast. Frequently, they wandered into the kitchen, perilously close to Madame's feet as she moved from meal preparation on the dinner table to the stove. When her patience could stand no more, she brandished a kitchen utensil in their direction and sent them screeching and skittering outside.

The open door admitted the local variety of small bees, as well. A number of them buzzed harmlessly around the table before settling on the window panes. Monsieur took it as his personal task to rid the kitchen of these pests. Brandishing a table knife, he stalked a bee at the window. When a deft slash of the knife had dispatched the offending insect, Monsieur with a satisfied grin on his face, wiped the blade on his trousers and returned the knife to its place on the table.

★ ★ ★

From across the room, I watched Madame prepare the evening meal. Yes, there were the usual green beans — *haricots verts* — I learned to call them, and a large kettle of potatoes boiled on the stove. At just the right time, she picked up a double handful of butter from the bowl on the table and splashed it into the boiling mixture. So that was how the potatoes had acquired their yellow hue, consistent to their core!

That night I drank cider without a murmur. I thought I might even grow to like the acidic drink. We had been joined at the table by the grandmother, who was deferred to, though she said very little.

As we were finishing our meal, someone came to the door. From the Croizé's attitude of acceptance, this man could not be an intruder. We were introduced, though I think we didn't hear his entire name. As Monsieur spoke with him, René explained that the man, with his wife and little boy, lived in the old house attached to the barn, just on the other side of the espaliered trees in the garden. He was a factory worker, René said, from a town south of Paris, who had lost his employment when the factory had been bombed. He had brought his family to stay in this out-of-the way place until after the end of the war. His wife and small son joined us almost immediately, remaining in the kitchen just long enough for this to be counted a neighborly call. Then they returned to their quarters between barns.

Though the bolster on the bed proved to be higher than the pillows to which I was accustomed, I slept well that night. Light was streaming through the eastern window when I awoke. The crowing of the roosters had not aroused me, nor had footsteps in the hall as the young Croizés went out to tend to the morning chores. Bob woke up then, too, and we dressed and descended to the kitchen.

Madame was busy at her stove; the table had been set with a deep bowl at each place. After a polite salutation, I went out the back door to the pump and filled the basin suspended from a bent wire near its spout. The cold water refreshed me as it splashed onto my face. Using the grayish chunk of soap thoughtfully left on the cement slab by the pump, I washed my hands and wiped them on the tattered towel hanging from a wire beside the basin. Bob, having followed me from the house, took his turn with the morning ablutions. By then, the men were coming from the barnyard, and they, too, stopped at the pump to wash off the grime accumulated from the milking.

Bob and I followed them into the kitchen where a kettle of milk was steaming on the stove. We took our places at the table, then, following the example of the others, crumbled thick slices of the brown bread into our bowls. Madame had transferred the steaming milk into a pitcher, which she passed at the table, beginning with her husband. He poured the hot milk onto his crumbled bread, then passed the pitcher to Grandmother, who passed it on to René. Madame lifted the blackened pitcher from the stove and brought it to her husband. Monsieur poured a little into his bowl of bread and milk. What poured from the pitcher was definitely coffee-colored. When my turn came, I discovered the thick brown liquid quickly altered the color of the milk. It tasted something like the "coffee" Eliane Hombeck had made by deep-toasting barley. Our breakfast of coffee-flavored bread and milk was a satisfying meal, somewhat resembling our breakfasts at the Dupases. However, we were not served coffee here.

The day was quiet, even boring, for we did not have a deck of cards nor access to a radio. Nor was there any reading material lying about. All that began to change when, late in the afternoon, I heard the familiar low rumble of a motorcycle. The rider was admitted at the gate and brought his cycle into the barnyard, concealing it from the view of any chance passers. We learned that he was our liaison from the Résistance. With him, but standing just a short step behind, was a young man, slender, with dark hair, and the light olive complexion I had understood to be common among Gallic peoples. The Croizés welcomed the guests, seemingly acquainted with the young man but not with the motorcyclist. We knew him as Gilbert Thibault, the Résistance chief for the north of France, whom we had met earlier at the Dupas home. The young man introduced Monsieur Thibault to the Croizés and pointed out his importance in the Résistance movement. Then Thibault introduced Bob and me to his young companion — his deputy, Roger Fontaine. Roger would be our direct connection to the Résistance as long as we stayed with the Croizés. Following a brief conference with the elder Croizés, Monsieur Thibault departed on his motorcycle.

Roger Fontaine, wishing to speak with us, remained behind. In fluent English, he bade us walk through the barnyard. It was the first time either of us had ventured that far. As we passed the little house abutting the barn buildings, we observed the small boy loitering near the doorway of the house, his mother visible in the interior. Roger led us beyond the courtyard, to the orchard north of the farm buildings. There we sat on the ground, in the shade of an apple tree, while our liaison proceeded to orient us to our new situation. Fontaine told us he lived in Ons-en-Bray, the village whose church spire we could just see, probably no more than a mile to the west. His father was an *avocat* — a legal counsellor — in the village. He then told us that his own family was sheltering two airmen from New Zealand.

Roger would never be far away should we have need of him, and would in any case stop by to see us frequently. René or Marcel could be depended upon to deliver a message to his home in Ons-en-Bray.

Then, anticipating that we might find days tedious on the farm, he took three books from his *musette*, saying that we could return them to him when we had no further use of them. One was a hardbound edition of the life of the famous Western gunfighter, Billy the Kid. The other two were paperbound books, in English, most likely prepared for use in classroom instruction: Lord Byron's narrative poem, "The Prisoner of Chillon"; and the other, by a Russian author, containing a story about the pursuit of riders in a troika across the snow by a pack of hungry wolves. We were grateful for his thoughtfulness, and since we lacked a deck of cards and access to a radio, those books were a providential gift.

On the following day, Bob and I decided we should clean up, but we had been unable to find a bathing place. We asked Monsieur where we might do so. He appeared puzzled by the question, but quickly grasped the intent of our query, and set out to satisfy our need. In the back yard he upturned the large tub, used as a drinking vessel for the geese and ducks, pumped a few strokes of water, and sloshed it around. After inspecting his job, Monsieur decided that the tub was clean enough for our purpose. He carried it across the barnyard to the rear wall of a building that served as an extension to the roadside wall of the farmstead. He set it down next to the small electric threshing machine. Towels appeared from somewhere, and a bit of wartime soap. The boys were enlisted to carry buckets of water from the pump. With a spirit of high adventure, they pumped, then fairly ran from the yard to the machine shed, where each poured the contents quickly into the tub.

Meanwhile, Madame was heating water in a big pan and the teakettle on the kitchen stove. Soon she appeared and poured the hot water into the tub. More followed, until the temperature of the water was warm enough for bathing. The stage then set, the Croizés gathered at some small distance from the shed, waiting expectantly for the unfolding of the next act of this drama.

Neither Bob nor I had expected our bath to become a public spectacle, so we, too, waited — uneasily — for the family to go away. It quickly became apparent that was not going to happen, and their voices urged us to undress and proceed with the action. I suggested to Bob that, since he was the officer, he should go first. Turning his back to the audience, he quickly undressed and stepped into the small tub, pulling his knees up under his chin in order to fit. Then, somewhat less exposed to view, he began soaping and splashing, to the manifest delight of the onlookers.

Meanwhile, I had stripped down to my undershorts, maintaining a faint semblance of decorum. As he prepared to emerge, I handed Bob the little towel. The Croizés, conversing among themselves, remained rooted to their spot; clearly both of us were to use the same water. As Bob toweled and made a frantic lunge for his clothing, I turned my back, shed my shorts, and stepped into the water. Though it had a grayish color and was still tepid, I found little to complain about. I splashed water on my hair, rubbed it a bit, then rinsed it as best I could. The rest of my body was more easily taken care of, but I was quite conscious of the crowd reaction outside. What were they talking about — the bath, or our bodies, or both? Well, by that time it didn't matter so much; we had been about as fully exposed as possible.

So I stood up, took the damp towel from Bob's outstretched hand, and rubbed off the water as best I could. When I stepped into my shoes, it seemed clear to the bystanders that the afternoon's diversion had ended. Helpfully, the boys came to the shed, dumped the water on the ground, and returned the tub to its usual location in the yard.

That evening, before supper, Monsieur seemed to have something special on his mind. Taking the water bucket from its place near the pump, he emptied it, then half filled it with water. Bob and I watched curiously for his next move. Sitting on the ground at the edge of the yard, he took off his shoes and stockings and rolled his trousers legs up to the knees, exposing legs that seemingly hadn't been in contact with water for a very long time. Then, towel in lap, he inserted one foot into the bucket and rubbed gently. He withdrew a lily white foot that probably had not been exposed to sunlight for a long time either. After drying, he repeated the process with the other foot. Then, with his footwear replaced, he stood up, splashed the water into the courtyard, replaced the bucket, and strode proudly into the house. Our public bath had been a good advertisement.

The following morning, as Bob and I were making our bed, I heard the roar of a low-flying airplane. Glancing out of the front window, I saw a sleek Focke-Wulf Fw-190 flying parallel to the road in front of the house, near enough that I could clearly see the pilot's helmeted head and discern that he was wearing a white scarf around his neck. Then, as quickly as he had appeared, he was gone. The fly-by served as a reminder that the Beauvais-Tille *aérodrome*, through which we had passed in the van, was only a few miles away — even closer, if measured in flying time. It seemed remarkable that this was the first evidence we had seen of the proximity of the war, excluding, of course, the distant drone of echelons of high-flying bombers, which passed overhead on a daily basis, and the far-off thunder of antiaircraft bursts reaching for their flight.

★ ★ ★

Lacking other activities, Bob and I spent time reading the books Roger Fontaine had brought us. Then, after supper one evening, we were told that René and Marcel would take us to the village of Ons-en-Bray. The family was close-mouthed about the matter, and refused to furnish additional details.

"It is almost dark enough for you to leave," was the most we could pry from the elder Croizés. And, in a few minutes, we did leave, following René and Marcel through the gate and onto the road. Cautioned to be quiet, we turned to the west and walked stealthily in the direction of Ons-en-Bray. The darkness was not opaque, and we could see ahead for some distance. The dark outlines of a town stood in relief on the next hill. The road joined another, which ran at right angles. René cautioned us to remain at that junction while he scouted the field ahead, then, climbing over the fence, he was soon out of sight in a cluster of trees. Moments later, his gray clothing showing in relief against the dark background, we could see him waving us to proceed. Marcel ushered us to the fence and waited as we crossed, then accompanied us up the sloping incline ahead.

As we approached a large house, René went ahead and rapped softly on a door. We were expected; the door opened, and we were admitted into a darkened room. René and Marcel indicated that they would return for us later. When the door was closed, the light was switched on. We were in a sort of utility room. Quite obviously, we had entered at the rear of the house. A well-groomed lady led us into another room, graciously appointed. Roger was there, for this was, as I had just guessed, his home. The lady who had met us at the rear door was his mother. Monsieur Fontaine, seated in a large chair, rose to greet us. And we also met Roger's younger brother, Claude, and his sister, Maryse, a pretty, dark-haired girl about 15 years old.

We chatted for a few moments, gaining confidence in this setting and my ability to converse with these people. Then Claude left the room, his footsteps padding softly on a stairway. A moment later he reentered, bringing with him two young men. As I had guessed, these were the two airmen of the New Zealand Armed Forces, who were harbored in the Fontaine home.

Their French was no better than mine, and they were as pleased as we to have the opportunity to speak English. Very quickly we exchanged information about how we came to be clandestine guests in France. The ANZAC's RAF plane had been badly damaged by antiaircraft fire over east-central France. Even so, they continued on the return flight to England. Finally, however, they were forced to evacuate the plane. One of their crewmen, who did not know how to swim, had parachuted into a pond. His body had been found the next morning, and the news relayed to these men.

Even more briefly then, for the benefit of the Fontaines, Bob repeated our story in French.

Madame told how, a few days after the two Allied fliers had been delivered to her home, a German staff car had arrived at the gate. The officer in charge had announced his intention to inspect this, the grandest house in the village, as to its suitability as a headquarters for the Forces of Occupation. Accompanied by several soldiers, he had politely but firmly insisted upon inspecting the premises immediately.

Painfully aware of the two airmen in an upstair's bedroom, Madame tried, as she accompanied the searchers, to close doors with a bang and otherwise alert the airmen to the danger. Then, with her heart pounding, she stayed with the soldiers as they peered into each of the upstairs bedrooms. Finally they opened the door to the room where the ANZACs were staying. To her surprise, the bed was neatly made, and there was no trace of anyone having been in the room recently. One soldier even checked under the bed. Another opened the door to the wardrobe and found nothing.

After descending to the front door, the officer announced that he had found the house satisfactory for the purposes of the Reich. He would duly report to higher authority. Madame would be informed of the official decision in the matter at a later date.

When the staff car had departed from the drive, Madame rushed upstairs to the "empty" room. Just then, the two airmen were extricating themselves from concealment in the wardrobe — one behind the hanging garments, the other from the shelf, hidden under blankets folded in storage.

That had been a narrow escape, and the family immediately began circulating among the villagers plausible reasons why their house would be an unsatisfactory headquarters for the enemy. Their strategy seemed to have met with success, for no notice to evacuate had been received yet.

★ ★ ★

The evening of genteel hospitality and camaraderie passed swiftly, and in response to some prearranged signal, our hosts bade us good night. A short distance from the rear door, René stood in waiting and accompanied us to Marcel, who was standing in the place where we had left him.

It was quite dark now, the way being illuminated only by the night sky. The buildings along the route loomed as black shadows against the paler canopy of stars. We four men proceeded quietly along the roadway until we reached the Croizés' gate. Only when we were safely in the house did anyone speak, voicing thoughts and experiences of the evening. Monsieur and Madame were still up, apparently awaiting our return. They did not question us about our visit with the Fontaines; their concern was, rather, that we had met no misfortune on the route. Bob and I said our goodnights, and went upstairs to bed.

Later, it was René who spoke to us of his father's need to visit "Ponkey Ponch," which, he explained, was a town just north and west of the farm. Ponkey Ponch, we decided, was a ridiculous name for a town — as unsuitable as calling those non-stinging yellow and black insects that clustered in our kitchen, bees. I laughed at the thought of anyone giving such a funny-sounding name to a place in which they lived. But sooner than I had imagined, Monsieur let it be known that he wanted Bob and me to accompany him there, to see "someone important."

As René disclosed the information, we came to believe that the proprietor of this farm lived in Ponkey Ponch, and that Monsieur wished to show us off to him.

Monsieur led the way, going through the barnyard, through the gate into the pasture, where Roger had led us for our first briefing. We continued through the fields until we met the highway we now identified as the Beauvais-Vernon road. There was no vehicular traffic at that moment, and we crossed, taking a small intersecting road. At that juncture I noticed a *borne* indicating that we were in, or approaching, the village of Le Pont Qui Penche. So that was what I had found so amusing, misunderstanding its name as "Ponkey Ponch." Le Pont Qui Penche, Bob told me, meant something like the "leaning bridge" or "swinging bridge." We didn't see any bridge that day, so we couldn't determine whether the name derived from some condition of a former bridge or whether a current or former bridge at this site had some very special feature of construction. It didn't really matter, we decided, now that we understood the general meaning of the name.

When we reached our destination, Monsieur approached the doorway first, rapping to announce our coming. Then he took off his cap and held it in both hands. When the door opened in response to his knock, his body bent forward as in supplication; ingratiatingly he responded to the salutation from within, and we three were admitted to the foyer. The proprietor waited in another room. After acknowledging Monsieur and being introduced to Bob and me, he opened the conversation with polite questions about each of the members of the Croizé household. Refreshments were served before the discussion turned to the business of the farm, the matter which was the occasion for this visit.

During the whole time, Monsieur Croizé fidgeted with his hat, responding to the conversational leads of his host, but initiating nothing. I wondered about this submissive demeanor, for though his ordinary conduct was not imperious, he normally expressed self-confidence and pride. Could it be that he feared the power of his landlord to cancel the lease, or might this self-effacement be a customary form of relationship — a holdover from the medieval pledge of servitude to lord of serf? It seemed unlikely that I would be able to settle that question, and knew I had better not ask. The business at hand was quickly dispatched, and we were soon bidding goodbye.

As we were ushered out the door, Monsieur replaced his hat on his head and walked erect once more. He smiled his satisfaction at having displayed to his proprietor that by risking the sanctions of the Occupation Forces in hosting Bob and me, he was serving the cause of France. He strode proudly on the return trip home.

★ ★ ★

Having been exposed to people living in nearby towns, Bob and I came to the conclusion that our hair had become shaggy and unkempt, and we needed haircuts. But we could not risk a trip to a barbershop; we would have to perform the task ourselves. From Madame's inventory of household necessities, Bob acquired a pair of scissors. We each carried our pocket combs, which would suffice, and walked to the back pasture where we could operate unseen and without risk of littering a floor in the house.

We selected a spot in the shade of an apple tree — a very good spot indeed, for Bob discovered a ripe apple. While Bob was busy eating the apple, I was assigned to cut his hair. On the ground, I knelt and began clipping hair gathered by the comb. It would be difficult to smooth the edges of the cuts so that they didn't resemble a thatched roof. As the comb edged nearer to Bob's ear, I became aware that his head was bobbing as he chewed, the ear rising and falling with each bite.

I don't know why, but just at that moment, I became very conscious of the difference in our ranks. Perhaps I had taken Bob's suggestion that I be the first to handle the scissors as a command. In our sharing of experiences, we had seldom been reminded of rank, though on several other occasions I had reverted to the officer-enlisted man distinction that had been drilled into us in training.

Wanting to avoid the impertinence of asking him to refrain from eating, I tried my best to avoid slicing the ear. My effort wasn't good enough, and Bob gave an anguished yelp as the scissors snipped a bit of skin from the top rim of his ear.

"Why did you do that?" he demanded plaintively. My excuse seemed lame even to me. When it was my turn to be sheared, Bob spared me unnecessary pain. But then I didn't even try to eat an apple.

★ ~ ★ ~ ★

Soon, the household acquired a new member, a wiry young man probably in his late teens, a resident of a nearby town. André Dubus, as he was introduced to us, would live with the Croizés, ostensibly as a farm worker, though the arrangement may have been more of a convenience to him than a boon to the farm labor supply. Now eight people sat at the table — Monsieur and Madame, René and Marcel, Grandmother, André, and Bob and I. Mealtime conversations remained about the same, with the Croizé men doing most of the talking and Madame speaking mostly about the food. "Do you need more potatoes? I have more meat heated on the stove."

Grandmother, André, Bob, and I contributed little, except to consent to a second helping or to request someone to pass the bread. And when the meal was finished, each person slipped away from the table to return to his normal job or pastime.

I saw little more of André until supper time. After the meal he had slipped away, while Monsieur listened to the radio news, reporting the snail-like progress of Allied troops through the hedge rows of Normandy. André did not appear before bedtime. Was he assigned a room in the house, or had a place been arranged for him in the little house with the refuge family, or even in the barn? Bob and I were invited to play cards with René and Marcel, which we did until bedtime, an hour or so later.

We evadees had never given up hope of returning to our air base in England. If we actually were successful, however, it was unlikely that we would be reassigned to flying missions in Europe. We could look forward to being assigned as crew replacements flying in the Pacific Theater of Operations. On that point, however, we were in agreement; a combat assignment would be far preferable to this inactivity, living off the hospitality of our many Belgian and French helpers impoverished by the war. We were eager to leave this rural sanctuary with the Croizés and to return to Debach, England, the base of our 493rd Bombardment Group. But this time, I thought, I would prefer riding to walking.

I had seen a bicycle in the machine shed, near the threshing machine. Hoping that this might become available, I went to investigate its condition. I hadn't seen anyone ride this bicycle, but the Croizés might have need of it. With our escape money, we might offer a price sufficient for them to replace this one, should it prove satisfactory for our purposes. And they might be able to locate a second one, as well. The bicycle appeared to me to be constructed for racing, though someone might call it a touring bicycle. Through a *derailleur* arrangement I had never seen before, it was geared for ten speeds. The handlebars curved downward, the saddle was a thin bit of leather suspended on springs, and the metal pedals were equipped with toe clips to secure the rider's shoes — far different from the balloon-tired, single-speed bicycle I had used as a boy, with a wide seat and widespread handle bars. And to ride it would require somewhat different skills, I soon learned.

Leaning the bike against some object, I stretched to lift myself onto the saddle, then tried to reach the pedals, laboriously succeeding in slipping my shoes under the toe clips. I felt it was a precarious perch, which was soon verified when I turned the bike and attempted to pedal. Gripping the handlebars, I was out of balance, and fell heavily onto my side. Tenaciously, I repeated the effort with the same effect once again. One more failure, and I abandoned the effort. Perhaps I might master the bicycle on another day.

Later, Bob and I were in our room when nature bade us to answer her call. We hurried down the stairs and exited by the main rear door very rarely used. As we sped through the back yard, I glimpsed Madame surrounded by a cluster of gray uniforms. Our impetuous dash through the yard did not escape notice. How could Madame explain the presence of two young men, of draft age for the labor forces in Germany? We had to trust that she could explain the situation. While occupied in the outhouse, Bob and I whispered our concern that if the German soldiers came to investigate, we had no easy escape route. No one came, and when we eventually returned, the soldiers had gone away. Apparently they were there to beg some foodstuffs, and left bearing a small offering. But Madame was visibly shaken.

That was but the first of many visits by knots of German soldiers. Apparently slipping through the narrow gap that American troops were unable to close near Falaise, they had succeeded in crossing the Seine River and had headed northeast along the Vernon-Beauvais highway. This farm, less than a mile from that road, invited foraging by enemy troops. On several occasions Bob and I went to the door or exited the house to find them demanding food or drink. Sometimes other members of the Croizé family were present when they came, but Madame met with them all. And, by a strand of hair trailing down her neck or by the flush of her cheek, the strain began to tell. She finally decided that Bob and I should eat lunch at some place removed from visibility through the open kitchen door.

Our meals were brought to a table in the bedroom occupied by René and Marcel. Overlooking the back yard and garden, we lunched on the fruits of the farm — the standard fare of buttered potatoes, *petit pois* — peas, green beans, roast beef, and bread; it was simple, but delicious. From the window we had a good view of the back yard, and when guests arrived, we moved out of sight.

Even with the generous productivity of the garden, the hungry mouths at the table finally overtaxed the supply. Just before lunchtime one day, Madame announced a moment of crisis. There was no bread, and her purse was empty. Quickly Monsieur, René, and Marcel searched in their rooms and examined pockets in the clothing they were not wearing at the time. Their searches completed, they assembled in the kitchen. Between them they had less than ten *centimes* — far less than the cost of a loaf of bread.

Bob and I still had, by comparison, the immense supply of unused money in our escape kits. Surely we could spare a little. However, we only had bills of large denominations. Would tradesmen be alerted to something amiss should these poor farmers seek to pass a large bill? We decided not to put them in that situation. We all had a breadless lunch that day.

But the Croizés were resourceful, and devised a way to supply bread for the table. Someone cut a cartload of the ripest wheat from the field and brought it to a room in the big barn. To provide a clean base to receive the forthcoming grain, that room was carefully swept even before the wheat was unloaded. René was dispatched to locate four short sticks, which he fastened in pairs with two lengths each of binder twine. The grain-laden straw could then be gathered in bundles of six to eight inches in diameter and secured by twisting the cords at the sticks, or handles. This I came to understand served as a sort of flail, and Bob and I were instructed to gather these bundles from the supply heaped in the corner of the room and to swing them heavily down on a beam placed on the floor. The grain dislodged by each blow fell on the floor, where it could be swept up and scooped into a waiting container.

We spent several sessions at this task. It was someone else's duty to crush the grains, which was done in the smaller barn across the courtyard, that also contained an oven, which we had not noticed previously. Large loaves of nearly whole-grain bread issued from that oven — both good enough and plentiful enough to satisfy us.

Bob and I were free to move about the farm during the day, making certain that German soldiers were not at the door when we left the house or when we wished to return. Passing through the spacious barnyard, we heard the roar of racing engines. Looking up, we saw a formation of German Messerschmitt ME-109s diving in attack toward a flight of North American P-51 Mustangs. The targeted planes scattered to the left and right — first entering a shallow dive to gain speed, then ascending in a climbing turn — an Immelman — to thwart the attack.

Bob and I scrambled to the rooftop to watch. This was like a scene from *G-8 and His Battle Aces*, one of aviation writer Robert J. Hogan's pulp novels about World War I that I used to read. Pairs of aircraft dived, climbed, and performed wingovers, all accompanied by the staccato *br-r-ups* of machine-gun fire. A P-51 was the first victim, hit by a burst from the initial diving attack. Trailing smoke, the aircraft dove toward the ground. Did it crash? We saw no parachute. Then two ME-109s afire fluttered down — and then another. As the battle continued, two other ME-109s, trailing smoke, left the fray. Finally, the three remaining German fighters, diving to gain momentum, fled to the east, five P-51s in hot pursuit. The air battle had lasted only a few minutes, but it was an exciting spectacle, adding credence to the report that this new American fighter was indeed superior in combat.

Late that afternoon André invited Bob and me into the loft of the small barn adjacent to the garden. There he removed a layer of straw, revealing a worn suitcase, containing a supply of hand grenades and rifle ammunition. A carbine rifle was concealed nearby. These weapons, he told us proudly, were his tools of the night. On most evenings, he said, he slung a *musette* loaded with grenades over his shoulder, took his rifle to a main road, and stationed himself in a tree. Then, when a German military truck passed under his perch, he would pull the pin from a grenade and drop it into the vehicle. In that way he had disabled many vehicles and not a few enemy soldiers. Cautioned into secrecy, Bob and I descended from the loft, and returned to the house.

One night we first heard a pulsing *whoosh*, traversing through the sky at a low altitude, flying in a trajectory parallel to the road in front of the house. By the sound, it could not be an airplane, because there was no hum from a propeller. Nor was there any sound of an internal combustion engine. Other members of the household had heard it, too, and we conferred, trying to fathom this mystery. Someone hazarded a guess that it might be a German V-1 rocket, a pilotless aerial bomb — the "buzz bomb" — of which we had heard reports. None of us had ever seen one, but the general consensus was that in the absence of any other phenomenon we had experienced, a V-1 appeared a logical designation. After that, almost every evening we heard others overhead.

On a later night, we saw a dark, winged, elongated shape trailing a tail of flame. That must indeed be a V-1 aimed toward England. At a preset time or distance the motor cut off, and the bomb fell. Reports from

England told of considerable damage from these bombs, which fell almost at random.

One night I was awakened for some unexplained reason. Almost immediately, our bedroom door was opened — did someone open it, or had it blown open for other causes? Sitting up, I saw the heads of Marcel and René peering in through the open doorway. And Bob was just rousing himself from the floor. Soon the elder Croizés joined the knot of spectators at our door. They had heard a loud noise, they said, and expected that Bob and I were the cause. But Bob's fall from the bed hadn't caused that much noise, and whatever it was had actually dislodged him from the bed. In the morning we discovered that a V-1 had gone off course and plunged into the orchard-pasture behind the barns, leaving a large crater. In the house, 100 yards or so away, the aftershock had blown open doors, rattled windows, and jarred Bob from his bed. I had slept through it.

From atop the roof of the big barn again, we watched as two American Republic P- 47 Thunderbolts attacked the train that plied the rails less than a mile to our east. The train was armed, and threw up a formidable barrage of bullets. The fighters reciprocated. When the P-47s turned back, apparently out of ammunition, the train traveled on. We were too far away to assess the damage to the train, but we had ascertained that it had received fire.

The attack was reported by BBC radio that evening; it must have been the train on the Paris-Dieppe line, the last connection between Paris and the Atlantic coast.

We witnessed similar attacks on successive days, and a neighbor reported that the gunner aboard the train, under the stress of a vicious attack, had beat his head on his own gun mount, resulting in his death. But the train continued to maintain its schedule.

Now the south breeze carried distant thunder of artillery fire. Grandmother went to the door as a little Volkswagen jeep loaded with German soldiers came into the yard in their quest for food and drink. The conjunction of enemy uniforms and distant gunfire caused her to tremble. Marcel, who had comforted her, told us that the old lady still had fearful memories of German soldiers sweeping west from the Alsace in 1871; she would not be comforted now until the last one had left the area.

Shortly thereafter, the boys produced spades and began to dig in the garden, protected by the garden wall and the farm buildings. They worked diligently for a couple of days, excavating a hole perhaps 16-feet long by 10-feet wide, and several feet deep. The excavated earth was heaped along the perimeter of the hole, supporting several logs, which formed a roof. Sealed to some extent by gunny sacks and other fabric, the remaining soil was shoveled over the top. Only a small entrance provided for fresh air. Upon being led to the spot to survey the shelter, Grandmother expressed some satisfaction. But the pounding of big guns could still be heard in the distance.

That day, at dinner time, there was great expectation in the house. General Charles de Gaulle was scheduled to speak on the radio that evening. Bob and I were invited to join the Croizés huddled around the radio. De Gaulle's voice was impressive as he likened the Axis Occupation to a rattlesnake coiled around France. In the climax of the address, all Frenchmen were urged to rise and strike that rattlesnake, loosening its hold forever. With exultation, Monsieur poured out several glasses of Calvados, which we drank as a toast before retiring for the night. From the shadows of the doorway, André, clad entirely in black, turned and carried his *musette* and rifle out into the night.

BBC radio had reported that despite repeated attacks from the air, the Paris-Dieppe train still remained in commission. As darkness fell, a burly young man whom I had not seen previously had come to the farm in search of André. The two had spoken earnestly at the garden gate for perhaps a half-hour before the caller left. They had given no clue as to their conversation, but by morning the Paris-Dieppe train ran no more.

As days elapsed, more Germans arrived at the door, making more evident the signs of strain on Madame. Cannon fire could still be heard in the distance, and the radio reported that Free French troops were about to enter Paris. Then a report came of fighting in the streets of the capital city. Soon we had no more electricity, and the radio was stilled — nor was power restored on the following day. Was this area about to become a battlefield?

Certainly, if we were to be discovered here, our presence at the farm constituted a threat to our hosts, and we did not wish to expose them to even more risk than they were already experiencing. Were we to remove that threat to the Croizés, toward what destination should we travel? Toward Paris? We wondered how long it would take to dislodge the enemy and when it would become safe for us to travel.

Bob and I considered alternative plans. If we couldn't enter the city from the north, say at Pontoise, our best chance seemed to be from the west, in the area already cleared by Allied troops. We were almost certain that no bridges across the Seine would be available to us. Could we chance locating a boat to take across the river? Otherwise, we might have to attach ourselves to some floating debris, which would act both as camouflage and float, as we swam across.

In any case, I would rather ride than walk to the river. I went again to the machine shed and tried to master the bicycle. After several tries, I abandoned the effort; it was too much for me.

The rumble of artillery seemed closer now. Possibly, Paris had been liberated and the battle lines were moving northward. Madame and Grandmother were now quite distraught; even the men showed evidence of strain.

Bob and I readied ourselves to depart, but for several days we had not seen our contact with the Résistance, Roger Fontaine. We might have to leave without announcing our intentions. By some means I exchanged my pair of patched trousers for a pair of gray woolen ones, belonging to Marcel. We gathered our few possessions in our *musettes*, filled our bottles with water, and added a Halazone tablet to each. Slitting open the lining of our caps, we inserted our Belgian *cartes d' identité* so that they would not give us away if a sentry asked for our papers. Earlier I had thought our dog tags might reveal our identity. So, acquiring safety pins from Madame's sewing supplies, we pinned the dog tags in our trousers pockets. We took care to affix them to the outer part of the pocket, away from the leg because, if we were ever frisked, the back of the hand is less sensitive than is the palm side.

As we descended the rear stairway, we helped ourselves to a handful each of sugar lumps from a box in a cabinet in the hallway. There was no one to bid goodbye.

Intent on circling the property before taking our set course, we went out through the barnyard and entered a lane through a field. Just then we met Marcel returning with his team of oxen to the barn. Here was someone whom we could properly thank for the family's hospitality. We told him that we were leaving, and asked him to extend our *adieus* to the rest of the household and to thank them for caring for us.

"We shall come back and see you in five years," I added, with greater assurance than I truly felt at the moment. Then we turned our backs and parted. The date was August 28, 1944.

Chapter 15

Detour on the Route to England

AFTER SAYING GOODBYE to Marcel, Bob and I continued on down the lane. Reaching a fence line, we turned east, away from Ons-en-Bray, until we were past the next set of farm buildings. We turned south, toward our destination, the Seine River. Cautiously, we climbed the fence, crossed the road, passed over the next fence, and entered the pasture on the south side of the road. No one was in sight in this or in nearby fields, and we soon fell into stride, the walking easy in pasture cropped short by cattle now absent from the field. Across the fence lay a field stripped of its summer crop. Out of sight from the road and its flanking farmsteads, we relaxed and proceeded at a pace that seemed more rapid than we had been able to achieve along the road north of Beauvais.

Several weeks had elapsed since we had been given sanctuary in the village of La Neuville-St. Pierre, and my sore foot had healed. Though the big toe on my right foot appeared to be pushed back nearly an inch into the foot, my formerly sodden shoe had accommodated to that change, and with dry stockings I was walking comfortably.

Coming upon a field where walking would be more difficult, we opted to angle westward on an agricultural access lane. Then, when a more southerly direction was possible over clear ground, we returned to our preferred direction. We repeated these actions as conditions dictated, until we approached the Beauvais-Gisors road. Our route had led us adjacent to the village of La Houssoye, south of Auneuil. We skirted the village, crossed the main road, and returned to the fields, angling toward a lesser road that would lead us eventually to the town of Marines. Our route allowed us the opportunity to consult the road map we had carried all the way from Belgium. The map had alerted us to and avoidance of habitations along our way.

Finally, before passing to the west of Bachiviliers, we took another five-minute rest, then joined and followed the little road for several kilometers. At this evening hour, and perhaps because it was a minor route, there was no vehicular traffic, which made for pleasant walking.

At a crossroad, we spotted a cluster of houses ahead, so bypassed them to the east. But then we came upon a small stream. We had to return to the road to cross the bridge. Darkness would soon be upon us, and we had to give some thought to shelter for the night, and to a bite to eat, for our stomachs told us the dinner hour was long past.

A village at the next crossroad did not appear hospitable, so we walked around it and decided to press on, hopefully, to Marines. We found a small stream, which we followed to the edge of the town. However, we discovered that what we could see of Marines was situated on a small but steep hill, which we would have to scramble up to seek assistance. With little opportunity to scout out the town before we entered, it seemed risky. In the dimming twilight, we trudged on.

Dwellings were scattered along the highway south of Marines. The road angled to the southeast and we walked parallel to it until we found a good place to cross. Then, by the light of a bright moon, we hurried down a gradual slope and away from the road. Distant shellfire made us very conscious of the danger of capture. Espying a small wood ahead, we walked to its edge, discovering an orchard bordering farm buildings. We were eager now to contact a friendly farmer. Perhaps we could beg a *tartine* and seek shelter overnight in the barn. But first we felt it necessary to assure ourselves that the buildings did not house German soldiers. We sat under an apple tree to reconnoiter.

Our hopes were quickly dashed by a loud commotion from within the barn. I could identify the sounds as the distress calls of geese, but I had never heard such a large company of them aroused at one time. Certainly such a disruption would bring someone to investigate. I drew up against a tree, the better to conceal myself. Bob did likewise. A shout came from within the barn, and the door was pushed partly ajar. A single shadowy figure emerged, moonlight gleaming on metal in his arm. He called, asking something like, "Who is trying to steal my geese?" With the likelihood that he carried a shotgun, I felt this was not an appropriate moment in which to reply in my imperfect French. What would I say, anyway?

I huddled closer to the trunk of the tree, comforted by the camouflage offered by my dark coat against its shadow, and happily aware that my light gray trousers matched the silver of moonlight on the grass. Bob, too, held his counsel, and we remained huddled as the farmer searched around the trees closest to the barn. Satisfied finally, he returned to the barn and closed the door. It didn't seem like a good time now to knock with our requests.

The geese remaining silent, we retreated stealthily through the orchard to a small road at its edge. The road sloped downward to the south, and we followed it for a short distance until we came upon a narrow lane leading eastward along the foot of the slope. There we tarried for a moment, considering the options. Though the moon was bright enough for to us see our way, it was too dim to allow us to refer to our map. Unsure of where this little road would lead, we opted for following the lane, likely a little-used agricultural access road. We might not find any farmsteads, but there might be a haystack or equivalent shelter for the night.

I led as we walked single-file through the uneven ruts of the lane, traveling less rapidly than had been possible in daylight. Clouds obscured the bright moon. After what seemed like a long distance, the lane came to an abrupt end, forking both to the right and to the left. Ahead, across a low fence, lay what appeared to be a level field. The southeasterly direction we had been taking pointed toward Paris, so we opted for the field.

Bob now took the lead as we climbed gingerly through the barbed wire fence. He led us cautiously for perhaps a quarter of a mile. Then, with a heavy thud and muffled grunt, he was stopped.

"What happened?" I asked. "Are you all right?"

"I think so," came a muffled reply. "I fell into this hole," he continued in a loud whisper. "It seems to be a foxhole. Lucky for me, this one is empty."

Bob was able to climb out of the hole, and we continued on, with him still in the lead, picking his way with care. We were very quiet, lest there be other foxholes nearby, perhaps still occupied by unfriendly soldiers.

The night was now so very dark that I could not make out any features of the terrain. Nor could Bob, for he fell again, with a thud that knocked his breath away. After a short interval during which he recovered, he reported, "This is another hole like the last one. It's empty, but I'll try to feel around to see whether anything was left behind."

Just then I caught the sound of an airplane above and south of us, flying at an altitude of perhaps under 4,000 feet. I was kneeling beside the hole when the plane dropped a flare. Suspended on a parachute, the bright bluish light descended slowly, illuminating the entire area in its glow. I remained transfixed, remembering that viewers more quickly detected movement, while inert objects tended to blend into the background. Without moving my head, I observed hundreds of gaping holes extended unevenly across the field. It was unlikely, I concluded, that these were foxholes; more likely they were the result of patterned shellfire. Even more likely, they might mark a massive aerial bombardment. I was at a loss to reason why that would be the case.

I remained motionless as the plane circled over a broad area. Then 400 yards ahead, in the direction in which we had been walking, loomed a massive shape, seemingly a haystack. That was the only distinguishing feature I could see. I tried to memorize the location of the craters along the way. When the flare had flickered out, I offered my hand to Bob, who clambered out of the hole and followed my lead toward the haystack.

Arriving without further mishap, we accepted the pile as our quarters for the night. The sides were too precipitous for us to climb, so we pulled hay from the lower part of the stack, making holes into which we could climb and try to sleep. Before retiring, we munched on sugar cubes and each had a drink from our water bottles, leaving some for early morning.

With difficulty I hoisted myself up into the little hole I had made, and turned so that my feet were toward the center. The quarters were cramped, but the hay made a soft mattress. In the dark it was impossible to determine the source of the cannon fire that punctuated the night at frequent intervals, nor to tell just where the projectiles, each heralded by a loud whistle, might land and burst. The shelling continued fitfully throughout the night; however, none exploded close to our resting place. From time to time I squirmed to improve my makeshift bed. I must have been wakened many times by the loud gunfire. But when early morning's light signaled the new day, I awoke well rested.

A rustling in the hay not far from my own sleeping place alerted me that Bob also was awake. Quiet until we could be assured that we were alone, I wriggled out of my nesting place and dropped to the ground. Joined by Bob, we walked around the haystack in order to survey our surroundings. We were on a large level plain with no evidence of a large encampment. What could have led to the bombardment here? Most likely, we guessed, this field had been used as an enemy airstrip, and had been bombed by the Allies to render it unusable. Our Michelin road map did not show the field, but later maps did.

A small farmstead was not far away, to our northeast. Though we could not see a road from our vantage point, we knew there had to be one leading past the farm and on to the village, barely visible to the southeast. A half-mile to our south, we could see shrubs and an occasional tree along a fence row that might be outlining the possible road. Just then, a horse-drawn wagon moved westward along that road. The lone driver was clad in the gray of a German uniform. For several minutes we watched as he drove by. We breakfasted where we stood, munching on sugar cubes and swilling down the remainder of our precious water. We would need to replace that soon.

We might refill our water bottles in the village, if the way were clear, and try to get more substantial food as well. Cautiously we walked toward the village. As we neared the road that we had expected to lead to it, we found only a rutted agricultural path, much like the one we had followed the night before.

We proceeded on until we noticed an intersecting roadway leading into the village. As we hesitated, hoping for some sign that we might be welcome there, bursts of machine-gun fire resounded from the town. Clearly, we would not be welcome. We heard the whistle of an incoming shell. We hit the ground and saw it hit a short distance ahead of us, scattering dirt over the area. Picking ourselves up, we hurried toward the hole, believing that another shell was unlikely to land in the same place — at least not yet.

Beside the crater, an older one contained a puddle of water. We scooped it up into our bottles, and as I was about to add a Halazone tablet from my bottle, Bob urged me on. We had not gone 50 yards when another shrill whistle heralded a second shell. In unison, we hit the ground. The shell burst almost exactly in the crater we had just left!

To remove ourselves from the fight going on in the village and the vicinity of bursting cannon shells, we abandoned that little road and moved quickly into the adjacent field, where shocks of grain stood in regularly spaced rows. We were on a small hill that obscured our vision of the road ahead. More importantly, we were screened from view by others on that road. Furtively, we split up and darted from the protection of one grain shock to the next, working our way up the hill. At the top we lay protected on the ground, while we surveyed the scene ahead. A second supply wagon moved along the road. We were content to lie in wait for it to pass.

A sentinel also walked slowly along the road. Apparently he had an assigned route, for upon reaching some point, he turned and retraced his steps. From his place of concealment nearby, Bob's low voice urged me to wait until the next time the soldier made his round, then to move ahead while he was facing the other direction. Together we scurried on and were able to move ahead the distance of two shocks before crouching again. After repeating this process several times, we approached the roadside. Between our last hiding place and the road was a unprotected space of perhaps 50 feet that we would have to move through, then cross the road, clear the ditch on the other side, and go nearly 100 feet beyond that to the next place for concealment.

Lying still, we timed the sentry's pace. We would have to move quickly. We did, running at a crouch, the whole time. We slipped by the guard.

The hiding places on this side of the road were not shocks of grain, but cleanings from a barn, no doubt brought here in a *tombereau* and dumped, awaiting a worker with pitchfork to spread them. Like the haystack we had hid in, these manure piles were large enough to conceal a man, providing he parted the material, crawled in, and pulled the extracted material over him as a cover. Crawling in, I was grateful that the stuff had dried for awhile.

Moving bit by bit, we succeeded in putting about 150 yards between ourselves and the road. Peering out through the smelly mixture, I noticed a string of German soldiers bicycling along the road, toward the west. Soon I heard the tell-tale scream of an incoming shell that landed and burst short of the road, less than 100 yards from where I was hiding. The sentinel was not in sight, so Bob and I moved a bit farther from the road.

Another shell landed closer to the road. Then another, this one farther east. We continued to move forward, keeping our attention on the road behind us. From time to time more German bicyclists continued to move along the road, all heading west. Then ahead, where the terrain sloped downward, we saw a hole from which a wisp of whitish smoke curled upward. We were not aware of any shells bursting from that quarter. Might this be a foxhole where a resident was prepared to remain for awhile? Certainly, a person stationed there could command a broad field of vision to the south, east, and west. Whispering our counsel, we elected to remain concealed in this spot and to survey the hole for any movement.

As we waited, rain began to fall from the leaden skies. Very soon I could no longer take comfort in the fact that the manure in which I was hiding was fairly well dried. As drops of water began to run down my face, I attempted to keep them away from my mouth. I need not recount how they tasted.

A thin trail of smoke continued to rise from the hole; still I saw no sign of movement from anyone who might have been within. We must have rested in those same manure piles for over an hour, by which time I was thoroughly wet. Hungry, I reached in my pocket for another sugar cube. What I found there discouraged my appetite; I emptied the rest of the wet brown stuff from my pocket, leaving it on the ground. Seeing no movement from the hole, Bob and I rose from our hiding places and circled to the west, leaving a wide area between us and the enigmatic hollow.

On a north-south road to our right, several gray-clad cyclists rode down the hill toward a village at its bottom. Possibly, I thought, that might have been the destination of the other cycling troops we had noticed on the east-west road on the hilltop. Several houses were visible in the village. If enemy troops were massing there, the town would be a poor place to seek refuge from the rain, or to acquire something for lunch. But there was a large barn-like structure, what our Belgian acquaintances would have called a hangar, at the north edge of the village. As we came closer, the hangar was revealed to have open sides, and was piled high with baled hay or straw. We might be able to find shelter, but baled hay offered a poorer milieu for concealment than would loose hay. Also, we could not see whether some enemy soldiers might have taken shelter in the hangar. To view the other side, we would have to cross the road on which troops had been traveling.

For the moment, we kept our distance, working our way down the hillside. A two-story brick house caught our attention. Its rear might be accessible from the field ahead of us, and perhaps we could contact a friendly resident.

An upstairs window facing the east was open. Bob and I lay on the ground, partly protected by tall grass in the fence line, and surveyed the prospect at length. Then a motion in the window revealed a German soldier, very likely a lookout. As we watched, he waved at someone to our left. Following that gesture, our eyes revealed a dark figure emerge from a house some distance away, hurrying along the path by the fence line, headed for the very house we had been watching.

As he moved across my line of vision, it occurred to me that although I surmised he was a German soldier, I could distinguish little more than the outline of his body and that his clothing was of a dark color in the rain. Possibly, the rain could mask our clothing, also, and help us escape detection if we moved through the open.

But what about the hangar at the village edge? Another group of cyclists approached it by the road, then passed out of my vision behind the building. Unable to determine that the hangar was a safe enough place in which we might hide, it no longer appealed to me. As we lay there waiting for the person on the path below to reach the village, we became aware that the artillery fire we had been hearing was directed in front of us and to our sides, as well as at the road behind us. We now discovered that the shell bursts were in wooded areas rather than in the open fields ahead. If we were to advance, we just might be safer in the fields. And it seemed that we must advance, for the last village we had passed was occupied by enemy troops and already involved combat.

With Bob in the lead, we crossed the fence and started across the field. As we crossed the little lane, I held my breath waiting for a challenge. There was none. Soon we had walked past the village and were in empty fields. Ahead, another town lay to our right, though a small highway and a stream blocked our way. We would have to approach the village in order to use the bridge at its southern extremity.

A knot of men stood conversing in our way toward the village. Bob continued on, altering our direction only slightly. As we neared them we could see their uniforms and weapons, but not clearly. We passed within 15 yards of them without a challenge. At the highway, we turned on the road leading south from the village and crossed the stream by the bridge. Very soon after that we were able to leave the road again and take to the fields.

Occasionally a shell burst in woods to our right or to our left, but most of the fire now seemed to be directed behind us. Remaining in the open fields, we were able to make good speed, and we quickly covered several kilometers. We had not seen German soldiers, or anyone for that matter, for some time. Then ahead there seemed to be a hill higher than the others, surmounted by a wood. The sound of small-arms fire seemed to come from just beyond it. We circled to the west, giving this hill a wide berth.

Quite suddenly, the rain ended, and we were quite exposed on a sloping field of stubble. The nearest woods offered our only chance of shelter, approximately 500 yards distant. We had barely turned in that direction when a shot rang out from the hill we had been trying to avoid. The bullet kicked up dirt near our feet. We stopped in our tracks, raised our hands in the air, and turned toward the sound of the shot. Three men manned a machine-gun nest dug into the hillside perhaps 100 yards from us.

Covered by the machine gunners, a rifleman advanced toward us. Fearful that my Belgian *carte d' identité* might be discovered, I doffed my cap and dropped it at my feet. Then the soldier arrived, took us in charge, and marched us up the hill. The men in the machine-gun emplacement seemed relieved at our capture. No doubt they had been readied for an armed assault around the side of the hill toward which Bob and I had been heading — but here were two wet, dirty peasants without so much as a walking stick between them.

Our capture had been observed at the hilltop, and soon an officer and several soldiers advanced to meet us. At the edge of the woods near the brow of the hill, a smart-appearing officer directed questions to us. Several soldiers alertly stood by. Showing our French *cartes d' identité,* we replied according to the information supplied on them.

Having rehearsed this in my mind, I indicated that we were French farm workers. Our native language was Flemish — that was why I did not have a better command of French. My companion — I forget what name was entered on either of these identity cards — was my cousin. We had received word that my grandmother was seriously ill and we were hurrying to be at her side. She lived, I said, across the Seine, in Chartres.

Why had we not come by the highway? Because that would have taken us far to the east of our destination, so we had chosen the most direct route. We intended to find a boatman to take us across the Seine.

The officer did not accept that explanation. Even to me it sounded thin. I suppose there was no good explanation for two young men wandering through fields in the rain — into an area of furious small-arms fire. Dismissing my reasoning, he took charge of the interrogation. He accused us of being English airmen, pilots of an observation plane that had been downed by ground fire recently. He continued . . . obviously we had stolen these working clothes and exchanged them for our own uniforms. Where was our military identification? We denied those accusations and resolutely maintained the veracity of my story.

The officer continued to question us in English, to which we did not respond. He was asking us to perform some bodily movements. He repeated each question in French, and we followed his commands. We appeared to be passing his test. Finally, in English he told us to get on our knees. Again, we failed to comply. Had he first expressed that in French, I would not have understood. But, assuming that he had merely repeated the same request, we knelt. He had missed an opportunity to trip us up.

Tiring of this line of inquiry, he said, "No matter. No innocent person would be foolish enough to walk into a combat zone. If you are not military, then you must be civilians up to no good. You will be shot."

In response to his several orders in German, the men about us sprang into action. Bob and I were escorted to the top of the hill, at the edge of the woods, and made to stand with our backs to the woods. A tall soldier carrying a Schmeisser machine pistol — a "burp" gun — came hurrying up, reported to the officer, and took position perhaps 20 feet in front of us. Meanwhile, another soldier brought a camouflage tarp and, with help, flung it over our heads. A brisk order cleared soldiers out of the woods behind us. Our interrogator's voice rang out, saying, I assumed, "Ready, aim . . ."

That's when I shouted, "*We're Americans!*"

The officer in charge called "*Halte!*" And to my relief, the tarp was quickly pulled from our heads.

Our erstwhile executioner walked up to us, saying in French, "You spoke up just in time — my finger was on the trigger."

Relieved to be alive, I regretted that we would probably not be free to continue on our way — this day, August 29, 1944. I wondered what could happen next.

Chapter 16

The View from the Other Side

ONCE WE HAD avoided the one-man firing squad, my apprehensions of having our luck run out abated somewhat. Certainly we were now prisoners, but this new situation was not devoid of promise.

I was not fully prepared for what happened next. To my surprise, with friendly smiles on their faces, several German soldiers hurried up to us. The first one to reach me offered a cigarette, which I declined, saying, "*Je ne fume pas, merci.*"

A second soldier offered chocolate, which I gratefully accepted. Not only did I like chocolate, but I was also famished, and this candy bar would take the edge off my appetite.

The soldier with the machine pistol tarried a moment before taking leave. "I must get back to my position," he said. "I have been holding the front line, only one hundred meters over the hill."

Meanwhile, Bob had been engaged in conversation a

short distance away, with a Sergeant. I overheard part of that conversation.

"Have you been in Chicago?" queried the Sergeant. "I was there for several years, attending the University of Chicago."

Bob countered that he was well aware of the university, for he had attended the University of Michigan; both colleges belonging to the Big Ten Athletic Conference.

"What was your subject of study?" asked the Sergeant.

"I majored in statistics," was Bob's reply.

"Then we have something in common," answered the Sergeant. "My subject was mathematics."

This conversation, quite normal in a different context, had a bizarre quality here on the hilltop, where the speakers were committed to be bitter enemies and the bullets whistling over our heads were being fired by our Allies.

The mood of welcome quickly changed as we were placed in the hands of a grim officer who had not taken part in the demonstrations of camaraderie. Accompanied by two foot soldiers, he urged them to herd us down the hill. Eager to please, they prodded us with rifles as we trotted to a path leading from the east. On the path we met several *SS* soldiers — the *Schutzstaffel*, the elite military and police unit of the Nazi Party — moving toward the front. Each time we came upon new arrivals, we were halted and exhibited as the American enemy. These young men glanced at us with simple curiosity and, it seemed to me, with insufficient hostility to satisfy our captors. The two riflemen eased their disappointment by jabbing us again vigorously with their weapons, and on we trotted toward the valley.

In a clearing at the bottom of the hill stood an isolated railway depot, rails snaking across the valley floor. I just had time to register the fact that an American jeep was parked by the station when a man dressed in khaki ran forward to meet us. Though he displayed no insignia, he appeared to be an officer of some kind, for the men with us quickly deferred to him. Weapons still pointed at us, the riflemen stepped aside as the man charged at us, his fists flailing. It was pointless to resist with their threat of weapons. Most of his blows landed on my ribs or midsection; one, however, caught me on the throat. After that, the rest of the pummeling was less painful. A greater pain resulted from my helplessness; I could not fight back, or even ward off the blows.

Weary at last, our tormentor backed away, then walked to the jeep, pointing out that the spare tire was flat. He ordered us to bring the tire to the door of the depot and to repair it. Then he went inside on some errand. With only tire irons as tools, and because we had not yet regained strength after our beating, it was a tedious job. In quiet whispers we agreed to feign inability to perform the task. This was my opportunity to remind Bob that he still carried his cap with the Belgian *carte d' identité* in its lining. He managed to toss it aside, where it lay unnoticed. When the khaki-clad man emerged from the depot, he observed that no progress had been made on the tire. Glaring at the two of us with disgust, he ushered us to the jeep.

With a rifleman standing on either side, Bob was made to sit on the driver's side fender, and I on the opposite one. That was not a secure perch, and I grasped the windshield with my left hand, while hooking my fingers of my right hand under the flange of the fender. I was sure that we were about to face an ordeal. I was not mistaken. Gunning the motor, the driver threw the vehicle into reverse. Perhaps 30 yards from the station, he slammed on the brake, threatening to dislodge me. Abruptly, he shifted into a forward gear and raced toward the brick building. I thought I would be dashed against the wall. Then, with only a yard to spare, he slammed on the brakes again, halting the jeep just short of a collision. Somehow, neither Bob nor I had been dislodged. The driver repeated this maneuver for what seemed an interminable number of times; still, somehow, we clung to our precarious perches. Tiring of the harassment, the driver turned the jeep and bade the Captain to take the front seat beside him. The riflemen climbed in the back, each with a gun pointed at us.

With the motor racing, the driver engaged the clutch and sped along a little road east of the depot. Instantly it was clear that this was not going to be a pleasure ride, at least not for Bob and me. The driver jerked the jeep from side to side, each swerve designed to dislodge us. I became certain that this was his plan, then have us shot as escapees. Somewhere along the route I saw a *borne* indicating that Pontoise lay 15 kilometers ahead. Maintaining a grip on the jeep required steadfast determination and reserve strength I didn't know I had. As we swerved down the road we passed many German soldiers, some carrying *panzerflugs*, the sort of personal antitank rockets the Americans called bazookas. Until then, I had seen only drawings of them.

Careening pell-mell down this little road, my attention was focused on retaining my grip on the machine, so that I have only fragmentary memories of the route. But I did see another *borne* indicating that we were in Pontoise. There was no cluster of buildings, so we must have arrived at the commune limits, rather than the city. Mercifully, it was only a short distance later that the driver rolled up before a brick building from which flew the swastika flag, and slammed on the brakes. We were ordered to dismount, and led into the building.

Guarded in the hallway by the two riflemen, we heard the officers report in an adjacent room. Shortly after, these riflemen were replaced by two different soldiers, and the four men from the jeep strode down the hall and left by the front door. The hallway, which extended completely through the building, was sunken by three or four steps, effecting a vestibule by the rear door. At the top of these stairs, a short wall jutted out from the south side. Bob and I were made to face that wall, an arrangement that curtailed any impulse we might have had to attempt an exit by the rear.

I was summoned first into the room at our right, where an officer seated behind a large desk addressed me. A junior officer stood at his side; another armed soldier was stationed by the door. The interrogator held the dog tag that I had been carrying.

"You are Green, George, Sergeant in the United States Army. Is that correct?"

"No," I replied. "My name is Cupp, William L., serial number 17097098. I am a Sergeant in the United States Army Air Corps."

The officer was agitated by my response. Was I an impostor, a spy, or really a soldier? I gave the lame excuse that I had lost my identity tags and, when I found these, I had appropriated them, knowing that I might need some proof of my military status. With a snort, he rejected that explanation. Pointedly, he informed me that any military person dressed in any non-uniform fashion was to be defined as a spy and treated accordingly. Pressed for additional information, I repeated my name, rank, and serial number. Impatiently, he continued his questioning, and I replied in the same fashion. Angrily, he concluded the session, demanding that I empty my pockets and place the contents on the table at the end of the room.

Onto the table went my collection of European coins, my French *carte d' identité*, and my escape kit, including the emergency escape money. The other officer rummaged through these possessions as I was expelled into the hall. Then it was Bob's turn in the room.

All the while we had been in the building, a field piece located behind the structure had been firing repeatedly at intervals of about three minutes. Obviously, an observer at some distance was monitoring the bursts and telephoning corrections for sighting.

Standing by the door and facing the wall, I could hear much of Bob's session. Questions and answers were near duplicates of my interview. Like mine, Bob's dog tags did not correspond to his statement of identity and status. The interrogator's expression began with a level of agitation reached only a bit later in my interview.

Loudly he proclaimed that whether we were actually spies or the American airmen we claimed to be made no difference. "We have not taken a captive alive for more than a month!" Clearly, he did not expect us to be exceptions.

He issued a command in German, and the soldier at the door hurried out of the building. As Bob joined me, gray-clad soldiers began entering the vestibule. I believe there were 11 of them, with weaponry of various sorts, prepared to carry out the execution.

In spite of these bleak prospects, I tenaciously clung to the belief that somehow the good fortune that had accompanied us all these days would not desert us now, and that we would still be extricated from the doom promised us. I stood, facing the wall, and tried to construct some scenario by which we could effect our escape. Meanwhile, the cannon in the rear garden continued its sporadic thundering. From the interrogation room came sounds of irritation, with voices raised both in pitch and volume. Then the door opened, and Bob was pushed roughly into the hall.

When I was called back into the room, both officers stood by the table, eyeing the contents of the two bags of coins lying before them. They had noted the similarity in our collections and suspected that these represented some coded message. The explanation I offered was not satisfying, and they called Bob in to replace me.

Now there was artillery fire in answer to the shots from the cannon. Shells were landing in the vicinity, but not yet near. I took some comfort in these delays, thinking that our lives might yet be spared. This time in the interrogation room they suspected that some other messages might be concealed in our clothing. The junior officer searched my jacket, slitting seams in the lining and lapels. They found nothing. As the jacket was discarded, I sensed a minor triumph in that no one had yet searched in the outer breast pocket, where the Benzedrine pills were stashed. Then I was made to take off my shoes, and the officer searched in vain for a place of concealment in the heels or soles. Thwarted again, he handed me my jacket, and I left the room to the shout, "*You will be shot!*" This time, it was believable.

The soldiers in the vestibule were becoming restive, fingering their weapons as if they were eager to get back to their previous pursuits. I knew that Bob's clothing was now being searched and that he would soon be ejected. I could picture both of us being led to a wall in the rear and forced to stand while this squad prepared to fire. I could conjecture no escape from that wall. Then my imagination raced again. After we had been shot, and left lying on the ground for dead, the Allies would quickly advance. Then someone would discover our bleeding bodies, not yet lifeless. In the building they would find our dog tags and conclude that they belonged to the men lying by the wall. Checking the blood types on our dog tags, they would offer transfusions and save our lives. The idea gave me some courage. Then I remembered that those dog tags had been for other men, and that the transfusions of incompatible blood would kill us. Now I understood the expression "to be shaken up." I wilted, trying to think of all the people to whom I would like to say goodbye.

Then came the *whoosh!* of an incoming shell, and from the back yard a mighty explosion rattled the doors and windows. The vestibule was emptied by a rush of feet. Bob was taken out the door, accompanied by the soldier who had been attending our interrogation. Another *whoosh!* was followed by rumbles from above us. Then a shell burst just beyond our building, having passed through the attic. Plaster dust blew down the stairway, and as we looked up, a portly officer with his monocle flying, in an Afrika Corps uniform, ran down the stairs. Reaching the ground floor, he shouted something, which must have been "*Save the files!*" and raced out the front door.

The cannon behind the house was now silent. And, apparently having accomplished its purpose, the Allied artillery turned its aim elsewhere. One of the officers came out of the room and urged the rifleman to have us sit on a table next to the wall. My mother would have called it a library table — a long, narrow affair of the sort one could place behind a sofa in a large room, as much to define the space as to have utilitarian purpose. We raised ourselves up to this perch, facing the rifleman, who sat on a chair along the opposite wall. The officer went back into our erstwhile interrogation room, I supposed to busy himself with packing up the files.

As long as Bob and I sat close together on the table, the rifleman posed a threat. But if we were separated a bit, he couldn't point the weapon at both of us at the same time. Observing him, he seemed to handle his gun clumsily. I thought that he might be much more at home with a typewriter than with a rifle.

I knew Bob might be entertaining the same thought as I. If we sidled ever so slowly apart, we could spring at the guard, one on each side of his rifle, and disarm him. We cautiously edged apart. He didn't appear to notice. A moment later, we repeated the maneuver. Bob and I were acting in synchronized fashion. Just a couple minutes more, and we would be poised to spring.

Then the front door swung wide open. Beyond the soldier framed in the doorway was an incredible sight — a 1939 Lincoln Zephyr sedan, painted in the dull green-gray of German military vehicles. The soldier came in and entered the office behind us, and our plan was put on hold. There was a "*Heil Hitler*," followed by the click of heels, then a quick exchange of words. With pistol drawn, the soldier came into the hall and motioned us to walk toward the waiting car. The driver waited, also with a drawn pistol. The rear door of the sedan was opened and we were urged to enter. The new escort climbed in the front seat and turned, his pistol pointed toward us. The driver put his gun away and set the car in motion. Could we be on a one-way trip?

Then the man spoke. "Are either of you from Chicago?" he queried. "I used to work in Chicago!"

That disclosure took the edge off my anxiety. I marvelled that of two enemy soldiers we had spoken with that day, both had been in the States, and in Chicago! I was reminded of a humorous, recurrent theme in the programs of Kay Kyser, a popular American dance orchestra leader. One of Kyser's musicians by the name of Ish Kabibil who, when a member of the audience was introduced, and named his place of residence, replied, "___! I used to work in ____ (whatever that place was)!" In this case, I could have inserted "Chicago"!

The rest of the journey did not produce memorable discussion, nor did it reveal animosity against us, which helped my composure. The car pulled onto a small roadway through a woodland and stopped in a wide clearing. We were told to get out. From a knot of men there, one short, stubby man separated from the others and hurried in our direction. His appearance brought back my uneasiness, for he was dressed entirely in black. I had seen pictures of men in black — *Gestapo* agents, I believed. Most notably was the cover on a popular American magazine, depicting a lanky black-clad figure bearing the *SS* insignia and standing in gore, a picture of evil most difficult to dispel. At that time I did not know that the uniform of the *Panzer*, or tank corps, was also black. This man was assigned to the *Panzer.*

He spoke with the two men who had brought us. I understood none of what was said. Turning to us, he asked, "*Essen*?"

Essen, I thought; he knows that we are from a bomber crew and wants to know if we were the ones who bombed his home town. I hastened to answer in the negative. "No, not Essen. We bombed only targets in France."

Fortunately for Bob and me, he seemed not to understand my reply, for he strode to a little trailer attached to a truck parked nearby. Raising the lid, he revealed soup thick with noodles. It smelled good, and we accepted a portion gratefully. Except for several lumps of sugar and the candy offered by the German soldier just after our capture, we had eaten nothing since noon the day before. It was now late afternoon.

A handsome blond soldier, very young, was assigned to guard us. We were seated on damp earth under the trees, protected from the moisture by the poncho we shared with our new guard. Hungrily, we made short work of the soup before our containers were surrendered to one of our captors. Our guard took his duties seriously enough that he did not initiate conversation, so we sat quietly, taking in the scene around us. Soldiers displaying evidence of having been separated for several days from bathing and shaving facilities lounged around the several trucks parked among the trees. On a tarp spread on the ground nearby, some played a game of cards; still others dozed as they sat, leaning against the trunks of trees. All in all, they gave the appearance of a bored and weary troop.

One man came up to us, bearing in hand a triangular shoulder patch. "What unit is this?" he wanted to know.

I confessed my ignorance of such insignia. Not only did I not know the designated unit, I had never seen this one before.

"There are black men in it," he asserted with strong emotion. "They run to the attack, and even when you put four or five bullets in them, they keep on coming!"

Somehow this declaration of apparent approbation, coming from the nation that professed superiority over other peoples and races, surprised me. I had expected utter disdain for enemies of a different race.

I grew apprehensive as two of the scruffiest men, one swilling cognac from a bottle, wandered over to our place on the poncho. Our young guard looked puny when compared to these toughs. He would be of little help should they be intent on harming us. The shorter one bent over us; his breath reeked of alcohol. He asked if it were true that we were American fliers.

Bob, very likely fearful that the fellow held some grudge against people who had bombed his homeland, allowed that that was the case. I wasn't very comfortable when the fellow shooed our guard away, but the soldier did not become menacing. The taller fellow, appearing even more interested in the conversation, squatted down beside the first.

They weren't angry with enemy fliers. On the contrary, they were delighted to meet people with kindred interests. The short fellow had been an aerial gunner in the *Luftwaffe*, but after having been wounded over the Soviet Union, was taken off flying duty and assigned to the paratroops. His companion had been a paratrooper from the very beginning, but aspired to be a flier. They looked upon us as brothers under the skin.

Addressing our status as prisoners, they told us how lucky we were. "You will be taken to Germany and placed in a camp with other men like you. It will be a wonderful place, with comfortable quarters, good food, tennis, and swimming. And there will be parties, where girls will come in for dances. You will like it very much."

The fellow had tears in his eyes, probably comparing those prospects with his own situation — dirty, damp, and in frequent peril.

Bob was instantly sympathetic. "We don't deserve such fine treatment," he responded. "Why don't we trade places, and you be the prisoners? You could hide us here, and go off to Germany in our stead."

Cognac must do marvelous things to the powers of reason, for our new friends agreed and became our conspirators. Immediately one pointed to the fuselage of a crashed airplane, down at the edge of the woods.

"We can take you there," the tall one asserted, "and when the truck goes to Germany, we will be on it in your place."

His happiness, though, was quickly extinguished as a staff car drove into the wood and slid to a stop. A rider stood up and shouted some announcement. Apparently, the enemy was advancing fast, and the area would have to be evacuated quickly.

In a trice, our young guard was back, and the poncho snatched up and rolled for transit. Our two conspirators disappeared. We were loaded on the back of a truck, accompanied by our guard. Motors revved. Loud commands were issued, and the convoy moved out, leaving behind the empty woods.

We were pointed north, away from the front. We learned a bit later that these soldiers had been on a brief respite from combat, and when we were brought to them, they were expecting to move forward again. Now they expected to be beating a strategic retreat, to regroup and attack with greater force.

With escape ever-present in our minds, we continued turning onto intersecting roads — all of them minor — for what seemed a long distance, though the vehicles probably never exceeded a speed of 25 to 30 miles per hour. Our truck was followed by a little German jeep bearing about six men. Crowded in as they were, weapons were carried high, so that the vehicle seemed to be fairly bristling with weaponry. Several trucks followed behind the jeep. If we were to escape, it would be necessary to neutralize our guard. Then we must avoid being seen by men in the vehicles trailing us. Were they alert? Watching them, I believed that they were.

The convoy turned onto a larger roadway, and we were passing through a town. In the business district many people were on the sidewalks, going about their evening affairs. Perhaps we could find a time to bolt the truck and escape into a shop. I looked for opportunity.

When the convoy halted on a curve in the street, I tried to make eye contact with curious passers-by. None displayed any emotion toward these Germans. Surely people would be sympathetic to our plight, as civilians riding under guard. Though many people saw us, I noted no reaction. Perhaps they thought we were collaborators. Or they may have realized that there was nothing they could do. There was nothing we could do, either.

A short distance ahead, the convoy paused in front of a church. The drivers were directed to turn and stop on a side road. Men from the vehicles crowded in the space in front of the church while a leader of some sort orated from the church's entry stairs. Now there were distractions, but where could we go? Some men, like our private guard, occupied each of the vehicles I could see in the line.

Our blond, curly-headed guard relaxed and became talkative now. He told us that he had been stationed in Italy, and was in the abbey of Monte Cassino when it had been bombed by the American Army Air Forces. He described what seemed to him to be days of intense bombardment, resulting in displacing sturdy parts of the stone structure. After the bombing, he was moved back to Germany, for recovery and rehabilitation. He had spent two months at home, he said, before he was able to hold a cup in two trembling hands without spilling the contents. He was now 18 years old. I felt compassion for his experience, and knew that it would be difficult to kill him, even if we escaped from our own captivity.

★ ൭൭ ★ ൭൭ ★

Eventually the convoy moved out, progressing slowly down this small, one-lane road. As the shadows of evening deepened, the vehicles moved by fits and starts; why they stopped, I could not tell, nor could I understand what occurred to prompt them again into motion. Then there was heightened vigilance as we moved along a dense wood. Our guard confided that the *Maquis*, an armed French Résistance group, often fired upon convoys from their places of concealment among the trees. I could hope so, but I didn't want to become the innocent victim of friendly fire. The convoy tightened its ranks, with the jeep behind so close that I could make out the details of their faces.

Darkness fell as we left the woods, turning north onto another small road. Some distance beyond, the convoy came to a stop. In the darkness I could make out the silhouette of a farmhouse. We parked almost in front, apparently for the night. Three more men climbed aboard our truck, in search of a more comfortable place to sleep. Five of us huddled sandwiched on the floor, leaning against the tailgate and the cargo in front. I was tired, so managed to sleep in that position.

Sometime during the night I felt a powerful urge to relieve myself. I managed to shift my position and rise up to sit on the tailgate, ready to swing my legs over and to drop to the ground. But a firm grip grabbed my ankle. The man on the other end of that arm demanded to know if I was attempting to escape; if so, he would have none of that. Had I been able to do so, I most certainly would have. But I told him of my need. When he understood, he relaxed his grip and dropped off the truck with me. We moved a few steps, and to the side of the road. Then he accompanied me back to the truck.

★ ൭൭ ★ ൭൭ ★

Daylight woke me to a scene of activity between the convoy and the farmstead. What we did about meals is no longer in my memory, but Bob and I were eventually removed from the truck and taken into the farmhouse to view a sorry scene. Soldiers were rummaging through the place, emptying flour from the bin in the kitchen and carrying sacks out to the convoy. Nor was the furniture spared. In the living room with Bob and me were the truck driver, an Italian soldier, and his assistant who served as interpreter with the German army. Through the chaos, the Italian driver sat placidly amidst the plunder, bouncing the family infant on his knee and crooning lullabies to the child. Near him slumped the child's parents, all too aware of the seizure of their property, and of the magnitude of this loss.

When we remounted the truck, several more passengers climbed aboard. I could see now that the larder and furniture accounted for only a small part of the pillage of the farm family. A fine black and white bull was tethered through the ring in his nose behind our truck. The animal would be unable to keep up the pace set by the truck, so this would ruin him. And for what purpose? I asked that question of the soldier who had tied him up.

"We need a bull like that on my parent's farm," he replied.

Bob remonstrated with him, asking him to release the animal, but he refused. The other soldiers regarded the matter with an air of indifference.

The bull was unprepared to move when the truck began to roll forward, and was jerked ahead, blood running from his nostrils. Gradually accelerating to the customary road speed, the poor animal valiantly rushed forward, pulled by the taut rope. Soon his neck twisted with the effort; foam drooled from his mouth and his eyes rolled. We dragged the tormented beast for more than a mile before some passenger from the rear, finally prompted from inaction by the cruelty, called to the driver to halt, and the bull was released. When we resumed speed, the animal was standing unsteadily in the ditch, his head down and flanks heaving.

The convoy changed direction several times during the day, traversing only the narrowest of roads. Periodically the line of vehicles halted for rest. At such times men clambered off their vehicle and gathered in small knots, smoking, conversing, eating lunch. On one occasion the lead vehicle was intercepted by another one, bearing news of the Allied advance. Apparently, there had been a real breakthrough, and the convoy changed course, not just for an evasive maneuver but to hurry to a more defensible position.

The vehicles drew up in tight formation alongside a small hill. Carrying their weapons, men jumped down off their conveyances, scaled the steep slope, and began to establish their defenses. Others, for reasons I didn't understand, discharged excess gear and heaped it on a fire in the field opposite. Brandishing an automatic weapon, a soldier ordered us to remain on the truck, seated on what we learned later was a box of rifle grenades. Since he took up a position just above us, we considered it expedient to remain in compliance.

Then, with a blare of its horn, a staff car roared up from behind, brakes squealing on the cobblestones, and an occupant stood up. Apparently he announced that this position was about to become entirely encircled by American forces. How quickly the trucks were filled with soldiers and were roaring down the road!

Our driver took an independent course, turning to the right on a small road, sailing along at what was high speed for this truck. Then ahead, we saw an American tank lumbering toward us! This was not the way I wanted it all to end — a victim of one of our own cannon shells. The driver swerved, bumped through the shallow ditch, knocked out one or two fence posts, and, trailing barbed wire, bounded back onto and across the road. After clearing out a section of the opposite fence, he high-tailed it back in the direction from which we had come. Mercifully, the gunner on the tank did not fire. At that time and for the next few minutes, we riders on the truck took aboard several soldiers fleeing from the fields. What a mixed crew they were — paratroopers, infantrymen, and black-suited tank men! We distanced ourselves from the danger.

As the afternoon slipped away, our convoy turned at an intersection onto a wider road. On our right side flowed a large river. We came to a city, where barges were docked along the riverside. This appeared to be an important inland port, which I learned was Compiègne. I knew the Armistice had been signed in that city ending World War I. I thought that meeting had been held in a forest, but I didn't see one.

Following the others, our truck turned to the left and groaned up an overpass over several railroad tracks. Descending again, we turned to the right and headed northward past the railroad depot. A short distance on, the convoy turned on a side street and stopped for the night.

Trouping in through the rear garden, we entered the glare of bright lights in the kitchen area. Already many soldiers were in the house, judging from loud voices upstairs. In the next room, they were congregated around a large table, drinking lustily from a bottle and singing off-key. Two men with rifles blocked our entry beyond the point where we had come in, and we were ordered to sit on the floor with our backs to the wall.

The black-and-white tiled floor was both hard and cool. How cool, we would learn later when we were forced to lie down to sleep on our backs. Though the festivities continued late into the night, I was able, finally, to sleep. I awoke later, stiff and uncomfortable from my position on the unyielding floor. I might as well move about a bit, I thought. A soldier sitting on a chair near the door protested my attempt to sit up, but I persuaded him that nature called. The darkness offered some chance of escape, and if I could get out of the garden and onto the little street, perhaps I could get lost between houses. But the guard remained doggedly close to me, his rifle at the ready. My stiffness somewhat overcome, I returned to the lighted kitchen and lay down again on the cold, hard floor.

On the street in front of the house, and parallel to the railway tracks, the convoy reassembled in the morning. Without fanfare, we were headed north once more. For some reason, there were no vehicles following us closely. Perhaps no more than three or four miles from the city, one of the men on our truck spotted four Allied P-47s following our roadway. A rider alerted the driver, who brought the truck to a skidding halt. All of the passengers jumped off. As we attempted to follow them, someone menaced us with a weapon, admonishing us to remain on the truck. As the several soldiers hid themselves behind a large boulder among the trees, some were aiming their guns at us. If bullets hit the box of rifle grenades, we would have a quick ride to eternity.

"Maybe," said Bob, hopefully, "these planes have been on a strafing mission. They might be out of ammunition." As the planes dipped low in approach, I hoped that he was right.

The planes flew over, then circled for a second pass. Then they flew on. The men from our truck returned from their hiding places. As they neared the road, Bob taunted them. "What brave soldiers you are, running away from the airplanes and leaving us here with no protection!"

One chap, seemingly in a position of leadership, appeared chastened. As they piled once more on the truck, Bob muttered to me. "They've scouted this convoy. No doubt they're radioing our position to their air base. We can expect another sortie — this time with ammo."

Bob's prediction was correct; two low-flying fighter planes came into view on the road behind us, and the truck was evacuated in a tangle of bodies. Had there been any woods beside the road, the occupants would not have had sufficient time to take cover. But I thanked our good fortune to have stopped alongside several slit trenches, provided for just such an eventuality. By the time I had righted myself after my dive into the trench, bullets were raking the roadside. Then the planes circled and repeated the attack, this time from the opposite direction. Cautiously, though foolishly, I raised my head to witness the action. For my folly I was rewarded by an eyeful of dirt, kicked up from the roadside by bullets. The air attack had disabled several vehicles, but ours, though fully exposed on the road, sustained no appreciable damage. We clambered aboard with the full complement of our fellow riders, and the truck pulled ahead, maneuvering around defunct vehicles on the road, resuming its way.

Later that day, when the convoy stopped for a rest break in a town along the route, soldiers clustered by vehicles parked along the curb. Some smoked; others ate from their personal supplies. From under the tarpaulin on our truck someone pulled out a large round loaf of bread. On its crust it bore the stamp "*1941 Afrika Corps*." Failing to cut the tough crust with a knife, he seized the loaf in both hands and struck it over his knee. Shattering, large areas of blue-green mold were revealed. It must not have been fully palatable in that condition, so the soldier reached under the tarpaulin once more, bringing out a large slab of bacon that looked raw, but must have been cured somehow. He placed a slice on his chunk of bread and ate it as a sandwich. Soon others followed his lead, and one soldier handed a bacon sandwich each to Bob and me. Our strong teeth bit into the bread, and the greasy bacon must have made it easier to swallow. The ensuing thirst was assuaged from a canteen offered by one of the soldiers.

A short distance away, the sweet sounds of "Indian Love Call" wafted to my ear, and I recognized the clear voice of Jeanette McDonald singing, of course, in English. Surprised to hear such music in this unlikely place, I glanced at several soldiers gathered around the phonograph. Three of them wore the arm bands of field medics. I learned later that they had been students of the medical college of the University of Vienna, assigned to perform their clinical duties in a combat area. They carried a considerable collection of the songs of Nelson Eddy and Jeanette McDonald, the famous American operetta team of the 1930s, which they played at every opportunity for rest.

At some time on this retreat, our blond guard became criticized for undue gentleness with Bob and me. He was replaced by a well-propagandized soldier — one who proposed a much tougher approach to these American prisoners. Confronting us with an epithet — *Juifs* — he began to call us each "Isadore." I suppose the name represented a stereotyped name applied to Jewish males in general. Surely, he considered that Americans could be Jewish.

I was tempted to ignore this, but Bob Donahue was not. He responded by calling the soldier Isadore in turn. Our new guard recoiled at the name, but retreated. After that, Bob and I each called him Isadore.

★ ★ ★

The convoy was attacked again from the air on numerous occasions, but never again was our seasoned Italian soldier-driver caught in such an exposed condition as on the first strafing. The passengers on the rear of our truck kept constant watch on the skies and alerted the driver each time aircraft were sighted. And each time he managed to steer his clumsy truck into a nearby barn or into the shelter of a house and out of the clear path of attacking planes. Then, standing aside from the spectacle of attack, he observed the savagery inflicted upon the less lucky members of the convoy. When the planes left and all was once again clear, we remounted the truck, which threaded its way through the derelicts littering the road and pursued its course.

★ ★ ★

At one of these stops Bob and I became better acquainted with our driver and his interpreter-assistant, a Tyrolean, who had prepared for medical training in his home town. He told us that he had enrolled for medical training in a college in Spain, and was there during the Spanish Civil War. His relatives lived in Washington, D.C., and from their letters and photographs he had aspired to engage one day in medical practice in that city.

On a weekend excursion by train, he overheard an exchange of sorts between a Spanish officer, a German officer, and an Italian. The three were having trouble communicating, so our assistant-driver, adept in all three languages, volunteered to translate for them. To his regret, he was drafted immediately into military service, and his course of study had to be abandoned. Later he served elsewhere in Europe, where he used his resourcefulness to stay away from combat. There he had met this Italian soldier with whom he was now paired.

Our driver, a seasoned professional soldier, also had a revealing story to tell. As an airman, he had been on the flight of an Italian military aircraft that flew to the Chicago World's Fair in 1934. During peacetime, he had assignments in both Argentina and Japan. In the North African campaign, his unit had been captured by British troops. Freed by Axis aircraft from the sand dune where he was held, he returned to his own army, picked up his equipment, and fought again. He was captured again, this time by Americans. After comparing their food rations with those of his first captivity, he tried never to be captured again by the British.

The *Luftwaffe* had dominated the North African skies at that time. When their planes roared over the sand dunes where prisoners were held without fencing and only by several soldiers, the prisoners had fled. The Italians had returned to their units and continued the war. But when they became hungry, he said, they threw down their rifles and gave themselves up — to the Americans — and ate well again. He licked his lips at the memory of C-rations. Altogether, he said, he had been a prisoner of the Americans 21 times!

Back on the Continent, he was commandeered by the German army to drive a truck. Pleading that he did not understand the German language, he was linked with the multilingual Austrian, and the two men were now together in a joint effort to keep the war at arm's length.

Chapter 17

Retreat in Desperation

IN THE CITY of Cambrai, the convoy entered, dispersed, and parked on a nine-hole golf course. With the prospect of assembling the troops for a lengthy stay, preparations were made to prepare a meal in the two portable cookers that had been towed behind the trucks. The convoy's soldiers made arrangements for their own comfort, and a number of them went into the city. Most returned in time for the evening meal of thick soup, some joyously displaying bottles of cognac they had procured at a warehouse. There was plenty of plain food to eat, but after the fare of moldy bread and raw bacon, I had no complaint. At dark, knots of soldiers sat about, conversing, while others listened to music on the radio.

Bob and I, having no bed rolls of our own, spent the night on the back of the truck, diligently guarded by Isadore. The park-like golf course provided a peaceful setting for sleeping. Wakened in the morning by the bustle of movement in the clearing, I watched as soldiers milled about, each with his own agenda for the hour.

One of the men from our truck approached us and led us to a small pond — a water hazard, perhaps — where he supplied us with razors and a high-quality cylinder of shaving soap. We knelt by the edge of the water, using the surface of the pond for a mirror, and splashed the icy liquid on our faces. Despite the condition of the water, the soap lathered well, and we were much refreshed. Bob's face, which I could see, looked much better groomed, so I concluded that mine might also.

Back at the truck there was something to eat — real bread, I seem to recall — and German military-ration coffee. The morning passed as hours often do when soldiers wait — time suspended until orders are received for action. Some of the troops played cards; a few wrote letters; some engaged in idle talk; a few dozed; others listened to the radio. As prisoners, Bob and I could only partake in that activity as observers. So we sat, listening to the music that others had selected, much of which came from the BBC.

Shortly after noon, as several men clustered around the radio, soldiers switched to a German station reporting the news. The attitude of the listeners changed to one of dismay, then to stunned apathy. The circle of listeners edged farther away from us. Someone turned the dial again to the music of the BBC. Hoping to learn what had produced the consternation among these soldiers, I waited to hear the news in English. But when the news program was introduced, someone abruptly changed the station back to a German-language program. Shortly thereafter, "Lord Haw Haw," the renegade English-speaking propagandist on German radio, announced the news. One of the soldiers explained, "Now you will get the correct news — not British propaganda."

Even discounting his message as being favorable to the Nazi cause, the news we heard was surprising to us.

"Allied troops have bypassed Amiens and are now driving north toward Cambrai," Lord Haw Haw reported.

Considering the rapid movement of our retreating convoy, the speed of the Allied advance was astonishing — small wonder then that the soldiers of the retreating army were disheartened. For a time, the little knot of men seated around our truck just sat in stunned silence. Then one soldier tuned the radio back to a station featuring music.

Isadore was the first to shake off this lethargy. He sprung up on the truck, returning with his large-caliber weapon and an oily cloth. As we watched, he carefully wiped off the visible working parts of the gun, now rusty from disuse, and brought them up to a glossiness that would satisfy an inspecting officer. As he put the cloth away, Bob pointed out to him that he had omitted cleaning the bore of the weapon.

"It will do you no good to fire that rusty thing," he warned. "With that rusty barrel, the gun may explode."

Isadore hesitated just long enough to reply. "That doesn't matter. When I meet the Americans, I shall die fighting, and I want the gun to look good for Hitler!"

And he hurried off to another truck, retrieving an antitank weapon as large as a drain pipe. Bearing the formidable *panzerflug* on his shoulder, he set off on foot and alone to meet General George Patton's armored tank forces.

Isadore was spared the necessity of that pointless sacrifice before he even had left the quiet grounds of the golf course. A staff car came tearing down the access road, its horn blaring. As it came to a halt, an officer stood up and called for the convoy to get underway immediately. The soldiers, losing no time in complying with that order, piled hastily onto the trucks, which then followed the staff car to the gate. We were met by Isadore, who obligingly clambered aboard as our truck swung onto the fronting street and pulled close behind its predecessor.

Soon the air was heavy with the exhaust fumes of many vehicles, and the roar of their engines thundered in the streets. Near the edge of Cambrai we were halted for a priority convoy. A large number of ambulances and trucks emblazoned with the Red Cross emblem were being passed through ahead of us. The true nature of that convoy was perhaps revealed by an *SS* soldier riding in one of the ambulances. With a reassuring grin, he displayed his arm from the window of the ambulance, showing a bandaged finger, as if to indicate that he was truly wounded.

The three-lane highway northeast from Cambrai was clogged with traffic. I had never anticipated so massive a retreat. All lanes on the highway were filled with trucks, automobiles, horse-drawn wagons, and motorcycles. Disabled vehicles held up traffic, which swerved around in any space they could find to maneuver. In the ditches, and often for a distance of 100 yards into the fields on either side of the road, throngs of men plodded along with no thought to maintaining ranks — impelled only, it seemed, by the goading desire to outdistance the tank battalions behind them. The line extended as far as the eye could see. There must be more than 100,000 men moving slowly on that road — perhaps double that number. Where were our planes now? They were missing an enormous opportunity.

The convoy may well have altered its course, for at what seemed an interminable time later, and on a two-lane road, someone reported that we were now crossing the border into Belgium. We came to a small town, similar to many others strung out along the main road. We had passed through the town square, I believed to be Quiévrain. As we curved northward, one of the soldiers spotted an approaching P-38 Lightning. Our driver responded instantly to the banging on the roof of his cab and veered into the driveway between two houses. The plane, flying one-wing down through the narrow street, whizzed past, spitting a hail of bullets into the less fortunate vehicles ahead. Satisfied that the truck was safely protected from aircraft following that same route, our driver and his assistant went to the rear door of the closest house and engaged the occupants in conversation.

Bob and I remained close to the protecting wall of the house and watched the strafing. The first P-38 was followed by several others. Then came a flight of P-47 Thunderbolts, their machine guns chattering. The truck's occupants had fled into the protection of houses along the street, to avoid the onslaught. Their vehicles had not, however. Flat tires, broken glass, and fires testified to the power of this raid.

The Thunderbolts were followed by a flight of P-51 Mustangs, and then by several Supermarine Spitfires, the only British planes deployed in this attack.

While the raid continued, one of the soldiers from our truck showed me his Luger pistol. Extracting the ammunition, he handed it to me. A bystander fidgeted anxiously with his own weapon until he was certain that I could not find means to load the pistol in my hands; then he relaxed. Curious as to how the Luger compared with the mechanisms of the Colt .45, which I had been issued, I field-stripped it on the spot, then reassembled it and returned the weapon to its owner. I liked the Luger; my Colt .45 was a large weapon, really too large for my hand. The Luger, I decided, was about the right size. Having familiarized myself with it, I could now hope that the knowledge might serve me well at some future time.

When the last Spitfire pulled up, the onslaught had lasted for a full hour. With the sky quiet again, our driver, chewing on a slice of bread, came out of the house, trailed by his Austrian assistant. After the briefest survey of the wreckage behind him, he started the engine, and when his men and Bob and I were once again on the truck, he backed onto the street and threaded his way through burning vehicles and dead horses, and out of town.

By this time 40 men, including Bob Donahue and me, were crammed in or sprawled on the truck, which lumbered along more or less independently on a road that bore only occasional vehicles. By the time we drove into Mons that evening, our truck had witnessed 27 attacks by Allied aircraft, in addition to the first fly-over just north of Compiègne. At the edge of Mons, a huge German *Panzer* tank was parked by the edge of the road. After being routed by their enemy, the riders on our truck were cheered by the presence of so formidable a weapon as this. But we never saw a second one.

In Mons, a large body of men and vehicles were marshaled around a park while officials attempted to bring the ragtag elements into some sort of order. The scene was illuminated by bonfires near which loud voices exhorted the troops to turn and repel their pursuers. The officers just might have been more persuasive to these dispirited men had it not been for the latest arrival — a small tank so badly in need of grease that its squeaking could be heard long before it came into view. The *Panzer* that we had passed near Mons was nowhere to be seen.

Only a few of the soldiers from our truck had joined the military pep rally; the rest seemed more inclined to dwell on the futility of counterattacking an Allied tank column with trucks and wagons, when led by the minuscule and ill-lubricated tank. Their companions returned from the bonfire with little enthusiasm for such an encounter. There was no need for putting the matter to a vote; the truck engine growled into life and the truck made its way past other vehicles, and stole out of town

We were now on an open highway, traveling alone in the dark night. The broad roadway unraveling behind the truck reminded me of the road Bob and I had crossed on that first night's walk after leaving the Hombecks' farm. And here we were approaching that area again. Now, if I could drop off the truck, I was certain that I could find my way back to the *Chapelle du Buisson* and find sanctuary. There would be help, even if I did not ask the Hombecks or neighbors known to be sympathetic to take me in; I felt confident that I could elude captivity in that area I had come to know.

I was reassured as my fingers felt the tiny bulge of the cellophane-wrapped Benzedrine tablets overlooked by my interrogators in the outer breast pocket of my jacket. If my efforts to escape became overly taxing, I could count on the Benzedrine to give me extra energy. I would wait awhile, for the last soldier to doze off, before dropping off the truck. In my mind I went over the maneuver — my legs over the tailgate, hanging on to the back, then, facing forward, dropping to the roadway. I would have to swing my legs up so that the momentum of my body would not force me upright, pitching me forward on my face. Expecting that my departure would have been noticed, I would need to roll toward a ditch and out of the line of gunfire.

Having had no previous experience at dismounting from a moving vehicle, I could only hope that the plan was workable. Only a couple of men now showed any sign of wakefulness. When the one closest to me fell asleep, I would alert Bob, and we could exit together; I could convey my idea to him by gesture.

Exhaust fumes from the truck made it hard to keep my eyes open. I rubbed them, fighting sleep. Why didn't the fumes put that last soldier to sleep? The time for escaping was now so near. . . . Then I, too, must have dozed off.

Some change in the sound of the engine — or was it a clashing of gears, or an abrupt change of direction — startled me into alertness, too late for putting my plan into effect. The truck was pulling up in front of a large official-looking building, its facade dimly lighted.

Pulling to a stop, the paratroops' sub-officer got out — the one with the four propellers on his sleeve, ascended the steps, and rang at the front door. He was admitted, but returned shortly after, accompanied by a smartly uniformed officer. The officer glanced at the truck, spoke to the driver, came around back to peer at Bob and me, then reentered the building with the sub-officer in company.

When he returned, he bore a sheet of paper. The truck started ahead once more, and traveled a short distance down the broad street before turning on a lesser street and then into a compound of some sort. At the far end of a square, a dim light illuminated a doorway. The truck pulled up to that door, and Bob and I were ordered to get off. Accompanied by Isadore, we followed "Four Propellers" into the building.

L'Abbaye de la Cambre, the wartime *Gestapo* prison in Brussels, Belgium.

Though I did not know where we were at the time, much later I learned that this was the *L'Abbaye de la Cambre* in Brussels, formerly a convent but used during the Occupation as a *Gestapo* prison and headquarters.

The clatter of hobnailed boots echoed down the narrow hall. In a room off the hallway, an officer scanned the paper given him by Four Propellers, summoned two soldiers to take charge of Bob and me, and dismissed the other two men, who returned to our truck.

Bob and I were ushered through the dimly lit corridor and down a narrow staircase to the basement. While one soldier made certain that we remained docile, the other unlocked a heavy door and swung it wide enough for us to enter. We were pushed into a large room illuminated only by a small bare bulb dangling from the ceiling far above. As the door closed behind us, I took in my surroundings. On the lowest level of a bunk bed slumped a middle-aged man clad in a business suit. He appeared to be the only occupant of this place. Bob addressed our fellow occupant, learning that he had been confined for black market activities. On the floor in front of other beds was a large bucket, whose purpose was not difficult to imagine. That was about all I was able to discern.

As the man told of his fears concerning *Gestapo* justice, my eyes grew accustomed to the dim light, and I glanced idly at names scrawled on the wooden post supporting one corner of the bunk on which he was sitting. There, at eye level were penciled the names of Cecil Pendray, Robert Mathie, and Irving Norris, our three crew members who had been captured where they landed after parachuting from our stricken plane. So they had been brought here, too! I wondered what had happened to them.

I slept well that night, though I do not recall how late it was when I awoke. A guard brought in a piece of dark bread and something for each of us to drink, then left, slamming the door closed behind him. The dial of the watch I had acquired in a trade with one of the Résistance workers in France had long ago lost its luminosity. I didn't know how long we sat there before footsteps sounded again in the hallway. There was a rattling at the door, and Bob and I were ordered to come out. *For what?* I wondered. Could the authorities have some reason to suspect that we had some ties to Belgium — some information they wanted us to divulge? I confess to some anxiety as we climbed the many steps back to the office we had visited the night before.

That concern was dissipated quickly, for awaiting us were two German soldiers from our truck; they had returned to reclaim us. They had already presented authorization for our release and appeared to be in some hurry. We were hustled out to our vehicle, which pulled out of the courtyard, passed under an imposing archway, and wound its way to a major thoroughfare. From the soldiers who had known us longest we learned that Brussels was in peril of being liberated, and that the men with us were to return to Germany for redeployment. We were to ride along with them.

The avenues down which we traveled were broad and flanked by impressive buildings. The soldiers lounging on the back of the truck sat alertly, gazing like tourists at the scenes along the route. Then the truck turned from a large street and entered a very narrow one. Those around us were excited, and pointed out some small monument on the street ahead. The truck halted momentarily beside it, a fountain from which a stream of water issued from the figure of a cherubic, small boy. "That is the Mannikin Pis!" Isadore reported to us. Then, as the truck moved along down the narrow street and into the open square, the Grand Place, at its end, these soldier-tourists attempted to explain the mythical story of the Mannikin Pis. The truck threaded its way through many back streets before arriving once more on a broad avenue.

We were within the city for a long time. I was conscious that we were traveling east, a direction opposite from Œudeghien, and I was eager to get off the truck and set out on foot. But that was impractical for now; it was daylight, and we were joining other vehicles moving in the same direction. I remained hopeful, however, at least until we entered Louvain. In the company of other German army vehicles we passed through an area of the city that boasted several ornate buildings in the Gothic style. The Nazi flag waved prominently over the scene. The swastika led me to believe that, somehow, we had penetrated into Germanic, at least Nazi, culture. How could I find help from these people if, indeed, I could escape the truck? I fell back into semi-resignation to this captivity.

Soon we were bumping along over rough paving stones and into a city the road signs designated as Tirlemont-Tienen. This town had a lesser display of Gothic architecture — a matter that should have brought me some comfort, but we were now much, much farther from Œudeghien than we had been when I fell asleep northeast of Mons.

Isadore, on the other hand, became more agreeable with each passing mile. The sharing of a common peril from air raids had taken the edge off his original animosity toward his American captives. The fact that he had shared his name with Bob and me had gradually transformed the name from epithet to humor. We had entered what anthropologists call a "joking relationship," and though he continued to take seriously his task of guarding us, he now also took us into his confidence.

"When we get to Germany," Isadore told us, "you will see what a beautiful country it is. Once there, we shall part and you will go to join other prisoners like yourselves. We Germans will go to a military installation where we will be reassigned to our own units. After that, I may go home and see my family and my fiancée. But before I do that, I am to go to a special compound where they keep many Aryan women. And there I am to make a baby for Hitler."

Isadore responded seriously to our questioning about his fidelity to his fiancée. "She will not be offended at all," he replied. "She understands that I must do this as a duty to my Fatherland, and that, by obeying this order, I betray her in no way. We true Aryans have an obligation to add to the numbers of a new Aryan generation."

Neither Bob nor I succumbed to the temptation to remark that, in our views, Isadore didn't fit the image that we entertained as Aryan. His dark hair was as different from the propaganda posters displaying the ideal, blond Germanic type — as was the dark-haired Hitler himself. Nor did we challenge the notion that bedding with a stranger "for patriotic purposes" was exempted from the requirement of faithfulness to a future wife. The conversation closed on the confidence shared by our captor.

As the border of Germany came nearer, the other soldiers on the truck, those who had most recently come aboard, gave voice to their hostility toward Bob and me. One Air Infantryman in particular threatened us repeatedly, fingering the concussion grenade at his belt and suggesting that he would like to drop it in our pockets, then push us off the truck. As his overtures became more menacing, those who had journeyed with us the longest dissuaded him from carrying out his threat.

The truck rolled through several almost-deserted towns, none of which featured the Gothic architectural features that had so alarmed me in Louvain. On the south side of the road, we passed an airfield, its large hangars and other buildings camouflaged with oversized windows and doors so that it might, from the air, be mistaken as houses and outbuildings. Though the exteriors were made to resemble the brick buildings common in the region, the layout reminded me of the military airfield at Syracuse, New York, where low clouds had impaired vision sufficiently to dissuade us from trying to land. I guessed that our own pilots would not be fooled by this camouflage.

The truck descended a long hill and entered the city of Liège. After what seemed to be a long ride through the streets, we came to a large open space bordered on one side by commercial buildings and on the other by substantial residences. On the side opposite the commercial buildings, the truck reversed to the curb in front of a house. There, Four Propellers alighted from the cab and addressed the riders in back. In essence, he said that he had a lady friend that he wanted to tell goodbye, before returning to Germany. The driver was instructed to wait here until his return. Then Four Propellers walked down the street and out of sight.

It was a quiet and serene location, for there was very little action in the square, other than people walking by on the distant side of the town center. There was very little vehicular traffic or movement, except the occasional swooping over by a flight of pigeons. As another hour elapsed, men on the truck were becoming uneasy with the waiting.

An ambulance pulled up beside us. Highly polished, it presented an unaccustomed contrast to our truck, so mud-spattered and covered with wilting branches for purposes of camouflage. Two men descended — men perhaps in their 50s, clad in what must have been the dark uniforms of the ambulance service. With attentive care, they assisted an old woman from the vehicle and supported her as they moved to the door of the adjoining house. This activity was noticed by everyone on our truck, and prompted comment by some of the soldiers.

"Just look at that!" exclaimed one man. "Two able-bodied men wasting time and effort on one person too old to contribute anything to society. It would be better were she helped to die, so those men could do something of value."

As several voices were raised in agreement with that statement, I reflected on the opposite view so common among my relatives, friends, and neighbors at home. They would hold that a frail and elderly person had probably contributed much already in life, was likely very dear to other people now living, and thus deserved all the assistance needed at this point to live as easily as possible.

After the ambulance drove off there was little to occupy the attention of loungers on the truck, and they became increasingly restive. More than two hours had elapsed since Four Propellers had gone off to his lady friend, and impatient voices were suggesting that the truck continue on its way, leaving the tardy soldier to his own resources. The driver finally complied with this request, we wheeled out of the square, through city streets, and back to the highway once more. No one seemed concerned that now the highest rank represented on the truck was a Private First Class, a man classified as a cook.

As the sun hung low, the truck turned east, passing over a couple of bridges, and began the climb up the steep hills edging the river valley. The road slid beneath our wheels, and the mood of the riders became lighter, more expectant. Isadore told us that we were on land that had been German until the treaty ending World War I, but now belonged to Belgium. Nevertheless, despite its designation on the map as Belgian, he still considered it to be German territory. The buoyant mood swelled to excitement when a soldier pointed out the markers signifying the border between Belgium and Germany; the soldiers began to sing. They were glad to be home. The singing continued mile after mile as the truck approached Aachen.

We entered the city under the light of a bright moon. But here the ebullient mood quickly faded, for what the moonlight revealed was the mere hulks of buildings that had once held homes. Block after block, the ravages of war were evidenced by gaping windows, roofless walls, and piles of rubble along these ghostly streets.

Aachen appeared to be a city devoid of people. There was no longer conversation among the men on the truck; they were sobered by the sight they beheld. At some intersection with another street I noted one building, perhaps four or five stories high, which stood tall, yet moonlight could be seen beyond, through a large vertical crack. We turned, and on the other side of the street I saw what I took to be a railway depot, its dark brick facade fronting a tangle of twisted girders. This, I thought, was the result of RAF bombing missions; pattern bombing at night spared very little in the target area.

Our truck twisted through silent streets, arriving apparently without error at a military barracks. At least the words over the gate indicated that it had been a barracks area. Inside the damaged wall, jagged lines of brick-work recalled the substantial buildings of a prouder era. Those buildings could no longer boast a single usable room.

I fully expected that our driver would soon take us from this place in search of another locale in which to spend the night. We were gratified, then, when we were taken to a doorway of a building and led down its dimly illuminated stairway to the basement area. Inside, blankets were issued to Bob and me, and the truckload of men was told to bed down on straw-covered troughs set up on the concrete floor.

Chapter 18

Joyriding in Germany

IN THE MORNING, after a breakfast of brown bread and coffee, the truck was loaded, and we departed the bombed-out city of Aachen. Our route led us through flat lands, eventually into Cologne, Germany. The truck stopped on a wide street from which the Cologne Cathedral could be plainly seen. I believe this street was the Ring Road. The debris from bombed-out buildings earlier had been removed between the road and the cathedral, hence our clear view.

From my vantage point it was evident why the edifice held such a lofty place among the architectural masterpieces of the world. The huge Gothic structure appeared to be wholly intact, a matter of little surprise to me, for I recalled the D-Day caution to our bombardment group, to avoid damage to the church at Lisieux, the shrine of Saint Therèse. I thought our bombers would have been ordered to observe the same caution when targeting an area close to this important landmark.

Some of the men piled off the truck in search of diversion

nearby. The rest remained, surrounded by the boredom customary among soldiers who have no immediate assignment. Soon a smiling lady dressed in a house frock walked up to the truck, her arms holding a large pan of red apples. She greeted the soldiers, and by her manner more than by her language, I understood her offer of apples to each of the riders. Outstretched hands quickly diminished her supply, but when she offered apples to Bob and me, one of our captors dissuaded her, saying that we were prisoners of war. The implication was that enemies were undeserving of such delicacies. Rebuffed, the woman departed, entering one of the houses along the street.

After gobbling down their apples, several more of the riders descended and disappeared on their own pursuits. A few minutes later, two small children emerged from the door of the house into which the lady had disappeared, and approached the truck. From their pockets they produced two apples, which they offered to Bob and me. No one on the truck objected to this gesture of friendship by small children. Apparently, children were considered incapable of making the distinctions between persons in general and enemies of their country. Or, perhaps, the soldiers least charitable to us enemies had been the ones to get off the truck. The apples were delicious.

Hunger brought the rest of the soldiers back and took all of us to a downtown restaurant. They did not hesitate taking two prisoners in with them. Could they have left us unguarded on the truck? Inside, the restaurant was an attractive place, its dark woodwork highly polished — in contrast with the gleaming table linen. Waiters dressed in formal attire solicited our orders, and it was agreed by the consensus of our captors that we would all have the same fare. I wondered how the food would be paid for; neither Bob nor I had any German currency, and I didn't expect that any of our captors would care to pay our share. But I was hungry and had no disposition to complain.

We were placed at a long table at the rear of the restaurant, Bob and I with our backs to the other diners. I was unfamiliar with much of the food that I was served, but found it to be as tasty as it was plentiful. I was particularly impressed by the sauerbraten, but also enjoyed the dish containing cooked red cabbage, neither of which I had ever encountered previously. I had quite eaten my fill before the arrival of dessert and coffee, but was feeling the pain of the sudden change to a rich diet. As one of the soldiers paid for the dinner by signing the bill, Isadore accompanied me to the bathroom, and even in my haste I saw that Bob, escorted by another soldier, was losing no time in following. I noticed, too, a table occupied by several officers dressed in smart black uniforms. They cast quizzical glances at me as I passed by, so poorly suited for the elegance of this restaurant, and curiously, also, in the company of Nazi soldiers. I inferred that they were *Gestapo*, but was in too much of a hurry to let that worry me just then.

That tasty dinner had given me little nutritional benefit, and as I turned to wash my face, there was a sharp knock at the door. While Isadore hurried me toward the street, I was aware that another soldier was hustling Bob in the same direction. Coming out the door, I heard the truck engine roar into life. As it raced away from the curb, we swung on board. Looking back, I saw the *Gestapo* agents waving furiously and futilely at us all.

Directly opposite the restaurant was a tall building. High on its walls someone had painted, in English, "THE TABLE IS LAID," and below that, the Morse code "V," used by our Allies to symbolize victory. So, despite their massive display of power, the Nazis were vulnerable.

Our Italian driver drove swiftly down the street and rounded a corner onto another. At some safe distance from any possible pursuit, he pulled the truck to the curb, where the occupants laughed about the adventure and decided what to do next. Someone knew of a tavern in a small town a few miles down the Rhine River, and we set out.

We unloaded from the truck, parked directly in front of the tavern. With Isadore, Bob and I waited until the others had entered the establishment. A long bar extended almost entirely across the rear of the room, with a few small tables in front. A larger table was positioned directly next to the window, in the space created by the recessed entryway. Isadore bade us sit at the front table, and detailed one of the soldiers to stand with his back to the bar where he could keep an eye on us in case we should try to escape.

Very soon the tavern became the scene of camaraderie as all the celebrants were served. Noting that Bob and I were seated quietly at the front table, someone spoke to the barmaid, who saw to it that our glasses were never empty. It was the beginning of a long afternoon. The man detailed to watch us from the bar was replaced by another, then another. The

Tyrolean assistant to the truck driver, in a generous mood, went to the truck, procuring from some place in the cab a foil-wrapped loaf of very black bread and a tube of Italian cream cheese. The barmaid brought two small plates and a table knife, and Bob and I began to replace our lost lunches, washing down the rich bread and cheese with beer.

When evening approached and the men at the bar began to give thought to other diversions, they told us to leave with them. By that time, I was suffering acute discomfort and, bloated by gas, could not stand erect. The barmaid provided directions, and two men supported me as we went down the street and around the corner to the next block. Then, behind the tavern in which we had spent the afternoon, we entered the town jail.

The jailer, probably the town marshal I thought, was a tall, erect man. His uniform, topped by a metal hat surmounted by a tall spike, seemed to be from a past era. Though I was too uncomfortable to pay more than passing attention, his manner was far more gentle than that suggested by his uniform. He opened the wooden door to display a narrow cell that surely would not invite criticism of him for coddling prisoners. The bed was a narrow wooden affair, slanted from the raised wooden pillow at the top to a lower level at the feet. The sleeping surface was wooden also. There was no sign of mattress or bedding. Still doubled over with pain, I sat on the edge of the bed, my head in my hands.

The jailer's wife entered a few moments later, moved by the news that a young man was suffering in her building. Though language was a barrier to our communication, her manner exuded compassion and she quickly left the cell, returning a few moments later with her arms full of blankets and a soft pillow. These she tucked around me, making me as comfortable as was possible. She or her husband checked on me at several intervals during the night.

In the morning, I was feeling better when the jailer brought breakfast. His wife looked in on me also before the soldiers from our truck arrived to take me away. Memories of her kindness and that of the lady with the apples would linger with me no matter what treatment I was to receive later in captivity.

★ ★ ★

The truck, which was waiting nearby when Bob and I were ushered out of the jail, followed the Rhine back toward Cologne. Just out of Cologne, on a road rising from near-river level toward the bordering hill, the truck was hailed by a man dressed in tweed jacket, hat, and riding breeches encased in long stockings, who appeared to be having car trouble. His manner proclaimed authority, and the truck halted beside his auto.

The trouble was a flat tire, and the man saw no incongruity in a civilian halting a truckload of soldiers in the expectation that they would repair his personal vehicle. Quickly a number of soldiers jumped off the truck and set to his task. Then, like an inspecting officer, he walked to the rear of the truck, examining its cargo and the men who had not descended to do his bidding. His curiosity aroused by our dress and appearance, he learned that we were American airmen, captured in civilian clothes.

In his mind, prisoners were to be interrogated, and airmen berated for the damage they inflicted on his native land.

"What kind of barbarians are you," he demanded in English, "to bomb such a splendid monument as our lovely cathedral?"

I replied that from what I had seen, it had been spared. He thought otherwise, and spoke of broken glass and damaged masonry. I told him that I was quite certain that our bombardiers had been issued orders to preserve important cultural landmarks, and that if there were indeed damage, it was due to accident, not intent.

Furious, the accuser was not through with the argument yet, and railed on. Bob then pointed out that there were important targets nearby, and that if, in targeting the bridge, antiaircraft fire jostled a plane, its bomb load would fall in an unintended trajectory, possibly damaging the surrounding area.

"Then you should not aim at the bridge!" he shouted.

Bob replied, " If you have such a target near your cathedral, you should not fire at our planes when they come to bomb it."

Whether it was that retort that ended the exchange or the fact that the tire had been repaired I do not know. But our contingent of soldiers climbed aboard the truck, and we continued on downtown. Where we might have headed later I do not know, but I could see that the soldiers were becoming increasingly restless. Whether it was their eagerness to rejoin their units and sally forth to repel the advancing enemy, or the tension evoked from the conflict between their desire to see family and sweethearts and the obligation to rejoin their units, I could not say. But they now decided that the time was appropriate for them to deposit their prisoners in some place equipped to deal with them.

Increasingly, now that they were in their homeland, they abandoned speech in French, except when they needed to address Bob or me, and I failed to understand much that was said. But they had decided that, as airmen, we should be put in the custody of the *Luftwaffe*. And where could they find the *Luftwaffe*, if not at an airfield?

Some time later, after rumbling through the streets of Cologne and elsewhere, we arrived at the edge of an air base. At the gate, the driver's oral statement of his mission gained us entrance, and the truck swung in a wide arc through the extensive area in front of the administration building. As the truck was being parked, a sporty dark red Mercedes roadster pulled up alongside a low building. The driver paid no attention to us, but he attracted notice from everyone with us. On the rear seat or bench of the roadster perched a large red chow dog, groomed as if for exposition. As the driver disembarked, his presence appeared like a fitting model for a *Luftwaffe* recruiting poster. Tall, slender, and blond, his immaculate blue and gray uniform was accented by an impressive array of medals.

I do not know what he did next, for one of the soldiers from the truck prompted Bob and me to descend and follow him into the administration building. After a short flight of stairs and down a long hallway to our left, he halted us at the door of an office. Inside, a gray-haired, bespectacled officer sat behind a desk. By his insignia I guessed that he might be, perhaps, a Lieutenant Colonel. Upon learning that these two disheveled men in tattered civilian clothing were to be turned in as prisoners of war, he announced that he was not in charge, and that action on this request would have to await the arrival of his commandant. As he turned back to his paperwork, we three were left standing in the large outer office.

But we were not there for long, for footsteps could be heard coming down the hallway. They stopped at the door of the office, which opened swiftly. In stepped the handsome flying officer we had seen disengage himself from the Mercedes roadster.

The older officer nodded to us, signaling that this officer was the base commander. The soldier who had escorted us into the building addressed him, explaining that we were American airmen captured in France, and were to be handed over to the *Luftwaffe*.

This news touched a sore nerve with the officer, enraging him. As he unbuttoned his holster and whipped out his side arm, he asked, "Who is the pilot of you? I shall shoot him!"

We tried to explain that neither of us was a pilot, but he was inflamed beyond comprehension, and stormed at us with curses from several languages.

"I will shoot you!" he repeated.

At that point our guard became our protector. He moved between the officer and Bob and me, then swung open the door. Bob and I lost no time in bolting out and rushing down the hall. Our captor had swung the door closed as he left the office, and followed us down the hallway and out of the building.

Those on our truck seemed to know our haste, and the truck was already moving through the front lot, not hesitating as we piled aboard, our escort swinging up behind us. The truck gathered speed through the entrance gate, slued around the corner to the fronting road, and sped away. At what seemed a safe distance from the air base, our driver turned on a joining road and halted the truck. There the occupants had a hearty laugh, and shared their knowledge with Bob and me.

While we were in the administration building, some of the soldiers had occasion to talk with enlisted personnel at the air base. They had learned that the base commander, a Colonel, a pilot accustomed to victory in aerial encounters, had recently been vanquished in combat with an American P-51. The proud owner of two Iron Crosses had lost his prized FW-190 airplane and was forced to fly an older ME-109, held together by baling wire. Not only that, but with this substitute plane, his opportunity to win his third Iron Cross seemed remote. "And he *would* have shot you, too!" they laughed.

Our captors remained steadfast in their desire to turn us over to German military authorities, and later that day drove up to the *Wehrmacht* headquarters in a nearby city in hopes of leaving us there. The truck, loaded with its mixed crew of combat troops, drew the attention of the young girls in the school beside us. They crowded to the windows to see what was happening below. No doubt few had ever witnessed a mud-spattered military truck adorned with wilting greenery. The highest ranking soldier still on board was the Private First Class, the cook who had jumped aboard as American tanks had come perilously close, north of Paris. Now he was delegated to speak to the officer in charge of this local headquarters.

A large, robust man, the cook strode confidently across the street and up to the door marked by the swastika flag. We could see the head of an officer peering out the window. Very shortly after, our delegate returned, trailed by a small pudgy Captain. The officer peered with distaste on these two civilian-clad men, then walked around the truck, giving it a cursory inspection. What he saw angered him.

"We do not accept *Luftwaffe* prisoners here," he growled. "And what are you doing, joyriding around Germany in a military vehicle, wasting good German gasoline?" That much I could understand. He continued with an order. "Clean up this truck, and leave it here with me."

The officer's dictum was received with resentment by our captors. They came to the conclusion, probably correct, that the rear-echelon brass had no idea of the unfavorable dimensions of the war in which their country was engaged at this time. Instead of commending the soldiers for having survived against great odds, they were berated for using the gasoline that had saved their lives.

As soon as the officer was in his building, the big cook took off his helmet and slammed it on the brick roadway. The resounding clang brought more girls to the windows above, and a call from the officer in the local headquarters. The cook was summoned immediately to the building. Shortly after that, the big cook returned, his face reddened. He had been slapped soundly for his display of insolence.

Somehow, the truck was quickly emptied of its cargo and the faded twigs and branches were removed and carried out of sight. From someplace, a bucket of water and cloths materialized, and with diligent application of elbow grease, the truck was ready to pass inspection, which it did. The men shouldered their gear, ready to walk to find another form of transportation. What remained was a sizable wooden box resembling a footlocker I had used early in my Army training. Bob and I were told to carry that, and we trudged off. The box was heavy, and it seemed a long way before we arrived at our destination — the train station.

Perhaps our Italian driver and his Tyrolean aide had remained with the truck. At any rate, I do not recall their being with us during the ensuing days. On the way to the station, our captors decided what our destination was to be, but Bob and I were not privy to that information. The men had no difficulty in securing passage; it appeared that a military uniform served as a train ticket. I do not know what was done to provide passage for Bob and me, but there was never any doubt but that the group intended to keep an eye on us.

★ ~ ★ ~ ★

We were in a passenger car on the train, a sort of day coach with seats on each side of a center aisle. Bob and I were seated together, the box at our feet. Some time after my stomach alerted me that it was mealtime, one of the soldiers opened the box, which contained a variety of canned foods. Bob and I were privileged to share in the meal. Now I was less regretful that the box had been so heavy to carry to the train.

Many of the stations through which we passed showed signs of major damage, though most of the debris had been meticulously cleared away. Between stations, the roadbed was often bumpy, evidence of patched-up bomb damage. Our captors, having so recently been exposed to assaults from the air, seemed to dismiss the destruction along the way, so happy were they to be once more in their homeland.

It may have been mid-afternoon when the men got to their feet at a station and, summoning Bob and me to join them, exited the train. With one of them leading the way, we boarded a streetcar. We captives had no idea of our destination, but at some point the streetcar was halted and the whole group got off. After walking double file for few hundred yards, our guide stopped at an iron gate, swung it open, and entered the walk leading to a house, the entire group following. The guide hurried up the steps and rang the doorbell.

"Mama!" he shouted, embracing the middle-aged woman who answered the door. With considerable emotion, she called the visitor's sister to the door. The happy reunion was enjoyed vicariously by the man's companions. Finally he turned away from his mother and sister and introduced each of them, ending with "and our two prisoners of war." Shortly, mother and sister retreated to the house to gather appropriate wraps, and we all trouped down the street to take a promenade through a neighborhood park.

Though it was not a long walk, we had thoroughly covered the area of the park, and when the circuit was completed, we took leave of the returning soldier and his family members; we never saw him again.

As the remainder of our group strolled back to the bus stop, the men discussed what they might do during the rest of the day. Some wanted to locate a hospitable bar; others chose a cinema. The others suggested finding a means to make new acquaintances. A couple of the soldiers, determining that two *kriegsgefangen* — prisoners of war — would otherwise provide a damper to their pursuits, escorted Bob and me to the city jail.

There we were booked and shown to a room. The two beds in our quarters provided the same level of discomfort we had met earlier — wooden slats nailed to a frame, with a raised ledge to serve as a pillow. But there were blankets on the bed, and we had arrived in good time for supper. The fare was Spartan, but the food, having been prepared for German citizens, was better than might have been served to American prisoners, had we been expected.

No one tucked me into bed that night, and I felt fortunate that no one thought it necessary. Though the bed was hard, I had no trouble sleeping, and was wakened in the morning by the arrival of breakfast — plain food, too, but filling. We also had the opportunity to wash, a rare luxury. I no longer recall what arrangements, if any, there were for Bob and me to shave.

The morning was not far advanced when our captors arrived and resumed custody of us. Soon we were at the railroad station, where we met the rest of our contingent. We boarded the next train and traveled much as we had on the previous day, except that we changed trains once or twice. Arriving at another city, the events of the preceding day were repeated, with another soldier reunited with the female members of his family, another promenade, and our being turned in at the local jail.

The holding units of the jail were located on the second floor, above the police station. Bob and I were ushered into a large room, separated from another large room in which a number of prisoners were lodged. The two rooms shared a door, the glass window of which afforded some privacy by virtue of a blanket draped on the other side. The noise of our entry aroused the curiosity of the men, and the blanket was pulled aside, revealing several faces at the window. We exchanged glances at one another's milieus, but were unsuccessful in bridging the language barrier, so as the blanket was pulled down once more, all of us returned to our own affairs.

Our room was furnished with two bunks, located on opposite walls. The one on the far side of the room looked very much like those we had seen in other German jails. The other one, though, on the inside wall near the stairway, was much higher than ordinary. A large blanket covered not only the bed but also draped to the floor. Bob chose the more distant bed, leaving me the higher one. There seemed no great advantage to either of the two beds. Near the foot of my bed a barred window set into the wall looked out on the walls of adjacent buildings. Since there was no street, the view was not particularly interesting. The bars in the window did not budge against my testing, so I turned to making my surroundings as comfortable as possible for the night.

Supper was, as I expected, a simple meal and was quickly consumed. Bob and I chatted for awhile, recalling the events of these past few days and imagining what might be in store for us next, before the light was extinguished for the night. I had climbed up onto the high bed and had fallen into the sleep of one who had become accustomed to irregular and unpredictable situations.

A piercing sound shattered the stillness of the night. In terror, I fairly flew out of the bed, seeking meaning to this continuing scream. The sound was coming from under me, and the tone first rose, then lowered. Now I recognized the air raid siren, and the focus of my terror shifted from the sound itself to its meaning. Was a British raid aimed at this city? If so, pattern bombing would create peril for all persons, including us. I dashed to the open window and placed all my weight against its bars in an attempt to loosen them. No matter how hard I pulled and pushed, they remained stubbornly in place. Through the window I could see searchlights probe the sky, and antiaircraft guns roared, the burst of their shells following shortly after. But no bombs fell near us, and after an interval the siren sounded again. The sound of the "All Clear" was indistinguishable from the earlier warning.

The siren shrieked its warning and its "All Clear" several times that night. Each time I rushed to the window in a desperate attempt to loosen the infernal bars. Now, terrified and sleepy, I became more able to appreciate the dread that night bombing raids could produce in a population — here, or in England, or anywhere.

Morning brought a jailer to lead us across the hall to the toilet for morning ablutions, followed by a breakfast of bread and a warm beverage. Then two of our companions came to reclaim us, and again we boarded a train for another unannounced destination. This pattern, with visits to soldiers' families, persisted for the next several days.

During those travels, I was surprised to note that we passed through the rail connection at Kassel what I thought was possibly eight times. I learned later that Kassel was a major connecting link in the German rail system. We must have zigzagged through a wide swath of what was east-central Germany. However, my count may have included other rail journeys, after we parted with our captors. It might have been that we had passed through Kassel less often during that particular week. During those days, however, the number of German soldiers in our company had lessened considerably.

What stands out most clearly in my mind is the last evening I spent with these men, though I do not know the name of the city at which we had detrained. In the company of Isadore and another soldier, Bob and I sat at a table in a large waiting room. A number of Hitler Youth boys arrived on another train. As the group broke up to go home, a young boy disengaged himself from the others and came over to us, apparently mesmerized by the presence of our captors, who bore the stamp of real soldiers.

The five of us lingered at the table, the soldiers talking of recent events and the young lad sitting quietly but in rapt attention, until I became very uncomfortable, wondering why he was permitted to stay out until so late an hour.

Excusing himself for a moment, Isadore's companion procured a copy of the German army newspaper, which apparently had just arrived by train. Both soldiers examined it eagerly, telling Bob and me in French the news they thought would be of interest to us. From personal experience we knew that the Allies' Western Front had been moving swiftly. Though we questioned the accuracy of some of the information, we had no way of checking its veracity. It had been two weeks since we had heard news from the Eastern Front, but for the Nazis, that news was not good either. The two soldiers were worried and seemed to regard these reverses with deeper concern than the rout that we had just witnessed on the Western Front.

Upon impulse, Isadore turned to us and speaking confidentially said "You are both better men than I expected. Perhaps the Americans are not so bad after all, just misled in fighting against us Germans. Why don't you Americans join us and fight against the Russians?"

Bob Donahue's body tensed as he answered, "We will not do that!"

His response was quick and unequivocal. Bob and I had seen some of the destruction visited on Belgium and France by the Nazis and we knew of the Occupation army's harsh demands for forced labor and material goods from the people of those countries. I had enlisted in the struggle to counter the atrocities for which the Nazis were responsible, and neither of us had any intention of recanting that purpose, nor of waging war against our Allies.

"But," Isadore persisted, "you do not know how much you have been misled by your Generals who have financial interests in this war. They have led you into battle against us, while your real enemies are Russians."

I replied that I believed that it was they who had been misled, especially by the German arms manufacturers, and by their national leadership.

"Not so!" retorted Isadore. "I myself have seen the battle tanks produced by your Generals, Sherman and Lee. It is they who have misdirected you."

Seizing upon the error in this bit of clinching evidence Isadore offered, I thought to ask, "Have either of you men studied the history of the American Civil War?"

Isadore's companion volunteered that he had done so, in *gymnasium* — high school.

"Do you remember the name of the famous General of the Confederacy?" I asked.

"Yes," was the reply, "it was General Robert E. Lee."

"That is right," I answered. "And what was the name of the victorious General for the Union?"

Hesitating only a moment, he responded, "It was General Grant — General Ulysses Grant." His eyes widened as he began to understand the incongruity of the belief that General Lee could be an arms manufacturer now and also a General in a war ended 80 years earlier.

I persisted in the questioning. "And do you recall the name of the Union General who set fire to Atlanta, then marched his troops through Georgia to the sea?"

Isadore's companion did remember the name — General William Tecumseh Sherman. At that point, both soldiers came to the realization that their beliefs, previously unassailable, might conceal great errors. How much more had been sheer propaganda?

I had never seen men so thoroughly shaken. Both sat with their shoulders slumped. Then they got to their feet. It was time to see that their prisoners were locked in for the night. They dismissed the young lad who only moments earlier had been enthralled by their heroic presence, and sent him to his home. One of the men procured a flashlight, and together we left the waiting room and walked out on the scarred and twisted platform. A building on the platform was to serve as our jail for the night. Isadore pointed the flashlight through the doorway, revealing a chaotic ruin of gritty remains from an earlier bombing. The light revealed several small stools and scraps of canvas strewn in disorder about the room. The men offered an apology, and suggested that Bob and I pull some stools together to fashion a bed; the canvas would have to suffice for covers. Then they were gone, the door locked behind them.

In the dark, as we tried to assemble some places to sleep, we began to understand why the men had kept us up so late in the station. They knew what facilities were awaiting us this night, and had helped make the night as short as possible. They had done us a favor. There were not enough stools to construct two beds that could extend the full length of our bodies, but we were able at least to elevate our bodies above the filthy concrete floor. The bits of canvas were stiff, dirty, and too small to cover us entirely, but they did serve to ward off some of the cold. The arrangements were not good for sleeping, but we managed somehow to slumber fitfully.

When morning came, we were grateful to be released from our quarters. Hot drinks and a bite to eat were available in the station before we boarded the train one final time.

It was after noon when we arrived at another town and were delivered to a hospital. I believe Isadore had brought us to a military hospital in Blankenburg or Wernegrode, only a short distance from Halberstadt.

Isadore spoke with an official, apparently making arrangements for our transfer. Two doctors, conversing as they strolled past, slowed to look at us. Their unfeeling gaze reminded me of rumored stories I had heard of medical experiments on prisoners in the concentration camps. With a brief goodbye, our military retinue parted, and Bob and I sat uncomfortably in the waiting room of the hospital, guarded by an unfamiliar soldier.

Chapter 19

In Company with Other Prisoners

THROUGH THE HOSPITAL'S large windows I was aware of activity in the office nearby, and that a telephone call was being placed, very likely about us — the two newly arrived prisoners. Still, Bob Donahue and I sat on a bench in the stark waiting room for an hour or more, fidgeting at the unaccustomed silence and solitude. Eventually, a soldier entered and reported at the office. He spoke with our guard, and the two of them ushered us to a small vehicle waiting on the parking area outside.

Just a few miles later, we arrived at the edge of Halberstadt. The name on the road sign again brought back memories of World War I flying ace G-8, and the biplane by the name of Halberstadt that was frequently engaged in the combat stories. When the vehicle pulled up at a work camp situated beside a bombed-out factory, it was easy for me to believe that this was the very site where that World War I aircraft had been manufactured.

Inside a high barbed-wire fence, the work camp consisted

of a few small wooden buildings adjacent to the highway on which we had arrived. Just behind the camp, and separated by a narrow street, was a row of wooden barracks, behind which was a scene of desolation extending for perhaps 200 yards.

Apparently all of the prisoners were away on work detail. The office was staffed by a Sergeant, and he used this rare opportunity to play the inquisitor. Gruffly, he questioned Bob and me: what type of airplane we had been flying; where and when it had gone down; where we had gotten the French *cartes d' identités*; and where we had acquired these civilian clothes. Receiving no replies save our names, ranks, and Army serial numbers, he became increasingly belligerent. In the company of a guard, he led us to a small wooden building resembling a storage shed. Again he repeated his line of questioning and, dissatisfied by the lack of response, he threatened to withhold food until we told him all he wanted to know. We had not eaten since that sparse breakfast, and we were hungry; but we refused to divulge further information. He departed, locking the door. We were alone in the bare room.

Later, after a very long afternoon, sounds from outside our window announced that a truck had pulled up to the camp. There was a bustle of activity in the area close to the road, but out of our line of vision, from the small window in our room. Then the sound of male voices, speaking in English, suggested that a prison work detail had returned, and that they were persons with whom we could talk, if permitted. Quiet reigned for a few moments, while Bob and I continued to peer fruitlessly out the window.

The clamor of voices came from around the corner of a nearby building, then several men dressed in woolen trousers and cotton shirts, rolled up to the elbows, advanced to our window. The man in front, a lithe fellow with dark curly hair, shouted to us.

"That fool Sergeant has been unpleasant, has he? He said he had refused you food until you told him all about yourselves."

We responded in the affirmative, adding that we were American fliers picked up in the front lines near Paris, and we had been with the retreating troops since then.

"Well, you shall have a good supper, and if the Sergeant objects, we told him we would cut off his supply of cigarettes and boot polish!"

"What's the story on this huge building standing in the center of all this rubble?" Bob asked.

The response was a surprising tale of the sly planning of two air raids, carefully designed to destroy German morale by stopping production. The factory had been an aircraft plant, though it had been manufacturing Junkers aircraft, not Halberstadts. Standing apparently unharmed in the midst of the destruction was a large, new building. That had been the final assembly plant, a replacement for the one destroyed by bombs some months earlier. It had been scheduled to go into operation on the very day of the bombing. But with production at a halt because of the absence of the assembly section, the new building was useless — no parts would be available for assembly. As testimony to the accuracy of the bombing, buildings on the streets flanking the factory stood virtually unharmed — a very few roofs missing only a tile or two, and a very few windows broken.

Many years later, I learned that this splendid bombing performance had been accomplished by our own 493rd Bombardment Group. On August 5, 1944, 21 of our B-24 Liberators had dropped 500-pound general-purpose bombs and 100-pound incendiary bombs on the aircraft component plants. (Martin W. Bowman and Truett Lee Woodall, Jr., show an aerial view of this raid on page 58 of their *Helton's Hellcats: A Pictorial History of the 493rd Bombardment Group*.)

The man outside our window told us that the barracks standing inside the next barbed wire enclosure housed Russian women. "A couple of small fires had been started in there by the bombing, but there wasn't much damage," he said.

The women, he told us, did the hard work at the camp, picking up debris, and so forth, and were just then coming in from their work details.

Our visitors had to leave to prepare the evening meal. They promised to bring our food when it was ready.

We were cheered by the prospect of something to eat. We didn't expect much. After all, it was a prison work camp, and didn't seem to boast such frills as a good kitchen.

Our room was almost bare, and there was very little to do to pass the time, so we sat on the floor, leaning our backs to the wooden wall, and tried to maintain a conversation by speculating on our uncertain future. After what seemed like a long wait, someone approached our door. It was opened by one of the men to whom we had been talking through the window. We could see, across the road, a long line of ragged women, standing in front of the barracks. Our prisoner-hosts trooped in, bearing a feast of proportions such as we had not imagined.

"You Brits are good providers," I complimented as I dug into a large portion of corned beef hash.

One of them thanked me, replying however, "But we're not British. There isn't one in our entire camp. We are Colonials of the Empire. I'm South African, . . . this chap is Scottish, . . . and he is Irish. We are proud of that, and what we have in common is our dislike of the British!"

Somewhat surprised by this confession of Allied disunity, I took a big bite of bread slathered with apricot jam and washed it down with a swig of hot tea.

"Where do you get food like this?" Bob questioned.

"We have our daily rations of bread, potatoes, *ersatz* tea, and soup. And, as workers, we each get one Red Cross parcel of food each week. In our little kitchen we can mix the food to make a more palatable diet."

Another man chimed in, "And we sometimes get parcels from home — not much food, but what we do get can be traded for other things we want, including meat."

The South African, seemingly the camp leader, added, "Everything you have here tonight came from the potato and bread ration, plus one-half Red Cross parcel."

And it was more than we could eat.

With wood shavings for a mattress placed on the wooden floor, and woolen blankets supplied by our fellow prisoners, we fashioned an acceptable bed. Then, as the lights were turned off, we lay down with full stomachs, in quarters far cleaner and more comfortable than the night before, and we prepared for a sound sleep. I was aware briefly of the rhythmical probing of searchlights in the compound outside our building.

The sounds of the camp rising for the routines of a new day stirred me to wakefulness. Our British Colonial prisoners brought us breakfast, and gave us news that we would be transported that day to their own main camp, *Stalag XI A*, the one where prisoners were routinely rotated for medical checkups, recreation, and other administrative purposes. Shortly after, the motors of vehicles coughed into life and took these men to their work assignments outside the camp.

After a stretch of sterile waiting, the Sergeant opened our door. Despite the fact that the inmates had quashed his pose as officious interrogator, he attempted to salvage his damaged image, and acted as though he himself had decided to defer to official *Luftwaffe* interrogators, who would certainly extract the information needed from us. Then, accompanied by a guard, we were taken through the streets of Halberstadt to the railway station, where we boarded a train for our destination.

The train headed north, then east, and passed through Magdeburg via very bumpy tracks. Then, circling to the north, it headed east again, through smaller towns, past Loburg, and north again, stopping finally at a building that bore the sign "Altengrabow." We alighted on what appeared to be an industrial loading dock and walked to the north end, where steps descended to ground level. Perhaps a half-mile ahead, I could see large buildings that resembled an industrial site. The road at this stop was deep in powdery dust, which we learned later had been churned up by the treads of heavy tanks produced at an underground arsenal, beneath the prison camp. We were escorted a short distance to a brick building, which served as administrative offices. The official business there was transacted swiftly, and the soldier who had accompanied us on the train was replaced by two soldiers from the camp.

We were taken through an area that was part of a pine forest, intersected by several residential streets serving rows of nearly identical large, brick houses. Then we followed paved streets edging on sizable compounds of low brick buildings surrounded by high barbed-wire fences overlooked by guard towers. We were passed through a gate leading to a small area enclosing a large brick building, which resembled horse stables I had seen at several state fairs back home. A tall brick wall extended from below the eaves of the roof on the west side, near a compound containing low wooden buildings.

The center of this long building was empty, except for several supporting columns. Flanking the center space were brick walls, broken at intervals by stout wooden doors. The apparent similarity of this building to a large horse stable was made all the more striking by the way the cells were arranged on the outer walls.

The soldiers who had escorted us into the camp were dismissed and left the building; the door was firmly closed as they departed. Once inside, we were greeted affably by a large prisoner who, when given charge of us, addressed us in simple English. He told us he was Polish, and the trustee in this solitary confinement block. He apologized for having to lodge us both in a single cell, for the building was crowded. With that, he opened a door halfway down the confinement area, which would be our quarters. The sanitary facilities, he said, were located on the opposite side of the building; we would have the opportunity to use them three times daily — and at other times in case of urgent need. He could be summoned by a knock on the cell door. Food would arrive at our door three times daily, and opportunity would be provided each day for exercise.

Inside the cell, the original use of the building was obvious. My first impression was correct. In an earlier era, it had been a horse stable. That was amply demonstrated by the high cement trough situated against the far wall, divided with a deep section for hay and a shallower section for grain.

The cell was narrow, with sufficient room for a single wooden bed not unlike those we had encountered in several German jails, with a narrow aisle between the bed and the wall. The bed might be wide enough for both of us to sleep at the same time, providing we each lay on our sides — certainly not on our backs.

Above the trough was a window, its white paint peeling in small blotches from its panes. The door had a small peephole at eye level, covered from the other side by a shingle-like board, which could be pivoted aside to allow a guard or the trustee to peer in at will. The diminutive dimensions of our quarters emphasized the fact of our confinement and led us to try to explore the world outside. By climbing on the bed, we could crouch on the top of the trough and try to peer through small holes in the peeling paint on the window.

Though the view was limited, I could see the brick wall that extended parallel to the side of the building, perhaps ten yards from it. But I could not see what was between the wall and our cell. Over the top of the wall could be seen the rooftops of buildings in the next compound, and through a gap between the buildings, men could be seen boxing in a raised ring.

Though that was all I could make out about our surroundings, I took comfort in the restricted view, at least for now a part of my present world.

Having explored the area visible from our cell, Bob and I sat on our cot and tried to help pass time by conversation. By now we had explored most of the topics readily available for sharing, and we were at pains to reach deeper into memory for fresh items of interest. It had been three months since our plane had plunged into the brown soil of Belgium.

Our activity was interrupted by a knock accompanied by a scraping sound, as the cover was lifted over the peephole in the door. Looking up, we saw the trustee's face peering through the tiny pane. After opening the door, he carried in a large serving bowl full of shredded cooked vegetables. Evidently, our portion had been taken from the bottom of a large tureen of soup; the watery portion of the meal had probably been served to others. With a friendly grin, he closed the door behind him and shot the bolt as he left.

Placing the bowl between us on the cot, we used the two large soup spoons to attack the huge mass. We were able to consume only about one-third of the vegetables, and with reluctance to waste the food, we rapped on the door to summon the trustee. He displayed no surprise that we had not eaten it all, and communicated to us that there was another prisoner who would appreciate having our leftovers if we would be willing. We agreed, of course.

Shortly the trustee returned, admitting a painfully emaciated man in a Russian uniform. His face bore a large scab and was discolored from a beating. So hungry was he that he expressed his gratitude to us by kneeling and kissing our shoes. That would have embarrassed us under any conditions, but the gesture seemed especially little-deserved since the food, really only our leftovers, did not represent the slightest sacrifice on our part. Grasping the bowl, he rose to his feet, and saluted us; then he was gone. The trustee, who had observed the proceedings, firmly closed the door.

The narrow cot had no padding over its wooden boards; however, we slept that night. In the morning, as the trustee made his circuit, he brought us black bread and drink. All prisoners then participated in a period of cleanup. Though our cell did not appear dirty, we swept the dust out into the center area of the building, and with others we cleared that away.

Our brief period of relative liberty gave us a moment to speak with the trustee, who told us that the Russian soldier we had met had been placed in solitary confinement because of his disrespect for a guard. From his bruised and battered appearance I judged that the person he had offended had administered his own sort of punishment. I remarked that the other Russians I saw were emaciated also. The trustee confided that the Russian prisoners' diet consisted mainly of the peelings from the vegetables given to the other Allied prisoners. Not only were the Soviets subject to the intense hatred of the Reich, but they also were not signatories to the Geneva Convention. Neither did they take many Nazi prisoners, nor participate in the exchange of Red Cross parcels for prisoners. The Russian prisoner's plight was not envied by the rest of us.

Following our cleaning chores, the inmates were summoned to assemble for exercise. First, we were permitted to use the latrine, located on the opposite side of the building from our cell. While busy washing, I was able to converse surreptitiously with one or two prisoners. This was one of the very few times when it was possible for men in the solitary building to communicate with others, I was told. We also were advised that during the exercise period there were short intervals in which the guards could not observe the face of each man, and while the prisoners walked in single file, it was sometimes possible to whisper a message to the man directly in front or to the rear.

In the latrine area, after a guard had cleared out all the prisoners, we were lined up, counted, and marched single-file out the front door, turned to the right, and passed through a heavy door into the exercise area. As I had guessed from what little I had been able to view through the chipped paint on our cell window, the walled area seemed no wider than ten yards, and extended only the length of the old stable that now housed the solitary confinement quarters. Guards accompanied the line of prisoners into the area, one standing at either end wall; another guard supervised us from his platform atop the guard tower just beyond the wall. Our exercise consisted of walking single-file inside the walled oval.

Through a narrow canopy of sky visible overhead, I observed a flight of B-17 bombers on a mission — possibly, I thought, to Magdeburg. The density of the black puffs of exploding shells told us that the antiaircraft fire was formidable. The pulse of gunfire and flak bursts penetrated the steady drone of the formation's high-powered engines. On the return lap of our walk I saw one plane burst into flame and drop in a tight spin as it left the formation. The raiders had passed out of sight before the end of the brief period allotted for exercise.

Alerted to the possibility of communication, I braved the opportunity to whisper some observation to Bob, who was directly behind me. I was not caught in the act, but it occurred to me that the message had probably not been worth the risk of detection. Though we were observed during the entire time, we were counted once again before we were allowed to pass through the exit door. These Germans were meticulous in keeping track of their prisoners. Back in the building, the men entered into their cells, and the doors closed securely behind them.

Bob and I were again given a large portion of the lunch menu — the same reconstituted dehydrated soup. The trustee again ushered the Russian prisoner into our cell to supplement his meager meal with our plentiful leftovers, and again he displayed his appreciation for our easily given largesse with a display of profuse gratitude. Bob and I knew that his thanks should be more appropriately directed toward the Polish trustee, for I suspected that the trustee was under orders to deliver only the most meager portions to this unfortunate fellow. Through the huge portions given to us, he kindly fed the poor Russian, without having done so in a technical sense.

Bob and I remained in the cell only a short time before we were summoned to the front door to be taken, under guard, on another train ride. Our destination was Burg, the site of an air base that protected both Magdeburg and the air route to Berlin, though we learned that only by observing the names of stations en route. As we were whisked by vehicle from the railroad depot to the edge of the air base, I was surprised to see, parked on a revetment near a large service hangar, a B-17 bearing the insignia of a group from the Eighth Air Force. The bomber appeared much as it would have on its home base in England. Two or three smaller Allied military aircraft were visible on pads not far from the Flying Fortress. I wondered how those planes had come here, and what purpose they might have.

It was only after the war had ended that I learned that the *Luftwaffe* had successfully salvaged Allied aircraft that had gone down in Europe. Axis pilots would take the aircraft up, alone in the sky, then feign damage or malfunction to account for their seeming separation from their formation. The plane would then join an Allied flight returning to its home base, its mission completed. Once the Axis aircraft was in close range to this "sympathetic" formation, it used its cannon to destroy the closest plane. After separating from the remaining formation, the pilot returned to the *Luftwaffe* base.

The vehicle in which we were transported passed through a pine woods set on gently rolling terrain, then rolled to a stop in front of an administrative center. We were led into the stark, neat building. There was a brief examination of our clothing, and note was made of our military identities; my wristwatch was confiscated — the one that the Résistance man in France had exchanged for mine. Then we were led to another section of the building, the detention quarters of the air base, and locked into small cells. I reflected that now I had entered the realm of the *Luftwaffe*, and was most likely on the route toward becoming officially their prisoner of war, though earlier rejected by their representative, the irate Colonel.

The silence of my surroundings was complemented by the stark tidiness of my small cell. The walls and ceiling were white. On the metal-sprung cot was a thin mattress covered by a white sheet; a white cover enveloped a feather pillow at the head. Neatly folded at the foot of the cot was a blue-gray woolen blanket. The gray flooring was consistent with the near-monotonous interior. The only color in the cell was provided by two books, Adolf Hitler's *Mein Kampf*, bound in red, and the *Holy Bible*, in a dark binding.

Idly, I thumbed through *Mein Kampf*, curious to learn the source of its power over those who supported the Third Reich. It didn't take long to convince me that I would be unlikely to discover that power, as I could only guess at the meaning of the German words. Abandoning the volume, I picked up the Bible. Because I was familiar with the English-language version, I could make sense of some of the words; still, I couldn't read the German script. That concluded the inventory of pastimes open to me, so I stretched out on the cot, hoping to doze away the boredom of these uninteresting surroundings.

My idleness was interrupted by the sound of grating at the metal door of the cell. The door was opened by a soldier who urged me into the larger room outside. As I came out, Bob Donahue was leaving his cell also, and we were led from the room, through a hallway, and into another large room. Several men, clothed in the green, heated flight suits now issued to American fliers, appeared to be dejected; one held his arm as though it might have been broken. A couple of others appeared to be in some sort of pain. Around them, on the floor, were various articles that must have been with them in their plane, including inflatable Mae West life preservers and escape maps. Draped from a projection screen was a parachute, stained with blood.

A German officer in the room spoke in English, introducing us as American airmen, captives as were they. To us, he explained that this crew had just been recovered after their bomber had been downed in an air raid. With distrust evident in their eyes, the airmen glanced at us, and gave no signal of acknowledgment. I wondered why we were brought into this room. Did our captors expect Bob and me to evoke an outpouring of information about our respective units? If that were the case, it was an unsuccessful ploy, for as much as I would have liked to converse with fellow airmen, I would not do so in the presence of the enemy. I expected that these men would suspect us of being Germans posing as Americans to elicit information useful to *Luftwaffe* Intelligence circles.

No words were exchanged, and Bob and I were returned to our cells. From sounds in the detention quarters, I gathered that at least some of the newly arrived airmen had been brought into the cell area.

The next time the cell door opened, I was served supper — a plate of adequate though not interesting food, a slice of brown bread, and a warm beverage. Soon after, the door was opened once more, this time to retrieve the dishes. Then it closed, presumably for the night.

The lights were still on when the wail of air raid sirens sounded. The cells were emptied, and all of us were taken down a hallway and to a large underground shelter, with yellow walls and white ceiling. Besides cots, the only adornment was a large red sign imprinted in black with the message, *Nicht Rauchen!* — No Smoking!

The guards forced us airmen to gather close to one another, something the new arrivals were reluctant to do at first. Then we were joined by about 20 blonde young women, whom we were told were Norwegians, brought here for the pleasure of the *Luftwaffe* airmen. One or two of them had pine needles in their hair, but none of them displayed any signs of happiness.

They kept to their section of the room, close to the entrance door, and whispered only occasionally among themselves.

Through the walls we could hear the sound of antiaircraft guns, and I thought I could hear also the thunder of exploding bombs. It wasn't a peaceful interlude, and the young women fidgeted uncomfortably during the commotion. Then we were joined by another figure, a man clad like the others in the shelter with us, but whose head was swathed in bandages that extended as far from his face as did his nose; his hands were bandaged also. Apparently blinded, he was led by a guard who brought him to the cot next to the one where Bob and I were seated. Someone said he was the flight engineer, and he had suffered badly from burns. His crew members were solicitous of his condition, and spoke quiet words of comfort to him.

Soon a soldier arrived with a large bowl of soup and a tablespoon with which to feed the blinded soldier; it was obvious that he could not feed himself. One of his companions began the task of spooning soup into his mouth through the slit in the bandages — a difficult task, for only a small bit of soup could be directed into the slit. The handle of the spoon almost disappeared before the soup reached his mouth. When that man tired of the duty, I volunteered to help. By grasping the handle of the spoon at its tip, with thumb and forefinger, I could just barely reach until the spoon touched his teeth. It was a slow process, and he tired from the effort, resting for a long period before signaling that the feeding could be resumed. After awhile, he fell into merciful sleep.

When the siren sounded "All Clear," soldiers ushered us back to our quarters, where I slept much better on this cot, provided for the detention of German airmen, than on the narrow one of the night before.

A soldier wakened me in the morning to refresh myself in preparation for this new day. Breakfast consisted of a warm beverage and bread with jam. Shortly, the door to my cell opened and I was summoned, along with the other American prisoners, to depart by truck to the train station. There we boarded a coach for a long ride to Frankfurt am Main, and, we correctly guessed, to the *Luftwaffe* prisoner of war interrogation center at Oberursel, which we knew from our Intelligence briefings, apparently mistakenly, as *Dulag Luft*.

We entered the coach via a door at one end and proceeded down a narrow hallway to a compartment about midway through the coach. Officers were segregated from enlisted men; Bob Donahue joined the officers of the other crew we had met earlier, in a compartment not far from our own.

In the compartment, two long upholstered seats faced each other. Our guard made it clear that he would occupy one seat by himself, the better to observe his prisoners, who sat opposite. I believe that the badly burned flight engineer was retained at the air base infirmary, so our seat was only snugly occupied. One enterprising airman, a lanky man with an unruly shock of black hair, clambered up to a baggage rack and scrunched up on the steel rods to sleep.

The track, due to bombing, was in very poor repair and the train bumped along slowly. As we entered Magdeburg, we could see that the buildings along the track were in ruins, all except one. Amid a scene of general devastation it stood free from damage; even the International Harvester Company sign affixed to its roof proudly remained. The bombing of the Junkers plant in Halberstadt had demonstrated to me that surgical bombing was indeed possible, but amidst the general ruination of the enemy's industrial production, it appeared to be more than casual chance that an American factory had been spared.

I was seated next to the flier who was nursing a sore arm. He offered his name as Henry J. "Hank" Smith, whose home was in Scranton, Pennsylvania. He warmed up to me a bit, now that he could see that I was being treated as a prisoner, the same as he. He was depressed about the death of one of his companions, a gunner, whose parachute had been descending near his own. Henry saw a civilian on the ground point a weapon at his friend, and heard the shot. Then the man strode over to the point where Henry would land, and waited until he was on the ground. The man had no more ammunition, and signaled his frustration over his inability to execute Henry on the spot. Then he attacked him, using his rifle as a bludgeon. The rifle broke as Henry fended off the blow with his arm, and he would have fought with the man had not German soldiers appeared at that moment and intervened.

Periodically, as we rode, a German soldier walked down the aisle and glanced through the window into our compartment, assuring himself that everything was in control — and it seemingly was, until our young guard fidgeted with his rifle and discharged the gun. The bullet ricocheted off the train's curved steel walls, spraying sharp, stinging chips of ivory paint.

That startled the sleeping man in the baggage rack above, and he sprang down to the floor. Enraged at the guard's carelessness, he stood over him, berating him for his ineptitude, and threatened him bodily harm if that ever happened again. The gunshot brought the patrolling guard hurrying to the door, rifle at the ready. He found the penitent German soldier in our compartment cringing before the furious American prisoner. Quickly he calmed the situation and, with a parting scowl, the lanky prisoner returned to his lofty bed to sleep away the miles.

Air raid sirens were sounding as our train pulled into the Frankfurt station. The train was emptied quickly, and our guards herded us down into an air raid shelter beneath the station. I felt that we were in as safe a place as possible because a German General was standing near me. We heard the rumble of antiaircraft bursts and possibly of bombs exploding in the distance. The people in the shelter were tense; apparently they did not regard the bombing as routine.

Eventually, the "All Clear" was sounded, and our guards herded us out of the shelter and onto a train on a nearby track. Our small group was joined by others, until our car was full of men. I wondered if any of the succeeding cars were also filled with freshly downed airmen.

Wooden cars with wooden seats were not designed for long-distance travel, and this ride — probably less than half an hour — seemed as comfortable as I could expect as a prisoner of war. When the train halted, sturdy guards lost no time in evacuating us from the cars, and we passed through a tall fence and into a compound of vast dimensions. Whatever occurred inside the dreaded interrogation center, we had been told to be on guard to reveal nothing more than name, rank, and military serial number either to the interrogators or to fellow airmen, for they might well not be what they appeared.

"The walls are probably bugged," had been the words of the briefing officer at our home base, "so anything you say in that place can be known by the Germans; and the most commonplace thing may be of significance to the enemy's Intelligence service."

I was distinctive in this newly arrived motley group by the dirty civilian clothing I had been wearing for weeks. I wondered what information they could want from me, except to reveal those who had helped me.

★ ~ ★ ~ ★

Chapter 20

Interrogation and Transportation

WE WAITED IN line until we could be escorted, one by one, down a stairway and into a concrete hallway, its expanse broken on either side, at short intervals, by steel doors. My guard ushered me more than halfway down the hall before stopping at an open door presided over by another uniformed guard. After being directed in, I entered and the door slammed behind me with a chilling metallic clang.

This small cell, about two meters wide and three meters long, was furnished only with a metal cot and a pail, obviously to be used for sanitary purposes. I sat on the bare wire springs of the cot — no mattress, pillow, or blanket — and surveyed these surroundings. Why did I have this sense of uneasiness? An electrical heating device was embedded in the wall, but its metal rod gave off no glow, and the room was just a trifle chilly. A window on the outer wall was painted over, so it admitted no view of the outside; only faint light filtered through it. The bulb in the light receptacle embedded in the ceiling was inert. The room had no switch to control either light or heat.

So that was the reason for my disquietude — the cell had many indications of comfort, but none of them was fulfilled. No view through the window, no softness to the bed, no blanket, no heat for warmth. There was no way for me to control my environment. Nor were there books, even in German; nothing to drink, when thirst would arise. There was no graffiti on the walls, nor litter on the floor. References to comfort, unfulfilled, spoke incessantly to tantalize any person consigned therein. By artful design the room was starkly barren of interest.

All was silent in the corridor outside my cell. I sat on the cot, staring at the wall, struggling to conjure up some memory of activity that might fill this void. I recalled tales of men who had lost their minds in the solitude of captivity. I did not want that to happen to me.

Was there a pattern in faint cracks on the wall that might remind me of a picture, a map, some image, which might stir up mental activity to occupy my time here? Keeping track of passing time should provide an anchor for reality. *What day was this?* I thought I had arrived at Altengrabow on September 12, 1944. That would have been a Tuesday. I had been there for two nights, so it would have been on a Friday — September 15th — that I had arrived at the *Luftwaffe* base in Burg. Two nights there — that would have me on the train on Sunday, the 17th. And I had arrived here on the same day. So it must now be Sunday, September 17th.

I would have to remember that; I had no way of recording it on the walls of the cell. I thought that task should keep me mentally alert. But what would I do with the rest of the time? Better that I avoid recalling the events since our Liberator went down; that should not be fresh in my memory, in case I would be subjected to torture. I posed myself a problem in trigonometry — in the absence of pencil or paper, that should serve to keep me alert.

The silence was broken by the sound of hobnailed boots in the corridor. Beginning at the steps where I had entered the hallway, the clatter grew louder as they approached. Maybe someone was coming for me. That would relieve this monotony. The footsteps continued past my door, then faded as the walker went to the far end of the corridor. I heard a metallic grating as another door was opened. Some indistinguishable words — without doubt a command — were uttered. The door clanged shut again, and the harsh clatter of hobnailed treads returned, this time accompanied by another set of footsteps of an airman, now on his way to the dreaded interrogation. Silence again reigned when the footsteps were no longer heard. I returned to my trigonometry problem, trying to recall just where I had been in my calculations.

Grappling with mental problems calmed my mind somewhat, and I became less fearful of becoming unnerved in the solitude. Matters eased even more as, now and then, hobnailed boots tracked down the hall as before — a door swung open, then closed again, and the boots retraced their path through the corridor, each time accompanied on the return journey by another set of footfalls. I wondered just what befell those captives after they left their cell. I hadn't heard any screams, so perhaps the men were not being tortured. Nor, I reflected, had I heard gunshots, so they were not being executed — not yet or, at least, not here.

Eventually footsteps stopped at my door. The lock bolt slid open and the door swung ajar. An armed soldier stepped aside, ready to follow me down the hallway. Ahead, a harmless-looking man advanced to meet me, his hand thrust out to grasp mine in a friendly handshake. Harmless in appearance? The man was of slight build, with gray hair. I judged that he might be 60 years old, perhaps older even than that. He was attired in the blue uniform of the *Luftwaffe*, but wore no insignia of any kind. The absence of any display of rank was itself reassuring, and his manner was avuncular, as much as to say, "Buck up, Lad, things aren't so bad. You're with friends here. You will like it."

When compared to others who had waited, I hadn't been cooped up in that little cell for very long, but I now had a strong desire to speak to someone. This man seemed eager to make that possible.

"Where are you from, son?" he asked. "From the Midwest, I'd bet. I used to live in Denver, myself. I owned a large trucking firm there, but returned to Germany so that I could vote on some important matter. And here I am. It's a pretty nice country in which to live."

A trucking company in Denver? I had spent one summer vacation living with my grandmother in DeWitt, Iowa, working in a gas station along U.S. Highway 30. Two or three drivers from The Denver Trucking firm had made regular stops at my station. The trucks took a lot of gas, and the drivers usually drank a bottle of pop and talked with me as I filled their tanks. I could relate to the owner of a trucking firm like that one.

But I didn't want to reveal too much about myself. Again, I remembered the Intelligence warning back at the home base — "Just give your name, rank, and Army serial number." So I adopted an agreeably silent manner, and walked beside him to the table to which he led me.

The interrogator took a chair with his back to an open window, and I was positioned opposite him. Elevated as we were above the yard outside, I could see nothing but sky and trees, so I had no difficulty in focusing my attention on my interrogator. He began in a conversational tone, asking me about my home, my family — topics quite normal for beginning a conversation.

But I gave my standard reply. "Cupp, William L., Sergeant, serial number 17097098." This response seemed to chill our affable relationship.

The man stiffened in his chair, as though his offer of friendship had been rebuffed, his open manner betrayed. He tried another tack. "What sort of work would you like to do? Have you any plans for furthering your education?"

Hearing my standard response again, he sat back in exasperation.

Taking a package of cigarettes from his pocket, he selected one, tamped it, placed it in his mouth, and lit it. A breeze coming through the window carried the smoke to me. I had never smoked, and I had regarded with distaste the smoke-laden air on city buses leaving the factory at the end of the day. But the aroma of this cigarette, carried on the chill wind coming through the window, suddenly appealed to me. My questioner had slowly and deliberately placed the open package on the table between us. He had not offered one to me. I guessed that he hoped I would ask for one, and then he would have gained some control in our relationship.

I said nothing, and shivered from the cold. Quickly, with feigned hurt, he closed the conversation and called a guard to usher me back to my cell. His voice was steely, his manner icy when we parted. I was escorted back to my own cell. This time, however, I entered with more confidence than I had when I entered the first time; I had witnessed no torture out there, and I had a mental task to occupy me in the solitude of the cell.

The interrogations continued in the same routine. Periodically a guard marched up the corridor. A door grated open, some command was uttered, then the door closed again and footsteps retraced the distance back down the hall. In the cell, after having examined the small room carefully to ascertain that nothing had changed in my absence, I occupied myself once more with mathematical exercises. Because my watch had been confiscated at the Burg *Luftwaffe* base, I had no way to tell how much time had elapsed. But my stomach told me that a meal was due.

The guard once again approached my door. I was ushered down the corridor, up the steps, and back to the same large room where I had been interviewed earlier. I was seated away from a window, in a more distant part of the room. A different questioner sat before me. Like the earlier one, he wore no insignia on his *Luftwaffe* clothing. This time the interrogator fingered a portfolio on the table in front of him. He gave me the opportunity to introduce myself by name, rank, and serial number. Then he leaned forward. "We know all about you. One of your aircrew members has spoken to us this morning." Feeling that I knew Bob Donahue's nature better than that, I doubted that he had divulged anything during his interrogation.

"Three other members of your crew passed through here some months ago," he continued, "so we know the identity of your bomber group, the mission on which your aircraft was lost, the location where your aircraft crashed, and the identities of your crew members.

"There is a problem, however."

I fully expected him to demand explanation of our activities and whereabouts since the day I had parachuted. I was relieved to learn that that was not his question.

"We need to be certain that you are who you say you are. We do not propose to accord the dignity of the status of prisoner of war to an impostor. Spies, of course, according to the Geneva Convention and our policies, are to be executed. You must convince me that you are not a spy."

The ragged civilian clothing I was wearing had not yet been mentioned, nor the absence of a genuine dog tag, but because of these factors the allusion to espionage appeared to carry a plausible threat. As the questioning unfolded, I was gratified that there were no inquiries about my whereabouts or helpers during the 11 weeks before my capture. He asked for information about things I had forgotten, or never known: what were the tail markings identifying my bombardment group; how many antiaircraft gun emplacements protected our air base; what caliber were those guns; where were they located?

I could not honestly answer any of these questions, but any anxiety I might have felt about establishing my identity as a legitimate member of the Allied armed forces was largely dispelled by the next actions of the interrogator.

Referring to the file folder before him, he proceeded to recount to me my own trail of assignments, complete and accurate from the date of my enlistment in 1942 until the 493rd Bombardment Group had arrived in England earlier this very year. It was most unlikely that any of my crew members would have known each of the places to which I had been assigned and the dates. Seeing my surprise at the completeness of my dossier, the interrogator proudly informed me that the *Luftwaffe* had subscribed, in Sweden, to all of the hometown papers in the United States. They had operated a clipping service, noting all of the hometown stories about local men in the military services, their stations, training, promotions, and anything else considered to be newsworthy by local editors. These clippings were then sorted and filed for future use. What an immense undertaking! But the information repeated to me by this interrogator seemed likely to have come only from my hometown newspapers, the Tipton, Iowa, *Advertiser* or *Conservative*, both weeklies, that seemed to validate his claim.

To my immediate relief, my questioner summoned a guard, who led me out of the room and down a hallway. He stopped me at one of the many doors, signaling me to enter. The narrow room, with a window on the far end, held three cots along one wall. There was some padding on the cots, each covered by a blanket. On the blank wall was a glowing electric heater. Seated on the far bed was a fellow dressed in the olive-drab woolen shirt and trousers of the U.S. Army.

Just seeing him aroused my curiosity. I wanted to talk with someone, especially with a fellow flier. Where had he been stationed? When had his plane gone down? Where? Did all of his crew get out of the plane alive? Was he captured immediately? I recalled, however, that my training had stressed the fact that *Dulag Luft* was wired for sound to monitor our voices. I nodded a greeting to the man, then surveyed the room for the sign of a microphone. I didn't see any, but then, of course, it would be concealed.

My companion must have been entertaining similar thoughts, for we sat silently, letting time pass by. The glow faded on the heater on the wall. Sometime later, noises outside the door signaled an arrival. A meal was thrust through the door — two plates, with dark bread and something else, plus an eating utensil, and a cup of warm liquid. My companion and I ate from the plates. The heater regained its warm glow.

I ventured some words, such as, "I'm glad to have something to eat; it has been a long time since the last meal."

My companion grunted in assent. After what seemed like a short time later, a guard came to the door and took our utensils. Had they estimated the length of time required for us to finish the meal, or had they determined that from sounds in the room, transmitted somehow over concealed wires? We sat again in silence. I wished that there were something to read, especially so since the temptation to speak hung heavily in the room.

The silence was broken by loud scuffling sounds outside our door.

"You don't have to push me around like that, you dirty bastards! You just wait, and you'll get yours!"

There was a loud thump, and the door was thrust open. A dark-haired fellow was pushed roughly into the room by two guards, and the door slammed behind him. The new occupant quickly moved to the middle cot, which we had left vacant, and launched into a tirade against our captors. Just as quickly, he turned his attention to the bond we ought to have between us.

He blurted that he was with a particular bombardment group, and with good humor and animation asked what units we were with. However, his openness smacked of deception; if he were an American airman as he claimed, he should have been cautioned not to divulge such information. I hesitated, waiting to see how my companion would respond.

"It is better that we don't talk of such matters here," he said, firmly.

"I agree," I said, hoping to close the questioning.

"Oh, they can't hear us talk," the newcomer asserted. "And if they could, it wouldn't matter; there's nothing they could use with what we'd say here."

He persisted in like vein, but my companion and I edged away from him and sat in silence. The guards returned and took him away, presumably to another interrogation. I speculated that he would be placed in another room where the occupants also had not been revealing information of value to Nazi Intelligence.

A short time later, guards came to the door and escorted both of us out of the room and down the corridor. We were taken along an intersecting passage leading to a large room, possibly used as a warehouse. The guards stopped us as we approached a pile of discarded clothing on the floor. They told me to take off my civilian clothing, and as I did so, one rummaged among the clothing in the pile, finally producing a flying coverall, which appeared to be about my size. As he held it up, I could see that several bullet holes and blood spots gave testimony to the fate of its previous wearer. I wriggled into it as he ordered, and followed the lead guard through the building and out into a large open space. On the far side of the area a number of airmen were assembled near a wall. My room companion and I were directed to take places in the formation, and soon others joined our ranks.

A burly Sergeant, his close-cropped head pink under his military cap, was in charge of the guards who surrounded us. He commanded us to stand at attention as another guard read names from a list, and the men responded as their names were called. "Geisman, Lester," intoned the reader; the short fellow next to me answered, "Here!"

At this, the Sergeant rushed to the reader and checked his listing. "*Juden!*" spat the Sergeant, rushing up in a threatening way to the unfortunate Geisman. Even though untutored in German, I clearly understood the term to refer to a Jewish person.

Towering over Geisman, the Sergeant glowered menacingly. Terrified, the airman cowered. I wondered what we could do to protect him if the Sergeant became brutal. But, apparently satisfied that he had aroused fear, the bully returned to his former place, and the roll call continued.

As the last names were being called, a train chugged up on the other side of the wall. The formation was marched to the gate by which we had entered the compound, and herded into the rail cars. Houses were visible through the train windows as we rolled down the hill to the Frankfurt station, where we were transferred into a different train, again in passenger coaches. We departed, taking a northerly heading.

The mood in my coach was not a festive one. After all, none of us had a certain idea of our destination, and whatever that might be, none of us wanted to go there. After a while, some of the prisoners broke their silence. One chap, noting my bullet-riddled flying outfit, told me how after he and his crew members had bailed out of their plane, they had been rounded up and were being transported under guard in a canvas-topped truck. One of their officers had suggested quietly that they make a break for it. There were only two guards on the truck, and if, on signal, the men jumped each of them, they might disarm them, take over the truck, and make their getaway. They were halfway successful, having succeeded in overcoming one of the soldiers. But the other staved off the attack and raked the truck with bullets from his machine pistol. The bullets were of glass, he said, and splintered badly when they hit bone. This was probably, he remarked, his co-pilot's flight suit.

As we traveled, the scenery was varied, with cultivated fields, forests, plains, and short, steep mountains. At one place along the route, someone at a window pointed excitedly at a village on a hill, surmounted, it seemed, by a castle. Probably none of us had ever seen a castle before. I certainly had not, and the view was impressive.

Eventually the train reached the *bahnhof* — the railroad station — at Wetzlar, where we were unloaded and transferred onto trucks. After a ride up a hill, we entered a military compound of some sort and were dismounted from the trucks. We were formed into lines and taken to a small building where we were issued bedding. In a barracks, we were shown to double-decker bunks.

We were taken across the camp to a tiny building where a man I believed to be representing the Red Cross handed us postcards. The printed cards announced that we were prisoners of war and provided space on which we could inscribe our name, rank, and serial number and check off an appropriate message, such as "I am in good health." I addressed my card to my mother, adding her home address. Though news of my survival in Belgium had been radioed to England, I didn't know whether the information had reached my family. That had been nearly four months ago, and I had been uneasy about my parents, fearing that they would be worried about me. Though this postcard conveyed no personal message, it was a relief to have sent this news.

We were taken next to a small supply store, where each was issued a pressed-paper valise, courtesy of the Red Cross, similar to those used by American college students for mailing home dirty laundry, and in which to receive by return mail clean linens and perhaps homemade cookies. In the valises were sets of underwear, for both warm and cold weather; stockings and handkerchiefs; a sewing kit; bars of hand soap; several packages of cigarettes, a package of pipe tobacco, and one or two pipes; and a sweater, hand-knit by a patriotic volunteer in some city or town in the United States. These packages occasioned a clamor of hearty appreciation from those who received them. Those of us who were not in possession of a presentable uniform were taken to bins containing standard uniform-issue shirts, trousers, and blouses, with no insignia, of course, but their olive-drab color presented a military impression. We changed right on the spot, then took our valises back to our bunks in the barracks.

Men were milling about in the open area in front of the mess hall. I joined them, looking to see if Bob Donahue might be there also. I didn't see him, but recognized one man as a bombardier, I thought, from the 861st Bombardment Squadron, to which our crew was assigned. Still hesitant to give away any information to the enemy — and I thought that enemy agents might be planted here with the new prisoners as well — I approached the man, asking obliquely if he knew Sammy Hale. Major Samuel Hale was the Commanding Officer of the 861st and well-known throughout the 493rd Bombardment Group.

The man replied that he did know the Major, and that he was well. Though I was eager to know more about our group, I treaded discreetly, fearful of saying too much. But at least I had contacted someone with whom I had some affinity, however remote our relationship, and I felt a renewed connection with my own military unit.

The meals proved to be tasty, plentiful, and welcome. The mess hall personnel seemed to be prisoners of the *Luftwaffe* like ourselves. Perhaps they appreciated good food, for the products of their kitchen deserved commendation. German potatoes and food from Red Cross packages were converted into hash, much like that produced by the British Colonials at the Halberstadt work camp. And there was a supply of American margarine and jam for the dark German bread. There were other dishes as well, but the hash lingers in my mind.

At about this time, a loud blast of an air raid siren focused the attention of those in the yard. As other men poured out of the barracks, a flight of planes came into view over the trees. We could see that they were American medium bombers, Martin B-26 Marauders, flying at low level with their bomb bays gaping. They were on a bombing run. What could be the target? Not our prison camp, I hoped.

The formation, however, had released its bombs even before the planes arrived overhead. I watched in surprise as the bombs arced over our barracks and mess hall and on down the hill. Following their trajectory, I saw them hit their mark on a factory, raising a cloud of smoke and dust. No large-caliber antiaircraft fire challenged them, and soon the planes turned and disappeared in the distance. The air raid siren sounded the "All Clear," and we prisoners returned to our former activities. I wondered what the scene might be like at the bombed factory.

On the next morning the enlisted men were told to fall into formation, and the names of those who were to be transported were read aloud. We who were named received a Red Cross food parcel and were taken to trucks for the return trip to the train station. Officers were to be sent to a separate camp.

Coaches on the train waiting for us had two rows of wooden seats separated by a middle aisle. The guards counted us off as we entered, and as each coach was filled, the next in line were herded into the following coach. Just behind the cutoff point, I was seated at the head of my coach, with just one man between me and the window.

With my clothing valise and Red Cross parcel stowed under the seat, I took stock of my surroundings. The passages to either adjoining car were guarded by soldiers with rifles at the ready. A toilet was at the far end of the coach, but nothing else of interest could be seen. As usual at these stations, the neighborhood showed evidence of bomb damage. I sat back and prepared to view the passing scenery, but I saw little that I could recall that was similar to earlier train rides. The hilly country provided a varied panorama, but having only a vague idea of our location and no idea of our destination took the edge off my curiosity about the scenery along the route.

My fellow passengers must have been becoming bored as well, for some of them began to explore the contents of the Red Cross parcels. Besides foodstuffs, each parcel contained three or four packages of cigarettes, but since the smokers had just received a similar quantity of smokes in their valises, they commanded only scant attention. Someone complained that his parcel contained no Lucky Strikes. I'm sure that he did not expect the shortage of those popular cigarettes to persist for the many months he was to spend as a prisoner of war.

Once the parcels were opened, it seemed a good time to sample their contents. Except for small packages of cheese and K-ration biscuits, the food was packaged in tin cans, and each parcel contained a tiny can opener, ingeniously designed for efficient use. None of us had eating utensils, but the bent lid of a can could be used as a substitute. The not highly prized K-ration biscuits, when slathered with jam, became very palatable. At some point, guards brought us hot liquid to quench our thirst.

Men settled back on their wooden seats and began conversations, often contrived to bolster egos damaged by their final mission and the disgrace of captivity. Now many found a need to reassure themselves that they were good, competent American airmen.

The suspicion that to become a prisoner of war was less than honorable had been fueled by the Hollywood film, *B-17*. The hero, played by the popular actor John Garfield, had emerged from his crashed bomber with a heavy machine gun in hand, firing at the strafing enemy planes until he succumbed to their bullets. This manner in which a soldier confronted the enemy, even against overwhelming odds, became the norm by which to judge valor. Many of us had accepted John Garfield's sacrifice as fitting behavior, at least until we learned that we were not permitted to carry handguns or knives on our persons during missions. But we wondered, would our families and friends back home mistake our helplessness for cowardice?

On this trip I met several new men. One of them stuck out in my mind because he was two or three years older and larger than many. I learned that he had been a first-string tackle for the powerhouse University of Southern California football team. Muscular, he may have weighed 175 pounds or more, adequate size for a lineman on a fast, shifty team in the early 1940s. He seemed to be a self-confident man, even-tempered, and with a sense of humor.

Much later in our travel that day, the train entered a large city, which the passengers correctly identified as Berlin, as corroborated by one of the guards. For miles we could see little but ruined buildings. But near them was neatly piled rubble; it seemed that the Germans had little tolerance for messiness, and we concluded that they must have had an abundant supply of hand labor to pick up and sort the debris.

The train swung north on a different track and moved slowly through what must have been a subsidiary station. Though ruination was everywhere visible, electric lines had been restrung, and an electric train moved relatively smoothly on an adjacent track.

We knew now that we were being transported beyond Berlin, either to the north or east. That was a long way from England, the home base for many of us. Speculation on our destination ceased, and the men sought other ways to relieve the tedium of the journey. Someone broke into song and others joined in. "Down in the Valley" was sung several times, until the leader was satisfied that we had it right. Other tunes from the reservoir of old favorites followed. Perhaps it isn't surprising that the spirited marching songs of our days of military training were omitted; few of us could have mustered the enthusiasm necessary for that mood.

The singing tapered off as hungry men dug into their Red Cross food supplies once again. There Spam, corned beef, and tuna, even without bread to make sandwiches, were filling and tasty. And each parcel had a bit of chocolate in an army-ration D-bar, dense tropical chocolate that was less sweet than the candy bars we had eaten as youngsters. Strong teeth were required to gnaw on them, but they were chocolate, after all, and lasted longer than the Hershey bars we knew from home.

An odd-shaped can of meat, narrow in diameter and tall, was identified as liver paté. I had never heard the term before, but when opened, it emitted the familiar aroma of liverwurst. I enjoyed the spread on a K-ration biscuit. Judging from their exclamations, other men had opened their paté also, and amidst howls of disappointment, several men pitched their cans out of the train window. Obviously they expected more food to be forthcoming, and were particular about their victuals at this point. Like them, I had no reason not to expect more Red Cross parcels when we reached our destination, but it pained me to see good food wasted in that way.

The train rumbled over a long bridge. Who knew what wide river this could be? Later we learned it was the Oder River, which became the postwar boundary between Germany and Poland.

The names on the railroad stations we passed were unknown to us. Few, if any of the men had flown beyond Berlin, and these towns may have been relatively unimportant in our schooling.

The train chugged along tediously for what seemed a very long time, passing cultivated fields and occasional woodlands. I was paying scant attention when it passed a sawmill at the edge of a tiny village and whistled for the station at a place labeled Kiefheide. After readjustment of boundaries following the war, it took the Polish name Podborsko.

The train continued on for a few hundred meters, then ground to a stop. Through the window I could see no reason for the halt. Just across from the track was a single brick house; beyond, only a continuation of the forest. I scooped up my Red Cross box and valise and hurried to the door as the guards hustled us out of our coach. On the ground, I saw another small building, nothing more. A husky soldier, obviously in charge, shouted at us to line up in a column of twos. He was roaring in German, but his meaning was clear. Bearing our little baggage, we obeyed, taking in our surroundings. There could be no prison camp here; we were on the very edge of nowhere. What would happen next?

It was September 21, 1944. I could not know that our train journey was over, and that we were in the vicinity of a prisoner of war camp. How we would get to it would soon be learned.

Chapter 21

Stalag Luft IV

THE STOCKY MAN in charge gave a signal to the guards; to us, he shouted "*Raus!*" — Get Out! — We set off at a trot, passing around the house garden and onto a wide path into the forest. The pace was brisk for me, but rather too fast for some of the men still nursing recent injuries. But no lagging was permitted; the guards, with threatening shouts and bayoneted rifles, moved us swiftly along. Less than 100 yards ahead, two fresh guards waited, accompanied by fierce dogs straining at their leashes. Like runners in a relay race, they sped on as the other guards tired. Then they were replaced by other fresh guards, some rather old to serve as soldiers, I thought, and others, though younger, who appeared to be good candidates for exclusion from the draft. Burdened as we were with our valises full of clothing and the remnants of our Red Cross food parcels, it was not easy to maintain the pace. But guards and dogs urged us relentlessly forward.

Perhaps a mile farther, the trail turned abruptly to the right.

Fresh soldiers awaited there, too. But while the first section of the trail had been on an upgrade, this section was more on the level. I recall a narrow bridge across a small stream, where we were urged to turn again to the left. Only a short distance later we came to a clearing fenced in barbed wire.

Two soldiers, rifles at the ready, held open a gate. Inside the enclosure we were prodded between small buildings. Ominous guard towers loomed ahead, flanking a little road, also blocked by a heavy gate. At a halt, the formation was closed, and we were ushered into a low building. Inside, the building was sectioned off by a row of tables, in front of which were a line of benches. Another long room appeared to be flanking this one, but that was concealed by a pine-boarded wall.

Forming a line to the first table, we were ordered to place our parcels on the table, then to disrobe, placing our clothing on the table. The guard at the first table was assisted by another, who fastidiously searched through our clothing for anything that might be considered contraband. Before those men had searched through mine, I was at the next table, my body being inspected for anything secreted there. Machine-like, we were passed down the row of tables. The very last one was separated from our view by a shoulder-high partition. As I approached the table, a guard brought my clothing and placed it in front of me. Having passed by the partition, I was confronted by a huge Sergeant, very likely the largest man I had ever seen, who made it loudly clear to me that I was to dress.

I didn't see the Red Cross parcel again, but thought better of registering a complaint. I dressed, then reached for my shoes. It seemed only natural to sit on the bench while I put on my socks and shoes, but I was dissuaded from that by a mighty swat from the ham-like hand of the scowling Sergeant. I managed those tasks by teetering on one foot while placing sock and shoe on the other. Then, retrieving my valise, I was moving through the door to the adjacent room.

We came to know the Sergeant as "Big Stoop," who gained a reputation for savagery. His name was Hans Schmidt.

The man behind me was the sturdy football player I had first met on the train, and he was being accorded the same treatment as I. He sat down, with shoes in hand, ready to put them on. Perhaps this was a game to the Sergeant, for no one made any attempt to caution us against using the benches. Then this man, too, received a sound slap. My new acquaintance was not easily cowed; he stood up, faced the Sergeant, and shouted, "You will change your tune when the Ruskies come here!" Whether the

Sergeant understood the statement is anyone's guess, but the big man did know when he was being confronted, and he did not like it one bit. Quickly he came across the table, grasped the football player by the front of his shirt, and with one hand threw him through the doorway. His trajectory stopped with a crash at the outer wall of the building, possibly 20 feet away. His valise followed, banging loudly against the wall.

No one else in line affronted the massive Sergeant, so the group assembled, only slightly the worse for wear from the cuffs of his ham-like hands. We were marched out onto the small road running down the center of the camp, *Stalag Luft IV*. I later learned that *Stalag Luft IV* was located about 25 miles south of the Baltic Sea, near the town of Bialogard, Pomerania, in the German-occupied territory of northern Poland.

We could see two parallel compounds, one on either side, each containing one long building and numerous low barrack-like structures. Just beyond the long building on the left side of the road was a gate. We paused for it to open, and passed through, suddenly conscious that we were objects of curiosity to a horde of men in olive-drab, waiting within the fence.

Just beyond the long building was an area of large tents, to which newcomers were assigned. We left our valises on the straw-strewn ground of the tent, and returned to the open area outside. Somehow we obtained blankets — two old, thin short ones — far too short to reach from my chin and also cover my feet. I was issued also an overcoat; it, too, was old, thin, and short. I guessed that poor garment had been the property of some army conquered by the Nazis, if not acquired from an earlier war. Just after I emerged from the tent, I was spotted by Bob Mathie, the tail gunner from my crew. Only moments later, the other two men who had been captured with Mathie, Charles Pendray and Irving Norris, appeared also. I told them that I had seen their names penciled on the bunk-bed support in the sub-basement of the *Gestapo* prison in Brussels.

To become reacquainted, we four men made a walking tour around the compound. They pointed out the several gun towers and told me that the waist-high wooden rail surrounding the barracks area, just about 15 feet inside the barbed wire fence, was the "warning wire." Under no circumstances was a prisoner to touch or overstep that line, on pain of death.

Guards in the towers would open fire on any man who did so. I noticed that the guard towers each had an uncovered machine gun pointed into the camp.

My companions pointed out a water tank just beyond our tent area, and about the size of a swimming pool, which they called a "fire pool." This was the water supply to be used in case of a fire in the compound. As we strolled past, several men were sailing crude toy boats on its surface.

At the far end of the compound, near the fence, several other men were playing catch with a baseball. We strolled around the other barracks, five of them in the row near the compound where our personal effects had been searched. I noted that these buildings were raised just above ground level.

"That's so that prisoners can be seen if they try to tunnel beneath the buildings to escape," Bob Mathie told me.

Midway between the barracks were a large latrine and a laundry room. Turning the corner, we came to the long building near the gate where we had first entered the compound.

"This building has the kitchen, the first-aid room, and library," Pendray, my flight engineer, pointed out. "Your meals will come from the kitchen, and in the morning you'll see the line for sick call."

My crew mates walked me past the long building to the corner where the fence separated this from another compound. "That is *B Lager*," they told me. "This compound is *A Lager*. Across the road is *D Lager*; *C Lager*, just beyond that, is under construction."

Lining the fence in *B Lager* were perhaps 100 men anxious to learn whether any of their friends or crew members were among the new arrivals. To my surprise, I noted I had been acquainted with several of them previously, in one phase of training or another. It suddenly occurred to me that our side was experiencing far more losses than I had ever imagined. I would have liked to speak with some of those men, but the distance between the warning wires in the two compounds was too great, and the guards in the towers seemed fidgety when anyone called to someone in another compound.

We had now walked completely around the compound, and my companions took me through the back door of one of the barracks.

"My room is just up the hall here," confided Mathie. "Pendray and I are both in the same room, and Irving Norris is in a room just down the hall. You can look for us here when you want to see us."

Mathie opened a door, and we entered one of the rooms. Just inside the door, placed on a bricked square, was a small heating stove. Both walls were edged by three-tiered bunks, each bearing a somewhat unkempt appearance, for there were not enough slats on the bed to fully support the occupants. That shortage may have been caused by a limited supply of lumber, but it may also have been by intent. In other prisoner of war camps, prisoners had utilized bed slats to shore up tunnels dug for the purpose of escape, only a few slats per bed may have been a solution to that problem.

Several men were lounging on bunks, while a couple of others sat before a table in the center of the room. A double window was set into the outside wall. Clothing was hung on the supports of the beds. The room wasn't untidy, but it had the appearance of being cluttered.

"It's about time for evening rations to be brought in," said Mathie. "You'll be getting yours in the tent, I suppose. Then there will be another *appel*, or roll call, and we'll all be locked in for the night.

"I'll see you in the morning."

Just as Mathie had said, four men from my tent were summoned to the mess, and returned with a loaf of dark bread each. The loaves were cut into 12 pieces, I believe, and distributed to the men. Cutting was difficult, given the facts that the bread was solid and the table knives issued to us were dull. But the task was managed. Later, we would hone those knives on stones until they were sharp enough to cut bread, even wood. Each man was issued a small pat of margarine to go with the bread, and we were advised to consume the bread appropriately; this was a full day's ration. We would wait until morning to have a drink; the camp water was potable only after boiling, and we had no means of heating it.

We picnicked on our beds, then went off to the nearby laundry to wash, towels having been furnished with the clothing in our valises. A guard then summoned us from the tent to stand in formation for *appel*. We stood by our tent, not far from the men of the nearby barracks, as a guard painstakingly counted each man and reported to his superior. The count tallied, and we were dismissed to our unlighted shelter.

The night was cold, and we doubled our bodies under the short blankets, pulling the top one over our heads. Those who failed to do so woke in the morning with their hair and eyebrows covered with hoarfrost. That's when I discovered just how uncomfortable was the plight of the fellow bunking on my left side. Nerone "Tony" Franco's face was blotched with purplish markings. His B-26 bomber had exploded just after he had lost consciousness from the fire raging on his clothing. He had been blown out of the top escape hatch. He had awakened some hours later in a French farm home. Those compassionate people had summoned a doctor to care for him, but the doctor said that Tony's burns were too extensive for treatment outside a hospital. So the German forces occupying the area had been alerted and took him away to a military hospital. Tony's burns extended over much of his body, particularly on his legs and face, and he had remained under treatment in France for several weeks. His burns, though healing, were extremely sensitive to cold, and this condition would plague him through the entire winter — yet to arrive.

The gentle hospitality of our guards heralded by our earlier captors was not yet in evidence. Rough voices urged us out of our tents that morning, hurrying us to *appel*. Even from the distance at which we could view the guard towers, the men clearly were alert, fingering their machine guns. After the prisoners had been counted and found to be present, we were dismissed. There was just enough time to fold up our blankets and place them at the heads of our beds, scoop up our towels and soap, and head for the latrine and wash room before the morning meal.

The disappointing breakfast consisted of a reddish fluid with an unfamiliar taste, in a tall metal pitcher. But it had been heated, so was potable. We were expected to consume some of the bread we had received in the last evening's ration. If we possessed any food from the earlier Red Cross parcel, we were free to eat some. Now we were able to do as we liked within the narrow limits of what was possible in the camp. Sick call was on the regular agenda, and as I walked around the circumference of the *Lager*, I came upon a long line of men waiting to see a camp doctor. Some of them appeared to be in physical pain. Turning to a man who was walking near me, I inquired about those in line.

"These men came in to camp some weeks ago," he told me, "from a prison camp in East Prussia. They call them victims of the Hydekrug Run. After confinement in the hold of rusty steamers, they disembarked at Stettin. They were handcuffed, and sat in boxcars in the rail yards there for several days before arriving here. Then, still handcuffed, they were run to the camp, being attacked by dogs and bayoneted by guards. One man in line has more than forty bayonet wounds on his back and legs. Worse, the doctors have no medication for them, only iodine and aspirin."

Recalling the sting of iodine on a cut, that account made me sympathetic to the condition of these men. But why were they so badly mistreated while my group was only harassed?

Later, I discovered that the Hydekrug camp, *Stalag Luft VI*, had been operated with correctness if not humanely, until shortly before it was evacuated as the Soviet army approached. Then some change in personnel had brought harsher men into the camp, effectively blocking the official commandant. The transfer of prisoners in two old ships was conducted with brutality. The Captain of the Guard had arranged for *kriegsmarines* — naval personnel — to set up along the line of march to the camp, ready to fire if any man bolted. The same Captain was in charge of the run from the train to the camp in which I had participated. That my contingent was only harassed may be due to the fact that the earlier incident had been reported to the International Red Cross, which had advised caution in the treatment of prisoners.

The noon meal, brought to our tent in a bucket, consisted solely of some thin soup. Doled out by one of my tent mates under the watchful eyes of others, each prisoner was apportioned one cupful. Clearly the concoction had seen neither animal broth nor salt. Though the meal did not fulfill the expectations of men who had eaten Red Cross rations during the railroad journey, there was not much grumbling about this fare. The meal seemed consistent with the austerity of our present surroundings and the far-from-compassionate treatment we had experienced so far.

While we were assembled in our tent, we were visited by a delegation of prisoners. One loitered outside, at the ready to alert the other two in the event that a guard should pass by. The two who entered were very businesslike. They quickly caught the attention of everyone and introduced themselves as officers in the prisoner internal organization. The larger man, Frank Paules, announced that he was the leader of the organization. His was a commanding presence, and he quickly inspired confidence both in the organization and in what he had to say. The other man, whose name I do not recall, was the leader of this *A Lager*. They assured us of the importance of the organization, and told us that each element of the camp, from room to barracks to *Lager*, was integrated into the whole.

There were committees to deal with matters of importance to the prisoners in the camp. Among these were internal security (reports should be made on any prisoner's inappropriate fraternization with the enemy); reporting of brutality of our keepers; and an escape committee, dealing with requests for assistance with or authorization to escape. There was also a committee to deal with news of the war effort. It was important, he told us, to be cooperative in our living unit, to assure cleanliness, order, and morale. Soon we would be moved to the new compound, under construction. Then one of our first tasks would be to elect a leader of our room and a barracks leader, who would be incorporated into the camp organization. Our leaders reassured us that they were in regular contact with the International Red Cross organization in Switzerland, which knew of conditions in the camp and would ultimately assist in the redress of violations of the Geneva Convention.

Meeting with my crew members again that afternoon, I was informed of some of the events that had occurred in the camp since their arrival. An infirmary had been built in the *vorlager*, almost on the *A Lager* fence line. The *vorlager*, the front compound of the camp, included the building where I had been interrogated, warehouses for food and supplies, housing for the German camp personnel, housing for the prisoner medical staff, the camp infirmary, and the camp detention quarters. To make room for the new building, the fence had been moved inward, very close to the rear of the barracks at the south edge of *A Lager*. Only a narrow area remained between the rear entrance to those barracks and the warning wire.

I also was told that two German fighter planes had earlier buzzed the camp, then in an exuberant display, performed aerobatics in sight of it. One pilot apparently miscalculated, and his plane had plunged to the ground, killing the occupant. The aerial display had attracted the attention of the prisoners, who applauded when the plane crashed, and camp guards and officials reacted angrily to the applause. Some of my informants expressed the opinion that the shooting of a prisoner some time later resulted, at least in part, from that incident.

I learned as well that a workman had been inside the fence separating

A and *B Lagers* when he accidentally brushed against the electrified wire of the fence. The shock had killed him, and again many of those who had observed the accident exulted. It was only much later that the prisoners discovered that the workman was not a German soldier, but an Eastern European prisoner who had been forced to work at the camp. The misunderstanding may have been due in part to the failure of authorities to orient the prisoners to the presence of prisoners of other nationalities, men who were segregated from the American and British fliers. Perhaps the fact that we airmen held ranks as non-commissioned officers and were thus exempted from manual labor blinded our men from perceiving camp laborers as prisoners of war.

And finally, my crew members told me of a man in *A Lager* who had been shot by one of the guards. My informants had known the man, Aubrey Teague. According to their story, corroborated by many other men in the camp at that time, Teague had laundered some clothing in the wash room in his barracks. He had to walk down the hallway, out the door, and around the corner of the barracks, then part-way back to reach the clothesline. After finishing this task, he remembered that he had left one article in his room. Retrieving the piece, Teague decided he could just as easily step through the window of his room near the clothesline. The Captain of the Guard, who was standing in a guard tower, shouted in German at Teague, who did not understand the language, then shot him. Bystanders determined that though wounded, he was not dead. But for a considerable time, prisoners were denied permission to come to Teague's aid. Eventually he was moved to a dispensary in one of the barracks. Within a few hours he died. Several of his fellow prisoners, accompanied by guards, removed the body to an open area outside the camp, where he was interred. One of the camp chaplains had conducted a brief service.

Supper that day consisted of one cup level-full of mashed potatoes, with neither salt nor a substitute for gravy. We ate a morsel of bread with a pat of butter to complete the day's ration. The evening passed routinely, with a little opportunity for tending to one's personal matters, then *appel* and, shortly thereafter, we were confined for the night. It had not warmed up, and I was aware of my bed neighbor Tony Franco's discomfort brought on by the evening chill.

The following morning started out like the last, but it was now Saturday, and a different routine. At *appel*, and for most ensuing Saturdays, the men in the guard tower tested their machine guns. We new prisoners, along with the rest of our compound, discovered to our dismay that the chattering machine guns were kicking up dirt just in front of the spots on which we were standing. No one was hit, but the experience was intimidating, reinforcing the powerlessness of our situation.

This day was also my 21st birthday, of which my crew mates were aware. I was invited to Mathie and Pendray's room for a birthday party. Sitting on the third-tier cot assigned to one of the men, the other two — Irving Norris had joined us — were perched on the cot just one level down. Each of them had contributed one item accumulated from their meager Red Cross rations. One produced a packet of K-ration crackers, another a ration of cheese, and the third brought a chocolate D-bar to the banquet. Together we put slices of cheese on the crackers; then for dessert, we shared the chocolate.

As we ate, I began better to understand how precious were these supplements to the prison fare, and how generous was their act of sharing. Though each prisoner exiting the distribution camp at Wetzlar had received a full Red Cross parcel, the men here in *Stalag Luft IV* were given only one-quarter of a parcel each week. Those rations arrived item by item, in cans punctured by our captors, and each empty can was to be returned on the same day. A guard made a careful count of all the cans. The rationale for this latter practice was twofold: so that flattened cans could not be used to shore up escape tunnels, and to prevent the hoarding of foodstuffs — again to discourage escape.

Each day we heard the sounds of construction on the new compound into which we would move upon its completion. The call for us to transfer into *C Lager* came one morning just after breakfast. We were ordered to take our blankets and personal effects and assemble in front of our tents. We were accompanied by men from the camp leadership, who helpfully interpreted the orders given to us in German. In columns, we marched through the *A Lager* gate, turned left up the little road, keeping to the left, away from the bases of the guard towers set on the road. It was a short march, but across the fence were prisoners dressed in American and

British uniforms eyeing our procession. Just past the buildings of *D Lager* we passed the double fence comprised of two rows of tall barbed-wire-hung posts set a few feet apart. Tangles of rusty barbed wire filled the inner space.

Just beyond the front of the first barracks in the compound, we passed through a gate and marched on, past a duplicate of the cook house complex in *A Lager*. We halted in the open space beyond. The camp leaders again translated the orders, issued by a smartly dressed officer. Then, counted off by guards, men left the formation and entered the barracks, starting with the one closest to the narrow road up which we had come. As my section of the line entered a barracks — the third one on the near side — a guard ushered 24 of us into each room. I was among those at the end of the line, and was shunted into the last sleeping room on the right side of the hallway; the door frame was inscribed with the number 9.

Stepping to the right as I entered the door, I walked around a one-meter square brick base on which sat a small heating stove. Others had preceded me, so I deposited my belongings against the wall, adjacent to theirs. Except for a table, two benches, and a couple of wooden stools, the room was quite bare. One small, bare light bulb dangled on a cord from the ceiling, and one tall, tapered pitcher stood by the stove.

Our next task was to construct our mattresses; the components were outside beside the barracks. We found the piles of large paper sacks and heaps of wood shavings — the kind I had known as excelsior, a packing material. As the sacks were unfolded, they were indeed the largest ones I had ever seen, measuring perhaps two to three feet in width and six feet (possibly two meters) long. As small groups of men busied themselves at the piles of shavings, we began to exchange information about ourselves. The talk was normal enough, giving and soliciting names, hometowns, bombardment units, and the place of each man's last ill-fated mission. When the bags were stuffed and shaken down, we returned to our room and continued our acquaintance process.

I laid my mattress on the floor next to my valise and the Red Cross box, now nearly empty. The space to be taken by each man had to be adjusted, since there wasn't sufficient room along the side walls to accommodate 12 men, even sleeping on their sides. Eventually we hit upon the idea of making 11 bed places along each wall, and placing two men with their heads just below the double window, perpendicular to the others. That was managed by turning the table in the same direction as the two fellows whose heads were at the outer wall. Otherwise, while sleeping, our feet would be entangled with the table. That arrangement filled the room. During the day, our mattresses were to be folded toward the wall, allowing room for people to lounge on the floor. The table wasn't large enough to accommodate very many of us.

The discussion leading up to this arrangement had revealed something about the natures of the men in the room, each of whom introduced himself. Hank Smith, whom I had met at the air base at Burg on the day his plane had been lost, and Tony Franco, whose face testified to the seriousness of his burns, were both assigned to my room. So was Lester Geisman, the Jewish man who had been harassed while in formation at Oberursel; his bed site neighbored mine.

Beyond simple introductions, men staked out their claims to individuality. One man, Vincent Landolfi, had worked at a famous New York City night spot, and had supplemented that income as a freelance betting agent. Another man, William J. Knightley, a relatively unassertive fellow, had been in religious training at St. John's College, in Minnesota. During his schooling, he had been a part-time English instructor. Granted a leave of absence in order to sample something of the outside world, he had become an instructor at a university, teaching air cadet candidates, until he had been drafted. Another man, lanky Robert R. Read, claimed parents who had become wealthy from investments made during the Depression, a period when most of the men had known hardship. To emphasize that claim, he began a survey of men in the room, saying that after the war's end, he would invite them all to his capacious home and asking, "What is your favorite drink?"

My response, after months away from such treats, was, "My favorite would be a double-chocolate malted milk." My reply ranked near the bottom of the beverage sophistication index, the tacit objective of the survey. The ratings of the man who had served as a bartender soared, and he would soon be elected as room leader.

The man closest to the door was selected by us to fetch the noon meal. He returned with a bucket full of thin soup. The bucket was placed on the table, and the soup was dipped out by another man — with a clean cup, we insisted. Spectators clustered around the table, anxious to see that each portion was equal to the others, and all our cups were filled before we began eating.

After lunch, we were to send two or three men to the area of the potato cellar by the mess hall, to peel potatoes for the evening meal. Again we settled on a rotation basis for this assignment, and the men chosen went off to perform their duty. They returned with new information. The only utensils available for potato peeling were our table knives.

"They must be sharpened," they told us. "Dull knives just tear up the potatoes. And don't try to make thick peelings," they cautioned, "just take off the skins, then we'll have more to eat."

The rest of us took turns kneeling by the stove, honing our table knives on the bricks beneath it. After awhile we became skillful at dislodging the least amount of skin. The potatoes were returned to us at dusk each day, as a bucket of unseasoned mashed potatoes.

At about that time, I took an informative circuit around *C Lager*. Adjacent to our building, Barracks 3, was the wash house; it had a cement floor, built-in tables with a couple of sinks, and a small hand pump. Apparently, our clothing was to be washed in cold water, for the building boasted no means of heating water.

Fronting on the open space between rows of barracks was the latrine, set on a line perpendicular to that of the barracks and the wash house. It was to accommodate men from the five barracks on this side of the *Lager*. Inside, a large wooden box-like device contained 20 toilet seats. Just behind the latrine, perhaps at a distance of 15 feet, was a well with a hand pump. Said to be only 15-feet deep, it was our main source of drinking water. As the sanitary facilities received more frequent use, water from the pump became cloudy, then muddy in color. Boiling would be a necessity before drinking. And, we discovered, some flavoring would be required to counteract its taste.

Returning to the walking area near the warning line, I followed it past two more barracks buildings; then I turned, following the eastern fence line, past a somber guard tower, and on past the next barracks. All of the buildings were coated with a dull brown wash, as if to emphasize the already drab sameness of the camp. All of the barracks in the compound were raised higher off the ground than those in *A Lager*; possibly because the Germans had become more aware of the tunneling activities of prisoners in other camps. These barracks were high enough to permit dogs to circulate under the floors, to ensure that prisoners could not exit through the floor. To my surprise, I saw no evidence of a fire pool in this compound. How would it be possible to extinguish a fire, should one break out in the camp?

The vista on the walk along the north exterior fence was a mirror image of the route I had taken from behind my own barracks. Turning again along the fence by the interior road, I came to the building that contained a kitchen. Inspection revealed a couple of large boiling kettles; little else could be seen through the windows. We would refer to this building as a mess hall; however, we all ate in our rooms.

The north end of this building was reserved for the Commandant of the *Lager*, and perhaps a small staff. Neither on this day nor later did I notice people entering or leaving by the north door. The south end of the building contained a large room, presently in disarray. It would become a library, on rare occasions to be used as a meeting room or theater.

I walked around the mess hall, to the area along the warning wire. Behind the building was a hummock, very much like the cyclone cellars or root cellars familiar on farms in the American Midwest. This was the potato storage bin, where the men from our room had been sent that very morning to peel potatoes.

I completed my walk, having noted that the barbed-wire fence appeared to be electrified. I thought of the man who had been electrocuted while working on the fence, and wondered if, perhaps, all of the fences here were electrified — not just the external ones.

I climbed the couple of steps up to the rear door of my barracks, and stepped into a room for laundering and, I supposed, for bathing. Another room contained a two-seat latrine with one window, a real convenience for those long hours during which we would be locked in at night. The roving searchlights, visible through cracks in the blackout shutters, could be seen after dark. Adjacent to the latrine was my room; another door just across the hall led to Room 5. Midway up the hall were two rooms, one on either side of the hall, joined because the dividing wall had been omitted for some reason.

On up the hall were other rooms, just like mine. Men were lounging, as there was little else to occupy their time. Yet some men were absent from every room, no doubt due in part to avoid the crowded conditions, and so that they could get a change of scenery, explore the camp more fully, or exercise to remain fit for a future escape attempt — always present in our minds.

This day we received the first of our Red Cross food rations, a can of corned beef to be shared among four men. Discussion led to the formation of sharing groups, then one man from each group emptied the can and, under careful supervision of the other three, divided the contents into four parts. The irregular shape of the corned beef can made this a challenging task that allowed opportunity for dissatisfaction.

A few days later, after the room received two decks of cards, this cause for food-ration friction would be resolved by the cutting of cards, with the highest draw being first to select a piece, the others choosing in turn. Similar questions of equity arose with the distribution of bread and other foodstuffs and also with other supplies that entered the room in very limited quantities. These recurrent matters were resolved in the same way, by the drawing of cards. Much thoughtful effort went into the enterprise of seeking the exact location of the ace of spades, as men took turns at cutting the deck. To the best of my knowledge, no one attempted to mark the high cards, possibly because that would give others a similar advantage.

After we had emptied the cans, each room's ration was returned to an area beside the potato cellar. We were allowed one hour in which to return the cans. These were deposited neatly on the ground in the presence of a guard, who penciled a tally in his notebook. Dire consequences were threatened should fewer cans be turned in than had entered the compound less than two hours previously.

Supper again consisted of a bucket of plain mashed potatoes with no seasoning. But the men were free to use their daily pat of margarine or later, after the Red Cross margarine ration was issued, to flavor the potatoes from their own supply. After the evening meal, each man cleaned his cup and utensils as best he could in the water considered unsafe for drinking. We used that for brushing teeth, as well.

Until the days grew shorter, there was time after supper to stroll around the compound. There had been little else to do until the decks of cards had arrived, or until the library became functional. At dusk, two men were assigned to cover the windows with blackout shutters. During the day, these were stored on hangers adjacent on either side of the double window in our room. When in place, they effectively darkened the room, and admitted no light to the outside, either.

Then the other men in the room turned the table in line with the doorway, unrolled their mattresses, and spread their blankets for the night. Controlled from outside the barracks, the ceiling light came on, providing dim illumination. We knew when the light was to be extinguished; and because the room would be in inky blackness, we all would be in bed when the light went out. But darkness did not discourage conversation, for the quiet seemed to stimulate memories, which we shared.

Even in October the nights were chilly. The floor of our barracks consisted of a single layer of boards, very much like the sub-flooring of the houses most of us knew from home. Raised off the ground, the wind blew under and through the cracks between the boards. That bothered me a little, but I was protected by my thin mattress, a layer of blanket, and a neighbor very close to me on either side. But nights were especially uncomfortable for Tony Franco, whose burn-scarred body still ached from the cold. Tony, at that time, had only one man beside him. Although 11 men were arrayed along the other walls, they were drawn up to themselves, because of their short blankets. Tony had no one at his feet to break the chill. It was discovered that first night that the wood shavings in our thin blankets provided little padding from the board floors. In addition, if uncomfortable, a man simply could not shift his position on his own. We learned to shift on signal. The first man who could no longer stand his position would sing out, "One, Two, Three, *Shift!*" — and 22 men would flip simultaneously to their other side.

The chill air of morning penetrated our thin clothing as we stood in formation at *appel*. Men clapped their hands over their freezing ears to protect them. There was no penalty for these acts, for guards seemed more concerned that we stand in place, so that we could be counted, than in our standing strictly at attention.

Chapter 22

Barracks Life in *C Lager*

THOUGH THE ROOM was pitch-dark, we knew when morning had arrived, for the electric light dangling from the ceiling came on again. Soon our room was alive with the sounds of men talking, dressing, and pulling on stockings and shoes. Our neighbors on the floor were disturbed and awakened as their blankets were pulled off. Rasping sounds at the outer doors of the barracks intruded into the room as guards removed the bars that sealed us in at night. Heavy footsteps resounded through the hall, and our door swung open with a bang.

"*Raus! Appel!*" shouted the guard, menacing with his rifle. In whatever state of attire we were found at that minute, we thundered out of the door, down the hall, and out in front of our barracks. A guard formed us into rows, and we were called to attention as an officer strode to the center of the compound and uttered commands, which were relayed to others. A guard then passed behind us, counting the men in the formation. Another passed in front, counting from that vantage point. After a quick conference, the total was relayed to another guard, who collected the numbers from the other barracks and took them to the Commanding Officer of *A Lager*, clad in a tailored gray leather coat, standing in the center. There the compound total was added. The number corresponded with the number of men registered in the compound, and we were dismissed.

Back inside, we folded our mattresses back to the wall, turned the table and benches, and cleaned the room. One man was dispatched to fetch the morning drink. The "tea" was warm. However, another man, in his disgust with the taste of the brew, used his cupful as shaving water. On several ensuing days, others copied his behavior. All would become quite thirsty before the next day's ration. The rest of us sliced off a bit of our remaining black bread, bit into the sour mass, and washed it down with the morning brew.

I had rinsed out my cup from the tap in the wash room and placed it in my Red Cross box, now my cupboard. I rummaged through the valise given me at the distribution camp at Wetzlar. The sewing kit caught my eye. It had a quantity of khaki and olive-drab thread; more, I thought, than necessary for replacing buttons. To occupy myself, I selected khaki thread and sat on my folded mattress, saddle stitching my dress blouse. The finished product would be distinctive, and unofficial; but a blouse without insignia seemed unofficial, too. As I was plying my needle, a guard tried to open the door. He encountered a man sitting against it in the crowded room. Savagely, he kicked the door wider open, dislodging the prisoner from his seat. The guard surveyed the room, looking for what I knew not; but it was clear that we were under surveillance, and that no disapproved activity would be tolerated.

Later, someone brought in two decks of aircraft recognition cards, the kind we had been issued during training. On the face of each card, instead of the usual number of spades, hearts, diamonds, and clubs, were drawings of aircraft — our own, those of our Allies, and of Axis planes. Men sitting at the table quickly determined that from two decks they could assemble one deck of pinochle cards, which they put together and began a game. Putting aside my sewing, I went outside to take a turn around the compound.

As I came back to the barracks, Bill Knightley was also returning, bearing a cross about one foot long on its vertical dimension, and fashioned from short boards stained brown. Speaking fluent German, Knightley had bargained with a guard to procure the boards and to fashion the cross, at the cost of a few American cigarettes, for which he had no other use. Knightley then went across the hall to Room 5, where two of his friends were industriously carving small bars of soap. Their amateur, but painstaking, work resulted in a likeness of a crucifixion figure. When the figure was attached to the cross, Bill, using his shoe for a hammer, pounded a stray nail through the cross and into the outer wall of the room, readily visible to all who entered.

Soon another guard brought him some pine twigs, from which he fashioned a sort of wreath. The whole gave a credible approximation of a shrine. The two soap sculptors visited to see the final result of their handiwork, and returned to their own room quite satisfied with their contribution.

Charles J. "Charlie" Summers and Norman J. "Rich" Ritchie, had just performed their first, and perhaps only, carving. Both were Roman Catholic, which Bill Knightley had discovered quite early in their captivity. That factor in common may have given impetus to their cooperation in this project.

The next guard who entered our room stopped in astonishment at the crucifix, then wheeling back to the hallway, shouted for his companion to come. The two stood inside our doorway for a couple of minutes, staring in fascination; I believe it signified to them that here were prisoners who cared about loftier ideals. Then, nodding a greeting to us all, they went about their rounds. After that, and in our room where we could be identified, these particular guards always treated us with respect and consideration.

The barracks was now being visited on a regular basis by our camp Intelligence Committee, who had visited us in the tent at *A Lager*. As these men entered, a lookout was placed at each outside door, ready to give an alarm in the event that a guard should appear. They brought with them news of the war that seemed to be quite up-to-date. They also told us about events in the other compounds, such as shakedown searches by the Germans, and of shipments of Red Cross parcels and supplies arriving for distribution. And they encouraged us quickly to hold elections of our representatives to the *Lager* government.

Not yet interested in learning a new card game and stimulated by the success of my sewing project, I decided to make a pocket-sized notebook in which to record the names of my roommates and other fellow prisoners. For the note paper I collected the wrappers of cigarette packages as my companions discarded them; a flap from the cover of my Red Cross food box seemed fitting material for a cover. Trimmed and bent back on itself, the folded section held a quantity of papers and permitted me to sew them together as a unit. When finished, the back side of the inner wrappers provided a white sheet on which to write; their fronts had proclaimed the brand of cigarettes from which they came — Chesterfields, Camels, Raleighs, and, still, no Lucky Strikes. The interior wrappings of wartime cigarette packs had no foil. No doubt, like the green pigment used for packaging Lucky Strike Green, the foil had also "gone to war," used to make up the strips of radar-fooling chaff, which by now so plentifully cluttered the fields of Europe. Instead, the inner wrappings were of a dark gray paper. That made entries on those pages harder to read, but they had two virtues — they were there, and both sides could be used for notes.

With lots of time available to me, I used a dog-tag outline to space entries of the men in my room. Then I asked my roommates to print their name and home address inside those rounded squares.

As others returned from their activities elsewhere, I requested that they do the same. Then I went next door, to Room 5, and solicited names and addresses from those men. In the process, I became better acquainted with the men I had met earlier and made some new acquaintances, as well. One of these was Gerald "Rollie" Ralston, whose home town was Des Moines, Iowa. An Iowan myself, I wondered if there were others from my state. Rollie knew of several, and I listed their names. Being careful of my limited supply of paper, I bunched the names together, closer than those printed in the spaces defined by the outlines of dog tags. I resolved to get a complete list of the Iowans in *Stalag Luft IV.* My venture occupied many otherwise tedious hours.

★ ◎ ★ ◎ ★

In time, news came that the library was open. Books could be checked out, and waiting lists would be established for those most popular. I hurried over to the library, a large room adjacent to the kitchen, and asked for *Life in a Putty Knife Factory*, a book I had heard would provide entertaining reading. The book was already in circulation, so my name, number 238, was added to the list. If each of the readers took only two days to finish the book, how long would it take for my name to come to the top? I hoped I would not be a prisoner for that long. I asked for another, *The Stray Lamb*, also recommended. There were already more than 200 names for that book, too. There was no master list of the library's collection, and because the room was crowded, no one was being admitted behind the counter to look at the books in stock. I went away empty-handed and disappointed.

At about this time, the camp representatives encouraged us to see to our schooling, asking if there were men among us who could offer classes. However, with no room able to accommodate a large group of men from various parts of the camp, the classes might at first be offered to the men in a single sleeping room.

Bill Knightley suggested that he might be persuaded to offer a class in English grammar, and somewhat surprisingly, most of the men in our room indicated an interest in that. Shortly thereafter, Knightley stood in front of a crowded Room 9, along with several men from Room 5 joining us. Bill was a good teacher, explaining concepts better, most agreed, than had our teachers at home. He held our interest, as men took notes with stub pencils on the paper from cigarette wrappers.

After a few classes, Knightley announced that the class would be discontinued; he had covered the rudiments of basic grammar. But interest in classes had been aroused, and Vincent Landolfi, who had worked as a bartender in Manhattan, said he would teach a class in bartending. That class, too, was fully subscribed, and Vince, who relished being the center of attention, introduced us to the niceties of appropriate stemware, to a wide variety of liquors new to many of us, and to a vast array of concoctions, more plentiful than I had ever dreamed, even though there was absolutely no opportunity in our present situation to put this new knowledge to use.

Vince was subsequently elected our Room Leader, and John H. Beattie, of the double room 7-8, was elected Barracks Leader. Beattie, an outgoing and cheerful fellow, would now often accompany the camp Intelligence Committee on its rounds of our barracks. Almost daily they would arrive with fresh news of the war, usually attributed to the Armed Forces Network, and despite many conjectures about where the radio came from or was kept, very little was known about it. Much later, we learned that the small radio had come into the camp in a parcel, the package marked with a special code. The sorting team, naturally composed of key "organization" men, had contrived to slip it out of the *vorlager* past the guards. Its presence, however, was suspected by our captors, and became the impetus for several surprise raids on rooms throughout the camp.

The Intelligence team usually came in the afternoon, stopping by each room. Men clustered closely about these purveyors of information, who spoke in hushed tones, cautious lest they be overheard by a guard. The news they brought gained credence by its contrast to a second source regarding the war effort. About weekly, a German newspaper — I believe it was *Der Frankfurter Zeitung* — appeared in our room. We depended upon Bill Knightley to interpret for us. Bill had been in daily contact with Benedictines from Germany, flexing his language skills.

Compared with the bulletins brought by the Intelligence Committee, the German press reports tended to lag days or weeks behind what Armed Forces Radio reported to be the actual movement on those fronts. News brought in by the camp Intelligence Committee, then, became an important source of prisoner morale.

Our physical condition, meanwhile, worsened on the meager diet of the camp. *Ersatz* tea in the morning, thin soup at noon, and potatoes at night, supplemented by a small piece of bread and pat of margarine did not maintain our physical condition. Hunger became a constant companion, even after the evening portion of potato. Within a few weeks, the men's talk ceased to dwell on girls, and focused upon food. I wasn't the only one who craved a chocolate malted milk, but most desired something they could sink their teeth into.

"I remember a restaurant in Kansas City," one fellow exulted, "where the steaks are aged in a cool room in the back. They turn a bluish color, and on a sizzling platter, they are so tender you wouldn't believe it!"

"Back on the farm, Mother would put a fried egg right on the top of my pancake," said another, "and then I would smother it with butter and syrup. When I get home, I'll want a pancake sandwich for breakfast — two eggs on my pancake, covered with second pancake, then a big slice of ham, and another pancake — all smothered in syrup!"

A third man lamented a piece of pie left on his plate in a California restaurant. "I'd give anything to bite into that pie right now," he told us.

The eagerly awaited Red Cross supplemental rations provided a welcome variety to the monotony of our meals, and brought unexpected nutritional benefits as well. Hank Smith was not fond of liver paté, so we traded; I gave him my portion of tuna for his ration of paté. Together, this amounted to a weekly supply of about four ounces of paté for me and, spread on the black *brodt*, made the bread more palatable.

The American Red Cross #10 food parcel, the one most regularly received in camp, contained one 8-ounce tropical chocolate bar (for which M&M's were substituted in one package), 2 or 4 ounces of instant coffee (tempting to our captors, so that the cans arrived only about ⅓ full), 16 ounces of powdered whole milk (Klim), 8 ounces of lump sugar, 8 ounces of liver paté (occasional substitute, peanut butter), 7¾ ounces of salmon or tuna, 12 ounces of Spam, 8 ounces of cheese, 12 ounces of corned beef (occasionally, C-ration as a substitute), 6 ounces of jelly or preserves, and 4 or 5 packs of cigarettes. Not standard were 1 ounce each of salt and pepper, 2 bars of soap, and vitamin C tablets. None of us had ever seen M&M's before, but we found the candy to be very good indeed.

Some weeks later, when a guard came to the room to hustle us out for *appel*, Hank suddenly slumped while in the act of rising. After someone had helped him to his feet and supported him to the barracks door, he regained his strength and met the formation on his own power. After that incident, he regularly had difficulty in rising, unless he did so very slowly. His face had become more pallid than those of most of his fellows, and his lips had developed an unhealthy blue hue. That I had no such problem furnished a clue, and we decided that his problem must be anemia caused by a deficiency of iron. We came to the conclusion that his iron deficiency was caused by the avoidance of paté, while my absence of such symptoms was due to my consuming the rations for both of us. Henry then retained his small portion for his own use, and I began to experience the same symptoms.

One man in our room had unexpected success at the library and checked out a book by Damon Runyon. Don Housler was elated with his discovery, and quickly others — mostly fellows from the East Coast — were similarly affected. Runyon had been a widely read columnist for a New York area newspaper. His writings about the lifestyles of denizens of the *demi monde* had been republished in book form, most notably *Guys And Dolls*, later playing in legitimate theater and on film.

We decided that the reading of Runyon should be a group venture, and the men of the room were assembled from time to time to hear a chapter. Housler began, interrupted occasionally by his listeners, who compared the characterizations of persons in the book to men in the room. So Don Housler was nicknamed "Harry the Horse," Bill Knightley "Educated Edmund," and so on. As had been true for the period when our men offered their classes, for several days the focus of interest became the *Guys and Dolls* floating crap game and its habitués.

But the harsher realities of those days continued to be the routines of sharing too little food, too little water, trying to compensate for the chill in our room, and roll calls. One day, while standing at *appel*, I noted a man whose ears were covered by the flaps of a knitted cap. I was not the only one who made that observation, and the discovery led to a steady stream of customers at the knitter's abode. As others had told me, I carried to him the knit sweater I had acquired with the provisions at *Dulag Luft* at Wetzlar, and a package of cigarettes. In exchange for these, I would soon receive a billed knit cap with ear flaps and my sweater, now sleeveless. The knitters displayed an artistic flair, using some of the wool from the donor's sweater for the major part of the cap, and part of another man's sweater to finish the cap in a contrasting color. My new cap, maroon and tan, topped by a little tassel, solved my problem of cold ears, released my hands from covering my ears so that I could warm the hands in my pockets, and later became extremely useful as a container for cooked potatoes and other foodstuffs.

The knitters, as I learned later, were Richard Shearer, Norman Peterson, and Marion Saar, three men from Nebraska who had met as prisoners. Richard had acquired the skill before becoming a prisoner, and enlisted his new friends into the activity.

In the meanwhile, Bill Knightley had established a relationship with the *Lager* librarian. He had reviewed the books on the shelves and received permission to check out those that were not in high demand. He brought me a copy of Geoffrey Chaucer's *Beowulf* in the middle-English version, and coached me until I could understand the old language. Later he procured a set of 12 volumes of Joseph Addison and Sir Richard Steele's *The Spectator*, which I eventually read in their entirety. Those books were a more than welcome diversion, contrasting with the monotony of my daily life. Reading was a daylight occupation; the illumination from the single small bulb dangling bare from a wire in our ceiling made it all but impossible after the shutters had been closed.

Those windows were shuttered earlier now, as the daylight hours drew more quickly to a close. Then, after the evening ration of potatoes had been distributed and consumed and the eating utensils cleaned, a pinochle game resumed at the table — but not for long, for the space was needed by those who would roll out their mattress pads and seek some warmth under a blanket. For a while, until the room light was turned off by the unseen guard, there would be some general conversation, while individual men followed their more private inclinations, such as checking the meager supplies in their personal containers. Then we huddled in our short blankets, on our side, of course, to seek more comfort in sleep.

News came that the rationing of coal would begin. Each room was to send one man to receive the daily allowance. Cecil Smith, otherwise known as "Smitty" or "Okie," in recognition of his family's migration to California, was selected to perform this chore on the first day. That was logical, for he slept closest to the door. Smitty was a long time on that errand, and he returned with a Red Cross parcel box full of building-brick-sized briquettes of coal. This wasn't the normal ration, he was quick to explain. He had been first in line at the coal supply, and since the guard on duty did not want to dirty his uniform, he had asked Smitty to hand out the coal to the others. Each room received a single briquette, but when the task was completed, the guard told Smitty to take all he could carry, and to come back tomorrow to repeat the duty.

Eager hands rapidly kindled a fire, and the small stove was quickly encircled by men anxious to experience warmth. And warmth there was, for if one briquette could produce heat, two or three seemed to magnify the effect. In the interest of prudence, though, we opted to economize on our supply, so that it would last until the morrow. The radiance from that fire reached out into the room, creating a level of comfort we had not experienced for some weeks.

During the course of the evening we were visited by men from other rooms, bent on trading a can of grape jelly for a more coveted flavor, or to acquire powdered coffee for their room. The heat from the other fires was now gone, and the warmth from our stove became a magnet for our cold mates. Soon, men from other rooms entered and crowded around our fire, some of them finding one pretext or another; but others were more frank in the purpose of their visit — they sought relief from the cold. The room became crowded, and the body heat from so many men added to the comfort level. Smitty had brought us a bonanza.

Often the men hurried out of the barracks at the announcement, "*Mail call!*" The event was always welcomed, even though there were few letters to be distributed, for each communication brought a reminder that we were not entirely forgotten. I always joined the group clustering around the prisoner of war bearing the mail, even though I didn't expect to receive a letter myself, at least not until early November. But the men who had survived the perilous "run into the camp," when evacuated from *Stalag Luft VI*, had been prisoners for many months — even years — and there was usually mail for some of them.

Eventually, one man with whom I was acquainted, from Iowa, received a box in the mail. To the envy of all around him, it contained 24 Oh Henry! candy bars, his favorite. Perhaps he shared some of it with other men in his room. Certainly, the bars would have brought good trades in the camp economy, but I never heard any more about it.

The news was passed from the next compound, *D Lager*, of an American who had received a package containing his favorite cookies from his British wife. He was so happy about the gift and its implication of an enduring relationship that, while circling the compound on his routine walk, he shared that news with an RAF flier whom he chanced to meet.

He, too, was married, and their conversation quickly promoted a kinship between them. As their circuit approached the Yank's barracks, he invited the Brit to his room to share a cookie.

"Why, that's the same kind my wife bakes!" interjected the Brit. And their wives bore the same name, too. A train of similarities led to the discovery that the Yank's wife had indeed been married to the RAF flier. The latter had been a prisoner for a long time, and listed as Missing In Action. So his supposed widow seemingly had remarried, this time to an American airman. I can only imagine the shock of that realization. But the story was told that the two men vowed to stay together, and upon their eventual return to England, to go to the home of their wife and announce, "We're home, Dear!"

The story highlighted the fragility of the relationships of men so separated from their loved ones. Out of touch and just possibly forgotten, they became intensely dependent upon their pre-existing romantic attachments. But there was the worry — might they become doubly victimized by their imprisonment?

An item of mail that probably had the greatest impact upon the men of *Stalag Luft IV* was delivered one autumn day to a resident of *C Lager*. The addressee was a man who so appreciated the sweater given him with his supplies at Wetzlar that he used one of his precious letter forms to write to the lady whose name and address was affixed as a label. He had told her of the circumstances of his receiving her handiwork and the comfort afforded as protection against the cold Baltic air. He told her, too, of how the sleeves of the sweater had been detached and used to fashion a cap that now protected his ears and served at times as a handy container. He concluded with an expression of gratitude.

His letter was one of a very few received by the men who had been captured in the summer of 1944, and it bore the promise of a link established between the prison camp and a caring world back home. But the message of the return letter was far different from what was expected. The writer expressed indignation that she had spent countless hours knitting an object that would ultimately fall into the hands of a man so cowardly that he would surrender himself to the enemy.

In our camp, the effect of that letter was stunning. News of it quickly spread, and the expression of that sentiment depressed morale to a lower level than did even the news of German advances in the Battle of the Bulge, in December of 1944.

One Saturday during *appel*, the customary testing of the machine guns from the guard towers came to a close. We were respectful of those guns that the gunners were sometimes tempted to fire so dangerously near to us. This time, bullets strayed from the area in the center of our compound and cut through Barracks 4, the one neighboring mine. Dismay and rancor gave way to another emotion when it was discovered what damage had been wrought. One prisoner, to pass time, with table knife and a piece of glass, from bits of wood had fashioned replicas of military aircraft. Then he had hung his planes from the ceiling, using bits of thread. In one scene, a model of a P-51 Mustang was being pursued by a ME-109. The guard's bullet had shattered the German model, missing the P-51 entirely. News of the incident quickly dispersed through the compound, and was taken joyously as a token repayment to our captors for their treatment of us.

The prison diet, meanwhile, continued in its repetitious, frugal way. The ration varied occasionally, from a thin cabbage soup to an equally thin portion of dehydrated mixed vegetables, to — what I seem to remember best — a cup of clear liquid with several small, hard soybean-like entities rolling at the bottom of the cup. I dropped one of these once, and it bounced across the floor; they were as hard to chew as they are to describe.

A small but welcome treat was provided on Saturdays, when a special ration was doled out, varying between a cautious portion of malodorous Leiderkranz cheese, a tablespoon of sugar, six green tobacco Russian cigarettes, or a tablespoon of fruit spread. These rations, I thought, came from our captors, but later I learned that Frank Paules, our "Man of Confidence" — our liaison with the captors — received weekly a small amount of money per capita for the men in the camp and permission to leave the camp to make purchases for them. On another occasion, in December I think, each man received a bar of soap and, later, shipped in the same railway car, a package of Rob Roy cigarettes. The cigarettes had a perfumed aroma, no doubt entering the packages from the soap.

But gustatory treats were provided by our captors on more than one occasion. News rocketed through the *A Lager* grapevine one day that mutton was to appear on our supper menu. Even those who were dubious about their taste for mutton were elated by that information, for we had never received meat from our captors. Excited by that prospect, Hank Smith and I, on our circuit of the compound, stopped by the windows to the kitchen to ascertain whether this rumor might be true. There they lay, two dressed carcasses, laid out on a counter near the window. In our imagination we could almost savor the taste of meat. Then we noticed the lower extremities of the animals. They had no hoofs. Those were paws!

Another rumor had it that one of our friendlier guards — we called him "Jimmy Gleason" because of his resemblance to a character actor in films of that time — had been bitten by his guard dog, and the dog had been put to death. Could this meat be that animal?

Back in our room, we shared our observations with our neighbors. There was little doubt about it, we declared; meat was being prepared for our dinner. But it wasn't exactly mutton. Nevertheless, our neighbors were reconciled with the news that we would have meat, and our anticipation grew. However, we were little prepared for the quantity of meat to be provided by the two carcasses. When divided into 2,500 portions, the most any of us found in our cup of potatoes was two small strands of sinew — a "modest" portion of protein, indeed.

On a later occasion, the work detail from our room arrived at the potato cellar to learn that the evening's ration would be cut to one-half, but that the portions would be supplemented by sauerkraut, and suckling pig. Yes, a shipment of suckling pigs had already arrived at the kitchen, and were being duly prepared for mixture with our ration of potatoes and sauerkraut. Hope overcame our skepticism, and we waited, salivating in anticipation, for the arrival in our room of our bucket of supper. The man charged with apportioning the evening meal tried as carefully as he was able to place an equitable serving into each cup. Then, as each man inspected the contents, he found disappointment once again. Two men discovered animal parts mixed in their serving; one had two short strands of muscle. The other found a tooth and bit of gum. We learned later that for our meat supply that day, 12 baby pigs had been distributed between 2,500 men! And the volume of sauerkraut did not quite equal the volume of potatoes they were to replace

I continued to be in attendance when mail was brought into the compound. By this time, I thought that news of my capture might have arrived back home and that relatives would have my address. But time passed, and I began to experience a little disappointment. Lacking mail of my own, I was eager to learn what messages others were receiving. One day a man standing near me reading a letter from his mother uttered a pained expression. "They just don't understand!" he complained. "My mother tells me that things are difficult back home; the family gets only one pound of butter per week, has to stint on sugar, and can have a good beef roast only once a week!"

That prisoner received a lot of sympathy from men who could only wish that they could taste butter and roast beef just once in several months. News of that failure to understand the thin rations we prisoners of war were receiving traveled quickly. Could our home folks really fail to know the depths of our deprivation? Regrettably, many of them did not understand the suffering by prisoners. One mother wrote to her son that someone he knew from his hometown was a prisoner in Germany.

"Why don't you go over to visit him?" she asked.

Sadly, many were accused by family and friends of exaggerating their experiences.

Perpetually hungry, Room Leader Vince Landolfi arranged a football game between Room 9 and the adjoining one, the double-size Room 7-8. He proposed that the loser of the game forfeit their bucket of potatoes that evening, the winner to receive the ration as the prize. As Vince presented it, we had an advantage. We had just discovered that Mel Demmin, the very quiet fellow from Peoria, Illinois, and who slept next to me, had been an All-State high school quarterback. Vince and a couple of the other men checked out a football and encouraged Mel to practice passing it to other fellows in our room. Mel's passes had satisfied those who watched the exhibition, and those of us who had a bit of high school football experience. The idea of the competition was quickly accepted, but a number of us voiced concern that we might lose our supper as well as the game. Eventually, Vince's proposal won approval, and the game was scheduled.

A fiercely contested touch-football game was played in the center of the compound. Mel Demmin's passing ability lived up to prediction, but no one had taken sufficient account of the ability of the former University of Southern California guard, who was a resident in Room 7-8. The big fellow who had been so roughly handled by "Big Stoop" upon our arrival at camp was almost equally rough on those of us, linemen and backfield, who sought to protect our quarterback.

At first, I played on the line, being rewarded for that activity by having my knuckles stepped on. Later, I shifted to the backfield, attempting to guard Mel Demmin while passing. The big USC guard, even with his body mass reduced by prison diet, hurtled with punishing ferocity through the offensive line. Standing in his path, I crouched to block his intended assault. On he came with knees lifted high, and my ribs only deflected his advance.

With credit to Mel Demmin's passing, Room 9 won a narrow victory that day. However, the prize was rejected through the generosity of Vince Landolfi, so that our opponents could eat their slim, but well-deserved supper.

Several of us went to the *Lager* dispensary after the game. There was nothing to be done about my cracked ribs, of course, and the dispensary had no ointments or bandages to offer for skinned knuckles. Our doctor had several choice phrases for us — in essence, "Don't be so foolish as to risk your bodies in childish games! There is a shortage of medication. Don't you know there is a war on?"

Chapter 23

After the Coming of Fire

AFTER OUR ROOM was assured of a constant supply of coal, we began construction of a cooking grate to insert above the burning level in our stove. The steel strips of the grate were the tops of the weekly ration of the Klim powdered milk cans — removed with their affixed metal key. These pieces were saved, then, straightened out and woven into a round grate, which was then anchored high in the stove. At first, the grate was used much as an oven to heat cans of food. Later it was discovered that the black bread became more palatable when toasted under a layer of Leiderkranz cheese. When heated, the cheese fairly boiled, and percolated into the bread, giving it a zesty flavor.

Morning rituals were easier after we made our cooking grate. We had warm water for shaving and, used sparingly, for sponge baths. Water from the pump, with its characteristically brown color and its taste even *more* brown, could be boiled on the stove; and when powdered coffee was added — and sugar and powdered milk — its unsanitary condition and flavor were overcome. Although there never was enough hot water to thoroughly wash eating utensils, warm water served us well. Luckily, no one acquired food poisoning while we remained in camp.

In our small crowded rooms, interpersonal contact was intense, and the men in each began to acquire characteristics that set their abode apart from the others. Our room became distinctive for the pervasiveness of pinochle playing and for the adoption of personal features taken from the Damon Runyon book. We also were insistent upon cleanliness. To remain clean in body, we braved the icy chill of the barracks bath room to sponge off with tepid water. And we endured the scraping by oft-used razor blades in order to remain relatively clean-shaven. We used the tepid water and hand soap to wash our underclothing, rinsing them in cold water, then wringing them by hand before hanging them to dry. Early on, the clothes were hung outdoors on lines strung beside the barracks. Some were hung in the washroom, but that was too small for the amount of space needed. With the advent of a regularized fire in our room, shoelaces were tied together and strung across the room to accommodate clothing already beyond the dripping stage.

To guard against lice, we submitted to the attempts of our roommates to cut our hair. There were no scissors, but someone came up with the idea to use a razor, cutting against a comb. Eventually many of us acquired some ability at the practice, and a few exceptionally talented men were able to market their skills for the price of a few cigarettes. It wasn't just the matter of avoiding lice, but pride — we were American soldiers, and felt we ought to look as proud as possible.

That was the outlook and practice in our room. I was to learn that the other groups of men who associated closely with one another similarly developed standards distinctively their own. In Room 5, just across the hall, no one ever played pinochle; bridge was the card game always. That was true also in other small groups throughout the *Lager*, and adhering to the rules of the game became as much an obsession as was winning. Loud voices from our neighboring room expressed fury over the failure of a player to follow suit. One man became so incensed when his partner trumped the player's ace, that he chased him down the central hallway, finally trapping him at the closed door, and stabbed him with his table knife. That news fortified my resolve, and the opinions of my roommates, to avoid the game of bridge entirely.

The men in a room near our own went to extraordinary lengths to maintain a supply of hot coffee. Each time I visited, I found a can of the hot liquid steaming on the stove. I have no idea how they acquired a sufficient amount of fuel to keep their coffee hot, but suspect that they must have traded other goods for the briquettes. That was clearly true with respect to the supply of powdered instant coffee. Rations of coffee were very slim, and men from that room regularly appeared in other areas of the compound, eager to trade chocolate, fruit preserves, and other scarce items for quantities of coffee.

One room became quite careless about the tidiness of their quarters and their personal hygiene; they established a preference for what men in our little cultural enclave viewed as slovenliness. Many of the men became bearded and let their hair remain uncut. We grew concerned about the matter, which we referred to the barracks organization. Other rooms had viewed the matter as we did, and that room was told to clean up, or else face eviction from the barracks at night. In this case, mass opinion, backed by the threat of forceful action, had resulted in the modification of the behavior of those occupants. Later, when vacating the camp, we ascertained that there had been no infestation by vermin in our barracks. We attributed this condition to our emphasis upon cleanliness.

For some of us, there was another reason to tidy our personal appearance. Few special occasions — perhaps none other than this — prompted good grooming, except Sunday worship. I cleaned up each Sunday for the Protestant service. There was a Roman Catholic service, too, though I had no direct contact with the Catholic chaplain. My "minister," who may have been named Father Jackson, was said to be a civilian from one of the Channel Islands, sequestered when the Nazis occupied that area. He had volunteered for service in prison camps. I believe he was of the Anglican Church. I have heard of two other chaplains in *Stalag Luft IV*; certainly there was none of the Jewish faith.

Our services were held outdoors near Barracks 8, across the compound from mine. The minister remained standing throughout the service, while men clustered around him, sitting on the ground; a few in the back remained standing. We had no hymnals, so the pastor led us in singing old and well-known songs of worship, such as "Rock of Ages." In our confined condition, that hymn began to hold special meaning for me, and the singing, though unaccompanied, was spirited.

A uniformed guard hovered in the background, as if to report any seditious communication, causing some uneasiness among those in attendance. The sermons were directed at the discomfort associated with our captivity and to our concerns for loved ones elsewhere. Reference was made to battles being waged by our compatriots, and to the brutality of warfare, especially as conducted by our enemies. I always expected the guard to object to such references. If he did, he must have reported it to his superiors after conclusion of the service. The minister's prayers spoke to the matters that weighed heavily on our minds. He understood our condition, thereby easing our worries and developed a steadfast and faithful following.

During these initial days at *C Lager*, a fellow prisoner had told me that he had successfully smuggled into the camp a silk evasion map of wartime Germany, sewn into the lining of his clothing. He consented to loan it to me for a few days. I had plenty of time to examine the map carefully, plotting a grid by which to memorize the location of key cities and rail lines and noting impediments to passage over terrain should I be traveling on foot. Essentially, I was formulating a plan of escape, and pondering the risk of entering a Baltic port and seeking clandestine passage to Sweden — or alternatively, to travel east to meet Soviet forces. However, I could speak neither German, Swedish, nor Russian. Thinking the matter too risky to involve a fellow prisoner, I mentioned it to no one until I could gather some confidence in my strategy. Eventually, I knew, I would have to present a persuasive plan to the Escape Committee in order to gain their approval and cooperation.

I continued to make my twice-daily rounds of the compound, more intent than ever to discover some weakness in the surrounding fences. Often I walked with Hank Smith. Each time I circled the *Lager* I looked for places from which an escape could be made. The tangle of barbed wire between the double fences seemed a daunting challenge, but the dangerous mesh ended at the perimeter fence on the east side. The two guard towers commanded a clear view of that junction of the fences. . . . But wouldn't that be obscured on a foggy night?

As Hank and I strolled and talked, I turned over the idea in my mind, neglecting my earlier estimate that the fences were electrified. Suppose the wires were to be cut — would the sound of the snip be deadened by the fog?

Just after we had rounded the last corner and were approaching the rear of our own barracks, Hank spotted the familiar gait of a man walking near the warning rail in the adjacent compound. Across the no-man's land and fences he hailed the man, the flight engineer on Hank's crew, who answered his call. His face had been badly burned, but he had survived. As the two men exchanged questions and information about each other, their voices attracted the attention of the guard in the tower behind us. He shouted, then waved energetically for us to cease this communication. As he swung his machine gun in our direction, Hank and I stepped up into our barracks. Out of his sight, Hank continued the conversation with his crewmate, though not for long, for the other man was quickly intimidated, too. We learned that the treatment of his wounds had left a frightfully scarred face. He was bitter about that, but alive. Then he beat a hasty retreat from the path by the warning wire, ending the conversation.

I continued to mull over the prospects of escape. Rumor had it that two men had made their way out of the camp by concealing themselves in the food wagon. How they evaded detection once the wagon got to the *vorlager* I could only guess. My own plans had left many holes. Perhaps I could get more information from the Escape Committee. Certainly, I should need to acquire wire cutters in order to breach the barbed-wire enclosures.

John Beattie, my barracks leader, directed me to our *Lager*'s representative on the committee, and I was able to meet him in a quiet setting. I told him my idea, and had to acknowledge the risks in the operation — I had no backup supply of food, did not know German, had no foolproof way to evade the guard dogs, and had no precise knowledge of the railroad depots in the area. The committee apparently recognized those risks, plus the reality that the fence through which I wished to pass was electrified. They denied my petition for wire cutters and disapproved my escape plan. That was a severe disappointment, but I soon began to appreciate the weaknesses in my plan, and as bitter winter swept in, I came to realize the hazards of trying to venture into Russia.

At about that time, the YMCA created more diversions for us by bringing an array of musical instruments into the camp. Very quickly I became aware that Cecil Smith had acquired a guitar, on which he played Western music. Another man, William "Offsides" Smith, brought a cornet into the room. He had boasted of auditioning with some well-known big bands, and the prospect of hearing sweet melodies quickly faded when we discerned that his lip produced only the sounds of a beginner.

Down the hall, in Room 1, someone promptly displayed his mastery of the clarinet by playing "You Can Win, Winsooki." Having once played it through, he repeated the melody — and repeated it, and repeated it again. Soon the tune became tiresome, then irritating. I checked to see if I could identify the player. He was a loner in his room, the sole survivor of a bomber that had gone down in flames. His facial burns were clearing up, but his ears existed only as small pointed appendages. He must have considered himself to be grotesque, as his fellows did.

We had no skills among us to understand his psychological condition, which we would later learn to be post-traumatic stress disorder, and no competence among us to begin the healing process. His clarinet was the one comfort to which he could cling. But the same tune went on, hour after hour, almost without ceasing. His roommates at last cautioned him to limit his playing to daylight hours, and to pause for considerable intervals, on pain of being expelled from the room.

Nevertheless, there were musical treats in store. We learned that Charlie Summers, from Philadelphia, one of the soap sculptors whose work had contributed to the crucifix in our room, had a pleasing tenor voice. Charlie, who lived just across the hall, was prevailed upon to come to our room to sing to us after the lights were out. Perhaps it was modesty, but he refused to come when he could be seen. On many nights we were entertained with songs that became favorites — "A Pretty Girl is like a Melody," "Blue Room," "The Desert Song," amongst others. Interestingly, Charles became a priest after the war was over.

A small reed organ, probably of the sort used by chaplains in the field, had arrived along with the musical instruments. Its presence was announced by eerie notes emanating from Room 5, just across the hall. Henry F. "Frenchie" Jurgens, from Maspeth, New York, was playing the theme music from an evening radio show. But he could perform other music as well, and he, too, eventually accepted our invitation to serenade us after blackout, though darkness made transport of the little organ difficult, especially between the crowded rooms. We enjoyed his music — even more so, since we had so little of it at that time. Bedtime music became an expected part of our day.

Scenes like this must have been occurring throughout the camp, and would eventually result in a teamwork production for a Christmas show.

Thanksgiving 1944 brought an unforgettable treat — special holiday boxes from the Red Cross. Each man received a full parcel. Hungry men were inclined to overindulge, resulting in heavy traffic at the latrines. The intestinal upset didn't stop just when the doors were closed for the night, and there was noisy bumping and jostling in the dark hallway, and panicky exhortations from those in line to use the facilities.

The mass stomach discomfort was short-lived, but from the experience, many of us learned to observe caution about giving free rein to our appetites. Then our Red Cross rations were increased to a weekly basis — one-half package per man per week, just half the supplemental ration for which the parcels were designed. The food furnished by the Nazis remained about constant, so even the increase in rations did not assuage our hunger. But our diet became more rounded. Now, for example, we would occasionally discover a cellophane strip of vitamin C pills among our foodstuffs. And there was an occasional bar of soap that had escaped the hands of the plunderers.

Of great interest was the doubled supply of cigarettes. Since cigarettes served as the standard for exchange, it at first seemed probable that the values of other commodities would increase correspondingly with the influx of cigarettes. Curiously, that did not happen. The demand for tobacco, like that for food, was nearly insatiable, and many of the surplus cigarettes were smoked instead of traded, thereby limiting their impact upon the price of goods.

★ ★ ★

Chill winter winds now blew under our barracks, sending icy drafts through windows and cracks in our floor. Tony Franco suffered in his place under the window, so compassionate roommates offered him their thin overcoats to pile over his bed place, somewhat easing his discomfort. Then came snow; just a dusting at first, as a herald of the bitter winter that was on its way. Someone eyed the clean snow, fetched some in a Klim can, and brought it to our room. He covered a portion with jam, declaring that he had an "ice cream sundae" — ultra thin ice cream, but the idea caught on for a day or two. Shavings from a tropical chocolate D-bar, sometimes melted with a bit of snow water, made a sort of hot fudge sundae, too. Imaginations, where food was concerned, remained keen, to the point that snow could substitute for rich vanilla.

The snow began to accumulate, and the circular route inside the guard wire became a tramped-down path, as did the area where our barracks assembled for *appel*. Those who broke the path at the side of the barracks to attend to the blackout shutters soon found the mounting snowdrift deeper than they wished to wade through. So the idea was presented by our room leader at a barracks meeting that the snow should be banked up along the building. The purpose was two-fold: to clear a path for those detailed to handle the blackout shutter chore, and to insulate the floor boards from wintry winds. Working together, two or more men could manipulate the wooden shutters as a sort of snow shovel. That task was promptly accomplished, to the particular satisfaction of us who slept on the floor.

About that time, a few recently captured men were moved into the barracks. One had been in his own home for Thanksgiving dinner. We listened to his tale of speedy deployment to England and almost immediate loss of his aircraft on a mission. We were so impressed by his recent freedom that no one even thought to ask him what had occurred in the national elections of early November. He was assigned to Room 5, across the hall from our room. He had been there only a few days when he, like the rest of us when we first arrived, picked up needle and thread to relieve the boredom.

One day he was sitting on the floor, embroidering a handkerchief, when Big Stoop entered the room. With characteristic savagery, Big Stoop bent over and gave the man a mighty cuff, which sent him sprawling. When Big Stoop reached down to collar him, a dozen of his roommates jumped on the German guard and wrestled him to the floor. The sheer mass of their emaciated bodies was sufficient to hold him on the floor, his arms pinioned. The dilemma was that they could not release him, for he was capable of breaking the bodies of those who held him. Another man ran quickly to the office of the *Lager* Commandant, informing him of the predicament. Soon the Commandant arrived with two guards. The erstwhile captors were greatly relieved to release Big Stoop, and he was not seen in our *Lager* again.

Other events also occurred now, in rapid succession. Construction had begun on two additional compounds along the northern perimeter of the camp. Along with hundreds of other men impaired in health or physical ability, several men from our room, including Cecil Smith, John McCracken, Nerone Franco, William Smith, and one or two others, were taken by train from *Stalag Luft IV* to the *Luftwaffe* officers' camp, *Stalag Luft I*, at Barth, Germany. Contradictory rumors circulated, one claiming that they would receive better health care, another that they were destined to become orderlies for imprisoned officers.

Their places were soon filled by transfers from *B Lager*, which was being emptied, it appeared, to accommodate scraggly, weary refugees from areas to our east. We watched as these bent-over, dispirited columns trudged up our central street and through the gate into *B Lager*. Who were they — Poles, Russians? From their olive-drab clothing we could not tell. But there was no doubt that they were in misery. Many of them had bundled their feet with burlap or torn blankets, making walking all the more difficult through the snow. Later, we learned of the insistence of their hunger. Some of them had broken into the medical room in the *Lager*, and were now desperately ill after having eaten supplies of flea and louse powder. We surmised that they could not read the labels, and had mistaken the contents for food. Or were they so terribly hungry that it mattered little to them what they ate, just as long as they put something into their stomachs? That was a disturbing thought.

A shipment of games arrived, a sort of pre-Christmas present, providing a welcome diversity of amusement. Characteristically, the games of chance were seized upon as an opportunity to set up a casino, and our room became a gambling center.

Fortunes of "The Combine," composed of men who had pooled their cigarette resources, were on the rise. Their accumulated wealth provided them with opportunity to purchase additional food from the Red Cross rations. However, now they had to maintain watch over their possessions, for the hours of daylight and the early evening brought a stream of visitors to the room. But there were games less well adapted to gambling, and those of us not as bent on wagering retreated to our own areas to engage in them.

Rumors were plentiful in the camp. Some had a basis in fact; others resulted from conjecture, an elaboration of some observation or chance remark. Some, no doubt, were constructed from wishful thinking; others were fabricated entirely to introduce excitement into an otherwise monotonous existence.

One rumor in particular caught the fancy of the men in our barracks. Following closely on the heels of the shipment of musical instruments, this rumor seemed more than simply plausible.

Word had it that a shipment of 50 pairs of ice skates had arrived in the *vorlager*, and were to be distributed throughout the camp. We thought ice skating would be fun, but there was no pond in *C Lager*. The terrain had a gentle slope from the mess hall down to the perimeter fence. Nevertheless, we could overcome that; we could build a skating rink of our own.

The idea caught on, and crews of men scooped snow from the area beside the barracks to the center of the compound. With might and main they scooped, pushed, and shoved blackout shutters laden with snow, until a wall enclosed an area almost half the size of a football field. More snow was pushed into the center and tramped down to level out the natural slope of the ground. Then crews of men formed bucket brigades, catching water from the pumps and carrying it in the huge pitchers in which we received our morning tea. The water quickly froze after having been sprinkled over the "skating rink-in-the-making," forming a relatively smooth surface. With shutters replaced, we now waited for our skates to arrive.

A day or so later, while walking the circuit around the *Lager*, we saw men skating in *D Lager*. That afternoon, there was an indignant reaction to the news that all of the skates had been assigned to our neighbors; we would have none.

Nothing could be done. Discovering that our rubber-soled shoes slid well on the ice, clusters of men began to occupy themselves at that pastime. Then the idea arose that a hockey game could be played, even in the absence of skates. We would have to improvise both pucks and hockey sticks. I no longer remember how the materials were acquired, but sufficient equipment surfaced to equip two teams. Discovering that some men from the room had modest experience with the sport, several men in my room, who belonged to The Combine, saw an opportunity to gamble. They succeeded in organizing a hockey team, and promoted a contest.

For several days the hockey players practiced; activity on the rink drew a steady stream of spectators. As the contest was announced, The Combine was on hand to build team loyalties and take bets. On the day of the game, the snowbank defining the rink was lined with men who stomped their cold feet to restore circulation, their bodies warmed a little by anticipation of the contest. Though rubber-soled shoes moved more awkwardly than shiny blades, this was a spirited game, with much bumping among the players and cheering from the fans, their bodies warmed a little by anticipation of the contest.

At one point, Offsides Smith, near his own goal, cradled the puck and began a charge to the opposite end of the rink. A spectator, seeing open ice between and a teammate near the goal — and eager to alert him to that fact — shouted, "Offsides!" He got the message and passed the puck, resulting in a goal. But the opposing players, unaware that Offsides was a nickname, paused in their play in anticipation of a call from the referee. One man protested, "I was not offside!" But the score was allowed, and The Combine added to its already considerable coffers that day.

Another rumor averred that our *Lager* was soon to have bunk beds. That was welcome news, for bunks would provide each man more space, and elevate him above the drafty floor. But that prospect posed a problem for our room. We had amassed a surplus of coal briquettes, and fearing confiscation of our bounty, we had begun paving the floor near the coal stove. The coal had been concealed under the extended bedrolls of Merritt Knox and Mike Pesta. Now there was imminent danger that the cache would be discovered. We hit upon a plan to share the warmth with our barracks mates. Though we had no wrapping paper, each brick was tied with a red cellophane bow fashioned from the opening tabs of packages of cigarettes; these we presented to the leader of each room in our barracks.

With Christmas morning came a delightful gift for each man, Christmas food packages from the Red Cross. In eager anticipation, these were opened with much the same enthusiasm as had occurred in our childhood at home. On top of each box from the American Red Cross was a photo print of some scene from the U.S. Lester Geisman, whose sleeping place was next to mine, was elated to discover that his picture was of Ebbets Field, the home of the Brooklyn Dodgers baseball team. He lived in that very neighborhood, and the view was one he knew well. At last he had a real connection with his home, and he posted the picture above his bedroll. There also were cigarettes and pipe tobacco, soap, toothpaste, tea, and food delicacies, the like of which we had never expected, as well as canned turkey, cranberry sauce, date bars, candy, cigarettes, and so on.

I sat on my bedroll, examining these treasures one by one. We would be permitted this time to keep our cans for a day or two, which meant that we were not forced to eat all of the goods at one time. The turkey would be opened today, I decided, but I wouldn't and shouldn't eat all of it at one meal. I turned to my trading partner, Hank, to arrange a sharing of that can and any others he might wish to open at noon. That agreed upon, I sat in contemplation of the delicacies I would consume later. The realization that my thinking was focused so narrowly on myself brought a pang of guilt. Christmas was a time for giving, and I was intent upon consuming.

Gathering up some of these dearest objects, I visited the rooms of some of the men I liked. Robert "Jolly Ollie" Joyce was absent; I tucked the can of Prince Albert smoking tobacco under the blanket of his bed.

I visited several other rooms, leaving a date bar in one bed, a chocolate bar in another, and so on. My pockets empty at last, I returned to my own room, surprised at the mounting realization that the joy I was experiencing from this giving was accompanied by a lingering wistfulness for the delicacies I would not have for myself. Had I been foolish to surrender objects that would help assuage my hunger, and to do so anonymously, so that I would not receive credit for it? As I bent to sit on my bedroll, I noticed with amazement that it was lumpy. Pulling back the top blanket, I discovered that others had left similar gifts at my place.

My impulse had been widely shared by the men in our camp. Here, far from home, and so limited in resources to satisfy elementary needs — nor with surplus to give — these gifts assumed even greater significance. This was to be one of the most meaningful Christmases of my life.

With the holiday season came the presentation of a show, to which the entire *Lager* was invited. In the mess hall, the library area was rearranged so that the south end of the building became a theater. Because there was insufficient room for all of us to attend at one time, the show was staged on three different days, December 24th, 25th, and 26th. These were the first such public entertainment events in our compound and were well received, revealing previously unexpected talent among our men. We enjoyed skits, with dancing and singing — tunes such as "Sleepy Time Down South" and "Shortnin' Bread," as well as a small band made up of men, most of whom I hadn't yet met, who played well — such tunes as "MacNamara's Band." The program was a huge success.

We ate well and more wisely than at Thanksgiving. Then as a treat on Christmas Eve, we were permitted to remain outdoors until after midnight. With the compound lit by floodlights, we poured water in strips on the snow, then ran and slid on the glossy surface. Inside the barracks, in rooms illuminated by the small bulbs, many prisoners sought shelter from the brisk outside air and played some of the new games. By midnight, most of the men had returned to the outdoors and stood expectant of what, we did not know, but only felt, under a starlit sky. Then, from somewhere in the camp, began the strains of "Silent Night." The first line had only begun when thousands of voices joined together in the song.

It would be, indeed, a merry Christmas. We did not know at the time that news of our caroling would spread throughout the Allied world.

Finally, another rumor proved to be correct. Workers came to *C Lager* and constructed beds for us, though differing from the three-tiered bunk beds I had seen in *A Lager*. These were two-level beds, each level wide enough to accommodate three men. One bunk occupied each corner of the room, separated by a narrow space from its neighbor. Unlike our former sleeping arrangement, these beds could not be rolled up during the day, so the smaller space in the center of the room became our common area, used for games. But during the day, men not involved in that activity could lounge on their bunks, away from the central area.

Having finished with reading the many thin volumes of *The Spectator*, I now began David Fairchild's *The World Was My Garden*, the life story of a man who became perhaps the first investigator for the U.S. Department of Agriculture to travel about the world in search of new and hardy strains of products that could be commercially grown in North America. This book impressed me greatly, and invited me to return to it, both day and night, until its very end. The story held such fascination for me that while in the Miami area in 1945, I sought to visit the experimental garden the author had established, The Fairchild Tropical Garden, on the old Tamiami Trail.

My reading time was further extended with the advent of the coal fires in the barracks, for it had become necessary for each room to post a fire watch throughout the night. Learning that faint light emanated from the fire in our stove, I volunteered several times to sit up by the fire. There I held my book close to its light, reading and contemplating in the silence and solitude. The same practice was equally useful when I came upon a paperback issue of Plato's *Republic*.

In the days following Christmas 1944, our Red Cross rations returned to the half-box level, made tolerable by bits we had saved from the Christmas parcel. New Year's Eve was another special occasion, for again the barracks doors were left unlocked and men were allowed the freedom of the floodlighted outdoors. Men engaged in activities mostly in pairs, sometimes merging with other clusters of prisoners whose actions attracted their interest. It just felt good to have this unaccustomed freedom, to look up at the stars above, and to walk around the compound at night.

As midnight approached, men gathered in the out of doors, awaiting the coming of the New Year. We had high hopes for 1945 — fancies of release from this confinement, of return to our dear ones, and of the return to customary family tables and to meaningful, productive activity. The condition from which these hopes could be realized, of course, had to be Allied victory, and a world at peace. We fervently hoped for the end of the war as we brought in the New Year of 1945. And then we returned to our barracks, to our beds, behind a locked door and extinguished lights.

The chatter of machine-gun fire brought many of us to the rear door of our barracks, curious to learn the cause of this disturbance. A prisoner slumped over the barbed wire, his body draining of blood. Why would anyone make such an attempt to leave the compound, directly in the view of the corner guard tower? And why try to climb the wire, which if it did not carry an electrical current, was insulated from its posts for that very purpose? As the story reached me, this man had been assigned to work in our *Lager*'s kitchen. There he had used raisins from Christmas parcels and crockery from the kitchen to concoct a liquid, which was soon bubbling in fermentation. His mad dash had been caused by inebriation that had released his inhibitions against seeking immediate and direct measures to escape. A small procession of men, led by a clergyman and accompanied by guards, took his body to a burial site a hundred yards from the camp.

At about this time, yet another rumor emanated with reference to the mess hall. Meat was to be served at another meal, this time in plentiful supply. With only a little skepticism, for desire often overcomes the memory of disappointment, we waited for that meal to materialize. This time we were wholly mistaken, for the meat was to be the old, emaciated horse that had pulled the supply wagon. Indeed, we heard, the horse had made his final sacrifice to our cravings. But the men in the kitchen, so it was said, had strong cravings of their own, and they were discovered, after hours, frying horse steaks on the kitchen stove. I never heard what had happened to the remainder of that old beast, but was told that the offenders had been retired from the kitchen to a cubicle in the detention quarters. I could not verify this story, for the men in the kitchen were faceless persons to me, living and working in a separate place.

If December had been cold, it was followed by a January thaw, much like the ones I remembered from rural Iowa. The ice rink became a puddle, dammed by an edging of packed snow. Eventually that snow, too, melted. Not all of the water could immediately soak into the cold, hard sandy soil, so it ran downhill, accumulating in depressions made by many sessions of *appel*. We soon found ourselves standing in two or three inches of icy water. *Appel* had never been a pleasant formation, but cold, wet feet now made it even more distasteful. Even so, we must have become somewhat inured to the conditions, for I recall having become aware of a guard fixing me with a wrathful stare. Wondering why this should be, I soon realized that I was whistling. Whistling at roll call? Yes . . . and it was the "Marseillaise." Brought back abruptly to reality, I desisted.

The days of January rolled by, each a monotonous repetition of its predecessor. But there were rumors that the Soviet army had at last broken its long sojourn at the edge of Warsaw, and was now moving rapidly westward. With the sound of artillery fire in the air, we waited expectantly for our liberation. The thunder of guns swept from the east to the south, then rumbled on, to our west. No liberators arrived at our camp. Yet rumors continued to circulate, and we continued to hope for freedom.

Another rumor had it that we would march out of the camp under guard. Our camp committee advised us that in such a case, we must be careful to drink only water that had been boiled — water from wells could be contaminated. As if that rumor had reached the Red Cross in Geneva, vaccine arrived at the camp via airplane. We were advised to receive inoculation against typhoid. Though it appeared to be at each man's choice, no one refused, and the line to receive these shots wound around the central compound. Somehow, I was at the end of that line. When my turn came, it was my rueful discovery that but a single needle was available for use in this *Lager*. That needle, blunted by its use on 2,500 men, seemed to resemble a tent stake entering my arm. But I was content to have the serum.

On the fifth of February, we were told at *appel*, that a bathing facility had been constructed at the camp, and that we were to assemble our towels and soap and prepare to proceed in an orderly fashion to the showers. Having bathed only by a washcloth dipped in tepid water in the four months since my arrival there, I was eager to step under what I hoped would be a steamy shower. In formation we left the gate to *C Lager*, turned past the guard tower, and headed for the main gate. Ahead and just beside the *vorlager*, I could see the new wooden building to my left.

We filed in, and disrobed as instructed, leaving our clothing in an outer area. Through a heavy door, and on command, we passed as a group into a room that had many shower heads mounted on the walls. Looking upward, I noticed a sort of grate in the ceiling. A guard was stationed above — a curious thing. What trouble could our captors expect from unclothed men intent upon cleansing themselves?

I had no fear, however, as I had not known of the gas chambers in the concentration camps. I had no idea how close this shower facility resembled those lethal structures. Later I learned that some of my fellow prisoners did know of the manner in which prisoners were gassed in the death camps. Unlike me, they were terrified.

The water was warm, and I soaped and splashed quickly. We were allowed only a short while under the streaming jets, just enough time to remove most of the soap. Then the water ceased, and we were commanded to return to our clothing. We toweled off, dressed, and marched out of the building, returning to our own *Lager*. It felt good to be clean.

That afternoon a guard entered our room, informing us that we were to be prepared to vacate the camp the very next day. We would walk, he replied to questions. "You will go to another prison camp, to the west. It is only about one hundred kilometers from here."

When our camp officers arrived, we were cautioned to be prepared to walk even farther; the destination was not truly known. It would be a good idea to fashion some means of carrying our possessions, and to roll our blankets in such a way that they could be carried around our necks. They offered little more information than that, but this advice stimulated creative discussion among the men in our room. How would we manage packing our goods, keeping warm, eating, drinking, and caring for our feet? At the advice of our camp committee, we chose partners for the march. It seemed quite natural for me to choose Hank, with whom I had shared Red Cross foodstuffs. Most of the men paired up into what someone had called "combines," though there may have been one or two trios. No one attempted to face the ordeal alone.

With the pain of my sore feet on the walk into France still very fresh in my mind, I resolved to keep my feet dry if at all possible. I had been fortunate enough to draw the ace of spades when a pair of fine British woolen stockings arrived in the room, so I began this trek with about eight pair of socks, counting the mended ones. I decided to wear two pair at a time, putting them on my feet with care so that they were unwrinkled. The rest I affixed with safety pins on the inside of my overcoat. The heat of my body, I thought, should promote drying, and I could replace socks each day, preserving them as best possible until I was able to launder them.

Taking my spare shirt, I sewed the tail to make a sack, and stitched the cuffs of the sleeves to the lower sides of the shirt. Satisfied that it would serve as a backpack to hold a Red Cross carton fitting over my overcoat, I turned to matters I considered to be of lesser importance. Finding used shoelaces with which to secure my blanket roll, I thought my preparations to be complete. After supper, I was ready to spend my last night in my new bunk.

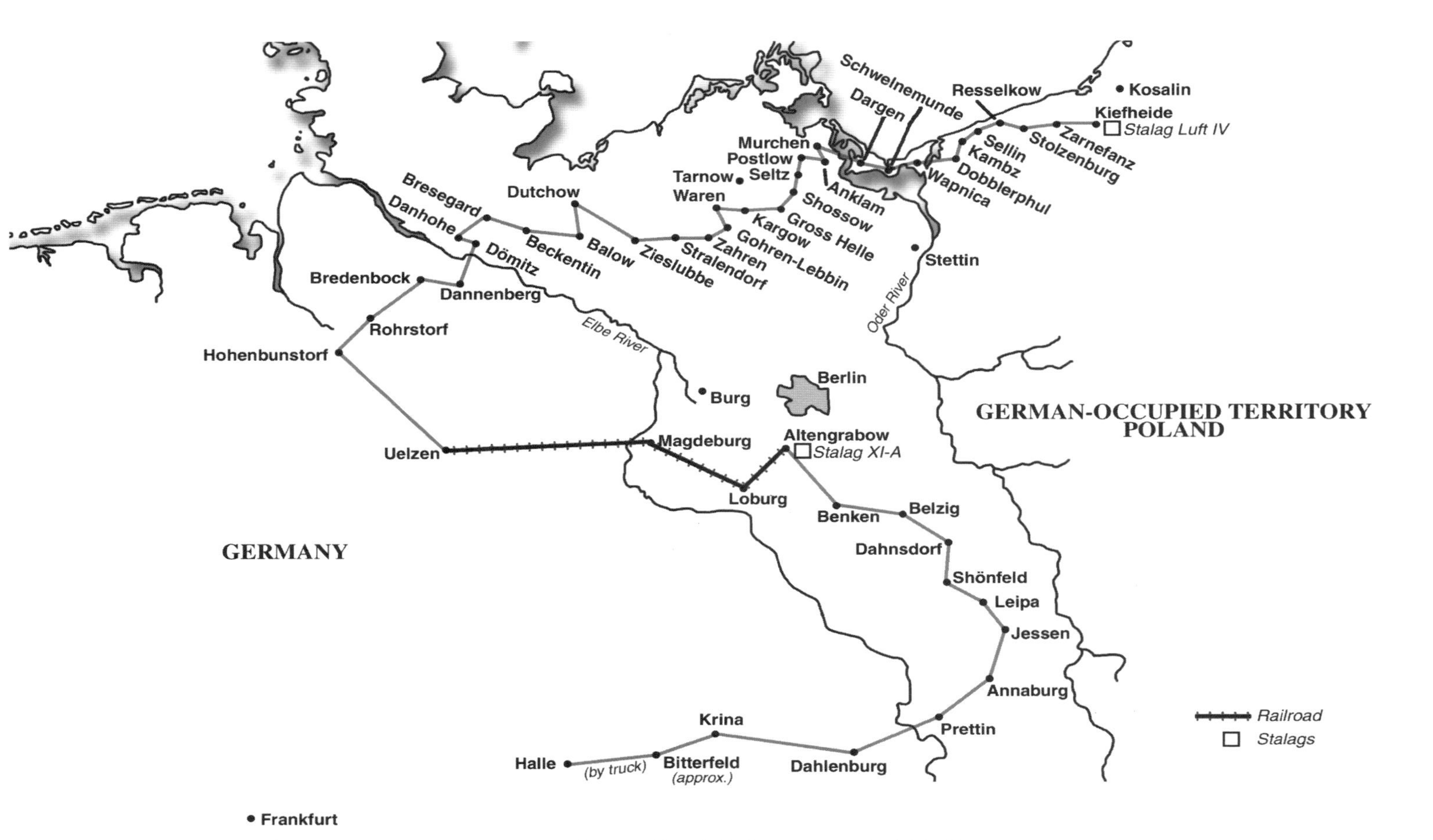

The forced march route from *Stalag Luft IV*, February 6, 1945, to freedom Bitterfeld, Germany, on April 26, 1945.

Chapter 24

Exodus

THE DIM BULB in our room lit up, signaling a new day — February 6, 1945. The rasp of the lock told of the guard's presence at the front door, and two men, today's shutter detail, awoke. Sitting on the edge of their beds, they dressed, then left the room. Soon one shutter was removed from a window, then the other. This would be the last time that particular chore would be performed in this camp.

Now everyone in the room was astir. I had just pulled on my clothing and was tying my second shoe when the morning pitcher of warm tea was brought in and set on the table. I pulled my box of personal articles out from under the bed, extracted the bit of black *brodt* left from the evening ration, smeared it with a bit of margarine, and took my cup to the table. After filling it, I sat on the edge of the bed to eat, sharing that spot with Mel Demmin and Les Geisman. Little did I expect that I would not be seeing them again.

With some of my belongings rolled into my blanket, I

shrugged into my makeshift backpack, a loose fit on my shoulders, holding only a few items. Joining with Henry, my partner, we were counted, admonished not to drink any water except that provided by our captors, and urged to move along and not tarry on the route. A bit later, counted again, we moved out of the barracks and followed the men from Barracks 2. Out of the *Lager* gate we turned left, past the guard tower, and marched toward the entrance of the camp compounds. Our column turned to the right and into the *vorlager*. Men from other *Lagers* had already preceded us.

A short distance ahead, men were clustered at stacks of Red Cross food parcels. I took one, stopped, and stuffed it into my backpack; Hank took two parcels. Ahead were two huge boxes full of cigarette packages. I scooped up about 20 packs, all I could cram into my various pockets, and hurried to join my partner. Clutching those two boxes of Red Cross packages, Hank, a non-smoker, had not hesitated at the supply of cigarettes but had walked slowly, waiting for me to catch up.

Activity in the *vorlager* had created disarray in the ranks of those from *C Lager*. Hank and I followed others out the side gate and to the right down a crude road. Though we were separated from most of the men from our room, we were with those from our *Lager*. What seemed most important just now was that the members of a combine should not become separated; we could already see the logic of cooperation.

Hank was beginning to tire from the unaccustomed weight of the Red Cross parcels, and I offered to take turns with him. For a long distance he declined my offer; he was both strong and resolute. When I did eventually take my turn with that spare parcel, I found it cumbersome to carry because of its five-kilo weight.

The road turned to the south, and now seemed recognizable; wasn't it the same road up which we had run from the train to the camp? Some time later, we exited the pine woods near a brick house that I recalled seeing when we had unloaded from the train. At that point we turned west again, and on a more substantial road we walked through a village, which must have been Kiefheide, the railway station nearest the camp. Several houses were visible, and men were working at a sawmill.

We continued, sometimes walking on low hills. I saw a pond or lake in the woods north of the road. After about an hour, our guards signaled that we should stop for a rest. I was ready, as apparently were many others. Several men, finding their loads intolerable, discarded some of their effects. Shortly, we arose and continued our walk. We were not required to march in step, nor to maintain a semblance of military progression; we just moved along at a constant pace, very much like a herd of cattle.

A bit farther down the road we approached an intersection, with a sign pointing north to Belgard (now named Bialogard) straight ahead to Zarnefanz, now Czarnowesy. At this point the pine forest came to an abrupt end, and we entered farming country. The road, bordered by trees, with only minor curves, headed due west. On this journey my feet were not sore, and though my physical condition was much weaker than during my walk with Lieutenant Donahue through Belgium and France, I seemed to have no more difficulty walking than did those around me. As we trudged along in route step, so-called by my leaders in training, we moved at a pace much slower than Bob Donahue and I had maintained a few months earlier.

Nevertheless, the hourly rest periods were welcome. As a guard would light his pipe, a prisoner near him would solicit a light for his cigarette. One cigarette was then lit from another, and soon hundreds of men were puffing. This was a time also when men would break out their meager supply of bread and eat a bite or two. Then, upon command, we arose and continued our trek along the road ahead.

★ ★ ★

At dusk we entered the town of Zarnefanz, 14 kilometers from our prison camp near Kiefheide. The column ahead turned to the right, and we followed along until we came to the crossroad. Ahead, men were turning off the road and approaching a large gray barn. Guards herded us past the barn and into a sort of courtyard, where a long line had already formed to receive a water ration. A large house with dim lights shining from the windows appeared out of the early gloom of evening. From a large barrel, a prisoner ladled out the portion of boiled water, each man receiving one cupful. Hank and I drank ours on the spot, fearful that some of the precious stuff might be spilled if we tried to carry it into the barn.

Then we followed what seemed to be a multitude of scrambling figures into the dark interior. Adjusting to the dim light, we averted the machinery parked on the floor in front of us and climbed a ladder leaning against the steep slope of hay piled from floor to near the rafters. Encumbered by our packs and Hank's extra parcel of food, the climb in the barn, now dark, required a great deal of exertion. The top of the pile being completely occupied when we arrived, we huddled on the slope, unwrapped our blankets, and made a bed for the night. Then we opened Red Cross rations and ate from one of the cans. Others were in a similar situation that night, clinging to wisps of straw to avert sliding down and falling on the machinery below. We didn't remove our shoes, there being no secure place to put them. In spite of our weariness, we slept only fitfully, hitching ourselves back up on the straw after having slid down to a precarious position.

The commanding voice of a guard awakened me to a scene of disarray illuminated by the faint light of morning. Carefully, I sat up and donned the overcoat I had been using for a blanket, then hastily I packed my bedroll and made my way down the ladder. On our way out of the barn, Hank and I were stopped by Bill Stroud and Bob Ice, two men from our room who had formed a combine together. Bill asked us if we would be willing to form a foursome.

"Practically," he said, "we can take turns standing in line for water or food when there is some, while one of us can guard the place we've selected for sleeping. And that fellow can also guard our personal effects. One of the others may be able to pick up his ration and bring it to him; if not, the rest can guard his things while he picks up his own rations. We can rotate those assignments, so no one will be shorted."

"Let's stay together this morning," I said, "while Hank and I think about it. We'll let you know."

On the ground, we were herded into formation while we were counted again. I found myself scratching; others were, too. We must not have been the first travelers to sleep in that barn. As we were waiting, one chap near me bragged that he had left the barn during the night. He had met a farm girl by the house, he said, and for two bars of soap he had had his way with her. He was quite proud of his accomplishment. If true, he must have been quite sneaky; I wondered why he hadn't used the soap to get something to eat, instead.

Then, with the tally corresponding to the one when we had entered the barn on the previous night, we were ushered out the gate and back on the road. Talking about our poor location in the barn that night, Hank and I concluded that we should try to walk fast enough to be near the head of the line at day's end; then we should be able to select a more advantageous location.

We were ambivalent about whether to expand our two-person combine into four. But Bill Stroud's suggestion made sense to us; four persons could more readily share whatever division of labor might be necessary on the road. If we were to walk 100 kilometers and had walked only 14 on the first day, we might expect to walk an average of 20 per day. So we would be on the road for four or five more days. We chose to try to meet Stroud and Ice at the next break and try to forge some sort of agreement on the sharing of our tasks and resources.

We slackened our pace and had no difficulty in finding the pair at our first rest stop. Bill then added one more incentive. He had grown up on a small tobacco farm in South Carolina; though he had become a smoker at an early age, the poverty of his farm had been such that the family had not been able to afford "tailor-made" cigarettes. He was accomplished at rolling his own, and he could do that for the combine. Then we could economize on the consumption of packaged cigarettes, and use those for trading for goods. Hank and I told the men that we were planning to walk as fast as was possible in order to have a favorable position in the column at the end of each day. Bob and Bill agreed to that, and Hank volunteered to add his extra food parcel to the resources owned jointly by the four-some. That was charitable of him, for since I had taken up the habit, he was the only non-smoker in the group. We agreed to link up, and when the rest period was over, we walked off together, passing others as best we could.

At the next rest period, Bill demonstrated his skill at rolling a cigarette. Using a package of papers and tobacco from the can of Prince Albert pipe tobacco saved from his Red Cross Christmas parcel, he deftly produced a hand-rolled cigarette. Begging a light from a neighboring smoker, he persuaded Bob and me to refrain from lighting cigarettes from our packages. Instead, he urged us to share the one cigarette he had just rolled. Then as we were urged to our feet again, he extinguished the short butt remaining from the much-used cigarette and dropped the tobacco into his watch pocket.

"When we get low on tobacco, I can make other cigarettes from the left-overs," he explained.

We repeated this practice at subsequent rest stops, adding at some stops a ritual of slicing off a small sliver of our bread, and rotating the task of cutting it into four pieces. Three of us drew straws to determine the order of choice, the cutter taking the last piece. It seemed fair, and each person who cut the bread took special care to divide the piece as equitably as possible, thereby getting his own fair share. Eventually, we became quite good at dividing the bread evenly.

The walk that day seemed very long, and the route anything but direct. We had followed this first road on a northwest course until we reached an intersection at a small village. We turned on the road to the southwest. This walking was difficult, and men grumbled about the change in direction. Increasingly at rests, tired men left behind some of the possessions they could no longer carry. At one stop I profited from finding a U.S. military overcoat in good condition, much warmer than the short, thin one I had been issued at the prison camp. Later, I found an American army blanket. Like the overcoat, it had come into the camp courtesy of the Red Cross, and had been "won" by some lucky fellow in a lottery in his room. The blanket was heavier than my original one, which I kept, thinking that it might still come in handy. With hopes high when we came to still another village, we felt that we had walked far enough that day. But no, guards marched us on.

The next town was Stolzenburg, a small town on a highway linking it to Kolberg (Kolobrzg) on the Baltic Sea coast. (Stolzenburg has been renamed Stawaborze). I breathed a sigh of relief when the column was led to a large barn. Near enough to the head of the line that we could lay claim to bed space on the ground floor of the barn, we spread out our blankets and placed our backpacks at our heads. I watched the places as my companions went into the courtyard to get their water ration. They were unable, of course, to acquire mine, so I went out later to the line with my cup. I would have liked to return to the barn in order to mix powdered coffee with the water, but I thought there might be opportunity to barter or beg some food from those in the house. A crowd of prisoners was pushing through the door, and I joined them. Somehow I got inside and into what may have been the dining room. Milk and bread were on the table, but the residents were unwilling to share. Anxious to protect their food, they called to a guard, whose rifle quickly cleared the house.

The water, though unmixed with coffee or milk, had at least addressed my thirst. But I was hungry, and no other food was forthcoming. I returned to my place in the barn, where I shared some K-ration crackers from a Red Cross parcel with Bill and Bob. Probably, I thought, as many as 2,000 men were packed into the building. There was less room for sleeping than there had been in our room at *Stalag Luft IV.* We could not stretch out our legs, for the heads of other men were at our feet. That, I was soon to learn, was to be a common condition throughout most of our journey.

★ ★ ★

On the previous night, an advance party had dug a shallow trench by the side of the barn, and a pole had been strung about two feet above it. Again this evening the same procedure set up the latrine. Those men were lucky who were fortunate enough to use it before bedding down for the night. Should the urge to use the facility come in the dark of night, there was no clear path to the door, and the air would be filled with angry shouts from those whose heads or bodies had been trampled by the man hurrying out into the dark.

I was glad that our effort to get toward the head of the line had resulted in a favored place to spend the night. Sitting on my bed place, I pulled out the little book I had made in camp and inscribed the name of the town, Stolzenburg, in which we were stopping. We had walked 28 kilometers that day.

We had eaten sparingly from our rations. We had no idea when, or if ever, we would receive another Red Cross food parcel, and our guards had said nothing about supplying us with anything to eat. Though we were now accustomed to going to bed with hunger gnawing at our insides, the marching was draining our bodily reserves.

If there was anything to distract me from my craving for nourishment, it was the itching caused by the increasing number of lice infesting my body. They were in my hair, in my armpits, they crawled on my back, my legs, my arms. None of my companions was better off, but fatigue from the journey eventually erased the discomfort, and they, like I, dropped off to sleep.

★ ★ ★

Because we were on the floor of the barn, it was easier to pack up the next morning. At the guard's call, men tumbled out of the building and stood in reasonable disarray while we were counted. After the recount produced the satisfactory number, we began to march. A bit north of the town, the column turned west, then north again on a still smaller road through agricultural land, now barren after the harvest. There were a few low hills, lending relief to the landscape. Our combine stayed close to one another, and at rest breaks Bill shared one of his rolled cigarettes with Bob and me. We were cautious about exhausting our foodstuffs, so one of us always tried to dissuade the rest from eating from our supplies. Other men gave in more readily to their appetites, and empty cans by the roadside gave testimony to our column's rest stop.

Trudging along, thankful for the earflaps on my knitted cap and wishing that I had gloves to protect my hands, I was glad nevertheless for the Army overcoat I had picked up the day before. I thrust my hands deeper into the pockets, conscious of how tiring this march was. But our guards were walking, too, and though their gear was being carried in a wagon, they each carried a heavy rifle and a small shoulder bag. Emerging over the horizon was a cluster of buildings — large ones — and I fervently hoped that we would rest there for the night. Some time later we were close enough that I could read a sign on the tallest building. Apparently it was a grain mill, and this was some sort of storage facility. There didn't seem to be much else in the town but this mill or factory.

Our column turned onto a larger road at an intersection. Disappointingly, this road took us on a southwesterly heading. Couldn't our leaders find a more direct route?

I eyed farms along the highway, hoping that one would be our destination so that I could rest my weary legs. Eventually, a number of guards assembled at a small crossroad and directed us to the right. Far ahead I could see a cluster of large buildings. That, finally, was our destination — Resselkow. We followed the road to its end, then turned right past a house and into a square bounded by large brick barns. (By 1991, the collective farm had the Polish name of Rzesnikowo. The large brick buildings had disappeared and had been replaced by low buildings used as an animal feeding operation.)

Drinking water was prepared for us and we hurried into line to fill our cups. As we headed for the barn, we were favorably close to the head of the line. We were to be bedded in the haymow, to which we had to climb a ladder propped against the hay. Below us, the parked machinery would be particularly hazardous if we rolled out of the hay. However, we were able to bed down so that the last one of us still had four or five men between him and the edge of the haymow. And we were in the first row of men next to the outer wall of the barn.

With one man guarding our places, we returned to the courtyard below to receive a ration of boiled potatoes — though we had nothing to carry it in. Most of us solved the problem by doffing our caps to receive the damp vegetables. They were not of table quality, we reasoned, but they were edible; the tubers would help ease the pain in our stomachs. The skins added nourishment, too, we concluded. Bob climbed up the ladder to relieve Hank, who was guarding our belongings, and Hank climbed down to take his own place in line. Seated on the ground, we ate our potatoes and shared some food from our remaining rations. Bob received a fair portion of that, too, which we brought up to our bed place in the loft. We had consumed all of the bread given us in camp, and now wished fervently for more.

Rumor had it that we would rest here tomorrow. I was thankful, for I was tired. We had walked 23 kilometers that day. With more than usual in our stomachs, and except, for waking occasionally to scratch those pesky lice, we all slept well that night.

The following day we arose and dressed. It was my turn to guard our belongings, so I stayed in the loft while the others went down to the courtyard. We learned that the rumor was true; we were not to march that day.

When I could do so, I retrieved the paperback copy of Plato's *Republic* and resumed my reading — but not for long. Several of the men were experiencing upset stomachs, and had exhausted their supply of toilet paper. I was asked to tear out and give them a page or two from my book, which I did, pulling from the part I had already read. Others, seeing my book as an important resource, implored that I share my "riches" with them. With all the first 60 pages given out, I had no more unread pages to spare; I pocketed the book and moved to another part of the courtyard, hoping to find opportunity to read more — and rapidly.

We received water that evening and, again, a ration of potatoes. Then I wriggled into the small space left between other men and, with my knees bent to fit the space, tried to dismiss the hunger gnawing at my innards and the lice crawling over me. I quickly fell asleep.

★ ∾ ★ ∾ ★

The loud, gruff voice of a guard brought me to wakefulness. He had mounted the ladder to the loft and, with his head showing above the hay, shouted for us to wake up and hurry down for the morning count. My companions were astir, busying themselves with pulling on their clothing, preparing their blanket rolls, and shrugging into their backpacks. Someone had already passed by my place and kicked my shoes out of my reach. In the darkness of the hayloft I could see nothing. As other men fumbled their way past me to descend the ladder, I groped frantically for my shoes. The hayloft emptied, and there was the guard again, shouting for me to hurry down the ladder.

I found the shoes, and thrust my feet into them, the two pair of stockings still stuffed into the toes. With no time to put them on properly, I quickly knotted the laces and made my way down the ladder. At the bottom, the guard followed me closely, his rifle jabbing into my back until I reached the formation. Hank, Bill, and Bob had descended much earlier and were not near my place in line. Our captors seemed to be in a hurry that morning and did not tolerate my bending over to retrieve my socks from the shoes. Standing there while we were counted and recounted, my feet, pinched as they were in the shoes, were becoming numb. I would need to correct that situation quickly, and hurry to catch up with my combine.

Finally, the order was given to march, and the column slowly walked out of the barn area and turned eastward down the narrow road. I stumped along, unable to stop to retrieve the balled-up socks from my shoes. I did, though, manage to move a bit toward the head of the line, closer to my combine companions. Ahead of me, the column reached the wider main road and turned to the west. I hoped I might be able to rest at the roadside for a moment and adjust my footwear. Though my cramped toes had become very painful by that time, I managed to push on past other trudging men and finally catch up with my companions. I told them of my plight and my intention to stop for a moment; I would catch up with them at the next rest break. I sat at the edge of the road, my back against a small tree, and pulled off my shoes. I fished my socks out of the toes of my shoes and was just pulling on my left sock when a guard, in obvious agitation, hurried up to me. He shouted something that I interpreted to mean "no loafing here," and threatened me with his rifle. Hurriedly, I pulled on the other sock, not bothering to adjust its smoothness to avoid blistering, and pulled on the right shoe, laced it quickly, and got to my feet.

This scene had attracted the interest of a burly Sergeant walking in the middle of the road. He called me to come to him, and when I reached him he shouted something that sounded very much like what the guard had said to me. Then suddenly he swung the club he was carrying, hitting me on my left ear. That hurt and left me faintly dizzy and with a ringing in my ears that lasted for days, then weeks, and bothers me still. I reeled back to the roadside and hurried to catch up with my companions. During that episode I had fallen far behind them, but I could now walk more comfortably, and did catch up with them at the next rest break. They noticed the blood now clotted on my ear, and, needless to say, I spoke with some feeling about the inappropriateness of that treatment. I carefully adjusted my footwear and was then able to walk with less pain.

A short distance ahead, the column left this road and took a lesser one intersecting with it and angling toward the northwest. Late in the day we approached a town that appeared to be of considerable size, as compared to the ones we had passed through. But just before reaching the town, we left this road, too, and took a small one heading north.

Some time later we came to our resting place for the night. The sign at the roadside identified it as Sellin. Here we each received one cup of meal soup, and again we were crowded into a barn. By then, some of the men had badly blistered feet. Two of them actually had blood showing through their stockings, visible above their army shoes. I recalled the sores I had experienced on the road into France, and though my sympathy was aroused, there seemed nothing I could do to ease their discomfort.

At this stop we each received a cupful of soup, made of some sort of meal — a change of routine, one which I hoped would be repeated often. On the next day we began by retracing our steps to the larger town we had bypassed the day before. There was some grumbling now, because of back-tracking distances that had been traversed with difficulty earlier. There had been grumbling the previous day, as well, when our course to Sellin had edged just a bit eastward on its northern path. Our destination, we thought, was to the west, and we begrudged every deviation from that direction.

When we reached the point where the two roads had diverged, we entered a town (Gryfice is its current name). Passing through it without incident, we took another road out, this time on a northwesterly heading. The grumbling continued. Why, some asked, had we walked toward the north, then retraced our steps, and were now heading toward the north again?

A couple of hours later we intersected with and took another road, this time bearing mostly westward, but a little to the south. A couple more hours elapsed before we passed through another village. Just beyond that, we halted again for a rest.

Three of us were now counting on these rests as opportunity for smoking breaks, to share our cigarette. To conserve our supply, we had taken to smoking only one-half cigarette at a time, then stuffing the extinguished butt into the watch pocket of our trousers. Again concerned about the duration of our supply, Bill fished some of those old butts from his pocket, produced cigarette wrappers included in the Red Cross's Christmas package, and expertly rolled a cigarette. He offered the cigarette to Bob, who drew in one drag before passing it on to me. I inhaled once, and passed it on to Bill. Though I didn't say so, the smoke had an old, burned taste. But, now addicted to nicotine, I would continue to encourage Bob in "rolling his own."

During this time, Hank had observed this ritual passively, giving not the slightest hint that the vice we shared was possible for us because he didn't smoke, and also because he had given us a portion of the cigarettes.

★ ೋ ★ ೋ ★

The roadside now bore resemblance to marshlands. The land was flat, and habitations were few. A chill wind blew in our faces. I kept my bare hands in my coat pocket, and my feet were cold. Then ahead, I saw the blue of water. Were we nearing the Baltic Sea? Others noticed the same thing, and the hopeful ones among us suggested that our captors might be taking us to a port. Weren't the Soviets battling the Germans somewhere south of us? It seemed plausible that we could be bypassing the battle area by ship.

Passage on a ship now seemed a luxury, compared to the deadly plodding on our icy feet. A few of us recalled the stories of discomfort and privation told by those men who had survived the Baltic journey from *Stalag Luft VI.* Our spirits were buoyed up at the prospect of a conclusion to this marching.

That evening we were ushered into barns at a place identified as

Kambz. (I believe that this locality is now known as Kamien Pomorski, Poland.) We stayed for two nights, and again received a ration of about two ounces of hardtack, packaged very much like the servings that accompanied soup in a restaurant. That quantity did not assuage our appetites, but it did at least signify that we were not altogether forgotten.

We did not embark on a ship from that point. Instead, we began to march toward the south, paralleling a waterway on the right side of our little road. The road veered away from the water, erasing hopes that our walking days might be over. We walked 18 kilometers that day, then rested in a large barn at Dobblerphul, which may now be named Partoko, Poland.

When we fell out to be counted the next morning, winter had settled in with a vengeance. A brisk wind blew snow into our faces, coating eyebrows and eyelashes with ice and clinging to our clothing. The journey was made even more difficult by our guards' urging us to walk faster. We crossed a narrow lake and pushed on, heads down against the driving snow.

During a rest period we sat with our backs against the wind, seeking some protection from the weather. All too soon, it seemed, we were urged to our feet once more. We stumbled along the road, heads down, shoulders hunched, our hands thrust deep in our pockets. The terrain now was undulating, and we walked down into shallow valleys and up modest hills. Snow on the ground made our footing slippery, but march on we did. Somewhere farther along the road, a sort of catering trailer was parked, and two German soldiers ladled out a cupful of cooked barley to each prisoner as we passed. We supped it while marching, very much as marathon runners drink the water thrust upon them by spectators. The warm food was a welcome treat for our stomachs, but soon I discovered that my thirst was now more demanding. We had been given no water.

Later, the snow abated somewhat and I paid more attention to our surroundings. The line of march came to an estuary that we crossed on a bridge. Just beyond that, a roadside marker proclaimed the town we were approaching to be Wolin. To our left, across a pasture intersected by a stream, was a set of low buildings which looked to be a factory. Nearer the road and just beyond, several tall structures of cement or brick stood resembling fingers pointing upward from a gloved hand. Were they the remnants from a bombing? Sections of a wall that had defied a fire? I wouldn't learn the answer to that, of course, but the memory of that structure remains with me still. We had traveled a greater distance than normal that day, but our guards urged us farther. There was no barn for us there.

Much later in the day — dusk was settling in by then — the column halted in a pine forest. This must have been as labeled Wapnica in the Poland maps — now called Wolinsky Park. Guards urged us off the road and into the wooded area on our left. This situation was not appealing; there was no evidence of drinking water at the roadside, and it appeared highly improbable that any boiled water would be available in the woods. What a way, I thought, to have spent St. Valentine's Day! We had been on the march eight days! Our guards were adamant, and we stumbled down the wooded hillside. A guard who had preceded us instructed us that we were to prepare our bed places here, but that we could forage for wood to use in campfires.

My combine selected a clear spot on nearly level ground. We dropped our bedrolls and backpacks there to reserve the spot and left one man to guard our belongings. We first scooped up armfuls of pine needles to cushion our bodies from the hard, cold ground. Then we gathered small twigs with which to feed a fire, and were fortunate enough to find a couple of larger branches, which would burn for a longer time. Old pine needles quickly burst into flame when coaxed with a lighted cigarette, and the small twigs were soon crackling in our fire.

Our bed site in place, I sought out the guards clustered along an access road. I wanted to ask, even assert, that we be supplied with drinking water. By my calculations, we had walked 40 kilometers that day, and we were all very thirsty. When I reached the guards, I saw that Bill Knightley was ahead of me, speaking on behalf of all the men on the march. Knightley was persuasive — perhaps even more so in German — but his requests were simply but firmly denied. Knightley became exasperated. For the first time ever, I heard him utter the word *damn!* I knew then that there was no use in my asking. We would just have to bear our thirst.

When I returned to my companions, I found the fire burning. Bob had spread his blankets over a layer of pine needles, but was already remarking that the chill from the icy sand was penetrating through both the layer of needles and his blanket. Heat from the fire did little to warm our beds, so we determined to rotate fire watch. One man would replenish the fire and seek more firewood while the others slept. That way, he could warm himself until time to return to bed.

Just as we were gathering firewood for the last time before retiring for the night, an air raid siren sounded in the distance. Almost simultaneously, our guards circulated among the campfires, demanding that we extinguish them immediately.

We hurried to comply with this order, and covered the scattered embers with a layer of sand. The ground, where the fire had been, was a bit warmer than the area where our blankets were laid out, so we moved our bed site to take advantage of that small difference in temperature. With half our blankets under us, the others used as covers, and wearing all our outer clothing, we crept into the bed and nestled in the fashion that had been our habit in the prison camp.

Accompanied by the sound of bursting flak, a flight of aircraft passed to the north of us. Moments later, the sound of bombardment came from south and east. The relighting of fires was not permitted, even when the roar of aircraft had faded into the distance. My right shoulder, on which I was lying, seemed to absorb cold from the earth below. I tried to dismiss thirst from my mind, and to disregard the cold. Eventually I fell asleep. We woke several times that night, switching positions, to shake the stiffness from our bodies.

Almost with gratitude I welcomed the dawn. At least I would get relief from the cold, hard ground. And perhaps, hopefully, our captors would have arranged to transport water to us.

They had not. We struggled to the road, fell in to be counted, then resumed our weary trek. At the edge of the forest we passed through a small village. Was it there that we had been permitted a drink of water? I don't recall just where it had occurred, but we did finally get a cupful later that morning.

It must have been afternoon when we halted at a wide expanse of water. Ships were pulling up, on which we were to embark. Somewhat disappointingly, they were small vessels, unlikely to take us out on the Baltic Sea. To my mind, they appeared to be tugboats or small fishing boats. Hank, Bob, Bill, and I jumped aboard one of them. When there may have been 40 or more men on board, all standing or seated on the deck, the ship turned about and headed for the far shore. We passengers debarked on a dock and joined others who had preceded us. The crossings were repeated, until all prisoners were across.

We had not been exposed to the indignities and hardships reported by our acquaintances who had sailed from *Stalag Luft VI* to *Stalag XI-A* earlier. We had crossed the Oder Estuary to Schweinmunde, leaving the scenes of battle perhaps 50 miles behind and to the south, on the opposite bank of the Oder River.

Chapter 25

Marching Onward

WE HAD ARRIVED in Schweinemunde, Germany (now Swinoujscie, Poland), on February 15, 1945. With our contingent gathered together, we set out on foot through city streets, heading south and west until we were in the countryside. On narrow roads, we traveled westward again, with blue waters clearly visible just to the south. We halted some distance from the small village of Dargen in near darkness. No structures were visible, and I was dismayed orders were given to climb into the adjacent plowed field and to bed down for the night. There was no fuel for fires, and the topsoil was rough, with large clods protruding through the thin crust of snow. We had no shelter at all from the winter air, but there was one improvement over the previous night; our captors brought a wagon with a supply of drinking water. A cupful per day was very little upon which to subsist, but it was better than none at all.

We spent another difficult night. The rough ground made a most uncomfortable bed, and there was no protection whatever between our blanket and the frosty soil. Huddled under our blankets, though, we provided each other at least some protection against the chill wind. I slept fitfully, and woke up the next morning with stiffness in the shoulders that persisted for several days and returned often in cold weather during the next several years. Woodenly we arose from the field, shook the dirt and snow from our blankets, arranged our gear, and assembled on the road. After we had been counted to the satisfaction of our captors, we started off again, across the flat sands of Usedom.

Some time later, a distraction was catching the attention of the marchers ahead. As we neared the spot, I saw a prisoner lying on the roadside. He was writhing in agony. An American medical officer, those around us explained, hurried to attend to him. I kept a watchful eye on the scene even as I walked past. The officer spoke urgently with a guard, and the word was passed forward that the man had acute appendicitis, and must have immediate attention. There was no provision on the island to deal with such a problem, so the stricken man was taken to a village lockup until help could be summoned. We never learned of his fate.

I believe the village was Stolpe. At the time, I was struck by the simple beauty of the church, which dominated the cluster of houses that I could see in the distance.

Later we neared a wide expanse of water, spanned at its narrow point by a long bridge. After trudging along the edge of a marsh, we arrived that evening at a farm where we were quartered in a large barn, at Murchen. In contrast with the frozen soil on which we had lain the previous night, the land around the barn was deep with mud that clung to our shoes.

On the following morning we walked south to the city of Anklam, where some whispered that the marks on pavement and walls were the result of an Allied strafing. Had the men of *A* and *D Lagers*, whom we thought had preceded us, been mistaken there for a Nazi troop movement? There was no answer to that, and we trudged on, to the west and south, staying that night in a barn at Postlow — just 15 kilometers that day.

There were mornings when men were absent at the *appel* count. Had they stolen away during the night, or were they hiding in the hayloft? Our captors took no chances with that latter possibility, and entered the barn, firing their weapons into the hay. We waited for the latecomers to run from the barn, wishing fervently that they had made their way safely during the night. Hopefully, the bullets found no cringing men, but put an end to some of the resident lice, instead.

We marched southwest the next day, on a road that passed through two larger towns. Getting through those towns was now becoming more difficult for our marchers, for dysentery was affecting many of us. The length of march through a city would, for many, require an impromptu, desperate, and demeaning halt along a convenient wall.

When we sat by the roadside at our rest stops, we sometimes broke out our meager supply of bread. This ritual served us well, for on most days our combine had at least one bite or more to eat. Others had responded to their hunger by quickly wolfing down any food they acquired, often resulting in upset stomachs, or worse.

Along the line of the march, we prisoners had surprising, though welcome, visitors. German military physicians, apparently learning of the condition of some of our men, came one evening to our barn. They sought out the two men who, by now, had feet so badly infected and swollen that they could no longer walk, but, incredibly, had crawled along the line of march. The physicians learned that another man, a paratrooper medic, had stayed with them. Each evening he had drained pus from their swollen extremities, using a jackknife. How, indeed, had the man succeeded in smuggling a jackknife past the wary guards?

The doctors commended the paratrooper for his attentions, saying that he had probably saved their lives. Then they escorted these two men to their car and transported them to a hospital for care. I never heard about them again.

Few of us knew how or why a paratrooper had been imprisoned with Air Corps non-commissioned officers. But it was not an error. The German military organization placed parachute troops in the same category as other fliers, so this was deemed the proper allocation of prisoners of this class. There were other paratroopers among us — at least one other, perhaps more.

February 18th was another hard day, as we walked 28 kilometers to the village of Seltz. We were doubly rewarded for that effort, as we were each given a cup of split pea soup and a rest in the barn for two nights.

On the second day we were rationed another cup of split pea soup. Not only was the warm soup welcomed, but the taste was a near-novelty, as well.

The next day's march was a disappointment, for we were backtracking, and there seemed to be no nearby prison camp toward which we were heading. But the distance was short, only 15 kilometers, and at the day's end we were issued one Red Cross parcel for each three men, and one loaf of black *brodt*, to be shared among every five men.

The following morning, after *appel*, we began to march south, then west. But as the day unfolded, our concerns surfaced once more, for our route circled back to the north, then west, and south, then straight toward the east once more. Speculation was rife among the walkers; were our captors unsure of our destination? Were they simply trying to keep us on the road?

We were moving along a narrow, sandy road when I saw a line of women standing between the road and the trees along its side. They appeared to be welcoming us, for some were smiling, others weeping. Frugally dressed, they must have been captives forced into labor on German farms. One raised her arm, tossing a thick crust of bread to the outstretched arms of those ahead of me. As I watched, the bread bounced from one hand to another, then fell almost at my feet into a pile of fresh horse manure. I stooped to retrieve it, brushed it off, and ate it. Hunger makes for eclectic tastes.

Only minutes later, the little road turned abruptly to the right at the edge of a town. The place marker identified it as Gross Helle, a name many of us thought apt, considering the corkscrew route we had followed that day. Our combine, near the head of the line, was diverted from the road into the nearest farm enclosure. At the gate stood a brick house and a couple of outbuildings. A barn smaller than those to which we were accustomed was situated just a bit farther along, on the right. We could see the rest of our company entering a much larger barnyard flanking the one we were in. In that enclosure stood a truly enormous barn. There would be ample room for us all to stretch out tonight.

We were able to make our beds on the ground floor, with a mattress of straw under our sleeping places. Drinking water was provided, and we soon received food, as well. Despite the unaccustomed space in which to stretch out my body, I lay awake for a long time that night, acutely aware of the discomfort of a hunger that transcended any I had experienced before. That gnawing pain remained with me most of the days we continued on this journey.

We remained in Gross Helle for nine days, lounging around during the daylight hours. We received one Red Cross parcel per man, and two-fifths loaf of bread, plus cheese and margarine; nevertheless, hunger persisted.

Seeking to occupy myself, I strolled over to the fence separating this barnyard from another small holding. As I neared the fence, a young woman came out of the neighboring house with a large bowl, and walked to the pigs' feed trough. As I watched, she began to dish the contents into the trough. I could see the mashed potatoes and sauerkraut causing the pigs' excitement. My mouth watered, and she must have looked up to see the begging expression on my face, for she paused in her chore, and approached me, bowl in hand. I was carrying an empty Klim can at the time, and as I held it out to her, she dished a heaping mixture of the contents into my container. The odor excited me as much as it had the pigs. But remembering my hungry combine buddies, I hastened back to the barn in order to share with them. It took many minutes before they were located, but not very long at all for us to gulp down this savory fare. I hoped that the pigs didn't suffer because they were stinted in our behalf.

Our last day at Gross Helle, February 27, 1945, was sunny and relatively warm. When I heard music coming from the vicinity of the house, I walked up to investigate. One of our men, who was said to have played clarinet in a Gulf Coast group named "Alexander's Ragtime Band," was playing the "Clarinet Polka." A sizable crowd, many of whom were farm workers, had collected by the time I arrived. We were an appreciative audience. The music was lively, and we were warmed as much by it as by the sun. A young workman who was standing by me was so moved that he indicated I must stay where I was until he returned. Moments later he emerged from the house with a bowl of meat and gravy. He wanted to watch me devour it, and I very much wished to comply, but I thanked him and hurried back to the barn to share the treat with my combine. It was very good indeed, though not very filling when split into four portions. I hurried back and returned the dish, murmuring my thanks.

The following morning we were led through the barnyard of the big barn, where we joined the rest of our contingent. We walked down a cobbled street and turned downhill on a road leading from the village. Our route wound down the hill and followed a valley, passed a mill, and then wound up a hill.

We ascended the high hill at a point that tourist maps would describe as having a panoramic view. Surveying the ascent from the valley, I doubted my ability to make it to the top, onto the opposite side. In order to summon more energy, I managed to acquire a lighted cigarette, and inhaled deeply. I must have reached the end of my energy reserve, for my legs became rubbery. Hank, who was walking beside me, sensed my predicament, and relieved me of my backpack and blanket roll. He strode on at my side, urging me on. I felt better after our next rest stop, and resumed my own burdens.

We arrived that evening at the village of Kargow. It seemed to boast of no particular distinction, but our quarters were at least different from any of the others we had so far experienced. We were in a low building, divided into a number of pens, that possibly had been used to house calves or pigs. But there was no odor of pigs, for which I was grateful.

We were supplied that evening with drinking water and a larger than usual ration of small potatoes. Up to then, the potatoes we had been given seemed to be of inferior size and quality, probably stored as feed for the hogs. These potatoes were small, too, but they were delicious! And there were enough to stuff some in our pockets, to eat on the next day.

Shortly after the beginning of our journey that day, our small road intersected with a highway leading to the city of Waren. The scenery changed, for we seemed to be in a district of lakes. As we entered Waren we were passing between two bodies of water. After leaving the city, the highway swung to the southwest, following a narrow spit between lakes. Then we left the highway, taking small roads to a place named Gohren-Lebbin, made distinctive by its two huge barns.

The next morning we rejoined the big road, being led on by the spire of a handsome monastery. Past that, the road followed a causeway into Malchow, where the narrow end of a lake divided the small city. I recall that while trudging across the bridge, my downcast eyes were attracted by the mechanism that swung the bridge laterally from its center in order for ships to pass. At its midpoint, the bridge floor had a circular plate, which pivoted to turn half the span at right angles to the road. I did not see it in operation, so I could only surmise its purpose. That thought served to occupy my mind for a time — a good thing — for by then my attention seemed to be filled with just placing one foot ahead of another, and keeping up with my combine partners.

At times like this, I tried to maintain contact with the life I had formerly known. On Sundays, in particular, I would gauge the hour by the number of rest stops we had made. Then, at what I deemed to be 11 o'clock, I would imagine a church service in the little country church I had attended in my boyhood. My mind retraced the entire service from opening prayer to final benediction. It would be disturbing a few weeks later to realize that a starving body would refuse to cling to such memories, and that I had become puzzled as to what part of the service followed another. I began to realize that the undernourished of the world simply could not be expected to devise remedies for their condition; they would need proper nutrition even before an attempt at a new life.

We walked up the hill past Malchow's church and cemetery, and continued on this highway for several kilometers, where we piled into a large barn for the night. Our route then parted from the highway, and I believe we followed a small track southwest. That next night we stayed in a place my notes — kept in the small cardboard-bound set of cigarette wrappers — listed as Zahren, then we moved on to Stralendorf, 15 kilometers away.

In seeking to retrace this route in 1991, my wife and I were unable to locate Zahren, for it is not on current maps. My guess is that the site might have been a local place name, and just east of Lubz. There is a village of Zahrensdorf about three days' farther northwest of Lubz, but that is two days farther on than Stralendorf, which we had reached on the following day.

★ ★ ★

In Stralendorf, we were housed in a large farm complex. Our combine bedded down in the hayloft. Leaving Bill and Bob to guard our bed site and our possessions, Hank and I ventured into the large open courtyard, in search of boiling water for drinking and, perhaps, to learn if a guard had purchased bread from a local person.

Though very little bread was rationed to us, our guards made a business of acquiring loaves from the local populace, then selling it to the prisoners. The standard price of a loaf was six packages of cigarettes, so prisoners most often exchanged only one package for one-sixth loaf of bread. Some of the prisoners had learned long before that American cigarettes were much prized by Europeans, and declared that prior to their capture they had personally exchanged one cigarette for a whole loaf of bread. Our guards, being sensitive to the profit to be made, endeavored to keep us away from the locals, thereby establishing a monopolistic trade route.

I overheard one guard boasting to another, "I am a rich man! I have a supply of two thousand packages of American cigarettes!"

While walking through the courtyard, Hank and I saw a *kriegi*e — a term we prisoners applied to our fellows, from the German *kriegsgefangen*, the word for a POW — a mere wisp of a man, who was crawling on all fours. Something was familiar about him; we looked more carefully at his face. Though his features were more drawn than we remembered and his eyes glazed, we recognized him as Edward S. Gates, one of our roommates from *C Lager*. He was able to tell us that he had a bad case of dysentery and that he had not eaten for several days. The companion member of his combine had been taken aboard the wagon of the sick, and with him had gone the supplies belonging to both men.

Hank and I helped him to the barn and pulled and pushed to assist him up into the loft. Once there, and with the situation explained, Bob and Bill quickly agreed that we should accept him into our combine, and that we should force some nutrients into him. Fortunately, we still had a small can of cheese and some biscuits from our last Red Cross food parcel. Reasoning that the cheese might arrest his diarrhea, we fed him the whole can. Later, when our potato ration was handed out, we built a small fire and charred the exterior of a potato. By morning, this treatment seemed to have been successful.

★ ∞ ★ ∞ ★

On the next day, we were attracted to the courtyard by angry voices coming from a small knot of men. It seemed that one of the men had been caught stealing food from another, and the loud accusations, protestations, and voiced confirmations were drawing a crowd. As I watched, the gathering took on the semblance of a court. Testimony as to the man's guilt was established to the satisfaction of the onlookers. The man accepted by those around him as leader declared that there were two alternative courses of action, one of which the guilty man must now choose. Either his name and the facts of this case be recorded and taken to military authorities after our liberation, in which case he would be subject to a court-martial, or else punishment would be administered on this spot and nothing more would be said of his misdeed. The punishment would be 20 lashes, administered with a GI belt. The accused accepted the latter option, and the erstwhile judge took off his own belt and whipped the man. It was painful to witness this scene, for even though the man with the belt was weaker than at his prime, so was the miscreant. When this activity was finished, the crowd melted away.

★ ★ ★

We remained at Stralendorf for three nights, during which Gates responded favorably to the food we forced upon him, and when the time came to resume the march, he appeared ready, though weak.

Earlier, I had come across another stub of a pencil and was again recording the names of the places in which we stayed at night. We now walked to Zieslubbe. Again we were ushered into a huge barn, but our combine was fortunate enough to be located in the center of the ground floor, perhaps 50 feet from the main barn door.

Many of the men suffered from dysentery. That night, one man with diarrhea tried to get from the loft to the front door. All along his route men shouted complaints like "Get off me!" "You stepped on my face!" He had just passed our sleeping place when I heard him mutter, "Oh, *Shit!*" The next morning a very soiled pair of Army trousers hung on the barn door, hopefully to dry.

Outside the barn I met several fellows from Room 5, just across from our room in *C Lager*. They offered me tea. Using the warm water rationed that day, one of them dunked a dirty, knotted handkerchief to hold a wad of tea leaves left from their Christmas parcel. They indulged themselves by "having tea." I partook, noting that the flavor had long fled, but felt privileged to share in this genteel custom. Along the route I had several times noticed groups of RAF prisoners — identifiable by their blue uniforms — gathered by small fires in fields by the road, drinking tea. Somehow they had been able to procure water as well as the privilege of leaving the line of march for the purpose of afternoon tea.

Then, standing by the doorway of the barn, I heard an unfamiliar sound. Two planes of a sort I had never before seen, buzzed by. Dark in color, with square-tipped wings, and bearing the German cross, they were jet fighters.

We continued on south to the small town of Dutchow. I think it was there where one of the most improbable events of our exodus occurred. A small truck pulled up outside our barn, and several names were called out, including that of Edward Gates. A number of men had been missed when Red Cross parcels had been delivered on a previous day, and our captors had actually taken the names of those men. This truck had a small cargo of Red Cross food parcels, and had been dispatched to rectify that oversight. Ed received a one-half sized parcel, which he insisted upon sharing with us, the members of his new combine.

We marched on to Balow. We managed to find a spot to bed down just inside the doors of the huge barn. We stayed there for nine nights, giving us greater opportunity to contact farm workers. Bob, his face beaming with good news, came to our bed site and pulled open his coat, within which he had concealed a large can of tinned beef. He had traded with one of the farm workers, exchanging his spare pair of woolen trousers for the meat. The five of us shared each bite with rich enjoyment. Once the can was open, we were fearful of spoilage, so we ate it all before sleeping that night.

We received rations from our captors, as well — five cups of soup, both potato and split pea. Then Hank came to us one afternoon, happily reporting that he had spoken with a Polish laborer on the farm, who had agreed to provide three loaves of bread in exchange for Hank's wristwatch. The freshly baked bread was to arrive that night. The farm worker was informed where our beds were located, and he had assured Hank that he would be able to get around the guard in order to make the delivery. For us, this was a great amount of bread, and we relished the prospect the rest of the day.

At about midnight, a cautious rap at the barn door wakened us. Hank crawled to the door, silently completed the transaction, and returned with the bread. Oh, but it smelled good! After consulting the rest of our combine about trying some of the bread right then, Hank placed the loaves in the shirt backpack at his head, and we sliced five pieces for this treat. The bread was still warm, and its consistency was soft to the touch. Obviously, the flour had been made from flailed grain, much like that of the Croizé family in France. The aroma of fresh bread aroused hundreds of famished prisoners, who protested, even begged for a piece. Though we regretted our inability to share with all, we accepted our own good fortune, finished the last crumbs of the piece we allowed ourselves, and went to sleep.

As we were leaving Balow, we received one Red Cross parcel for every five men. With Eddie Gates now in our combine, our little group had a complete parcel to ourselves. This parcel did not include the usual D-bar, but, instead, a small package of M&M's. Taking my share, I rationed myself one of the little tidbits on each hour of the day's march, delighting in the melting away of the candied covering before savoring the sweet chocolate inside.

Our distances were shorter during the next two days — 9 kilometers to Beckentin, then 16 to Bresegard. But the following day's march seemed very long. We traveled southwest, mostly on a small road, until it joined a larger one fronted by stately pines. We were close to a city, but as dusk settled in, we departed this road and climbed up a smaller road toward the north, stopping at what appeared to be a large farm with a milling complex. The place marker indicated that we had arrived in Danhohe. The town does not appear on current maps I have consulted, but perhaps it has been incorporated into the city of Domitz, Germany. The highways also have changed since 1945.

Weary, we slipped into our bedrolls for the night. We were wakened later by a noisy disturbance nearby, but could not ascertain its nature.

Early the following morning we learned about the din that had awakened us during the night from the prisoners distributing grain to us.

Apparently someone had set up a diversionary disturbance while others plundered the grain storage bins nearby. In the end, they had been fearful that they would be discovered — and anyway their packages were too heavy for them to carry — so we now benefitted from their enterprise.

As the grain donors gave us our allotment, we knotted our undershirts, poured a couple of pounds into them, then slipped in our arms, letting these little sacks hang freely under our shirts and outer clothing.

We retraced our steps back to the main road, walked on a street at the edge of the town, Domitz, and filed across a long span bridging the Elbe River.

The broad bridge had been severed by the Soviets or East Germans after they had gained control of the area. I have been told that this was done in order to prevent East German civilians from fleeing across to the West. It is possible that they wished to discourage traffic coming from the West, as well.

On March 21st, the first day of spring, light snow was in the air, and a breeze blew across the river; to me, it felt wonderful. A rumor circulated back from those in front that a train was waiting for us, and that our long walk would soon end. That news now seemed credible, and my mind wandered to images of Iowa City and of a line of trees clad in the new greenery of spring extending from the hill below the Old Capitol to the bridge over the Iowa River. I was inclined to enroll in the University of Iowa following my military service.

The thought that I might soon be going home began to register with me, and I realized that it had not passed my mind for a very long time.

As I walked along, I recalled in detail our trek from *Stalag Luft IV*, how my feet had become so swollen that Hank had helped me use a razor blade to make slits in the upper parts of my army shoes, widening them enough to accommodate my ankles. They remained swollen even now, but my feet were not blistered, thanks to the care with which I had layered my stockings, now four pair deep, to cover the holes in other stockings below. I recalled, too, that I had been so hungry at one time, when no food had passed through my mouth for a week, that I had stolen into a nearby field while the column had stopped to rest. I had dug out a partially decayed, partially frozen tuber from a makeshift bunker in the field and gnawed on the root as it thawed. Its bitter taste didn't dissuade me from eating much of it, but now I recalled the explosive intestinal consequences that night and on the following day.

But, now, as I trudged across the Elbe River bridge, those experiences were receding from my mind, and my thoughts were turning to the prospect ahead. Was there truly a train waiting for us on a track just ahead?

No track was found at the western end of the bridge. We had walked a long time before we saw a town — Dannenberg — and we averted the main street, walking some distance before crossing rails — but no train there, either. Accustomed to false rumors, I shrugged off the prospect of riding. I would just follow along the line of march as I had been doing for more than six weeks.

Outside this city that seemed to stretch out for such a distance, the column turned northward, arriving two or three rest stops farther on at the village of Bredenbock. Guards on the road ahead counted us as we passed by, then directed sections of us to small barns along the route. My combine was shunted into a small place. A barn and several small outbuildings stood behind a neat cottage.

Only a small portion of our retinue, about 150 men, I believe, had been assigned to this farmstead, and there was ample room to spread out. Our captors furnished each man with a cup of *ersatz* tea and a kilogram of sugar for the lot of us. We were told that we would rest here the following day. The host family had granted us use of their forage beet cooker, and water was piped to the barnyard. With this good news, we planned to grind the grain we had been carrying, and make a good meal for the next day. We stretched out in the spacious luxury of our bed places, and slept.

Another cup of *ersatz* tea was dished out in the morning, and then we sprang into action. Some men spread blankets in the small meadow behind the barn while others located old bricks to use as grinding tools. With the pilfered grain piled on the blankets, we knelt beside them, placed a handful of grain on a brick, then struck it with the other brick. Eventually the blankets were littered with a mixture of grain bits, hulls, and brick dust. Then each blanket was lifted by its four corners and shaken so that the gentle wind carried off the hulls and much of the dust. What remained was carried to the little building where other men had brought water to a boil in the forage beet cooker. To the water was added the grain meal and the sugar, which had been carefully guarded until this time.

Now that our common chores were finished, we were free to do as we pleased until the meal finished cooking. The day was sunny, the temperature spring-like, so I determined to wash my soiled shirt and trousers. None of my clothing had been so cared for since our departure from camp, and the trip had taken a severe toll. The cooking utensil was in use, preparing the main meal of the day, so it was unavailable for heating laundry water. Instead, I would use cold water from the spigot by the watering tank. I found some sort of container in which my clothing could be dipped; a bit of hand soap provided thin lather. I worked vigorously to scrub the grime from my shirt and pants, and when they had been rinsed and the excess water squeezed out, I hung them on the fence to dry. It was drafty work, for I had only underclothing and an overcoat to cover my skinny body. But at least it was done. Too bad I had lost track of my toothbrush, now that there was water in sufficient quantity to brush my teeth.

The gruel was cooked long before my clothing had dried sufficiently to wear, but the sun provided warmth in this protected place. We lined up and passed through the small outbuilding to receive our portion. Each man received nearly a whole Klim can of the cereal. I joined Hank, Bill, Bob, and Eddie in the pasture, where they had spread a blanket. The mixture of roughly pounded grain had melded into a porridge that must have been more nutritious than it tasted.

"I've eaten hot cereals for breakfast," commented Hank, "but none of them were as substantial as this. I just wish we had some milk to put in it."

It certainly was substantial. Could that have been duplicated without the addition of brick dust?

Comforted by this warm meal, we lazed in the sun, speaking frequently now of what we might do when we returned to our homes. Later that afternoon my laundered garments were nearly dry, so I put them on, hoping that the heat of my body would complete the process. Using myself as a form, I was able to pull the wrinkled fabric into a coherent mass.

In my blankets that night I was able to get to sleep quickly; the sharp pang in my stomach had receded for the time being, and the laundering had washed out the pestering lice. Two or three hours later, however, I was wakened by a familiar presence. The nits had hatched!

Nevertheless, I woke up refreshed the following morning. We gathered our belongings, submitted to a count, and walked to the road. Men from other barns were already on the march, and we fell in behind them, being joined, in turn, by men who had been sheltered in barns farther on. It was a bright, sunny day, and having had a good meal the day before, I felt invigorated, and strode off at the fast pace that had been set by others who must have shared my energy. Believing that each step now was bringing us closer to home, I rejoiced and took greater notice of my surroundings. We were climbing a hill, with a line of fir trees on the left, when I saw a small girl, perhaps ten years old, at the side of the road. She was skipping along, backward, and passed our entire company of men. If this was a brisk pace for us now, how slowly we must have walked for many days!

Shortly after, we turned abruptly from this northern heading and followed a narrower road, passing through neatly kept forest on both sides. At our next rest stop we sat on the edges of the road, with steep embankments on one side and a sharp drop-off on the other. Someone had remarked to a guard on the beauty of the area, and the word had been passed on that we were traveling through land that had been the Kaiser's hunting preserve. As we left it, we entered flat farming country. That evening, we were shunted north off this small road to a farmstead in the hamlet of Rohrstorf; we had walked 21 kilometers that day.

The following morning we headed westward again. In the afternoon we traversed a small city, Bad Bevensen. At its western edge lay a railway track. With some regret that no train was waiting for us, we crossed and continued on, arriving in late afternoon at the village of Hohenbunstorf. The barns there were neat, but not as comfortable as the one we had left at Bredenbock. Still, there was nothing here to complain about, and there was some excitement about what might occur next. We stayed at Hohenbunstorf for two and one-half days, being fed two cups of meal and two of bean soup.

At about noon on March 28th we were on the road again, retracing our steps to a larger highway, then heading south. While passing through the edge of a city named Uelzin, we crossed a railway, with some disappointment, because the rumor of a train ride persisted. We continued on some distance south to the edge of town. There, at a railway yard — at last — stood a train. Surely it couldn't be ours, I concluded, for it and other sets of carriages on the tracks were all small boxcars. My idea of a train ride was to have a real seat, even if only a wooden one, in a passenger car.

Still, guards gruffly herded us across several lines of empty tracks, and to carriages obviously intended for hauling freight. We were lined up, beside the small freight cars, as guards counted us and urged us aboard, through the gaping doors. The one closest to where I was standing bore the printed message, "*quarante hommes/huit chevaux*" — 40 men or 8 horses. As we struggled aboard, I discovered that 60 men were crowded into the car. There was scarcely room for all of us standing; without question, we could not all sit at one time.

The door was rolled shut, but the train remained motionless, doubtless waiting until all the men were aboard. After some considerable experimentation, it was agreed that we could all sit down, providing one man sat, legs outstretched, while another sat at right angles to him, placing his legs over the outstretched legs of the first man. The third man could then sit with his legs across those of the other two, and his back supported by the back of the number two man in the adjacent configuration. Changing positions would be both necessary and difficult, but it was preferable to fighting for a place to stand when the train began to move.

Very little could be observed from inside the car, for through the cracks in the boxcar one could gain a narrow perspective of what was outside. Then the door swung open and uniformed men were outside with a push-cart bearing both milk cans full of water and loaves of bread. Struggling to our feet, we learned that we had to perform this sequentially.

Each man received about one cupful of water, and there was a loaf, to be divided among six men. My portion was a crusty heel, which had the virtue of being less likely to crumble than a chunk from the middle of the loaf.

Someone able to speak German asked where we were headed, and why. The answer to the first question was vague, but the soldier indicated that a British spearhead was driving this way from Hannover, and the train would take us away from that.

The battle lines were hazardous, but I would rather have been moved closer to our Allies.

Chapter 26

On Foot Between Two Fronts

THE TRAIN LURCHED forward, jarring the men who had resisted the suggestion to sit on the crowded floor. They were thrown off balance, though none of them toppled, for there was no room to fall, packed tightly as we were. The point had sunk home. Although three-layered seating was going to be uncomfortable, trying to stand in the rough-riding car presented other hazards. Soon, all of the men had found places on the floor.

In order to squeeze into the cramped space available, we shifted our bulky blankets and packs. We turned our heads, to avoid too-close contact with the face of a neighbor with whom we had no prior acquaintance, and whose breath was offensive, too. Though the posture we thus contrived was far from comfortable, fatigue gradually overcame our discomfort and, lulled by the throbbing rhythm of carriage wheels on steel track, we fell asleep.

I was wakened, how much later I could not say, to some change in my environment. Was it the rumble of a bridge over which we were passing, a change in the train's direction or velocity, a whistle in the night? I could not tell, but I knew that my legs were numb from my cramped position. It was time to awaken the men between whom I was sandwiched and for us all to shift position. This disturbed those seated next to us, resulting in a general groping and trying to stand, the chafing of limbs that had gone to sleep, squatting, sitting, interlacing, and adjusting to new positions. It must have taken some time for the majority of us to fall asleep again.

How many times this scene was repeated during the night I do not know, nor how many times the train stopped on a siding while waiting the passage of a higher-priority train.

I believe we came to a halt at least once when bombers flew overhead, but the doors remained closed and locked. Eventually, morning light entered through the small windows high in the front and rear of the car, and through cracks between boards in the siding.

When the train stopped at an anonymous marshaling yard, footsteps crunched outside and the door was opened at last. Soldiers had brought a handcart alongside, bearing cans of water. With great care, they permitted some to alight, partly to allow space for movement inside, and partly as an answer to urgent needs of some of the men. The rest of us were allowed to come to the door of the boxcar and receive a ration of water. With a drink at hand, I broke off and nibbled a bit of bread from last evening's allotment. Getting to our feet had alleviated some of the cramping that had occurred during the night, making it more agreeable to resume our positions in preparation for another leg of the journey.

Much later in the day, the train diverted at a siding and proceeded on what seemed to be a different direction. When its brakes brought it to a squealing halt an hour or two later, the door was opened and we were ordered to debark. We saw a small station, and alighted on a long wooden platform. There was something familiar about this place; the sign on the station read Altengrabow. This was the very same prison camp, *Stalag XI-A*, to which Bob Donahue and I had been brought last September, shortly after our parting with the soldiers whom we had accompanied through France, Belgium, and part of Germany. Certainly, this large contingent of men could not be accommodated in the solitary confinement building where Bob and I had stayed. Perhaps, I thought, we would be assigned to a barracks in this camp. After weeks on the road, the prospect of barracks living now held some appeal.

★ ꩜ ★ ꩜ ★

Assembled by the guards, we descended the several steps from the platform and turned to the right. The street was ankle-deep in powdered dust, churned up no doubt by battle tanks moving from the factory, concealed under the camp, to be transported by railway. The plodding feet of so many men raised a cloud of dust in front of substantial brick homes, which accommodated the permanent cadre of the camp. We turned from this tree-lined street onto another. Barren of trees, this little road passed through open fields separating the camp personnel's living quarters from the prisoners' area. Ahead I could see familiar terrain — the solitary confinement building, and on the left, wooden barracks, which had housed Soviet prisoners when I was there.

However, the column turned to the right, passing beyond the rows of barracks. Camp guards opened a barbed-wire barricade. We entered, and were lined up alongside a large tent, labeled on its side "AFRIKA CORPS." It had previously been used as an aircraft maintenance hangar on the sands of Africa. In the background, behind the guards, stood clusters of dark-skinned observers, prisoners wearing uniforms of other countries.

We were counted and separated into two groups. Half of us, my combine included, were assigned to the tent by which we stood; the other half were to go into a second tent, just behind. We were ordered to find a space, to leave our belongings, and to return. Smith, Ice, Stroud, Gates, and I found a place along the outer wall, not quite midway from the north end. With some misgivings about the safety of our possessions, we dropped them as directed and left the tent. Outside, guards issued each man a large paper bag similar to those which had covered our mattresses in *Stalag Luft IV.* Assured that our belongings would be safe, and that the tents would be guarded in our absence, with our bags in hand we were marched down a narrow track into a wooded area.

We halted in a semi-cleared place while a guard pantomimed our chore. We were to harvest a wiry type of grass, he demonstrated, and fill our sack. When full, this would serve as our mattress.

Hundreds of men fanned out among the trees in search of this particular vegetation. The bulky grass in each sack had to be compacted in order to have sufficient density to protect one's body from the hard, cold earth. An abundance of this vegetation was found, and the task was completed in a fairly short time. Then, with sacks tied shut and hoisted over shoulders, we retraced our route to our new home.

Midway, we passed an area of perhaps two blocks in length and one block wide, in which stood rows of upright small boards. Somehow I communicated to ask the guard, walking beside me, what they represented. He told me that it was the burial ground for Soviet prisoners who had died while in the camp. The boards were grave markers. How close together they were! Many had died here. Recalling the wasted body of the soldier who had so gratefully received the food Bob Donahue and I hadn't needed while in solitary confinement, I guessed that many had died of starvation.

Once again at our tent, we put our mattresses on the ground next to our other belongings. The sacks, stuffed as they were with the springy grass, retained their round, inflated shape. I tested mine by lying down. It was soft, all right, and it did mash down a little, but much of that compression disappeared only seconds after I arose. We covered our mattresses with the blankets. There would be sufficient room in the tent for men to lie on their backs, without crowding.

Guards, accompanied by prisoners bearing soup and bread, passed by our tent. This sight produced a general press at the door as men hurried to get in line for dinner. We were rebuffed, and the food was carried to more distant tents.

One of our inmate officers conferred with the guards, then reported that we would receive no rations today.

"Nor tomorrow, either," he said. "I have requested that a German officer come to discuss the matter."

The officer appeared and explained that the officer in charge of our transport by train had reported that he had distributed rations to all men on board, sufficient for five days. For that he had been compensated, and there would be no more for the next four days. Argument did not sway the officer; the decision had been made. That bit of bread could hardly be counted a single day's ration, yet the officer had been paid for supplying us for five days. His graft must have brought him a tidy profit.

To take my mind off the absent dinner, I set out to explore the area. Beyond our own tent lay its twin, occupied by the remainder of our companions from *Stalag Luft IV.* The two adjacent tents, which may have been equal in size to ours, were occupied by prisoners from India. These men spoke English, though with an accent unfamiliar to my ears. The next two tents, smaller than the others, were inhabited by Moroccans. Standing at the entrance, I discovered a scene much different from any others in my experience. Somehow the men had contrived to suspend their equipment from tent poles or ropes from the tent roof. The scene reminded me of movies I had seen purporting to portray North African market places.

I walked on, resolving to explore more fully at a later time. Behind these last two tents, and separated by perhaps 100 yards, were two smaller tents. I had been told that the Gurkhas, said to be from mountains in the north of India, were fierce fighters in the British army. Obeying the cautionary advice of my informant, I kept at some distance from these tents, noting only that the men visible outside were small and wiry, and dressed in British uniforms. Returning to my end of the compound, I discovered a pipe and spigot where potable water could be obtained. I resolved to launder my clothes on the next agreeable day.

My companions and I went to bed early that night, hoping that sleep would erase hunger pangs. The bed was reasonably comfortable and the temperature was warm enough; only the lice continued to pester us. Hunger stalked us all the next day, and the next. After the weather had lost some of its chill, I went to the spigot and rinsed out my clothing, particularly my socks, which I scrubbed with soap for the first time since leaving the *Stalag*. They had given good service, and would need mending when they became dry. My shirt and trousers were the next to receive attention. I scrubbed hard, rubbing soap along the seams in the hope that it would destroy both lice and nits. When finished, I spread the clothes on the ground to dry. Then I took the liberty of a sponge bath with the cool water from the spigot.

By bedtime the clothes were dry enough to put on again. Though the weather had warmed, it was still too cold to sleep unless fully clad. It felt so good to relax without the annoyance of those crawling, biting creatures, and with only hunger to haunt me, I fell asleep. But that comfort was short-lived; a few hours later a new generation of lice had hatched out from the seams and were feasting on and exploring new terrain. Awake, I again became aware of incessant, gnawing hunger pangs.

To dismiss them from my mind, I strolled again around the compound, first speaking to a couple of Indian prisoners who were standing outside their tent. Almost immediately I became aware of my deficiencies in the geography of India, for I had no idea of the locales, which they declared as home.

I walked down to the next set of tents, for some obscure reason walking into the second of the Moroccan tents. Men were quietly sitting on their blankets on the floor, their possessions dangling from overhead. In English, I spoke to one. He responded pleasantly enough, but in French. Ah! Here lay the possibility of communication. He was not dismayed that I could not pinpoint his home community; he came from a small village, he said, but had worked as a taxi driver in Casablanca. I had, at least, heard of that. He was equally vague about the location of my home town, Tipton, Iowa, even the location of Iowa was something of a mystery to him.

But he was charitable about my limited command of French, and we sat, conversing together for some time. He grasped the fact that our rations were being withheld. As I made ready to leave, he invited me to visit him and to share his meal when his rations would be distributed on Easter Day. Touched by his generosity, I left the tent to return to my companions.

Rumors — or were they more than that — were flying when I arrived at my tent. One of our elected camp officials had formally complained to the commandant about our ration situation. The story continued, to the effect that the commandant had ascertained that a supply of American Red Cross parcels was in storage at a nearby city, and that they would be requisitioned for our use. If true, this was good news and, as usual, I accepted this with reserve, tempered by fervent hope.

That afternoon the announcement came that food parcels had indeed arrived, and were to be issued to our group only. The truck bearing this food had been dispatched from a warehouse in Juterbog, we were told. I had never heard of that place before, but it was said to be not too far distant. The spokesman emphasized that the Germans were not going to issue us rations until the food for which they had reimbursed the transporting officer were supposedly exhausted. With some grumbling about the unfairness of that decision, we gladly accepted these parcels. Each man received a portion of a parcel, just how large a portion I no longer recall, and the men in my combine characteristically exercised caution, eating sparingly despite our enormous appetites. I believe that this must have occurred on Good Friday.

Shortly thereafter, a ruckus commenced outside the next tent. When we went to investigate we discovered a few American prisoners facing off against three tall, lanky, accusing Indians. As the story unfolded, two or three American prisoners had traded a pound can of margarine to the Indians in exchange for a tin of corned beef, which their religion forbade them to eat. The exchange itself had gone off to the satisfaction of all concerned, but the Indians became furious when, upon emptying the can in order to divide it among themselves, they discovered that the bottom half of the can was not margarine, but sand. When these facts became known, these American cheaters were surrounded by hostile Americans as well as Indians. With apologies, the Indians were given the other half-can of margarine, and the incident terminated peacefully.

The following morning, when checking our supplies for breakfast, we noted that food was missing from our packs we had used for pillows. A neat slice had been made in the tent just beside each sack. Most of the men sleeping on the outside row of the tent ruefully reported similar losses. No one had noticed a disturbance in the night, not even when the opening must have been slit into our tent, nor when a hand must have been inserted into the shirt-backpack under our heads.

The general consensus was that the Ghurkas were responsible for our losses. They were known to be stealthy fighters. Perhaps we were fortunate to still have our heads. No one was inclined to confront those men; we let the matter rest and guarded the remainder of our goods between us and away from the tent wall. Our light meals were made from the goods shared by the members of our combine.

On Easter Sunday I went to the Moroccan tent, just in time for dinner. My host, seated in his customary place, greeted me and gestured for me to be seated. Almost simultaneously we were joined by another American prisoner, also invited to partake of this Easter repast. The ration, a half can of carrot soup, was shared equally by the three of us. Accustomed only to potatoes, the carrots, even without salt, tasted sweet and delicious.

★ ★ ★

Massive air raids, with heavy opposition both from the ground and the air, could be witnessed from the camp. The heavy activity was to our north and west. Most likely, the target was the marshaling yards at Stendal or the air base at Burg, where I had first become acquainted with Hank. We could see our bombers under attack, some exploding in air, others in a downward spiral. The war was becoming more and more a present reality to us.

Then the fifth day passed, and we were included among those who regularly received camp rations — the familiar black *brodt* plus the tasty carrot soup — so common in this camp. When men peeled off their outer clothing to bathe or change, it was surprising to see just how gaunt their bodies had become. How welcome were these regular rations!

Bill and Bob appeared at our sleeping place, excited by the news that they had struck a deal with an Indian prisoner to purchase a cooking container for two packages of cigarettes. The others in our combine were at first skeptical. We had few prospects of acquiring anything to cook in the container, and two packages of cigarettes might be used to purchase badly needed food. But Bill and Bob were enthusiastic, and persuaded us to at least meet this man and see what he had to sell.

The metal box, about 4 inches wide, 3 deep, and 14 in length, had a lid fitted to slide into grooves at its top. It would not leak, we were told, even when heated; and with the cover closed, it would serve as a container for dry comestibles, even if we were again on a march. Their enthusiasm persuaded us, and we walked back to our tent, the happy owners of a utensil we might never need.

On the morning of April 12th, with the ground under our feet trembling from the shock of distant explosions, we were herded out of our tents, led hurriedly down Altengrabow's streets, and onto a narrow, rough path on a southward heading. Artillery fire was intense to the south and west of us. The pace was quick and I struggled to keep up with my fellow companions. At the fence marking the south side of the camp, those men in front of me were stepping briskly around or over the collapsed body of a prisoner. I quickly quelled the impulse to stop and help, lest I lose contact with my combine. With a quick pang of guilt I stepped over him at the opening in the fence and followed the ragtag crowd now turning down the narrow road to the left.

With a single rest stop we hurried along this narrow road, then passed through a town named Gorzke. Our route maintained about the same eastward direction, but on a larger road. We stopped that night at the village of Benken. I believe we had walked 19 kilometers that day, perhaps a few more, counting the distance traveled within the camp itself.

Whether we all stayed in the same barn that night I do not know, but our group was lodged on the ground floor of a barn smaller than most in which we had stayed earlier on the march. The next morning I woke to find a big guard standing in the doorway. He had a message for us.

"I have bad news for you," he said, rather sympathetically. "Your President is dead."

I called out in answer, "So Henry Wallace is our new President!"

"Not so," he replied. "His name is Truman."

That response brought home to me just how long we had been out of contact with the United States. I had never heard of Harry Truman; there had been no news from the recent election. How could a man whose name I had never heard now be the President of my country?

The following day we moved through several small villages. News of our passage must have reached the inhabitants, just as had news of the death of President Franklin D. Roosevelt. Villagers stood silently in their doorways, some of them in tears, as we trouped past. Then it struck me that in life, President Roosevelt had been seen by these people as the leader of an enemy nation, but it may have occurred to them that he might have been kinder to them in defeat than his unknown successor.

We walked 21 kilometers that day before filing into a farmyard at the small town of Dahnsdorf. We were supplied with a larger than usual ration of potatoes that evening, enough to save a few for the following day.

In the barnyard, I noticed that our guards were less officious, gentler than those who had accompanied us from the beginning of our march. They wore the green-gray uniforms of the *Wehrmacht*, and some of the American prisoners of Polish extraction were able to communicate with them in Polish. Those guards let us know that they had been captured in their native land and given the choice of serving as forced laborers, or as German soldiers guarding prisoners. For better or worse, they had chosen this duty.

Somehow, the next morning, the five of us in our combine were able to assemble in one of the farm's outbuildings. Whatever its normal use, it was equipped with a narrow table. Boiled water for drinking was available to us from large kettles in the barnyard. While Hank and I stood in line to get our ration, Eddy and Bob nosed around the farm, returning with two eggs, for which they had traded our remaining two bars of soap.

Hank and I then guarded our belongings as the others stood in the water line. Upon their return, and with the help of hot water, we mashed up some potatoes and mixed in the two raw eggs. It seemed a hearty breakfast for the five of us, and we began our morning's march at a brisk pace.

Stopping along the road for our hourly rest, one of our group complained of an "upset stomach." With the good fortune of last evening's supply of potatoes, we quickly kindled a small bonfire, caked one of the already boiled potatoes with some mud found at the side of the road, and thrust it into the flames. We were there for only ten minutes, but that was long enough for the mud with which the potato was caked to dry, and for the outer skin of the potato to char. That remained our cure-all for diarrhea. The prescription was eaten, and there were no more complaints.

Sounds of war — distant shelling, low-flying aircraft, possibly attacks on bridges or railroads — were often borne on the wind. Later that day, walking along a road in very flat terrain, we observed a huge formation of bombers. Our guards shooed us off the road, asking us to lie flat. I found myself in a patch of rhubarb. Surreptitiously, I pulled the ones closest to me, stripped the leaves from their stalks, and thrust the stalks into my coat pocket. I stuffed the leaves underneath me, hoping that they would flatten out and remain unseen by the nearby guard when I stood up. I would cook the stalks on the first occasion.

The bombers passed over and we returned to the road. No one had noticed the layer of rhubarb leaves. Not long after, we heard a clucking noise ahead. A hen and trail of chicks were crossing the road, right through our formation. The cluck was followed by a throttled cackle, then silence. As we walked along we saw feathers littering the road.

That evening we arrived in the small town of Schönfeld. Only small barns were available for us. That night, I discovered a carefully guarded fire behind an outbuilding; some prisoners ate chicken for supper.

My sleeping place was hard and lumpy. In morning's light I discovered that I had been lying on a sack of barley. Feeling just a tinge of guilt, I opened and shared the contents of that sack with the men around me. They stowed it in their undershirts as we had done with grain on an earlier occasion. The several pounds remaining, I left in the bag and brazenly tossed it over my shoulder. I tried to appear nonchalant as I joined the morning formation. There were no comments from our guards.

On this day or the next, we passed close to a concentration camp. The ugly low wooden buildings seemed ominous enough. I remember seeing one man standing, the wind whipping a light striped costume around his gaunt body. He appeared to be more skeleton than man. That was all I saw, but the memory of that scene has stayed with me to this day.

We arrived that evening at the small village of Leipa, apparently a farming village, where the houses sat back from the road, enclosed by a wall at the street. We stopped at such a place; the tall doors were swung back, and we entered and climbed up into the hayloft. That night I was awakened by the deep-throated roar of engines and, from the street, the rumble of machinery. In the morning a guard told us that a Russian patrol, in battle tanks, had passed through the streets, apparently on a reconnaissance mission. We were closer to the Russian front than we had realized.

That day we walked through the edge of Jessen, probably the largest town we had encountered since leaving the camp at Altengrabow. We crossed a large highway, and what appeared to be a canal, then continued southward. At a crossroad we came upon a contingent of boy-soldiers dressed in German uniforms. Sitting on the roadside, they appeared dejected — far too young and too small to be sent into battle.

Soon we entered Annaburg, a city of some size. Someone passed along the information, apparently conveyed by a guard, that this was an open city — neutral and non-combatant. We would expect no assault or bombing here.

We walked down the street, past cafés and stores, crossed a railroad track, then moved by a fairly large factory. We came upon a small building, apparently a pottery factory. We left the main road and were marched in behind the building, past a pile of broken and discarded crockery, and to an open space near a large brick building. It might have been an annex to the pottery but, instead, had been an aircraft wing manufacturing plant. That was to be our shelter during our stay in Annaburg.

Inside the building stood rows of giant presses, perhaps 50 or more feet long; perhaps 32 inches above each low, flat steel deck was suspended the opposite pressing member.

There was no way to measure these dimensions. It just became important to bend when sitting on the lower deck, and to roll slightly to the outside before sitting up from a sleeping position. As it turned out, there was no material available to serve as a mattress over the cold steel plates. But, at least, I thought, we were not sleeping on cold snow or frozen clods.

That evening we built a bonfire in the open space at the end of the building and, recalling how the Hombeck family had prepared a barley beverage, I poured some of the pilfered barley into the shoebox-type container and popped it over the fire. Once popped, and boiled with rhubarb, it made a filling dish, though very tart.

My bed that night was warmed a bit from the heat of my body, and was sheltered from the wind. We must have lounged around there for another day, repeating, without much pleasure, the menu from the day before. Desiring some addition to our food supply, I enlisted Charlie Summers, our "singer" from *Stalag Luft IV*, to try to leave our place with me, in order to trade with local people. Well aware that anyone wearing the RAF uniform gained special privilege from our captors, we managed to borrow caps and blue jackets from fellow prisoners.

Charlie and I strolled with simulated confidence toward the main gate of the plant. As we neared the gate, we saw a crowd of prisoners noisily clamoring to be let out, armed guards firmly holding them at bay. Displaying the bag I carried over my shoulder, I nodded to the guards. We walked on past, opened the gate, and stepped into the street. Immediately as the gate closed I was struck by the realization that we were out from the scrutiny of our captors. This was the moment I had awaited for six and one-half months! But now what? To appear indecisive was to invite attention, a sure way to bring our freedom to an end.

We had to choose a direction. Across the broad street to our right was a wide, empty street. We chose to turn to our left, returning in the direction by which we had entered the factory enclosure. I experienced a sense of elation; we were free! But were we? The supplies we carried as trading goods were not truly our own, but property shared by companions in our respective combines. It would not be right to leave them, taking some of their precious foodstuffs.

We muttered such thoughts in nearly silent communication as we walked down the street. No habitations lined this side of the road, but a crossing street gave us the opportunity to get out of sight of anyone who might peer out of the factory gate and see us. We turned and unexpectedly came upon a barnyard not far from the corner. We thought there should be some food to trade here, and we entered the open gate.

At first it appeared that no one was around, but as we walked back behind the house we came upon a man forking something from a large pile. His appearance wasn't at all reassuring — he had a small Hitler-like moustache, and his black hair was pulled down to one side over his forehead, also in emulation of the Nazi leader. We tried in clumsy German to explain our mission. My message must have been unintelligible to him. Then I discovered that he spoke French; in fact, he had been conscripted as a farm laborer and assigned here as a replacement for the German farmer, who was in military service. Now with a language with which to communicate, I told him that we had coffee, cigarettes, and chocolate, which we wanted to exchange for potatoes, vegetables, or whatever he wished to trade. We would have to speak with the householder, he said, and dispatched the young girl standing nearby to call her mother.

Wiping her hands on her apron, a slender woman followed the girl from the doorway. With the French farm hand as interpreter, we began to tell of our trading goods. We were interrupted by a flight of low-flying aircraft winging directly overhead. The three residents wasted no time in running to the barn, where they disappeared. Charlie and I stood our ground, confident that this was an open city and that we would come to no harm. We stood there, gazing at the sleek silver craft until they passed out of sight. What kind of airplane were they, we asked each other. They resembled the twin-engine Douglas A-20 attack bombers — the Havoc — we were familiar with, but were longer, perhaps larger. Later, we found out that they were A-26 attack bombers — the Invader, a larger and more advanced version of the A-20, which we knew well from our classes in aircraft recognition. We were quite unaware that these advanced planes existed at this time.

The planes receded into the distance, and the farm family returned from their shelter. We resumed our explanation. Then the planes circled and returned once more. This time, Charlie and I accepted the family's frenzied invitation to join them in their air raid shelter. We followed them into a cave under the barn, fortified by large beams. The farm hand closed the heavy door behind us, and we sat together in dim light.

Quickly the notion was dispelled that this was an open city. Multiple concussions showered clouds of dust from the beamed ceiling. The locals huddled in terror. This may not have been their first such experience, but it was for Charlie and me.

When quiet was restored, we all climbed out of the shelter and walked together back to the place where we had first spied the farm worker. Resuming the talk of barter, the woman and her farm hand consulted as though they were equal partners in the farm operation. Finally they supplied some vegetables in exchange for our bit of coffee. The lady communicated that she might as well exchange some of her foodstuffs, for the Russians would undoubtedly arrive soon and take what she had. She pointed to a hole just outside the big barn door, a hole perhaps four feet in diameter and four or five feet deep, beside which lay a pitchfork. When "the Russkies" came, she said, she would jump in the hole to fend them off. She lived in obvious and constant terror of the Russians.

The "All Clear" sounded, and as I hoisted the sack of vegetables on my shoulder, I saw a cloud of smoke and dust rising from just beyond our factory. Many of our fellow prisoners had fled the bombing. Some of them were now in the meadow between the factory and these farm buildings. Home force guards were frantically trying to herd them back to the factory area.

Charlie and I took the direct route, over the fence and into the field. While crossing, we were stopped by a civil guard, intent on collaring us, we couldn't understand why. A prisoner dressed in RAF uniform came up and remonstrated with him. Distracted, the guard released his grip on us, and we hurriedly returned to the factory area.

Inside, on and by the huge presses that served as our beds, some men were groggily trying to get to their feet. One of them told us that he had been asleep on the press when a mighty blast woke him. He sat up quickly, knocking himself unconscious as his head struck the press. Apparently the planes had struck a fuel depot in woods only 100 yards from the factory.

The other men from my combine soon arrived. In the turmoil they had entered the pottery plant itself, where they had discovered cases of bayonets. They had scooped them up and had been selling them to other prisoners for ten cigarettes each. Now we had a huge supply of cigarettes, and many prisoners had concealed arms. A bayonet might have but limited effect against guns, but it was better than nothing.

Hank had saved a bayonet for me. Having for many months felt powerless in the face of overwhelming force, I found it comforting to have a weapon, just in case.

On the following morning, April 21st, we prisoners were assembled, many with bayonets concealed under our overcoats, to be marched westward down a city street, down a hill, and out of Annaburg. Twenty kilometers later, we arrived at a farmstead in the village of Pretten, where we were ushered into a large barn.

The next day we left that barn, and marched just three kilometers to another farm. The barn there had a large lean-to addition on its side. The men in my combine bedded down on the ground under the canopy of the lean-to; it seemed like camping out. The following morning, our captors evidently wished to feed us. They called for volunteers experienced as bakers; 15, they said, were needed. I doubt that there were any bakers among us, but offered the incentive to be near food, more than 15 men quickly volunteered and were taken away to prepare bread for us.

Men sat or stood in little knots around the barnyard, speculating on the length of time needed to bake bread. In anticipation of that prospect, there seemed little else to do. We were surprised, then, to hear intense small arms fire to the east of us. The small road that ran along the farm disappeared in a grove of trees up a small hill. It sounded as though a small battle was raging only a half-mile from us. We waited anxiously for signs that would convey the import of this development. Several guards gathered in a nervous conference by an outbuilding. We saw the evidence that our Allies were getting the best of this conflict, as a number of *SS* troopers ran down the road in our direction. One detoured into our area. He handed me a small cigar, saying, "If I am captured, you will tell them that I have been kind to you, won't you?"

"Small chance of that!" I said to myself.

He hurried off, away from the fighting.

Hastily, our guards urged us to pack our belongings and leave the farm.

There would be no fresh bread given out here today. I wondered what had happened to the volunteer bakers.

We had no rest stops that day, just the frantic urging for us to move as speedily as possible. We crossed the Elbe River on a bridge, walked southwest through the town of Domitsch, then on to Trossin. Just out of Trossin, at a fork in the road, we turned wearily to the north. We arrived at the wee village of Dahlenburg and filed into a barnyard. I remember only a large house set back from a large barn. We had walked about 20 kilometers since mid-morning at what was, in our physical condition, a brutally fast pace. At least, we had been provided with drinking water.

On the following morning we left Dahlenburg on a road leading south, up and over a high hill, to rejoin the highway on which we had fled Pretten. Polish-speaking prisoners told us that our guards were very concerned about the Russian advance. The Poles had sound reasons why they did not want to be captured by the Russians. When the Soviets had controlled eastern Poland, to 1941, they had starved the people, not allowing them to receive food; they forced Poles into the Russian interior for slave labor; and they were quick to kill any organizers of religious groups.

This day we were permitted rest stops; our guards were tired, too. One older guard was so exhausted that one of the prisoners took pity on him, carrying his pack for several kilometers. At the city of Sollichau, we left this road, heading northwest for several kilometers. Then we branched off, following a narrow road bordered by stately pines.

Toward evening, we arrived at a settlement displaying a cluster of farm buildings. A sign proclaimed it to be the village of Krina. We had walked 32 kilometers and were glad to shed our small burdens and rest.

The barn to which the members of my combine were assigned was the last in a series of small buildings. Standing perpendicular to the road and joined at right angles by a wall of some sort, its side defined an open space between that wall and the road. As the dim light of evening faded, I explored the possibility of eluding guards and escaping, at least temporarily, from this place. The guards appeared to be stationed on the other side of our barn, while one or two patrolled the road. There was ample space between the patrolling guards for me to slip out of the barn and, staying in the deep shadow close to the side of it, to seek a place by which I could leave this open lot. Just opposite from our barns was a field. A wagon was parked alongside the barn; I would investigate its contents later. At the exterior side of this open space, a low wall ran along the road. From my position I couldn't see any other buildings on this side of the road, but one or two houses, widely separated, stood on the opposite side.

The patrolling guard had turned and was heading my way. I took cover under the wagon until he retraced his route. What was on the wagon? It was loaded with small bales that didn't smell like hay or straw. Reaching up, I pulled out several wisps of dehydrated vegetables, the kind that had made up the rich soup Bob Donahue and I had eaten while in the solitary block at Altengrabow. I stuffed a big double handful of the dried vegetables into my pockets and scurried back to my place in the barn to report to my comrades. With some water and a fire, we could cook up a good portion of nutritious soup on the following day.

Hank and I pocketed some goods for trading, then stepped out of the lightly guarded barnyard, and set out to find bread. We knocked at the rear door of a house perhaps 100 yards away from the barn. After what seemed to be a long interval, a German soldier answered the knock. He appeared anxious for us to leave. Recalling that many German soldiers I had met in France had a passing acquaintance with the French language, I spoke to him in French. He seemed disinterested in talking. I took a pack of cigarettes from my pocket, tamped one on my knuckle, and lit it. Now he was interested.

Would he trade bread for cigarettes? He disappeared into the house, returning a moment later with three other German soldiers. I offered the first one a cigarette. The others were quick to accept one too. They had no bread in the house but, yes, they would get some, and trade. We must return in an hour or so. It seemed only courteous that I should stay, smoking with them, until they finished their cigarettes. Warming up to us, they told us that a fifth man was with them, but he had gone some time ago to contact the Americans. He wanted to become a prisoner of the Americans, not the Russians.

We returned to our barn, our absence undetected. Seeing Gates, Stroud, and Ice, we told them that we had been negotiating for bread and that at least one loaf would be forthcoming in an hour or so. After an appropriate pause, we returned to the house. The fifth soldier had returned, with depressing news. He said that the Americans had taken his identity card, stamped it POW, extracted the ammunition from his pistol, then returned the weapon to him. They declared that they could not accept his person, and that he must go back to his comrades.

The Germans were AWOL from their units and wouldn't have known where to find them even if they wanted to, which they emphatically did not. With the avenue to surrender blocked, they became despondent. Just then, an observation and liaison plane, one of the little lightweight "Grasshoppers" in use by American forces, flew over, out of which a number of leaflets fluttered down. One of the soldiers hurried into the field to retrieve the missive, and brought it for the others to read.

The message encouraged Axis soldiers to surrender. They must come to specified points in a group of no less than 125, led by an officer. The men were stunned; they numbered only five, and none of them was an officer. They asked Hank and me if we would be willing to accompany them to the American lines. Surely, if we Americans would vouch for them, they would be accepted as prisoners.

Hank and I thought the idea had appeal, but told "our prisoners" our party would include Bill, Bob, and Eddy. Reluctantly, the men accepted this condition, though they protested that the larger the group, the more difficult it would be to reach the American lines. They told us that they had access to a motorcycle, and would ride by our barn in the evening, to speak to us about the final details. With a loaf of bread in hand, we returned to the barn, eager to report this happy news to our comrades.

To our surprise, our buddies did not share our enthusiasm about these plans for imminent liberation. In our absence, a rumor had spread among the prisoners that a man had already left to meet the Americans. Hopes were high that American troops would enter the village in the morning to escort us to liberty. No, our buddies did not want to accompany us through what might be a no-man's land, when a safer route might be opened to them in the morning.

In anticipation of meeting the Germans in the evening and finding friendly soldiers who would care for us, Hank and I took our share of the remaining food supplies and hungrily ate them by ourselves. It seemed that darkness might never come. As daylight faded, a brilliant moon rose to replace the setting sun. Several guards patrolled the road.

Hank and I crowded close to the barn, waiting for our German soldiers to arrive on motorcycle. At last they came by, their engine backfired, feigning trouble. Hank and I approached them, trying to appear as curious onlookers.

The driver shook his head resignedly. "We cannot go tonight," he said softly, "a company of *SS* troops has camped along the road. We dare not try to pass through." Then he wheeled his motorcycle in the road and rode off toward the house in which they were staying.

Our companions received us without surprise. They had had no confidence in plans for escape at this late stage of our trek.

In the morning, we ate no breakfast; we had consumed our supplies the evening before. We again heard the rumor that during the night a fellow prisoner had walked through to the American lines and explained our condition to the authorities. When the man returned to our barn, he was accompanied by one or two soldiers disguised to look like prisoners. They had brought weapons and ammunition, concealed in a handcart, just in case we would meet trouble on this day's march.

Guards hurriedly ushered us out of our quarters and onto the road. The *SS* troops deployed along the road nearby had stolen away in the night, and a guard had told one of the prisoners that the Russians were only five kilometers behind us. There was no sound of battle, nor could we hear the roar of truck or tank engines. By then, we had appropriated two or three handcarts among us, piled with backpacks and blankets. I saw nothing, though, that suggested to me that any of the men pushing them were anything other than prisoners. I did not expect our guards to turn on us when we came close to the front, yet there was uncertainty about what might lie ahead. The bayonet under my coat lent a feeling of reassurance.

Chapter 27

To Freedom, and Beyond

AT THE VERY edge of the village, we departed the road, exchanging the hard paving for a needle-strewn path through a pine forest. Hank and I walked together now. The others from our combine had struck out separately, seemingly still harboring a sense of betrayal in our suggestion of leaving with the AWOL German soldiers in search of our own forces. Perhaps they were miffed by our asking for our share of the combine's larder after they had turned down the idea. During those months of codependence, we had forged a bond that would be difficult to sever, but now that bond was endangered. No doubt we would rally together when we were again free.

The guard in the lead turned us onto a path that angled sharply away from the one we were traveling. Other guards stood at the junction of these two paths, barring our departure from the group. Within the hour, we were led from the forest and to the edge of a town. The road sign read Plodda. We turned, then, to the south, walking past the edge of the town.

Many of the houses bordering our route had balconies from which fluttered white cloths, indicating surrender. A guard told one of the prisoners that the Americans had come this far, then pulled back to a nearby river. The town had surrendered, and was determined to maintain that status. Our ragtag band was watched from behind curtained windows, but no one gestured to us.

A guard happened to be walking beside me as we passed one of the houses flying a white flag. As I watched, he extracted the ammunition clip from his rifle, emptied it and slipped the ammunition into his pocket. Then he handed the rifle to me, saying, "We are your prisoners now."

We continued walking, much as before. The road stretched out wide before us, empty except for the line of fellow prisoners, which had been the constant view for these many months. Despite the guard's declaration, I did not feel free, and the road ahead seemed long. We stopped twice to rest. At the second stop, we came across Bill Stroud, Bob Ice, and Eddie Gates. They were lunching on the portion of food that Hank and I had left them the preceding evening. A bite or two from them would have been most welcome now.

Up ahead, we could hear a commotion. As we approached the disturbance, two American soldiers could be seen on the road, one on either side. *American soldiers!* What a relief! They were members of the 104th Infantry Division, posted as sentries and to assure that the German guards parted ranks to be processed as prisoners. Elated, I shouted out a salutation, but my voice was drowned amid the cries of jubilation issuing from the throats of hundreds of happy men. As I passed the GI on my side of the road, I clapped him heartily on the back. Didn't everyone? Had we not been so weak, our exhibition of happiness might have exacted brutal punishment on these two sentinels. I think these soldiers knew how happy we were to see them.

Only a short distance farther on, a path diverged from the road, bypassing a bombed-out bridge. Our guards filed off to the left, to be accepted as prisoners of war by American soldiers. Not one of us doubted that our erstwhile guards were relieved by this event; they were delighted to escape capture by the Soviets. Across the narrow Mulde River, a rude plank bridge, supported by cement broken from the former bridge, served as the actual point of our liberation. Our information at the time was that by international agreement, American forces were to halt at the banks of the

American prisoners of war, from *Stalag Luft IV*, cross the Mulde River to freedom near Bitterfeld, Germany, April 26, 1945.
10th Infantry Division, the "Timberwolves"

Mulde, the line dividing American and Soviet-controlled areas of Germany.

Maintaining our column, I threaded my way cautiously down the path to the bridge. Midway across the makeshift planks I had an impulse to leave all the vestiges of war behind. Reasoning that this weapon had already produced its quota of terror, I dropped my souvenir rifle into the river. Climbing up the far embankment, I regained the road, which bypassed Pouch, a small coal mining town. No longer in existence, the village had been chewed up by the huge machines used in extracting low-grade coal to fuel fires and to provide raw material for the local chemical industry.

Hank and I trudged up the hill, following the road that flanked the village. A passing infantryman called to us, "Stop one of the trucks as it comes by . . . they're carrying you liberated prisoners to processing!"

Trucks already loaded with happy ex-*kriegies* were passing us. Hank and I hailed the next one. Though the driver was headed toward the makeshift bridge we had just crossed, he stopped and Hank and I clambered aboard. Other men plodding along the road around us joined in, and the truck was half full by the time it reached the turn-around point at the bridge. Loaded to capacity, the vehicle swung around and rolled up the sloping road toward the west.

Soon we were passing through the adjoining city, Bitterfeld, located only a mile or so distant from the ruined bridge. Today, few, if any, of the prisoners who had been liberated that day remember Pouch at all. Bitterfeld, however, is almost universally noted as the place of liberation. That may be due, in part, to the fact that another contingent of men from *Stalag Luft IV* also arrived that day.

Now, on April 26, 1945, as passengers rather than herded plodders, the realization flooded in. WE WERE FREE!

Chapter 28

The Flavor of Freedom

THE TRUCK ROLLED past inactive open-pit coal mines and through the streets of Bitterfeld, then entered a veritable forest of smokestacks in its western suburbs. As the road passed beneath us, the boisterous euphoria of our release from captivity subsided into sporadic, muted utterances. Perhaps most of us had exhausted our repertoire of conversational topics during our long walk together. It was good, though, to watch the scenery pass by so much more rapidly than had been the case during the many painful miles since leaving *Stalag Luft IV.* I had logged approximately 504 miles in my notebook!

Eventually the truck turned from this road into the city of Halle and entered the main gate of a newly vacated military base, a *flakschule*.

Everyone piled off the truck, which presumably returned to fetch another load of weary walkers. At a table set in the center of what may have been a parade field, each man was requested to sign in, name and army serial number. Then we all hurried off to find a place to sleep. Recalling the subterranean quarters in the ruined military post in Aachen, I led Hank to the lower level of a nearby building. While our fellows hurried up the steps to other floors, we found a secluded spot in the corner of a basement room where we prepared our beds.

We scouted the base for food or a place to shower, learning only that there would be a delay in providing bathing facilities, but that the kitchen staff would be ready to feed us that evening.

A call went out for all ex-prisoners to assemble on the parade ground. Dinner would be served soon, to those who had meal tickets, and as our names were called we would receive the tickets. The men were brought forward in groups of six. Soon we heard "Cupp, William L., and Smith, Henry J." When we responded, we discovered that *eight* men had answered to the call. Improbable as it seems, another Henry J. Smith and William L. Cupp had come to the base together. I had no idea that there were other Cupps in the States, certainly not that another bearing my name would have become a POW. All eight of us were issued meal tickets, and we hurried to the mess hall. In line, I asked the other William Cupp what was his hometown.

"Atlanta, Georgia," he replied. That was the extent of our conversation. Both of us were focused narrowly on food.

The food had been prepared elsewhere. In the mess hall, only two American workers were visible. The meal was doled out to each of us, and I remember it consisted of a sort of gruel and black bread plus margarine, and coffee. There may have been more than that, but as disappointing as it was not to have been served steak, this food from German rations satisfied us.

Unaccustomed to going to bed on a full stomach, we slept peacefully on the basement floor that evening. When morning came, we took our breakfast tickets to the mess hall. A line had been formed; however, breakfast was not ready yet. Suddenly a horde of hungry ex-prisoners, many in uniforms unfamiliar to me, rushed the ticket-taker. Inside, they created utter confusion. Soon those inside threw loaves of bread out of the window to their friends. No breakfast would be served in this disorder.

Disappointed, Hank and I stood by the entrance gate, observing the confusion. This disruption, toward the end of the war, was not uncommon — probably in all armies — with the unavoidably fluid lines. Our own columns, even while prisoners of the Germans, had often been arbitrarily split at night; when one barn was full, the rest of a column would march to another barn.

With our liberation, the mixing and confluence of different groups was only increased. Some of my *Stalag Luft IV* roommates had gone to very different places than did I. And thus, as Hank and I watched, we considered whether or not it would be wise to venture out into the city to get away from it all. Besides, we thought it our duty to try to return to our own bombardment groups — wherever they were — as expeditiously as possible.

Just then a supply truck came by and the American driver asked if we would care to ride with him. It didn't matter where he was going; having been unable for so long to exercise choice, we climbed aboard. The driver, Corporal Jim Ecochard, of Company C, 294th Engineering Battalion, told us he was going to the airport to pick up supplies. We had heard rumors that all the ex-prisoners would be flown to a destination preparatory to return to the States. Now we would see the airport.

The runways were pockmarked with bomb craters, and the terrain between runways was filled with holes as well. No planes would come here in the near future. While our driver waited for his cargo, he pulled out small boxes of K-rations — not our favorite food, or at least they had not been before our capture. But we greedily dispatched the contents. Jim had more, should we wish them.

Noticing my enthusiasm for the tiny package of cigarettes in the ration box, Jim offered me a package of Raleigh cigarettes. "Have another pack," he added. "Folks back home send us these. GIs prefer Lucky Strikes, Camels, and Chesterfields, and the Army supplies us with those." I stuffed a second package into my shirt pocket.

Back at the base, the skeletal crew at the mess hall had been unable to restore order and the noon meal would not be forthcoming. Hank and I went to our basement quarters to await improved conditions. What we found was distressing. In our absence, someone had looted our meager belongings, blankets, and spare clothing — even the two bayonets. Unless the upper floors had room for us, we would have no place to sleep.

Standing again at the main gate, a truck rolled to a stop. Our friendly driver, Jim, heard our story sympathetically, then offered us a ride. This time, he was returning to his company quarters for the night. Gladly, we accepted his hospitality and clambered onto the rear of the truck.

A veritable parade of vehicles was traveling in either direction along the road. Hank stood beside me in the truck. I relished the wind blowing through my hair. It had been many months since I had moved at this giddy speed — possibly 30 miles per hour. A jeep passed and flagged the truck to a stop at the side of the road.

A tall, lean officer stepped out and barked at our driver. "You have men on this truck who are not wearing helmets. Regulations require that they be worn. There is danger from snipers. Tell these men to put on their helmets at once!"

Apologetically, the driver responded that his passengers had no helmets. They had just been released from a prisoner-of-war camp.

The officer strode to our position, giving us a closer inspection. Then he saluted saying, "Congratulations, men; I'm glad you're back. Now, try to get helmets as soon as possible, and wear them!" Flagging our truck on its way, he stepped into his vehicle, and continued ahead.

The truck left the highway following a smaller road for a short distance, then entered a village. Jim swung the truck into the courtyard and halted at a small farmstead. We three stepped down together. Jim informed the others of his visitors. There was no problem. Anyone looking at us could see that we might be hungry, and supper, they told us, would soon be delivered from a central kitchen. In the courtyard we washed from a large bowl, drying ourselves on a proffered towel. Inside the house, a number of soldiers were lounging about after completion of the day's assignment. They accepted us matter-of-factly.

In the courtyard, a Sergeant dished out the evening meal, a new menu, consisting of fresh vegetables and meat. Hank and I were given portions far larger than those doled to the other men. I wolfed mine down, then hurried into the barn to regurgitate this unaccustomed quantity. Still hungry, I approached the Sergeant for seconds. With a look of amazement, he filled my tray and Hank's again. The food was so-o-o good, but naturally, I became sick again; Hank was at my side, in similar distress.

In the house, we joined the others in conversation, then were treated to our first taste of C-rations — the food that had so impressed the Italian driver with whom Bob Donahue and I had ridden on the retreat from Paris. They were good, but everything was so heavy on my stomach.

One of the men, bound on a brief trip to a command post, asked if we ex-prisoners would like to ride along. There were showers there, he said. When we agreed, towels, soap, and a can of flea powder were thrust into our hands, and we hurried off.

The command post had the appearance of a public school. Inside a vast room, work coveralls were suspended from a high ceiling. These, we were told, were miners' clothing, airing there until they were to be used again; this was the main building for a coal mine. The adjacent large room was equally surprising. Showers lined the walls and more were installed on pedestals around the room; we counted 56 in all. Hot water soon gushed from all of them, and Hank and I paraded around the room, cheerfully taking care to visit each one. When scrupulously clean, we sprinkled flea powder liberally into our clothing and over our bodies, then showered again, until dusky gray skin took on a pink hue. It was with trepidation that we donned our filthy clothing, but the itching had not begun again.

Back at headquarters, our fresh-scrubbed appearance contrasted too greatly for our new friends. Someone remarked that suitable clothing should be found for us. The supply Sergeant was summoned. He declared that his clothing supplies were all but exhausted; he had only one woolen uniform and one pair of fatigue coveralls in stock; possibly, he had some underclothing. Despite his protests, he was persuaded to bring us the clothing. The woolen shirt and trousers fit me; the fatigues were larger, just right for Hank. In a corner of the room, we stripped and pulled on our new, clean clothing. On the floor where we had dropped them, our discarded apparel looked disgustingly filthy and shabby. Probably they should have been burned, but no one chose to touch them, and they lay on the floor during the several days we stayed in that place. Even after washing, those dirty trousers retained their filled shape, much as discarded football pants with padding.

With Jim, we drove to the site of a German military warehouse complex, comprised of eight four-story buildings, set in two facing rows of four. Jim and his helper had specific goods in mind, and received directions from a soldier in charge there. Hank and I were directed to the building housing chocolate.

We looked through three of the floors, sampling poorly labeled goods. One set of bins contained pellets of coffee. They tasted terrible, though they bore some resemblance to chocolate. At last we discovered the chocolate. We selected a round cardboard container looking something like packaged Camembert cheese. Inside were thick wafers of dark chocolate that had a marvelous taste. Having no containers except our pockets, we chose to take a large wooden box. Our problem was how to carry the bulky treasure. We attached a scrap of rope, but all of our combined strength was needed to get the box back to the truck where Jim and his helper hoisted it aboard. As the truck rolled out of the compound, we broke open the box. The temptation was as great as our incessant hunger, so we each munched on a thick chocolate wafer.

When the truck stopped in front of a store in a village, Hank and I climbed off to sample the flavor of a small town, no longer identified as vermin-infested prisoners. True to our expectations, passers-by did not shy away from us. A lady approached, leading a small boy. He looked like someone who would appreciate candy, so I pulled a package from my pocket and handed it to the woman.

She recognized it instantly and broke into tears. "My little boy is five years old, and he has never tasted chocolate," she said. "I shall make him a cup of hot chocolate."

Her strong emotion was thanks enough. How sad it was that the military stores were well supplied with cherished items withheld from the citizenry!

On another day, Jim took us back to Halle. We apparently had not been missed. There was hope that arrangements had been made, by now, to transport the American ex-prisoners on a leg of their way home. But the airfield remained a discouraging sight. The bomb craters dotting the airfield were untouched. We would not soon be flying out. While we had been gone, the ex-prisoners had been moved from the *flakschule* to the airport, where they could be seen huddling under a long, simple roof. Some were in makeshift "shelters" of blankets over their heads, trying to keep warm with bonfires built at the edge of the ruined runways, like the hobos in newsreels during the Great Depression. We thought that only "clueless" authorities would have expected us to be assigned to such a "camp."

Jim, too, was discouraged. I sensed that his superiors were eager to be rid of us, for we were not on their roster. Back at the house that afternoon, the Sergeant told us that two men were to be taken for training in Belgium. Would we like to travel with them? For me, that would be ideal. From any place in Belgium, I could go to see the Hombecks. That was fine with Hank, also. Secretly we were to meet the vehicle out on the road just past the house. Knowing that we were penniless, the Sergeant gave each of us ten dollars of invasion money; we could pay him back later, he said.

The Sergeant flagged down the Belgium-bound vehicle, and we climbed aboard. Our driver accepted us with cold indifference. Some miles down the road, he reported at Battalion Headquarters. Prepared to leave early in the morning, we were quartered in a nearby house. When morning's light woke us, we learned that our driver and his passengers had departed earlier. Hank and I were ordered to report to the headquarters, where we were roundly chastised for being AWOL from our ex-prisoner companions at Halle. We were threatened with court-martial for this transgression. . . . But that would wait until after lunch; the officer had an appointment that would not be put off.

Somehow, Hank and I found our way downtown, to the offices of the Military Government. There a sympathetic Sergeant heard our story and made out orders to the effect that we were to be assisted on our way to our homes without delay. We had evaded the threat of court-martial.

While waiting for transportation back to the Engineering Company where we had spent the past few days, I discovered an Army dentist, and contacted him about my chronic toothache. He wasn't busy at the time, and because I needed a filling, a Sergeant, the dental assistant, was called in to provide physical power to the drill. Grinding slowly and noisily, the matter was expeditiously completed.

Our return to the Engineering Company was met with dismay. The Sergeant was under pressure to dispose of Hank and me — and now we did have papers ordering our expeditious return home! On the following morning we were taken to a field where several Douglas C-47 transport planes were being filled with French prisoners on stretchers from a liberated military hospital. All had contracted tuberculosis and were being transferred to a hospital in Paris. Yes, there was room for two more passengers. In fact, another man was in line ahead of us. His baggage was a BMW motorcycle recently liberated from its *SS* rider.

The flight was uneventful, until a cry went out that we were over Paris. That evoked a rousing cheer from these poor, emaciated patients. I could see the Eiffel Tower out the window. The plane passed closely by, at the level of the second platform. Soon we landed at Orly airfield, and the business of transferring the patients was begun.

As usual, the first business for Hank and me was to find something to eat. It didn't take long to find a mess hall. Inside, we picked up trays and helped ourselves to prodigious portions. The mess Sergeant, silent through all this, now surveyed our heaping trays and asked whether we had been prisoners of war. He had seen others with such voracious appetites.

"You need to be debriefed," he said. "I'll phone Paris to send a jeep for you. And they'll put you up for the night."

Nevertheless, Hank and I went to the air terminal, relying on the orders issued by Military Government to expedite our travel to our homes. However, the orders were discounted, with the observation that these could not be honored. We were told that hundreds of men traveling on such orders could be absent without leave in the United States, where their officers could not find them. That was a bitter disappointment, and we trudged back to the mess hall.

The Captain, who had met us, drove us through lighted streets of the city. At last he drew up to a large hotel, the Francia. Inside, we were registered and instructed to come downstairs for breakfast in the morning. Our room was on an upper floor, accessed by a minuscule open-framed elevator. Alighting, we stepped onto red carpet. Our spacious room had amenities far beyond our expectations. And the bed had white sheets — snow white!

We each used the huge tub in the bathroom, then explored all the wonders of this sumptuous room, exclaiming over its appointments before going to bed. We slept until morning. Even then, we marveled at being able to do so, at not having been wakened by acute pangs of hunger.

Breakfast was served on the lower level, the *rez de chaussée*, and we were interrogated by a member of Army Intelligence. He asked a detailed account of our trek from *Stalag Luft IV.* In particular, he asked about Frank

Paules, the leader of the prisoner organization there. The officer was disappointed that neither of us had seen Paules since we had marched out of camp. I gathered that Frank was a much more important figure than we had ever guessed.

I was questioned generally about the weeks during which I had evaded capture, which provided opportunity for me to ask permission to visit my benefactors in Belgium. I was flatly denied, on the grounds that dissidents might learn of the aid given me by the Résistance, and that knowledge might bring harm upon the Hombecks and others. That seemed improbable to me, for it had been such a closely guarded secret all that time before liberation. There was, however, as I learned, some conflict between the patriots of the Résistance and the traitors as Belgium was being liberated, though the patriots quickly took the upper hand.

I dared not disobey a military order. I would try to contact those people, and to return to Belgium as soon as possible.

The interrogating officer then directed Hank and me to another table, where a correspondent from *Yank, The Army Weekly*, a U.S. Army magazine, asked us about our views of German civilian opinion. What about their expectations of Hitler, etc.? Really, we were not in the best position to report on the public opinions of the German people, but we plunged in, anyway. When I read our account in a later issue of *Yank*, I recognized the views I expressed as being an echo of my companions' comments on the march through Germany.

Though breakfast was provided in the hotel, we were issued a meal pass, valid at a restaurant on the *Champs Elysées*. Apparently the restaurant had been leased by the Army, for only soldiers were there when we entered. Though the lights were dim, fine furnishings and décor were visible. The food was good, but the fare was identical for each diner — after all, it was just an elegant mess hall.

The sky was dark when we departed the restaurant, but the broad street was illuminated by low-intensity bulbs. Hank and I walked slowly up the street, past stores that were closed at this hour. We had walked perhaps 200 or 300 yards when we came upon an unlighted area. We could discern a small yellow flame. Probably, we concluded, a smudge pot put there by construction workmen as a warning to pedestrians. We had not seen a single vehicle on the street. We turned and went down the other side of the street, passing a French automobile agency. Years later, after I returned to France, I recognized the darkened area was the *Arc de Triomphe*; our "smudge pot" must have been the Eternal Flame. So much for touring Paris without a guide book!

On the following day, we were relocated in "The Barn," a huge building, which I cannot identify by any other name. Hank and I were assigned cots in a dormitory large enough to hold several hundred men. We were given a small amount of money and a permit to purchase goods at a small commissary. I was in need of personal items such as razor blades, shaving soap, after-shave lotion, and items for dental care. They were not expensive, but I was conscious that it would be wise to guard my remaining money carefully.

Down the street I looked in at a barber shop. Reflected in the window, my hair was long and unruly. Reading the price list for services, I concluded that I had sufficient funds for a haircut. I went in and took a seat. At my turn, I requested a simple haircut and settled back in the chair. The barber guessed that I may have been a prisoner of war, which I acknowledged. When he finished, I thrust out the amount of money indicated on the list. The barber was agitated, and spoke rapidly. I pointed to the price list, indicating that he had been given the specified amount. He grew more excited and shouted to the other customers. Seemingly, he felt that he was being cheated. It was years later that I learned what was meant by *pourboire*. It was the customary tip that I had omitted, not the fee.

Shortly thereafter, our names appeared on a list of men to go by train to Le Havre, then to Camp Lucky Strike. On the train we heard that the camp was a processing center from which we would be shipped home. The train passed for hours along the Seine River, allowing me to see how difficult it would have been to try to swim across to the southern side. At Le Havre we were met by trucks and taken north. We stopped at some place where a large tent served as a mess hall, and ate a delicious meal of powdered eggs flavored with cheddar cheese.

Camp Lucky Strike was huge, with most functions taking place in tents. An officer addressed us, stating several clear rules about our conduct while there. We would eat simple meals; there would be no candy bars or nuts in the post exchange, for some prisoners who had eaten such rich foods had died. Our stomachs were not yet ready for that. I recalled the distress experienced so often at mealtime in recent days, and counted myself fortunate to have survived. We would have a physical examination and be issued new uniforms. Then, after processing, we would be shipped by boat from Le Havre, when shipping was available.

To men who had longed dreamed of sinking their teeth into juicy steaks, the food was simple, but plentiful and nourishing. And it rested easily on our stomachs. A cot in a small tent served as a bed, and I slept until reveille the next morning.

Our activities for the day were posted on a bulletin board. As had been announced, we had a physical examination and were issued clothing. For the first time, I wore a pair of combat boots — ankle-length shoes with a leather addition stitched to the tops, secured by a buckled strap. The Eisenhower jackets also were new to me. General Dwight Eisenhower had made this style popular; it resembled ordinary military blouses cut off below the waist. Fully clad, and wearing these heavy combat boots, I was weighed; I tipped the scales at 89 pounds. Having eaten great quantities for ten or more days, I wondered what my weight actually had been at the end of my captivity. I estimated that I had weighed about 150 pounds when captured.

On May 8, 1945, the camp loudspeaker announced the surrender of German forces. Our processing now completed, Hank and I were free to do as we pleased, as long as we remained in close contact with Camp Lucky Strike. We elected to take a walk along the coastal road. Walking was much easier now than when we had been under guard. We were better nourished, rested, and better shod. Easily, we walked several miles, coming to the edge of habitation. A sign indicated that this was Fécamp — was this the edge of a city, or the border of a commune by that name?

A small circus tent was being erected in an open area east of the road. Curious, we investigated. The unlikely crew — mostly children, and some incredibly old adults — in due time, succeeded in their efforts. Then the workers assembled in front of the tent, clad in threadbare uniforms, bearing an assortment of musical instruments. Their music lacked much of a professional sound, but it was successful in drawing a small crowd of people. An emaciated old man, wearing a tall hat and an old swallow-tailed coat, spoke in a cracked voice into a megaphone, urging the bystanders to purchase tickets and see the show. We paid, and joined the onlookers.

The war must have taken a huge toll on the circus. The performers were recent recruits, and the menagerie consisted of a small nondescript dog and a painfully thin, arthritic horse. Two small figures bravely climbed a pole to a 12-foot-high platform, where they timidly moved around the circular stage to the encouragement of the band's music. When it was time for the animal act, two small figures led the horse around the ring. It was evident that the horse was not strong enough to carry a rider. After considerable urging, the animal was persuaded to kneel. Then the two performers, assisted by the ringmaster, pushed it on its side. Grasping its legs, they rolled it over on its back, then on its other side. With great effort, they brought the horse to its feet, and the maneuver was complete. The dog was a bit more successful, and the show moved to a merciful conclusion. Unusual as the performance was, it has remained in my memory more vividly than the more polished performances I have seen since. Perhaps it serves as testimony to the determined persistence of that little group in the face of mountainous adversity. Their circus lasted until the war's end.

On the Camp Lucky Strike bulletin board we found our names posted for transport to the harbor at Le Havre. Seated on the back of a truck, we watched the miles whisk by. Le Havre bore distinct evidence of recent destruction, and we had heard that the residents bore a grudge against Americans, who had bombed the city. But we encountered no natives.

I was assigned to the *William D. Pender*, a Liberty Ship, for the homeward voyage. From its deck, I followed a line of men down a steep stairway. I found my assigned hammock in the middle of a five-level tier, put my new belongings on the hammock to reserve my place, then set out to scout the ship. On deck I made an acquaintance with a merchant mariner, who willingly pointed out the passing scene. In the harbor, several "Ducks," 2½ ton amphibious trucks — the *DUKW* — were plying about, delivering supplies. We departed Le Havre on May 10th.

About 500 passengers were on board, including about 20 combat troops who were being rotated home. Shipboard food was tasty, nutritious, and plentiful; especially good was the bread — fluffy white loaves cut into Texas-sized slices.

After whiling away several hours, it was time to try out the hammock, a strip of canvas laced onto a tubular framework, which resembled the litters for wounded troops. Getting into mine required considerable ingenuity. I tried to elevate my entire body in a horizontal position, then to slide into the aperture between hammocks. After several attempts, I succeeded in positioning myself. Lying on my back, my nose almost touched the hammock above me. But sleep was possible, as thousands of travelers had previously discovered.

Assignments were made for kitchen police duty on the following morning. Names were called in alphabetical order. Naturally, I was on this first list, but I didn't mind, for I was sure to have opportunity to eat, and I might never be called again.

When awakened the following morning, I struggled out of the snug bed, found my clothes in the dim light, washed up, and went to the kitchen. Providentially, one of the ship's cooks gave us instructions on food preparation and serving. Supplying the food line, cleaning up, and preparing the next meal kept me very busy that day, and I was glad to crawl into my hammock for the night. A few hours later I was rudely shaken to wakefulness. None of the second day's food workers could be found. Those of us who had experience were called again into duty. Well, I enjoyed eating, and worked hard, and I soon found myself in charge of the passengers' dining.

News came that the ship would put in at Southampton, England, to join a convoy for the Atlantic crossing. I was eager to put my feet on British soil, and not just on my own air base, as had been the case earlier. But I was requested to stay aboard and see to the food, while others spent several hours ashore. Regretfully, I remained aboard for the rest of the voyage.

Solid food still created problems for former prisoners. Meat was prepared in the crew kitchen and brought to ours. After steak was served, jaws ached for a week. Seven days later, roast beef was served, with the same result. For lunch and dinner on six days, we ate creamed tuna on reconstituted potatoes, alternating with creamed chicken on the same soft food. Between-meal snacks consisting of eggnog, delicious bread, canned butter, and preserves were filling and easy on tender stomachs.

My task became the preparation of the eggnog. At each snack I mixed two 30-gallon cans to which I added powdered whole milk. Adding water, I stirred the concoction vigorously to eliminate lumps. Twelve dozen eggs and a bit more water were added, then 20 pounds of sugar, nutmeg, and a pint of vanilla extract, and stirred again. The cans were placed into the walk-in cooler until serving time. The rich treat was much enjoyed by all.

The convoy that sailed from Southampton on May 10th was the last to cross the Atlantic and so large that it extended over both fore and aft horizons. In case of fog, each ship trailed a line pulling a log-like float, which left a wake visible to a nearby ship. But the pace was slow. The screw of the *William D. Pender*, riding high in the water, churned air about half the time. We may have progressed at eight knots, but from the deck I saw Ireland for three days!

One poor, skinny ex-prisoner was unable to process his food, and I gave him a key to the cooler so that he could help himself to eggnog, as needed. But that was not sufficient to help him, and a hospital ship was summoned alongside. In choppy waters, he was transferred via breech buoy to the other ship. I hoped that he would receive effective care.

Late in the second week out, the emergency siren sounded, calling all hands to general quarters. I was serving supper at the time, but snatched my life jacket and dashed up to the deck. Dense fog all but obscured the other ships. From the bow I could see the wake from the fog float. The ship turned, and then I saw an oiler passing across our bow, so close as to slash the hawser trailing the float. It was a narrow escape, but no damage was done to either ship. Later I heard that one of the lead ships had struck an iceberg. The convoy was commanded to change course; then the order came for a correction to that course. Confusion reigned in the fog. That night there were sounds like the clashing of tin cans.

In the morning, we heard that 23 ships had collisions. When the fog cleared, I could recognize none of the vessels that had been near us before that incident. Several ships were directed to St. Johns, Newfoundland, for repairs. The rest headed cautiously for New York City.

The voyage had taken longer than expected, and our regular rations had dwindled. We resorted to supplies of what the military mysteriously called "spam," not nearly as tasty as the real Spam. Now I understood why troops tired of it quickly. The potatoes were reconstituted, too, and the variety of canned foodstuffs limited. By that time, even we ex-prisoners were well enough nourished to complain about food that would have elicited gratitude a few weeks earlier.

We arrived in New York Harbor on June 3, 1945. The first recognizable sight was Coney Island. I couldn't see the Statue of Liberty, but I knew we were approaching home. Our voyage had taken 23 days. At the dock we were loaded onto a train, which took us to a military base. We were directed to a barracks where I claimed a bed. Then we trooped off to the mess hall. German prisoners of war, our former captors, served us. I felt a twinge to see them so near good food. My server forked two steaks onto my tray. I couldn't complain, except sore gums.

We had scarcely settled into bed when we were awakened. A train would take us to Jefferson Barracks, at St. Louis, Missouri. The cars were boxcar-like carriages, fitted out with tiers of Simmons sprung cots. Once in, I fell asleep readily.

Something — perhaps the train had stopped — woke me. My head was facing an unshaded window. Standing before a white-tiled wall, a sailor, his cap pushed back rakishly on his head, was wrapped in fond embrace with a girl. It took a minute for me to realize that I was indeed awake and that this was no dream. Then the train lurched ahead.

I woke again to an eerie view. Just enough light allowed me to see a man in the next bed rising and falling in steady rhythm. I raised up in my bed, now realizing that the bedsprings were responding to the steady clacking of the rails. My own bed, too, was following the same exaggerated rhythm. That understood, I quickly went back to sleep.

Jefferson Barracks had been organized for the rapid and efficient processing of returnees. There was a brief interrogation, then I was issued a paper declaring that I claimed to be William L. Cupp, Sergeant, Army Air Corps. Trusting in that, a paymaster issued me money and a train ticket to Davenport, Iowa. Telephone calls were *gratis* but I found long lines at the phones. Just ahead of me, a soldier from our boat was being rotated home after months of combat duty. He came away from the phone puzzled and dismayed.

"She hung up on me," he said. He had been overseas since before D-Day, and his unit had moved so swiftly that his mail had never caught up with him. He had received no word from his wife while he had been in Europe. She had been eager to tell him her news that he was a father. Accustomed to the banter of soldiers, he had responded as so many did, when fearful of bad news, "Is it mine?" One wonders just how often, if ever, a wife could be made to understand the origin and innocence of such a reply.

My call went through immediately. My mother was both surprised and elated to know that I was alive and near home. They had not received my letter from Germany as yet. I told her to expect me in a few days.

It was my turn to be surprised when I learned that I was then free to go. On the train I sat by an acquaintance also headed for Iowa. We stayed awake all night, watching the stations pass by.

When the train stopped in the morning at Galesburg, Illinois, I rushed into the station and frantically phoned home. No one would be expecting me this early, and my ticket would take me only as far as Davenport, some 50 miles from home. Under wartime restrictions, the speed limit was 35 miles per hour. It was a surprise to my parents, but I would be met. When I hung up the phone, the train was no longer visible from the station window. At the door I could see it picking up speed nearly a block down the track. I hadn't run for months, but adrenaline assisted my pursuit, and I caught the platform rail of the last car just as it seemed beyond reach.

As I stepped off the train at Davenport, I could see my parents and my brother, Wesley. They were expecting an emaciated figure often portrayed in photos of starved prisoners, and they did not recognize me. I was plump, having gained about two pounds a day since leaving Camp Lucky Strike. During the trip home we had much to chat about. I was eager for strawberries and chicken, as I had written mother from Germany. She still hadn't received my letter, but I was to be foiled on those two items. The strawberry season had just ended, and Mother had sold off her flock of chickens just a few months earlier.

There had been changes at home in my absence. Tipton now had a frozen-food locker and the family no longer relied on cold-packed meat. Instead, we had a wire basket or two of meat in the locker plant. Now, when someone went to town, they stopped at the locker. It had been far more convenient earlier to bring up a jar of meat from the basement, but there had been a sameness to our diet.

The house was no longer quiet. My little brother had acquired a saxophone, which he played for hours on end. How was that possible?

Earlier, while on the farm, my hours had been taken up with hand-milking a sizable herd of cows both morning and night, and in feeding the cows and cleaning the barns. That, too, had changed. The herd had been thinned, and only two milk cows were left. Wesley wasn't responsible for the chores, so long as he kept up his practice. His diligence had improved his technique. He would soon become an accomplished musician.

And I had returned home just in time for putting up hay. Manpower shortages during the war had necessitated altered techniques. Now the family truck pulled a loader — a machine that lifted hay from the surface of the field onto the truck bed. One person drove the truck while another, standing on the truck, forked the hay into a stack on board. When the load was filled, the loader was unhitched, and rested in the field until the truck's return. The truck was then driven to the barn, and the hay lifted into the mow. Dumped by the loading fork, I moved the hay to the edge, eventually leveling the fragrant green forage. It was hot work, and after each load, I went to the house, took ice cream from the refrigerator, added soda pop, and relished its refreshing taste. Each day some of my body fat was replaced by muscle, and I began to regain my former proportions.

Haymaking at an end, I was eager to see Penny, the girl to whom I had given my wings on my last visit home before going overseas. We had met at the age of eight at Red Oak Grove Presbyterian Church, a few miles from Tipton. We had been friends through school, and had discovered each other in a new way while she was in college and I in military service. Her father, a farmer, had also been our minister, and had been a comfort to the family while I had been a prisoner. He had valuable insights into the POW experience, having served in World War I with the YMCA, monitoring provisions of the Geneva Convention in an Austrian prison camp. My mother had maintained close contact with Penny during my imprisonment, a relationship that intensified a longstanding bond of friendship.

I had inquired about Penny on that ride home from Davenport, expecting that I might have arrived home early enough to attend her graduation exercises at the University of Iowa. But the academic schedule had been advanced that year, and graduation was past. She was working in Chicago, I was told.

I contacted her, and took a train to Chicago. The streets there held little traffic, but the first cab I hailed broke down after only two blocks. The same happened to the second and the third. With my bag, I trudged to the nearest elevated railroad station and completed my journey. Securing a room in a residential hotel, I returned to the Loop, the downtown area of Chicago. At her workplace I paged her, met her boss, and arranged to meet her later. She had been following the news about prisoners on the march in Germany, but had heard no news of my unit.

That first evening we spent at the Chicago Public Library, looking through atlases to discover the route of my forced march. I hadn't seen it on a map, either.

For several days we met at the YWCA where she lived, rode the train downtown, and breakfasted at a cafeteria. We arranged to lunch together, too, and to dine together at night. Most memorably, we dined one evening at the Walnut Room of the Bismarck Hotel. Naively, we joined the line waiting at the door. Tables were in short supply, but some of those in line ahead of us were ushered in, after the surreptitious passing of folded currency. My uniform stood out in the largely civilian setting, and the *mâitre d'* passed us in, and saw that we were seated at a good table. Few overseas veterans were visible in Chicago at that time, and this was but one of many acts of generosity shown me.

I returned to Chicago a few weeks later, and secured Penny's consent to marriage. Arguing that I was spending more money visiting her than she was earning, I persuaded her to return to Iowa City, where she moved in with her parents and soon began teaching school. I was less successful in arguing for a speedy marriage. The following semester I enrolled as a freshman at the University of Iowa, and we were married in April.

I insisted that at the end of the school year she should quit her job, and let me be the principal breadwinner. She agreed, but soon accepted part-time work at the university, as did I. But I had not reckoned with the sudden rise of prices when the OPA, the Office of Price Administration, ceiling on foodstuffs was lifted. With dwindling reserves, Penny again sought full-time work, and I continued part-time employment at the university. In our spare time we enjoyed athletic events, drama, concerts, and tennis on the university courts. I became very active in the International Relations Club which, because of a regular program we sponsored, went by the name of The World Affairs Forum. Soon that group brought us most of our closest friends.

The framework offered by sociology for the analysis of events had attracted me to that major field of study. And my experience of helplessness as a prisoner of war led me to take a course in criminology. Was it likely that convicted persons were led to experiences and attitudes similar to my own? I began to think so, and registered for additional courses in that field.

However, my more serious interest lay in discovering the source of attitudes that led people into conflict situations, and I became interested in public opinion polling as a means of assessing the attitudes and values of various national peoples, with the hope of discovering means of reducing those conflicts. When I decided to take further study to prepare myself for that activity, I took more courses in social psychology.

Chapter 29

Thanking Our Helpers

JUST BEFORE LEAVING the Hombecks in 1944, I had written a message vowing to return, in five years, to visit and to thank them properly for their aid. Marie's powder box had seemed a safe place in which to hide the scrap of paper. Ever since my return to the States, my promise had been an elusive goal. But eventually, Penny and I had made some headway toward this end. Then I received a timely pension for veterans and a stipend unexpectedly distributed among former POWs from the reparations from German assets that had been frozen during the war years. We were able to return to Europe during the summer of 1949.

Because I would have felt guilty had our trip been one of pleasure only, I had devised a research project on youth hostels in Europe for the thesis for my Master of Arts degree in sociology. But even more urgently I wanted to visit and thank the people who had so selflessly given me aid when our aircraft had been shot down in Belgium and to show my wife, Penny, the places about which I had told her.

★ ☙ ★ ☙ ★

With our clothing loaded on bicycles purchased in England, and with a valise carrying 50 pounds of questionnaires in English, French, and German, we crossed the North Sea from Dover to Oostende, Belgium, then traveled by train through Brussels to Ath. There we mounted our bicycles and headed west on a cobblestone road toward the Hombecks' home in Œudeghien.

I was quickly reminded that I did not know the route from Ath, having arrived at the Hombecks by bicycle by a different route and having left through the fields at night. But we did locate a bumpy road out of Ath, on the route to Œudeghien. At Mainvault the road dead-ended at a café. No signs directed us on to Œudeghien, so I inquired at the café, asking for directions to the *Chapelle du Buisson*. The bartender, no doubt perplexed by my accent, hesitated to answer. But a young man there came up to me and asked, "Are you Bill Cupp?" As a relative of a neighbor of the Hombecks, he had seen my photo in their home, and knew we were expected to visit that summer. He led the way to his home, where his mother made us comfortable and telephoned the Hombecks. We waited for them to come for us.

Our bicycles and baggage were loaded into a war surplus jeep driven by Eliane's husband, and we went quickly along a winding road from which we could see the little chapel at a distance. Much was the same as when I had left, except that the red brick house now had a yellow brick facade, refurbished at the time of Eliane's wedding. And the bars had been taken from the windows.

What a welcome we received, not only from Marie, René, and Eliane and the dogs, but also from Eliane's husband, Roger Ronsse, when introductions were made. Penny and I remained there as guests for several days. During that time we were taken to the village of Œudeghien for a dance, met several neighbors from whom my presence had been concealed during the war, and partook of a festive meal at the Hombecks, where we met additional members of that family.

On a weekend, Roger and Eliane took us to a park, *le Bois de la Houppe*, located on a high hill almost visible from the Hombeck home. There we hiked and dined, using the opportunity to become better acquainted. Later, René accompanied us to Renaix to visit his sister and brother-in-law, Gaston Termonia. It was Gaston, who during the war, from

Eliane Ronsse, an uncle, and Marie Hombeck in front of the Hombecks' home, 1949.

his spacious home by the site of his textile mill, had maintained contact with authorities in England, acting as a liaison between the Belgian Résistance and the Allies. His two-way radio had been hidden in the garden behind the house.

It was a pleasure to see him once more, and to thank him for having lent me books to read while I stayed at the Hombecks.

★ ★ ★

After Elaine's marriage to Roger, the two of them had come to live with her parents. A large bedroom was constructed in an addition above the milk house. Eliane's former bedroom was removed in order to provide space for a stairway. The closet, into which a visitor had been so unceremoniously pushed to permit Bob and me to escape detection in a front

Marie and René Hombeck, Œudeghien (Hainaut), Belgium, 1949.

room, had been converted into a doorway from the kitchen to Roger and Eliane's quarters. Roger had purchased the jeep to use as motive power for his fledgling commerce in livestock. In lieu of a trailer, he transported his animals in a wagon drawn by the jeep. At other times, the vehicle served as the family vehicle.

From left: Gaston Termonia, Penny Cupp, René Hombeck, and Yvonne Termonia at the Hombecks, Œudeghien, Belgium in 1949.

Below: The Croizé family, René, August, Madame, and Marcel, Ons-en-Bray (Oise), France, 1949.

Monsieur Totis and Madame Irma Totis-Binutti near Bapaume, France in 1949.

Roger, Monsieur, Madame, and Claude Fontaine, Ons-en-Bray (Oise), France, 1949.

One day, while Roger was away on business, Eliane borrowed an old sedan from a neighbor and took Penny and me to visit people who had helped me before my first arrival at the Hombecks. We were successful in locating the tree into which I had parachuted and the farmhouse where I had first sought sanctuary. We were greeted by Lucien and Denise Guerlus and their two daughters, Jeanine and Nadine. Quite contrary to the information I had while an evadee, they had not been executed by the enemy, though they had been visited by a Nazi search party just minutes after Doug Hooth, Bob Donahue, and I had left.

We visited the field where we three men had evaded on that fateful day, meeting one of the men who had brought us supplies that first evening. Paul Thomas, accompanied by his young son, Julian, had guided us to that line of trees where we had lain all day. I could still find the hollow trunk through the knothole of which I had surveyed the area. Though Eliane tried, we did not at that time locate any others of our helpers, but we learned that the man I had known as "Jean" had married, then left Belgium very soon after the liberation, to live in the Belgian Congo. It wouldn't be until my next trip, in 1967, that I learned the true identity of Jean.

We were at the Hombecks at the observance of a major holiday, and thus accompanied Eliane and Roger to the dance hall in Œudeghien. There were so many people to meet that I could not keep track of them all, but I recall seeing Paul Thomas, who introduced me to his brother, who lived in a house adjacent to his.

Soon Penny and I mounted our bicycles and began a journey to retrace the route Bob and I had followed into France. Somehow we did not encounter any of the Belgian people we had contacted on that route, but rode over bumpy cobblestone streets, which were covered by layers of coal dust, and witnessed the painfully slow recovery from the ravages of war. North of Bapaume, by the still unfinished canal, we spied the brick kiln and little house on the hill where Bob and I had begged a cup of coffee and chance to shave. We rode up wholly unannounced for, as usual, I had not asked the name of the householder.

Madame emerged from the kiln, her countenance smudged with coal dust. She seemed to recognize me immediately as one of the Belgians who had come to her door. Quickly she summoned her husband, then entered the house to refresh her appearance. Now we learned her identity — Madame Irma Totis-Binutti — and met her husband, whose first name I do not recall. Monsieur Totis avowed that he would not have mistaken my accent for that of a Belgian, and declared that had he known that Bob Donahue and I were in need of sanctuary, would have hidden us in the base of the kiln's chimney. He had done the same for other passers-by during the early 1940s. In the meantime Madame had returned, freshly washed and wearing a colorful cotton dress. Penny and I accepted their invitation to join them for dinner and the night. We rode on the next day.

Riding rapidly downhill on the rough road going south in Bapaume, we turned onto the cinder bicycle trail. Unseen was a ditch cut across the path, and we spilled in a heap from our bikes. Penny's bike wheel was badly bent, and she suffered abrasions and a severe sprain of her right thumb. After tending to the worst of these injuries, we proceeded to the nearest railway station and boarded a small train on to Auneuil. We took a room in the small hotel by the railway tracks. Our bikes repaired, we rode down the hill to the Dupas' home.

From the street, the house appeared much as I remembered it. But Monsieur Dupas had died, and Madame had moved to the little house just next door. We were made to feel very welcome, then accompanied Madame Dupas to the cemetery where she wept over the grave of her husband, Lucien. Back at her home we learned how very different her life was now. It seemed that she had brought most of the furnishings from the big house to this one. There was little unoccupied space in the house, so before taking our leave, we conversed with her in the front garden.

Next, we rode our bicycles to Ons-en-Bray to visit the Croizés. We found Marcel in the courtyard, his head hidden under the hood of an old car. Hearing my call, his grease-smeared face emerged from the motor.

Seeing us, he called, "Hello, William!" then thrust his head back to his task.

"Aren't you surprised to see me?" I asked.

"No," he replied, his head reemerging from under the hood of the car, "You said you would be back in five years, and you are just on time!"

Little could he know, that on our scarce resources, just how close we had come to being unable to make this trip.

We received an effusive welcome from the Croizés, who invited us to dinner and insisted that we stay overnight in their home. In the interval since Bob Donahue and I had departed, the old grandmother had passed away. The family income seemed to have improved. Also, the refugee family had departed the old house by the courtyard. Otherwise, little else seemed to have changed.

Penny and I then pedaled the short distance to the village of Ons-en-Bray to visit the home of Roger Fontaine. Roger had been my direct contact with the French Résistance when Donahue and I had been in that area. This time we entered by the front door. Roger, appearing weak and yellowed by jaundice, took us to his room to view his current issues of *LIFE* magazine and other literature in English. Obviously, he read them with full enjoyment and proudly exhibited them. When we returned to the street level, Roger's father was at home, and we conversed with Madame Fontaine and Roger's brother Claude. Maryse, Roger's sister, was away at the time. In front of their home I took a picture of the family. Later I learned that this had been the last photo ever taken of Roger; he had passed away a few days later.

This had concluded our visit to helpers in France that we knew by name. We kept in touch by mail with them, mostly at Christmas time.

Financial considerations — graduate school and two children — and my work, which brought a most modest income and required my employment during summers, delayed another trip to Europe. In 1965, Eliane wrote us that Marie Hombeck had passed away. René, she reported, was very lonely and expressed a desire for us to visit him. I was not needed in the classroom in the summer of 1967, and was able to make the trip. I hastened to leave at the close of my college semester, but our children's school was still in session. Alan still wanted to attend summer camp as he had been promised, and so we arranged for him to be taken care of until Penny, Amy, and I would return. Penny and Amy were to depart several weeks later than I.

René and Eliane had arranged for us to live in a house abandoned suddenly by a widow upon the death of her husband. Gradually it dawned on me that this was the home of Madame Destrebecq, where Penny and I had waited in 1949 until the Hombecks had come to transport us to their home. But, they said that it would not be suitable for me to stay there alone, and arranged for me to stay temporarily until Penny and Amy arrived, at the home of Eliane's cousin, Evelyne Horlay, in the very center of the village of Œudeghien. With a borrowed bicycle I commuted between the village and the little house by the *Chapelle du Buisson*, dining and visiting René, and Eliane, and Roger Ronsse.

Roger's business had prospered since my earlier visit. A Studebaker truck had replaced the jeep, and Roger dealt with larger quantities of animals. Often I accompanied him at his work. One day he was to deliver a package of meat to a householder at some distance. The route excited me.

We passed the farm where Bob Donahue had stayed with the Ponchauts. They no longer lived there, Roger told me; they had all moved to Brussels.

Soon I recognized that we were on the route on which Jean had taken me to Lessines, when we sought out the "little tailor." I had just told Roger this when we came upon a cluster of houses by a little chapel. I told him that I recognized this place. Roger was skeptical. Then at a familiar barn, Roger turned onto a smaller road. Here I had ridden with Adolphe on the day when the Résistants had feted the airmen down in the area.

By now, Roger was becoming impatient with my improbable recollections. The truck turned on a small road leading toward a village, then turned again. I told him I thought that I had walked on this little road the evening of the day my plane came down. He grunted, unconvinced. Turning twice again, he drove to the courtyard of a small farmstead. Alighting, he knocked at the door.

I took this opportunity to check the rear of this place. Sure enough, a narrow footpath passed behind this and other buildings. I was now certain that I had been led by here toward the safe house on the day our plane had crashed.

But Roger shrugged off this observation also. When the lady for whom he had been waiting approached by bicycle, they greeted one another, then the lady asked just who this stranger was in Roger's company.

"He's an American who is visiting my wife's family," Roger replied. "They sheltered him during the war."

Evidencing excitement, she addressed me. "Do you know Douglas?"

"Yes," I replied. "Douglas Hooth was my co-pilot."

She ushered us both into the house, telling Roger to put the meat in an adjoining room. Quickly she produced an album and pointed out a photo of Doug. Roger, astonished, peered over her shoulder at the album.

"Douglas was hidden by Marie-Louise and Emile Deltenre," she said. "They live just a few minutes away from here." To me, she asked, "Do you know Abel Coton?"

The name at the time had meant nothing to me, though I had been photographed with the members of Coton's "safe house" in 1944. She thumbed through the album, producing a picture of the man, whom I recognized as "Jean." That was sufficient to convince her, and Roger. This lady's sister, Laure Rémy, she said, had been working in a field with Marie-Louise Deltenre-Auverlaux when Dick Wright's parachute had hung up in a tree. The two had assisted Wright until a known member of the Résistance — Abel Coton — arrived and took charge of Wright, who was limping on a broken foot. She then insisted that we all go immediately to meet Marie-Louise and Emile. We did, and that opened up a whole new line of persons who had helped members of our crew.

Emile and Marie-Louise lived in the same small farmstead in which they had sheltered Douglas Hooth during the summer of 1944. There was only one outside door to the house, clearly visible from the street, perhaps 75 yards away. The outdoor toilet was attached to the front of the house, but the way to and from it was fully visible to passers-by. While staying at that home, Douglas had been unable to avail himself of the outhouse. The house was supplied with electricity; I do not recall whether it had a water spigot. The major change to the house since the war, as at the Hombecks, had been the removal of the bars from the windows. Emile had continued to work as a laborer in the big quarry at nearby Lessines, and Marie-Louise sometimes prepared and served food for weddings, funerals, and other festive occasions. Her fine culinary art was now displayed in her girth, as generous as were the servings of her tasty food.

Emile made good use of the small plot of land at his disposal, mowing the front area with a scythe and feeding the cuttings to animals, which in turn contributed to the family larder. A few chickens ranged freely, providing eggs and meat for the table. Behind the house was a large garden, weedless and productive. A combination stove in the living room provided warmth for the room and heat for cooking. It was fueled with small twigs and branches cut from the trees at the back edge of the front yard. Pots and pans were stored in the small kitchen, and the counter space was so tiny that one could marvel at the quantity of food this cook could prepare. The showplace of the house was the dining room, furnished with oaken table, chairs, wardrobe, and a sideboard, containing a supply of table service. It was apparent that the couple used the dining room sparingly, except to store a pie or cake to be served later to company. Regularly they ate in the living room, at a table that could accommodate four.

Prominently displayed on the wall was a commendation from General Dwight D. Eisenhower, the certificate of appreciation thanking the householders for their assistance to an American during the war. A door from that room opened to the couple's bedroom. While hiding in the house, the dining room had been Doug's bedroom. When German soldiers had come to the door, Doug had hidden in the wardrobe.

Madame Deltenre volunteered that she would contact others who had aided members of my crew, and arrange that we must all meet. The acquisition of an automobile, a shiny red Volkswagen Beetle, and the arrival of my wife and daughter, set the stage for extending knowledge of those who had aided members of my crew. Daughter Amy's highest priorities lay in the activities of her age mates. While Penny and I visited with the older set, much of Amy's time was spent with the Ronsse girls, Monette and Nicole. Monette was about one year older than Amy, and with the aid of a French-English dictionary, they quickly discovered many differences in their respective lifestyles and experiences. Soon the dictionary became tattered through use. Nicole was about five years younger than Monette, and her experiences were less interesting to these teenagers.

We subsequently traveled to France, this time discovering, just north of Beauvais, the village where Bob Donahue and I had been given sanctuary, La Neuville-St. Pierre. I had not recalled its name — nor that of our benefactors — but I recognized the village from the main highway and drove up the narrow road. All of the houses had a sameness about them, with walls of the farm buildings that fronted on the streets, sealing off the houses from view. I soon found an open gate, with a man working in the garden.

I felt almost foolish to ask in this way, "Twenty-five years ago, I was an American flier who sought sanctuary here. The proprietor of the house had a long mustache; his wife was plump and did some sewing. They had a daughter who was in her late teens. Do you know of them?"

The answer came swiftly. "Yes, he is the mayor, and they now live in the house next door."

My knock was answered by Mr. "Moustache" himself, as Bob and I had first identified him when we had arrived there — Georges Debailleux. To my surprise, he promptly greeted me by name. His wife reminded me that Bob and I had professed to be hungry, and she had given us all the meat she had in the house, but we had fallen asleep while eating. Apparently she understood our condition at the time, and had long since forgiven us.

The Debailleux's welcome was more than cordial. We learned that Monsieur Debailleux had turned the farm over to his daughter and her husband. As a retirement activity he had become a distributor for seeds and fertilizer in a large area of northern France and Belgium. Their daughter, Jacqueline Tabary, and her husband, René, both toiled on the extensive farm. We learned that after the war, the 18 or so workers had sought other kinds of employment; machinery and long hours of toil by the proprietors made up the difference.

Back in Belgium, in Brussels later that summer, Penny and I had dinner at the home of Raoul and Rosa Ponchaut. Raoul was at that time employed by one of the larger automotive dealers in Brussels. His mother had passed away, but Néry Ponchaut, Raoul's father, was living with them, as was the twin daughter, Oda and her husband. The other twin, Odette, was living not far away with her husband, and they made it a practice to join the larger family for the evening meal. The two girls had married brothers who had grown up on a farm not far from their own home, and both couples were now employed in Brussels.

With Marie-Louise and Emile we met Gilbert Hoebeke, whom I remembered as the man who had shown me and my fellow fliers the subterranean hideaway at the safe house. Gilbert and his wife Lea lived at La Cavée, a minuscule settlement fronting on a chapel of the same name, a scant half-mile away from the "safe house." In his tiny Fiat, Gilbert and his wife, Lea, led us to Isières and the home of Monsieur and Madame Henri Keldermans, who had sheltered Casey Bomar in 1944. There was an additional connection — Madame Gilberte Keldermans-Boucher, Henri's wife, was a niece of the older couple, Ghislain and Hortense Boucher, who had resided in the safe house. During World War II, Henri had been employed at the *aérodrome* in Chièvres. During the days he had bent nails into configurations that, no matter how they fell, would expose one point in an upright position, just right to puncture a tire should it be run over. Only Germans, he reasoned, had access to automobiles at that time, so he opened a seam in his trousers pocket then stuffed the pocket with those sharp objects. Walking home in the evening, he had strewn the nails along the road, resulting in punctured tires on numerous enemy vehicles. Henri retained that adversarial attitude even to old age.

We all spent a most pleasant outing together, picnicking at Ronquières, near Charleroi, at the monumental lock — an inclined plane on which barges were transported in huge tubs down a steep incline from one river to another.

Somewhat later, Gilbert and Lea drove to the Hombeck home to bid us goodbye before our departure. On the very next day, Gilbert, on an errand to a nearby town to procure votive candles for the little chapel of La Cavée, was struck during a heavy downpour by an unscheduled locomotive at the crossing near his home. Penny and I attended his wake before we left.

In 1970, a research grant enabled us to spend an extended year in Belgium. One aspect of my research required that I draw a random sample of households in Œudeghien. In calling upon one house, I met Juliet Hubin-Duvivier, who informed me that she and her husband had sheltered my crewmate, Lieutenant Richard Wright. They had been living at the edge of the commune of Lahamaide during 1944, but after her husband's death, she had moved to a small house in Œudeghien. Finding her led me also to her son, Odon Hubin, the proprietor of a café in Mainvault. Through the years, Dick Wright had maintained a brotherly attachment with Odon, who had been active in the Résistance, and we became acquainted with him and his wife Carmen, as well.

We seized the opportunity on that trip also to visit my wartime helpers in France. In passing by the brick factory north of Bapaume, we stopped at the home of the Totis family, finding a much more substantial house. We arrived as they were being visited by their daughter, Norina, and her husband, Angelis Chretien, and his parents. The Totises were preparing to move to a new home in Tinques, northwest of Arras. The house had been constructed by their son-in-law, proprietor of a large building-supply business, the brick a gift from a grateful owner of the brick factory for which the couple had toiled for many years.

For me, it was fortunate that we had arrived when we did, otherwise we might have lost track of the couple completely. Subsequently we visited them in their new home, located next door to that of their daughter. Set on a plot of land large enough to accommodate a fine garden, vineyard, and chicken houses, it was a fine testimony to the builder's art. There the Totises lived well, thanks to years of deferred expenditures. Monsieur Totis passed away in March of 1978.

René, Marcelle, and Marcel Croize, St. Pol (Oise), France, in 1971.

Growth of the city of Amiens had obliterated some of the landmarks that had led me out of that city, and I was unable to recognize the farmhouse in what I believe to be the town of Cagny, where a displaced Belgian farm family had fed Bob Donahue and me and allowed us to sleep in their farm that night.

Notified in advance of our coming, Madame Debailleux had made elaborate preparations to host us. Crossed over her front door were two flags, French and American, and a newspaper reporter was on hand to interview me. Before this visit, Monsieur Georges Debailleux had died suddenly in an automobile accident, just a few miles from his home. Madame arranged for her daughter, Jacqueline, her husband René Tabary, and their son, Michel, to take us to a quaint Norman restaurant some 50 miles away. There, in a large room reserved for our party, the table decorated with small American flags, we dined sumptuously.

Later, Jacqueline Tabary led us to a small dress shop in Beauvais, *Chez Dany*, where we again met the widow of Georges Vitasse, the man who had taken Bob Donahue and me from the Debailleux home through the *aérodrome* and on to Auneuil. Madame Henriette Vitasse spent workdays in *Chez Dany*, the shop of her daughters Danielle and Arlette, where the three of them made pleasant each visit of customer and friend.

On subsequent visits to Belgium I learned of more persons who had come to the aid of my crewmates. Raoul and Rosa Ponchaut returned from Brussels to Mainvault, moving into the home of Rosa's parents, August and Augusta Leleux, now deceased. Raoul told me the address of Adolphe Clément, still living in the old café to which he had led me en route to the home of the Hombecks. Raoul's directions also led me to Ostiches and to the building that in 1944 had been a café. Adolphe had indeed been incarcerated by the Nazis, but his imprisonment in the former Belgian barracks of Casteau, later the site of SHAPE — Supreme Headquarters of Allied Powers, Europe — had been of short duration, and he had returned to his home.

After the death of his parents-in-law, the Rivières, Adolphe and his wife had continued to operate the café. By the time I had discovered them, the café had closed and had been converted into their home. The couple spent their days mostly in the kitchen, which was warmed by a combination heating and cooking stove. The part of the house formerly used as the café had been decorated with murals of rural scenes, which had been preserved when the rooms had been converted to domestic use.

On a subsequent visit, Madame Clément had passed away and Adolphe lived there alone, comforted somewhat by visits from a widowed neighbor and his dog, and by occasional visits from his son and his family.

★ ★ ★

I had often wondered about the identity of the man who had beckoned to me from the field where I hid after shedding my parachute. One day while making a social call on the Deltenres I met a man who was visiting Emile. Emile introduced me as an American flier who had parachuted into the area, a crewmate of Douglas Hooth. Quickly alert, the visitor asked me the date when I parachuted, and where. Then I learned that he was Gilbert Rasson, who lived in Ogy, the man who had come to the field to lead me away from that parachute, dangling like a beacon on the hill. With Lucien Guerlus, who farmed that field, he made off with the parachute, thereby removing the evidence of my landing.

Through an acquaintance in Œudeghien, I learned that Lucien Guerlus and his family had moved away from their Ogy farm many years earlier and now lived in a small town near Charleroi. In Charleroi, Lucien had developed a brisk business in wholesale foods. After his retirement, the business was in the hands of a daughter and son-in-law, whom we also visited.

★ ★ ★

During my stay in Belgium I attended a meeting of the Rotary Club of Ath. No program had been prepared for that date, and I was asked to tell what had brought me to this place. The *patois* — the dialect — that I had acquired and which had been useful, even at times necessary for communicating in Œudeghien, was difficult for these urbane members to understand. A man seated near me was appointed to interpret for me. Naturally, I told about the reception I had been accorded in 1944.

At the end of my talk the interpreter made himself known to me. He was Jacques Empain, now an insurance agent from Ath, who had been the interpreter at that party given by Résistants. His cultivated charm gave little hint of his wartime activities as a demolition specialist for the Résistance. I saw him again at other meetings of the Rotary Club, and I sought him out on several occasions after that. Later I found him to be a willing and able organizer for a special ceremony held on the 45th anniversary of the day that our stricken B-24, *Won Long Hop*, plowed into the field in Wodecq.

As I had met the people who had courageously given aid to the members of my crew, I learned that each of them proudly displayed the certificate, signed by General Eisenhower, commending them for their assistance to the Allied cause. There had been no compensation for the food, clothing, and other goods they had provided for the airmen they had so selflessly sheltered, and none of them seemed to have expected it.

Although the U.S. government did not compensate these brave people for the care they so generously provided our downed airmen, the Air Forces Escape and Evasion Society (AFEES) did not forget their perilous sacrifice. Founded after World War II by men whose evasion from capture was made possible by people in Occupied countries, the Society was established to thank those responsible for their safety, even their lives. I had learned of AFEES while attending a reunion of the Eighth Air Force Historical Society. At that meeting Scottie David, an enthusiastic recruiter for the organization, and wife of Clayton C. David, one of its founders, told me of the AFEES mission. Though my own attempt to return to American control had been unsuccessful, I was eligible for membership.

Eventually, through the efforts of an AFEES network in France, I learned the identity of and address for Pierre Schapendonk, the second man in the delivery vehicle through which Bob Donahue and I had been transported between the Debailleux and Dupas homes. Pierre had announced that Bob and I had been the 27th and 28th Allied airmen they had safely escorted through the Beauvais *aérodrome*.

Originally from the Netherlands, Pierre had settled in Beauvais, not very far from the airport. He had worked for several companies as an engineer, and in several countries. He was retired, and with his wife Jacqueline was situated comfortably in an apartment or townhouse.

Because Pierre spoke English, we had hopes that the Schapendonks would travel to the United States, and be honored guests at an AFEES reunion. However, we had become acquainted just a bit too late for this, considering their health.

The Air Forces Escape and Evasion Society provided an incentive for the former helpers of downed American airmen to visit the States. At the annual reunion, any known helper was hosted *gratis* by the organization, providing they could come to the reunion site at their own expense. Marie-Louise Deltenre-Auverlaux took advantage of the offer. After the death of her husband, she was able to fulfill the long-held dream to visit Douglas Hooth, whom the couple had hidden in 1944.

Due to the necessity of caring for his invalid wife, Douglas had been unable to visit his former hosts in Europe, nor was he free to travel elsewhere in the U.S. Knowing that, Penny and I had offered to host Marie and to take her to visit Doug, if and whenever she could come to the States.

In 1990, the adventurous, but little-traveled, lady flew to Chicago, transferred to another carrier, and arrived at the Minneapolis-St. Paul airport.

In a state of perpetual excitement over the many comfortable innovations she found in our home, Marie-Louise visited us for four weeks. During that time we took her to see the Hooths, who lived just outside of Lansing, Michigan. Doug insisted that she stay overnight at his home, while Penny and I were put up in a hotel. The visit proved to be a very meaningful event for Doug and Marie-Louise, and seemed to mean a great deal to Nadean Hooth, too, though her health prevented her from conversing.

We subsequently drove from Lansing to Memphis, Tennessee, where the AFEES reunion was held in the splendidly restored Peabody Hotel. Marie-Louise enthused over every aspect of the program, including a boat ride on the Mississippi River and an excursion to the site of the famous B-17 bomber, the *Memphis Belle*, whose crew, of the 324th Bomb Squadron, 91st Bomb Group, was the first to complete 25 combat missions in World War II. At the banquet Marie was presented to the gathering, where she told the story of her assistance to Doug, became acquainted with several people with whom she could converse in French, and ate well —

a matter of exceptional pleasure for her. Without doubt, this was a second high point of the trip for her.

AFEES gave an equally warm welcome to all of the Dutch, British, Belgian, and French helpers at that reunion. Though this recognition in no way compensated for the material gifts provided airmen during the war, the warmth of their welcome may have, at this time, seemed adequate payment.

Considering the many persons who had helped our downed airmen, only a relative handful could ever attend a reunion in the States. On several occasions, the organization had sponsored tours to Europe, visiting persons and places remembered by members. I had never participated in one of those tours, but I wanted to give special recognition to those people who had assisted the members of my crew. By the time I had assembled a list of helpers and discovered their present whereabouts many, including Marie and René, were no more.

In 1989, 45 years after the crash of *Won Long Hop*, I enlisted the aid of AFEES to honor those of whom I knew. The airstrip at the former Chièvres *aérodrome* was still in use by SHAPE, and I hoped to arrange for some sort of ceremony at the Chièvres chapel. The AFEES organization supplied me with tokens of recognition — a citation of remembrance hand-lettered with the recipient's name, signed with the facsimile signature of President Ronald Reagan, and also a handsome lapel pin. On its blue background, the circular pin displayed a parachute descending into an outreached hand, and around the edge was printed "AFEES — We will never forget."

My request for space and arrangements for the ceremony were mailed to the Chièvres airport. In case there was insufficient time for a reply to reach me at my home, I supplied the address of Penny's brother in Germany, where he worked for *The Stars and Stripes*, the official newspaper of the U.S. Armed Forces.

We went directly to Germany, there to discover that no response had arrived. In a rental car, we drove to SHAPE, and went immediately to the office of the chaplains. There I found attentive ears, and obliging personnel drove us to the headquarters building where matters were quickly expedited. The date, June 14th, observed as American Flag Day, was free

Julien Plume praises the Allies for liberating Europe from Nazism as Lieutenant Colonel Stanek and Bill Cupp stand by at the Air Forces Escape and Evasion Society ceremony, NATO/SHAPE Support Group (80 ASG), Chièvres, Belgium, June 14, 1989.

The Air Forces Escape and Evasion Society's award given to Oscar Carlier (r) by Bill Cupp, at Chièvres, Belgium, June 14, 1989.

for this assignment. I learned that the Chièvres station was now assigned to the U.S. Army Signal Corps, and that local arrangements would need to be made there.

At the Chièvres base, a civilian, Monsieur Charles Herbaut, Public Affairs Officer, quickly agreed to all I asked, then added that refreshments should be included. He had no budget for that, but he phoned a man in Germany who offered him sufficient funds for his request. The planning was in progress; now it was necessary to issue invitations.

In Ath I visited Jacques Empain, the Rotarian acquaintance who in 1944 had served as interpreter at the festive gathering of downed airmen

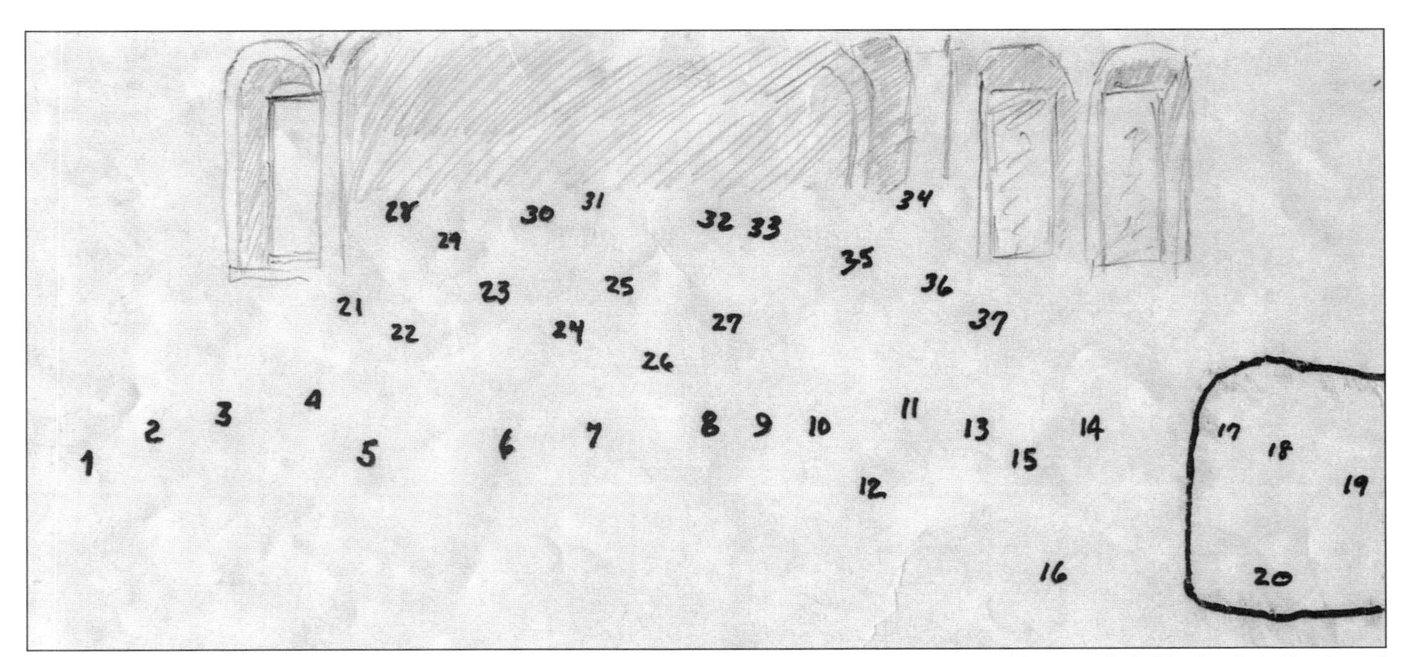

The Air Forces Escape and Evasion Society's Awards Ceremony at Chièvres, Belgium, June 14, 1989. (Honorees in bold print; their friends and family members in normal print.) 1. **Paul Thomas**, 2. Robert DeChevre, 3. Roger DeChevre, 4. Josiane Coton, widow of **Abel Coton**, 5. **Laure Rémy**, 6. Marie-Jeanne Pettiau-Houbeke, 7. **Marie-Louise Deltenre-Auverlaux**, 8. Penny Cupp, 9. Bill Cupp, 10. Emmanuel Keldermans, 11. **Rosa Ponchaut-Leleux**, 12. **Adolphe Clément**, 13. **Gilbert Rasson**, 14. Guy Termonia, 15. Monette Derotteleur-Ronsse, 16. Mehdi Derotteleur, 17. Infant Thomas, 18. Julian Thomas, 19. Josiane Thomas-Vanderhole, 20. Veronique Thomas, 21. Unidentified, 22. Maurice Moulard (who may have procured the *cartes d'identité* for Robert Donahue, William Cupp, and others), 23. Odon Hubin, 24. Unidentified, 25. Madame Carmen Hubin, 26. **Raoul Ponchaut**, 27. **Henri Keldermans**, 28. Unidentified, 29. Unidentified, 30. Unidentified, 31. **Gabrielle Keldermans-Boucher**, 32. Roger Bogaert, 33. Michel Keldermans, 34. Albert Moulin, 35. Madame Adelson Fontaine, 36. Evelyne Gorts-Horlay, and 37. **Eliane Ronsse-Hombeck**.

In France, on November 11, 1989, Marcel and René Croizé receive an Air Forces Escape and Evasion Society certificate of commendation, from the mayor of Chappes, France.

and who on my later visits to Belgium had assisted me as well. Jacques eagerly consented to contact the Belgians on my list and to communicate with Monsieur Herbaut. Reassured that arrangements would be completed, Penny and I hurried back to our hosts in Germany.

We returned to Belgium with little time to spare for the ceremony. We learned then that the entire list of honorees, or their deputies, had accepted the invitation — all except Jacques, who after contacting all the honorees, had suffered a severe heart attack and was hospitalized in Brussels. His award was hand-delivered during his convalescence.

The chapel was filled for the ceremony by honorees, survivors, family members, and several other interested persons. It was my intent to observe and photograph the proceedings, so Penny and I took places at the front. Monsieur Herbaut, who acted as master of ceremonies and translator, had other ideas. I was requested to actually hand out the awards. The murmur of voices stilled as a signal brought the assembly to its feet and the crisp cadence of marching feet sounded the advance of the Color Guard. Three flags — American, Belgian, and NATO — were placed before the color guard retreated.

Monsieur Herbaut then introduced Lieutenant Colonel Stanek, who spoke proudly of the role of the Allies and of the Belgian people, who so stoutly persevered in resistance to their Occupiers and played an important role in the Allied victory over Nazism. To my surprise, I was asked to say a few words. I did so, expressing greetings and appreciation, and words of welcome from crewmen Douglas Hooth, Robert Donahue, and Richard Wright, as well. This was followed by the presentations. Several honorees were summoned to the front again to place a rose in a vase in remembrance of their departed relatives.

Then Julien Plume, who had requested time on the program, took the podium. The man who had given me a pistol as we walked across the fields toward the safe house in 1944 delivered an address, lauding the airmen who had left countless trails across the sky during that great conflict. The *Bourgmestre* of Chièvres, Madame André, followed with a brief but warm tribute to the hardships experienced by and the wartime efforts of her countrymen in countering the oppressive might of the Occupiers.

After the Color Guard had lowered the flags, Monsieur Herbaut concluded the ceremony, requesting the assembly to go to the front steps for a photograph. Most did, but I learned later that some distinguished guests had gone unnoticed. Among them, I learned later to my chagrin, were two celebrated members of *Comète*, the Belgian organization that had transported downed airmen toward their home bases.

The honoring of our French helpers, scattered as they were, required contacting municipal officials in several towns. Penny and I subsequently visited the *maires* of Beauvais, Tinques, and Chappes — where the Croizés lived at that time — and arrangements were made for delivery of the awards at times appropriate in each community, each event coming as a pleasant surprise to the recipients.

The ranks of those many good people, to whom we owe our lives, have thinned considerably, but the memory of their patriotism, courage, and good will always remain.

Epilogue

THE CREW OF *Won Long Hop*:

Floyd Addy, pilot, lost his life in averting destruction to the Belgian village of Wodecq. He was posthumously awarded the Distinguished Flying Cross. His wife Barbara, bore a daughter, Ann.

Douglas Hooth, co-pilot, completed his education under the GI Bill, then worked as an engineer in the Michigan Highway Department. Douglas and Nadean had one son. Nadean contracted multiple sclerosis, resulting in Douglas's early retirement to care for her. Marie-Louise Deltrenre-Auverlaux, Douglas's helper, was a visitor to the Hooth home before Nadean's death.

Robert G. Donahue, navigator, now of Wethersfield, Connecticut, is married to Wanda and they have two sons. Until his retirement, Bob worked for Phoenix Mutual Insurance Company, of Hartford.

Richard Wright, bombardier, currently lives with his wife, Rosalie in Houston, Texas. He was a consulting engineer, contracting for the building of shopping centers. Richard and Rosalie have visited helpers, the Hubins, and others in Europe. The Wright's had several children.

Cecil Pendray returned to his native Detroit. I believe he was employed in advertising. With his wife, Betty Lee, they raised four children. I spent an evening with him in about 1956. He passed away some years later.

Irving W. Norris, nose gunner, returned to his home of Greenville, South Carolina. He owned and operated an auto parts store in Easley, South Carolina. He and his wife, Virginia, raised three children. Virginia passed away in 2000.

Hugh Casey Bomar, armorer and top turret gunner, who had been cared for in Isières, Belgium, was tricked into reporting for his liberation just days before Belgium was truly liberated. He escaped from a guarded train and was subsequently repatriated. I never saw him again, but he returned to El Paso, Texas, where he died at a relatively young age.

Frank McPherson, after his liberation, served as radio operator in Major General Jonathan Wainwright's plane following the General's own liberation from imprisonment by the Japanese. Frank returned to Belgium for a visit.

Some of my comrades in *Stalag Luft IV*:

William J. Knightley was counseled, after the war, to pursue graduate work in English. He married, and later taught at the University of Mississippi. I discovered him, in 1986, in his hometown, Wichita, Kansas. In company with another man he had established the Central Business College in Wichita.

I have been delighted with that visit with him, for he was the first ex-POW of my acquaintance to speak kindly of our captors. That drives home the point that sharing a common language is favorable to communicating and understanding. Knightley had remained with his captors for several days after they had themselves been captured. He involved himself in returning the rations which his Allies had taken from these German soldiers. Knightley died in March 1987, just five months after I had seen him.

My companions on the forced march:

Henry J. Smith was with me on the *William D. Pender,* though I had little opportunity on that ship to converse with him. On visits to the families of his own crew members, he visited me on my parents' Iowa farm later in 1945, where we had occasion to reminisce.

Later, when I was teaching at the Upstate Medical School of New York, in Syracuse, we visited one another in Scranton, Pennsylvania, and Syracuse. Much later, we visited again at national Ex-Prisoner of War conventions. Henry and his wife, Evelyn, have two daughters, Michele and Kimberly. For 35 years, he worked as financial manager for Commercial Credit Corporation.

Robert E. Ice returned to southern Illinois, where he worked for some time as a coal miner. He married Eleanor, and was eventually elected sheriff. Later he became warden of Fitzgerald State Park, a delightful position for him. The Ices have retired to Hemphill, Texas.

Edward Gates and **William Stroud** both re-enlisted in the Air Force. Though for several years we were in touch with members of their families, I have been unable to contact them in recent years.

Sources

Bowman, Martin W., and Truett Lee Woodall, Jr. *Helton's Hellcats: A Pictorial History of the 493rd Bombardment Group* (Paducah, KY: Turner Publishing Company, Inc., 1998).

Fairchild, David, assisted by Elizabeth and Alfred Kay. *The World Was My Garden: Travels of a Plant Explorer* (New York: Charles Scribner's Sons, 1938; Miami, FL: Banyan Books, Inc., 1982).

Kramer, Marie. *Out of Barbed Wire into a Nazi Death March . . .* (Henderson, NE: Service Press, 1995).

Shoemaker, Lloyd R. *The Escape Factory, The Story of MIS-X* (New York: St. Martin's Press, 1990).

Index

by Lori L. Daniel